HARVARD
An Architectural History

HARVARD
An Architectural History

Bainbridge Bunting

Completed and Edited by
Margaret Henderson Floyd

The Belknap Press of Harvard University Press
Cambridge, Massachusetts, and London, England · 1985

This book is printed on acid-free paper, and its binding materials
have been chosen for strength and durability.

Designed by Marianne Perlak

Library of Congress Cataloging-in-Publication Data
Bunting, Bainbridge.
    Harvard.
    Includes index.
    1. Harvard University — Buildings — History.
I. Floyd, Margaret Henderson.   II. Title.
LD2151.B86   1985   378'.1962'097444   85-794
ISBN 0-674-37290-5

Frontispiece: detail of pen and ink drawing of Harvard Square, copy-
right 1890, D. W. Butterfield. Courtesy The Harvard University Archives.

Foreword

Margaret Henderson Floyd

Harvard architecture is unparalleled for its sense of place and as extended urban design: a contextual campus in intimate dialogue with the City of Cambridge. This history, written after three hundred and fifty years, aims to record, articulate, and assess this architectural identity.

The intersection of planning and design that is intrinsic to the American college campus attracts a high level of popular attention today, as it did in 1909. The critic Montgomery Schuyler began his series of ten articles on the architecture of American colleges, written for the *Architectural Record* in that year, with the oldest campus, Harvard. Since then, interest in academic architecture has persisted, and recently a number of monographs on individual college campuses have appeared. Evident in these works is a growing concern for cityscape, for environment, and for vernacular as well as monumental building.

Classic campuses such as William and Mary College in Williamsburg, Thomas Jefferson's University of Virginia, Thomas U. Walter's Girard College in Philadelphia, and Joseph Ramée's Union College in Schenectady, New York, all are notable as unified planning endeavors as well as for their individual great buildings. These classical campuses have conditioned our ideas of what the architecture of a college should be, yet the models they provide sidestep the complexities of engagement with the urban environment. Indeed this avoidance was the intent of designers who sought a division between the college campus and the world outside. Their ideal solutions were never constrained to address the realities of urban life, whereas, with more relevance, Harvard has faced a continual challenge to maintain its open spaces and to protect them from encroachment.

By Schuyler's day many architects of the City Beautiful movement had tried and failed to introduce into Harvard Yard the ideal of axial symmetry and vista that so influenced other Beaux Arts university campuses then rising from coast to coast. Charles McKim's designs for Columbia University and additions to the University of Virginia were models for a whole new generation of college campuses. At Stanford University and at the University of Chicago Harvard's architect Charles Coolidge maintained axial symmetry. But all grand plans for alignment of Harvard Yard or even the chemistry quadrangles to the north were abandoned. While the gothic towers of

Princeton and Yale and the monumental dome of M.I.T. were erected as academic compounds, the Harvard campus was drawn instead through Cambridge toward the river.

The colonial image of Harvard extended into the urban landscape, northwest to the Radcliffe Quadrangle and the Longfellow residential compound on Brattle Street, and south to the River Houses, whose variegated plans and siting along the banks of the Charles have no true counterparts elsewhere in American collegiate design. In this sense we are not dealing in this book with the history of a traditional college campus. The very nature of Harvard's architectural history dictates an examination of the cultural mission and background of the institution rather than a mere perambulation through a clearly demarcated academic compound.

At the time when Charles McKim's elaborately sculptured brick and iron fence was beginning to cloister the Harvard Yard, Schuyler commended the strength and "comity" of Harvard's "scholar factories" (as President Lowell had termed them), the honest brick designs of Massachusetts Hall (1719) and Harvard Hall (1764) and their successors Hollis, Stoughton, and Holworthy. But what he could not accept was the randomness of Harvard's plan. "Patriotic piety apart, could anything be uglier or more of an effort toward a convenient and effective grouping than can be made out from the actual aspect of the yard," he cried. "There is no grouping, there are no vistas. No building borrows any increase of attractiveness from any other, nor lends any to it. There are American colleges, very likely, of which the actual building is more discouraging than that of Harvard, which, indeed, in its oldest examples, is not discouraging at all, but supplies a negotiable basis and point of departure. But there is none in which the chaotic want of foresight and arrangement in the relations of the buildings renders any real rectification more difficult."

Schuyler continued his critique more specifically, in a vein that twentieth-century Harvard did not always heed: "And indeed, as the architecture of our older colleges goes that of the College Yard of Harvard is not so bad. There is not in it, on the part of each succeeding builder, that itch to signalize his work by difference from that of his predecessors which is responsible for the chaotic miscellany of so many campuses. The characteristic is rather of deference than of difference. And so, on the whole, and taking its two centuries altogether, while one would be puzzled to designate a work of genius, he finds a series of examples of decorum." In contradistinction to the traditional American campus, Harvard's quality of design stems from its focus on deference: an architectural strength drawn from the totality of its buildings rather than from individual, assertive monuments. The successful visual impact of Harvard derives more from that human scale which invites exploration than from heroic architecture. And architects with heroic dreams have been the least successful at Harvard, except when they have adjusted to the somehow indomitable spirit of irregularity that characterizes the campus.

It was this quality that attracted Bainbridge Bunting. He recognized the coherence of Harvard architecture, which he saw as an ordered progression, in a near-ideal relationship to the educational objectives of the university: "The order that was finally achieved in Harvard Yard—that grew organically over the generations—derives from more than half a dozen spatial units, which key together in lively, unpredictable ways . . . it must be explored unit by unit . . . Unexpected pockets of order appear, each with a character of its own, yet all these fit together to form a coherent pattern. Such a varied, individualistic environment, offering choices in its variety, is appropriate for a university that encourages each student to pursue his own interests and to develop his own particular talents."

The extended yards of Harvard and Radcliffe now sweep in an arc from the Charles River northwest to Brattle and Garden streets. Contained within this crescent are multiple districts shared by the city and the college. Harvard and Cambridge, in their endless dialogue, have not reached their present form, however fine in ambience or flawed in parts, without struggle. The rationale of the development of Harvard architecture has not resulted from an overall plan; rather, as Walter Muir Whitehill said of one of America's great urban spaces, Copley Square in Boston, "it has stumbled into being." Some inner energy at Harvard has foiled repeated attempts at apparent logic in planning. While overt architectural devices serve to define the classic American campus, each person leaves Harvard with his own strong visual impression. These impressions are the more powerful because of the variety of individual perceptions. In the driving climate of urban economics and politics there have been mistakes: errors in visual judgment have been implemented; fine buildings and much of the neighboring Cambridge streetscape have been lost. Yet in the end this inner energy has somehow controlled, united, even dictated the design objectives of the architects who have been most successful here, who have given Harvard its force and shape, who have made it somehow, as Louis Kahn might have said, architecture that is "what it wants to be," engaged with the City of Cambridge yet maintaining a strong sense of its distinction as a unique institutional place.

Preface

Bainbridge Bunting started research for *Harvard: An Architectural History* in 1964 while serving as director of the architectural inventory of the City of Cambridge and began to write the book after completing *Old Cambridge,* the fourth volume of the Survey of Architectural History in Cambridge, of which he was major author. When he died in Beverly, Massachusetts, on February 13, 1981, he left unfinished this work of more than fourteen years. In completing *Harvard: An Architectural History* I have edited Bunting's text, written a number of missing sections throughout the book, and selected the illustrations.

Bunting's notes provide the basic framework of the bibliography, but I have expanded these to encompass additional information on individuals, commissions, and firms that amplifies the text and furnishes the documentation he intended. The original manuscript comprised six chapters in near final draft and a seventh incomplete chapter. The book that follows includes all this material, but it has been augmented and in a number of places rearranged. Bunting's Chapter 4 on Eliot has been subdivided to make parallel treatment of the presidencies of Eliot and Lowell. To the section covering the second phase of the Eliot administration I have added the history of the early athletic facilities, Soldiers Field, and the stadium. I have substantially enlarged treatment of the Colonial Revival at Harvard throughout, drawing on my own research on Guy Lowell, A. W. Longfellow, Jr., and Charles McKim. The common style, architectural authorship, patronage, and objectives that unite certain buildings of Harvard and Radcliffe beginning in the later Eliot administration have thus been made explicit. Chapter 6 on Radcliffe and Chapter 9 on Gropius and Modernism contain Bunting's visual descriptions but I have researched and written contextual and historical material and provided the documentation. The chapter on Radcliffe has been inserted in chronological position between the epochs of Presidents Eliot and Lowell; Bunting's part appeared in *Old Cambridge* but was not included in the manuscript he left. The final chapters of Bunting's manuscript were incomplete or in outline form and notes, but his views were clear. The last sections of the book now combine his text with my own, particularly for recent buildings in Chapter 11.

From century to century authors and critics have commented on the character of Harvard architecture. Quotations from many of these in the text provide a picture of the evolution of architectural objectives over time. Particularly for more recent buildings, critical assessment is required in a book such as this. During our twenty-eight years of professional association Bunting and I of course had differences of opinion; yet our general agreement was profound. For the most part our differences were based less on varying criteria and method than on differing familiarity with particulars or vision of critical purpose. Because my editing and additions to the text have necessarily been pervasive and we were fundamentally in critical accord, no distinction of attribution for criticism has been included except as specified above.

Evident in his *Houses of Boston's Back Bay* (1967) and his work on New Mexico in the 1960s and 1970s was Bunting's longstanding practice of studying architecture in cultural and historical context. The book that follows is likewise neither an encyclopedic inventory of any explicitly defined category of structures or geographical region (readers wishing comprehensive information on minor works can refer to the Cambridge Historical Commission files) nor exclusively a search for great architecture. Rather, it traces Harvard's architectural history in terms of environment as well as design, in terms of the events and people who created the buildings that record Harvard's material, cultural, intellectual, and design evolution over three hundred and fifty years.

I want to thank first of all those who are unknown to me and thus impossible to name who worked with Professor Bunting on the initial phase of this publication. Throughout the 1960s the vision of the late Walter Muir Whitehill and especially of Albert B. Wolfe through the Cambridge Historical Commission made possible the enormous undertaking that has become the inventory and Cambridge Reports. The intellectual exchange of these years provided by students and many others nurtured Bunting's idea for the present book. At an early stage Antoinette Downing generously shared the techniques developed in the earlier College Hill Study in Providence, and Elizabeth B. MacDougall, Eleanor Pearson, Robert Bell Rettig, Susan Maycock, Robert Nylander, Paul Turner, Charles Sullivan, Arthur Krim, and many others worked with Bunting; each contributed to the endeavor in these years. In my later research Susan Maycock and Charles Sullivan, the latter now executive director of the Cambridge Historical Commission, provided comments on the manuscript and visual materials from their files. Robert Nylander's review of maps and generosity in making available his research, completed since Bunting's death, on seventeenth-century Cambridge and Harvard architecture is noted in the early chapters. Robert Bell Rettig, author of the classic *Guide to Cambridge Architecture: Ten Walking Tours* and the third Cambridge Report, *Cambridgeport,* was centrally involved in the development of data collection management for the inventory, and consistently believed in the importance of this book. Robert Neiley A.I.A., present chairman of the Cambridge Historical Commission, first located the Bunting manuscript and over a long period of time encouraged both Professor Bunting and later me toward its completion.

My own portion of this book was enhanced and expedited by the interest of many colleagues. Professor John Coolidge made available his encyclopedic knowledge of Harvard in reviewing the manuscript and in other ways too numerous to count. I particularly appreciated his views and writings on the Sackler Museum and his firsthand assessment of my work in bringing together Harvard in the era of President Conant with the architectural milieu of Walter Gropius. Christopher Hail of the Loeb Library, Graduate School of Design, shared his authoritative research on building and construction dates to refine the chronological list of buildings. Professor Paul Turner of Stanford University kindly answered several of my questions. His recent book *Campus: An American Planning Tradition* (1983), an outgrowth of earlier work at the Cambridge Historical Commission, records the history of academic planning in America, of which the architectural history of Harvard is a part. Anthony Alofsin of Columbia University established through his research many details on Professor Langford Warren and Harvard's Architectural School and kindly shared them with me. Juliette Meylan Henderson furnished documentation on the development of Harvard's athletic facilities and the philosophy of its early leaders in physical education. The comments and insights of the late Professor Kenneth Conant and more recently of Ellen and Theodore Conant were invaluable for my assessment of the architecture of the Conant presidency. Professor Leonard K. Eaton of the University of Michigan, Carter H. Manny of the Graham Foundation in Chicago, Robert Shaw Sturgis F.A.I.A., and Jean Paul Carlhian F.A.I.A. of Shepley, Bulfinch, Richardson and Abbott shared with me their views of the Gropius period, during which all were students at Harvard. A final enlightening and essential perspective was furnished by Robert C. Dean F.A.I.A. of Perry Dean Shaw and Hepburn in reviewing his work at Houghton Library and that of his firm at Harvard and in Williamsburg.

I selected all the photographs and visual materials for the book. This task would have been impossible without the help of my research assistant Sylvia McKinney Sanborn, Master of Arts candidate at Tufts University, who contributed a special dimension to this portion of the book by patiently, exhaustively, and imaginatively culling through the vast Harvard visual collections, locating many photographs that Bunting specifically discussed, and preparing a final selection group for me. Her efforts in locating much documentary and research material enabled me to complete the manuscript in the available time. Many others at Tufts contributed to research on the architecture of this neighboring university. Professor Cynthia Zaitzevsky, architectural historian for the Harvard Planning Office and my colleague at Tufts, reviewed the manuscript and enhanced this book with many details, and Professor Madeline Caviness provided documentation on the seventeenth-century stained glass in the Naumburg Rooms of the Fogg Museum.

The cooperation of Dean Frank Colcord and of my colleagues and the staff in the Department of Fine Arts has been heartening; and I researched, analyzed, and documented recent Harvard buildings with Pia Wortham, John Barnes, Tom Rourke, Andrew McNabb, David Lazarus, and Lisa Raffin in my Architectural History seminar in the fall of 1983.

Many architects and others have provided visual materials: Joseph Maybank F.A.I.A. and Martha J. Perkins of Architectural Resources Cambridge, Inc.; Graham Gund A.I.A.; Robert S. Sturgis F.A.I.A.; Huson Jackson F.A.I.A. of Sert Jackson Associates; Lana Uppstrom of Hugh Stubbins Associates; Steven Rosenthal; and Robert C. Dean F.A.I.A. of Perry Dean Rogers and Associates. In particular the help and assistance of Jean Paul Carlhian F.A.I.A. and Katherine Green Mayer, the latter librarian at Shepley, Bulfinch, Richardson and Abbott, in allowing me to review their firm's historical files and in providing photographs of much of the firm's enormous Harvard oeuvre is gratefully acknowledged.

The assistance and interest of the following persons in the Harvard collections, who have provided visual and other research materials with comments and documentation, is gratefully acknowledged. Robin McElheny, curatorial assistant of Visual Collections, provided a "processing cart" that made possible a thorough review of photographs at the Pusey Library Archives with the assistance of Robin Carlaw and Barbara Meloni, curatorial associates, Thomas Sexton and John Trepasso, reading room assistants, and Charles Schille, curatorial assistant. Assistance of many sorts was provided at the Semitic Museum by Carney Gavin, curator, and Judith Nathans, senior research assistant; in the College Library by Kenneth Carpenter, assistant director, Research Resources; at Houghton Library by Melanie Weisner, library assistant, and Nancy Finlay, assistant curator, Prints and Graphic Arts; at the Fogg Museum by Jose Matteo, staff assistant, Leonie Gordon, administrative assistant to the director, Marjorie Cohn of the Conservation Laboratory, Richard Stafford and Martha Heintz of Photographic Services, Louise Ambler, curator of the University Portrait Collection, and Phoebe Peebles, archivist; at the Busch-Reisinger Museum by Emilie Dana, curatorial assistant; at the Harvard Planning Office by Robert Drake, librarian; at Baker Library by Florence Bartosheski, archivist; at the Harvard Law School Art Collection by Bernice Loss, curator; at the Radcliffe College Archives by Jane Knowles, archivist, and her assistant Barbara Harris; at *Harvard Magazine* by Jean Martin; at the Harvard News Office by William Tobey and Grace Choi; and at the Eda Kuhn Loeb Music Library by Michael Ochs, librarian. Nancy Locke Doonan at the Cambridge Historical Commission helped review the visual collections as well.

Manuscript production began with Juliet Floyd's lightning transcription of Bunting's often illegible pages into the computer. Editing and word processing arrangements over three years have been developed and provided (for this work on his alma mater) by William Floyd, who with my Tufts art history student Mary Speare moved the manuscript intact through many stages. Dorie Bunting has provided for me the impetus and the vision for this arduous endeavor as she has over the years for so many others.

Margaret Henderson Floyd
Medford, Massachusetts

Contents

HARVARD
An Architectural History

1 Seventeenth-Century Harvard

The debut of Harvard College was not auspicious. Almost immediately after the college was created in the summer of 1636 it became clear that neither the financial arrangements for its support, the faculty that was to staff it, nor the first buildings provided to shelter it were satisfactory. The financial needs of the young institution were never entirely met, the faculty (of one man) had promptly to be dismissed, and within eight years the first college building needed to be replaced. Nevertheless the leaders of the Massachusetts Bay Colony did not falter in their determination to nurture the school, for they viewed it as essential to the continuance and well-being of the divinely inspired experiment in which they were engaged. To succeed, the colony required leaders with the training to interpret and expound God's Word. The move to the New World had been made under the leadership of men who had the advantage of the best education available in England in the seventeenth century, but within the foreseeable future they would be retiring and replacements would be needed. There was no time to waste. Not only preachers but government officials must be educated, because it was expected that secular administrators would be guided by the same principles and insights that directed the ministers.[1]

Some idea of the importance the colonists attached to the college can be derived from the fact that the sum appropriated to it was more than half the entire tax levy for the colony in 1635 and almost one-quarter that of 1636. The economic prospects of the region in those years were fairly good. People were emigrating to New England as the result of straitened economic conditions in England and increasing pressure by the Crown on nonconforming religious groups. In 1633 ten shiploads of immigrants arrived in Massachusetts; seventeen came in 1634, and thirty-two in 1635; the population of the Bay Colony grew from approximately nine hundred settlers in 1630 to eleven thousand six hundred in 1641. Nevertheless one marvels at the early action on so bold an undertaking as founding a college, a matter that any other group probably would have deferred until times were settled, the population larger, the economy stabilized.

The earliest building used by the college, the house of William Peyntree, was purchased before the college adopted the name of its first benefactor, John Harvard. Peyntree, who had probably erected the house in 1633, had sold it by 1638 when he joined many other Cambridge residents in the Hooker migration to Connecticut.[2] In June of 1638 Nathaniel Eaton, the ill-starred first head of the college,[3] moved into the dwelling, and by September instruction in it had begun. The building must have been fairly spacious, because it housed Eaton's family and servants and perhaps as many as ten students. Its appearance and plan remain conjectural; yet early New England houses tended to be quite uniform, and it must have resembled the adjacent Wigglesworth House (fig. 1). The middle of Massachusetts Avenue in front of Wadsworth House can be identified with certainty as its location. Remains of the structure were discovered in 1909 during construction of the subway, and the positions of its front corners were marked by brass plates set into the pavement of the street.[4]

In 1644, within eleven years of its construction, the Peyntree house was replaced by a new dwelling for the president, the second in a long series. Again no visual record remains, but it too probably differed little from the typical seventeenth-century dwelling with a room on each side of a central entryway and a huge center chimney. Later, a lean-to kitchen may have been added at the rear. That it was large, as befitted the president, can be inferred from the appropriation of £150 by the General Court for its construction, whereas an ordinary house and lot in Cambridge at this time sold for £40 or £50.[5] But the college was not profligate with the space, for a room on the main floor was occupied by President Dunster's printing press, and students were housed in the building when the need arose.

There can be little doubt about the shape of the neighboring house bought from Edward Goffe in 1651 to accommodate the overflow of students from the first Harvard Hall, which had only recently been completed. Goffe College, as this small structure was rather ostentatiously called, was clearly a typical two-story, center-chimney house with lean-to kitchen; the 1654 inventory of college property describes it as "conteyning five Chambers, eighteen Studyes, a Kitchen Cellar, & three garretts." It takes little imagination to see how these were arranged: two rooms per floor plus back kitchen, with three small studies off each of the rooms plus three more studies fitted into the attic. The house was purchased with £124 derived from the sale of brazilwood sent by grateful Puritans in the Bahamas whom the people of Massachusetts had aided in 1650. Goffe College, along with the second president's house, was demolished, probably in the 1670s when the enrollment was at a low point.

These first two presidents' houses and Goffe College differed little from ordinary domestic structures of the time in Massachusetts, except perhaps in size. Before proceeding to a description of the first edifice erected specifically for college requirements, a word should be said about the relation of the college grounds to the village of Cambridge. When this story begins the village was still known as Newtowne; not until 1638, after it had been designated the seat of the new college, was its name changed.[6]

The original form of Cambridge was a small gridiron of streets occupying a gentle slope on the northeast bank of the Charles River (fig. 2). The townsite was divided into between 50 and 60 house lots, which varied in size from 1/8 acre to 1 1/8 acres. Although these sizes permitted small gardens within the village, the fields and pastures lay beyond the gridiron. A restriction that confined the earliest houses to the townsite, relaxed in 1634, was clearly intended to keep the population together in case of an

1

The Shepard-Hooker-Wigglesworth House: sketch from memory after its demolition in 1844.

2

Map of Cambridge in 1670. The College is the large U-shaped building at the upper right on the outskirts of the city. Indian College and the President's House to the west had already been constructed by 1670.

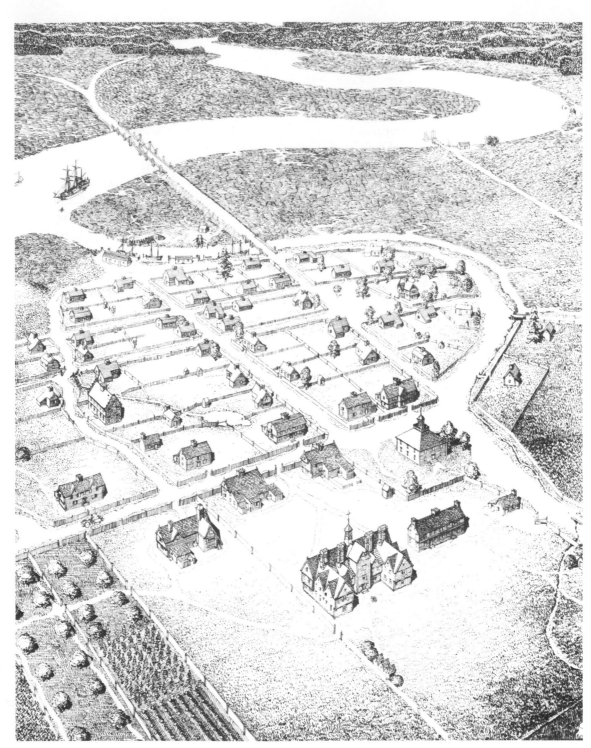

3
*Cambridge in 1668. The
Cambridge Historical
Commission has established
many inaccuracies in this
well-known reconstruction (by
H. R. Shurtleff, c. 1933), but
the basic street pattern and the
location of the college (in the
foreground) are correct.*

enemy assault; it also helped to create an urban context for the seat of government.

The grounds the college first occupied and those it would acquire in the course of time were located on the northeast fringe of the village (fig. 3).[7] House lots fronting Braintree Street (the present Massachusetts Avenue) were narrow and extended back about 100 feet, separated by a lane from cowyards behind. The low ridge on which they were built formed a barrier to the drainage of the land behind (to the northeast), so that in wet weather it became rather swampy. This area is now the Old Yard and the site of University and Thayer Halls. A shallow brook, which sometimes flowed, meandered south through the Yard where Matthews and Straus Halls now stand, across Harvard Square, down Brattle Street to Eliot Square, and from there into an inlet of the Charles River at the foot of Dunster Street.

Traffic in those days moved along very different routes from today. The only through roads were those leading northeast to Charlestown (the modern Kirkland Street), west to Watertown (Brattle Street), and Water Street (now Dunster), "the high road to the river" where a ferry connected with a road to Brookline. In 1660–62 a great bridge was built at Boylston Street. Both sections of the present Massachusetts Avenue were local streets, the eastern branch running to fields and salt marshes beyond what is now Central Square, the northern to planting fields, pastures, and wood-lots controlled by the town. But as the settlement of the outlying parts of Cambridge was allowed, Arlington (then called Menotomy) grew up and traffic along the northern road increased.

Another topographical feature should be mentioned: the small swamps on both sides of Kirkland Street and one of considerable size that extended from Oxford Street to the Somerville line. The latter area, which long resisted development, constituted a good part of what became Harvard's North Yard. Much of the land to the north and northeast of the first college, although it had been divided and granted by 1638, was too poorly drained for agricultural use. There was some disposition on the part of the town fathers to assign to the college acreage from the common lands, but as Harvard expanded over the years it had to purchase most of the land it needed.[8] Thus from the very beginning, except for some advantageous purchases after the Civil War, limited available land has been a controlling factor in the physical growth and development of Harvard.[9]

The first structure erected for academic purposes, construction of which began in the summer of 1638, was the largest building undertaken in the English colonies up to that time. Never given an official name, the building has been referred to in a variety of ways: The College, Harvard College, First Harvard College, and Old College. But its successor was also some-times called Old College. In order to avoid confusion and to underscore the chronology of the school's three early main buildings, we will refer to this first academic building as Harvard Hall I and to its two successors as Harvard Hall II and Harvard Hall III.

The building of Harvard Hall I was undertaken in the summer of 1638 on the strength of a grant of £400 promised by the colonial government and before the receipt of a £375 legacy from John Harvard, who died in September of that year. After two years and an expenditure of £577, the building had been enclosed, but with the exception of the main hall, it had "no floar in and above ye hall layd, no inside separating wall made, nor any one study erected throughout ye house."[10] Under President Dunster's supervision the building was sufficiently complete by September 23, 1642, for the Commencement banquet to be held in the hall. Next day the students, many of whom had been "disposed in the town and miserably distracted" while occupying rented rooms, moved in. Some of the studies, however, were not finished for another three years. The total cost was about £1000, of which one-quarter had to be scraped together in small donations from colonists and sympathizers in England.

As with the dwellings mentioned earlier, no visual record of Harvard Hall I remains, but scraps of information gleaned from college records, coupled with knowledge of seventeenth-century domestic structures in the colonies and of collegiate buildings in England, permitted a reconstruction of its plan and appearance (fig. 4) by Harold Shurtleff and Samuel Eliot Morison in 1933.[11] Like most New England houses of the time, this edifice of two stories plus garret was framed in wood, sheathed with clapboards, and roofed with shingles. Its windows were iron casements, and the large chimneys were of brick, possibly laid in clay below the roof but above it in a lime mortar made of oyster shells. It is safe to assume that except for size the building looked much like contemporary houses with dark weathered clapboards (since paint was not yet in common use). The front elevation (fig. 5) was probably fairly simple with a small gabled projection somewhere toward the center, judging from financial accounts of the time that refer to a small room above an entrance vestibule. The 1693 Franquelin View of the college suggests that there may have been two gables on the south elevation — yet there is no mention of attic rooms that would have required gables on this side of the building.[12] On the rear elevation, however, several gables and dormers must have been needed to provide windows for suites of rooms on the third floor of the two north wings and to cover the tower. "Ye turrett," as this feature was termed, contained the staircase and the back door, which provided access to the service yard where the privy was located.

The fenestration of Harvard Hall I was surely in actuality less regular than it appears in Shurtleff and Morison's reconstruction, since we know from college accounts that some rooms had as little as one square foot of glass, the equivalent of a small single casement, while the hall had 112 square feet, which must have been arranged in large banks of windows. Even among the studies the quantities of glass mentioned vary from one to $2^1/_2$ square feet. From information such as this it seems unlikely that there was a modular system of fenestration.

It is possible, however, to arrive at some notion of the plan of the first Harvard Hall (fig. 6), because the early records often indicate the functions of rooms and sometimes their orientation.[13] Most important was the hall, the all-purpose room that was occupied every hour of the day. It was used for lectures, recitations, commons, prayers, and college functions, the most important of which was the feast that came at Commencement time. If students were allowed any free time, they probably congregated here as well, at least in winter. No record exists of its exact size, but the hall must have been large enough to contain about sixty persons. Across one end ran a parclose, a wooden screen that partitioned off a passageway that ran between the front and back entrances in the manner of great halls in England. In addition, the ground floor contained a kitchen with pantry and

4
The Old College, Harvard
Hall I: north elevation.
Twentieth-century conjectural
restorations and perspectives
of Harvard Hall I were more
regular and balanced than the
actual seventeenth-century
building, yet provided a
romantic and picturesque
silhouette.

corn room, a buttery, one chamber (that is, bedroom), six studies, and a stair tower. As Morison observes, the buttery was to store and dispense beer, not butter, and the corn room served for storing the large quantities of cereals used to feed the college community and in which a large part of the tuition fee was paid.[14] Near the kitchen was a cellar. The second floor (fig. 7) contained the library, three large chambers, fourteen studies, two "cabims," and two single chambers, each with its own fireplace and study. The dimensions of the library need not have been large; as late as 1654 the collection of books numbered about one thousand, by 1723 only three thousand five hundred. On the third floor were two suites, each comprising a chamber and four studies, and four more studies were provided in the upper part of the stair tower. Some of the chambers were really small dormitories containing beds for all roommates, each of whom had a study of his own. The great (or long) chamber across the south front of the building may have had sleeping accommodations for as many as a dozen freshmen, to whom studies were not usually assigned. Morison cites diaries to show that students generally slept two to a bed and that trundle beds were often employed for younger classmates. Since furniture was scarce, such a chamber was not crowded.

The most intriguing feature and also the most elusive in attempting to arrive at a likely plan for Harvard Hall I is the study. This was little more than a closet furnished with a window, to which the student might retreat to study or to be alone. Very small, perhaps no more than $4^{1}/_{3}$ by 5 feet, it was ceiled with boards or plaster but in only two instances provided with a

5
Harvard Hall I: south elevation. Conjectural restoration drawing by Singleton P. Moorhead (c. 1933).

fireplace. No matter how small and simple, such a private space was undoubtedly a welcome adjunct in the otherwise highly communal life of the school. The private study, which originated in medieval times, was still being used in building English colleges in the seventeenth century. Morison spent a summer in England looking at early university buildings and found several examples of chambers with small attached studies, as in the Perse-Legge building of 1618 at Gonville and Caius College, Cambridge.

Although the student at Harvard appears to have paid nothing for the quarters where he slept, rent was charged for his study. These rents were an important source of college revenue. At Wadham College, Oxford, Morison discovered records indicating that when funds ran short during construction in 1610–1613, the college required the first occupant of each study to finish it off at his own expense. Upon graduation he was credited with the sum he had expended minus a reasonable deduction for depreciation. Harvard appears to have employed a similar method of financing. Evidence for this can be found in early student accounts under the confusing term of "Income," the meaning of which appears to have been the amount a student paid on coming into his study.[15] The records also indicate differences in the cost of finishing studies, with variations of from £1 to £5, and explicit items also vary, such as the number of board feet of lumber or square feet of glass used in a given study. This suggests that studies may have varied in size more than Shurtleff's plans indicate.

Another possibly confusing reference encountered in the records is to the "cabims" located in the great chamber above the hall. A "cabim" appears to have been a closet equipped with a bunk similar to that of a boat or the "lits-clos" of Brittany. In Corpus Christi College, Cambridge, for example, Morison discovered similar windowless recesses intended for sleeping.

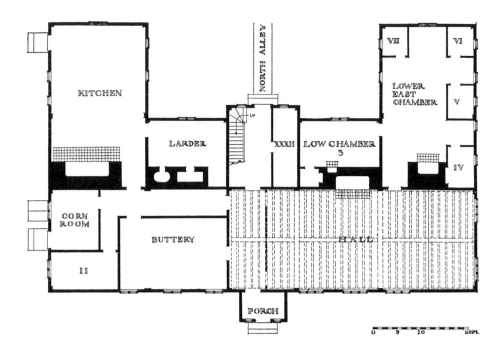

6
Harvard Hall I: first-floor plan. Conjectural restoration drawing by H. R. Shurtleff (c. 1933).

7
Harvard Hall I: second-floor plan. Conjectural restoration drawing by H. R. Shurtleff (c. 1933).

In each of the six suites of Harvard Hall I the cost of outfitting one study is substantially greater than that of others. This conforms with our knowledge that one "fellow" (instructor) or "domus" (candidate for the M.A. degree) was housed in each suite, where he was expected to maintain discipline and to see that the underclassmen spoke only Latin.

Although it would be fruitless to attempt to push the hypothetical reconstruction of Harvard Hall I further than have Shurtleff and Morison, several minor questions about their design should be registered. Seventeenth-century builders in New England were less concerned with symmetry and window regularity than were later designers (including twentieth-century restoration architects) who had been conditioned by the Renaissance. As mentioned earlier, it seems likely that the variation in the size of study windows produced a less regular system of fenestration than is indicated in Shurtleff's drawing. Similarly, the overall plan of the building was probably not so symmetrical. For one thing, the original plan was changed after construction had begun to permit an enlargement of the building, and it is unlikely that the original nucleus, which amounted to little more than half the final cost, could have been augmented with so much regularity.[16]

Shurtleff is undoubtedly correct in envisioning the stair tower as structurally independent of the main part of the building, because in 1679 the latter remained standing though the "turrett" had collapsed. But it is hardly necessary to suppose a fourth floor in the tower to contain the four upper studies. Placing the flights of stairs over one another — a more usual arrangement than on opposite outside walls — would make it quite possible to fit these studies into the corners of the third level. Each of these studies, noted in seventeenth-century accounts as the most modest in the building, could have had a small window above the adjacent second-story roof.

It may seem academic to ask who designed Harvard Hall I, since there were no professional architects in the colonies at this early date, but Morison makes an educated guess. After noting similarities in arrangement between Harvard's first building and the Old School quadrangle at Eton College, near Windsor — the presence of a large dormitory above the hall, individual studies, and a stair tower — he observes that John Wilson, minister of the church in Boston and member of the Board of Overseers of Harvard when the hall was being planned, had lived near Eton as a boy and attended school there. This nomination is probably as good as we shall ever have. The builder was John Friend of Ipswich.

Several bits of information regarding early seventeenth-century building practices can be deduced from the Harvard Hall I accounts.[17] The construction timetable for a frame building appears to have called for the erection of the wooden frame before the construction of the masonry chimneys. Evidence for this is Nathaniel Eaton's small expenditure after one year's work for bricks delivered at the job (£3) or for the mason (£6) in contrast to the £252 for shaping, hauling, and erection of the wooden frame. Lime was burned on the property. That there is a charge for "ffeling, squaring, Leading [hauling] timber" but not for the wood itself is explained by the fact that citizens of Cambridge could obtain a permit to cut trees on the common land for the purpose of building or repairing a structure.[18]

The completion of the hall undoubtedly contributed to the optimistic frame of mind of the Harvard community at mid-century. Besides having erected the new building, the school had survived the financial crisis of the early 1640s, it had friends in England who were now highly placed and willing to lend aid, its graduates had been accepted by Cambridge and Oxford as candidates for the M.A. degree, enrollment had so increased that an additional building (Goffe College) had to be purchased, and the curriculum was about to be extended from three to four years to conform with English university practice. But tempering this satisfaction was concern of a practical sort as Harvard Hall I, only a few years after its completion, began to manifest serious structural problems. In July 1647 a petition from President Dunster to the Commissioners of the United Colonies (Massachusetts Bay, Plymouth, Connecticut, and New Haven) stated, "Seeing from the first evill contrival of the Colledg building there now ensues yearly decayes of ye rooffe, walls and foundation, which ye study rents will not carry forth to repaire." Eight years later the Corporation informed the General Court: "The Colledge building although it be new groundsilled by ye help of some free Contributions ye last year, yet these ceasing & ye work of Reparation therewith intermitted, it remains in other respects in a very ruinous condition. It is absolutely necessary that it bee speedily new covered, being not fitt for Scholars long to abide in, as it is. And without suche Reparasion some time this summer both ye whole Building will decay and so ye former charge about it be lost."[19]

Such revelations are not surprising considering that the wooden sill of the frame was placed not on walls of a cellar but directly on the ground, on rocks laid in a trench. The cellar that was built was undoubtedly small, constructed for the storage of food rather than for the support of a superstructure. In 1654 the ground sill had to be replaced at a cost of £127. The roof required reshingling in 1663; for this purpose the town of Cambridge (as the early town record tells us) gave the college permission to cut timber from the common lands ("granted to the Coll: liberty for timb: to shingle the rooffe"). The original siding made from unseasoned wood apparently had shrunk, allowing for uncomfortable leaks of cold air. Between 1654 and 1663 repairs on Harvard Hall and the second president's house cost £337; during the next five years, another £139. Yet the average academic budget (excluding commons, that is, without meals) during the Dunster administration was only £175 per year. By 1671 it was evident that the structure was not worth repairing, and a replacement, Harvard Hall II, was begun. From then on the old hall deteriorated rapidly. The library was transferred to the new building in 1676; students were evacuated a year later, and just in time, because in 1679 the old structure was reported to have "fallen doune, a part of it."[20] Soon the remainder was demolished, a humiliating end for the structure that Edward Johnson had lauded in his pamphlet *Wonder Working Providence of Sion's Savior in New England* (1651): "The scituation of this Coledg is very pleasant, at the end of a spacious plain, more like a bowling green than a Wilderness, neer a fair navigable river, environed with many Neighboring Towns of note . . . The building [is] thought by some to be too gorgeous for a Wilderness, and yet too mean in others apprehensions for a Colledg. It is at present inlarging by purchase of the neighboring houses. It hath the conveniences of a fair Hall, comfortable Studies, and a good Library."

Whether it was inexperience in building for the harsh New England climate, poor supervision during construction, or something more mysterious like termites that caused the premature decay of Harvard Hall I we do

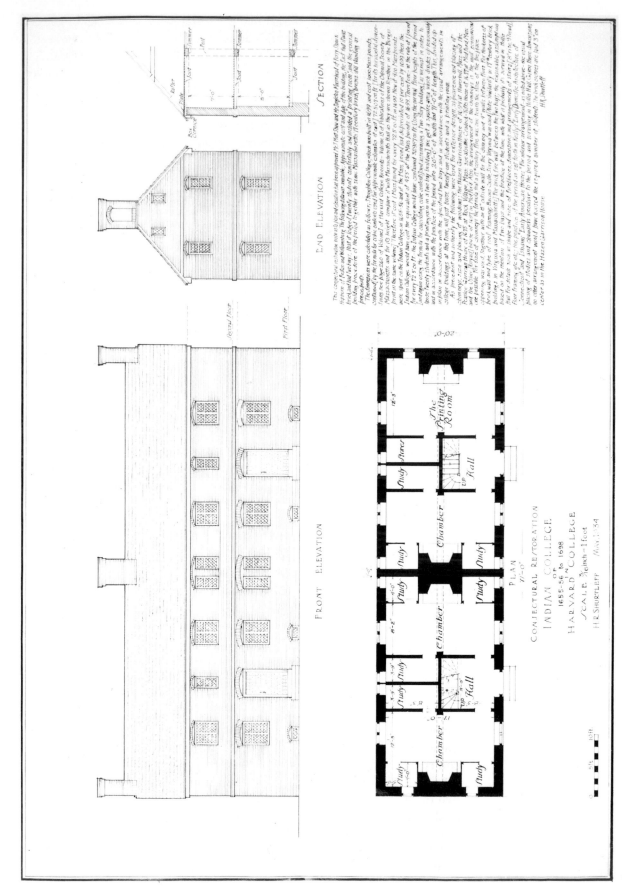

8 *Indian College. Conjectural restoration by H. R. Shurtleff (c. 1933).*

not know. Early supervision was sporadic. At first it was entrusted to the notorious Professor (not President) Nathaniel Eaton, who in the process of supervising the construction may have embezzled £1000 of college funds. The project was next entrusted to Overseer Samuel Shepard, but in 1641 he departed for London "leaving/ye work in ye Carpenters and masons hands without Guide or further director." Responsibility then fell on President Dunster, who was already overburdened, giving twenty lectures each week, hearing recitations, disputations, declamations, and commonplaces (practice sermons), as well as watching after college business matters, overseeing the commons, and keeping an eye on student conduct and morality.[21]

Even with adequate supervision, many early Cambridge buildings proved structurally unsound. For example, records for the Lee-Nichols house, built at 159 Brattle Street about 1686, show that it required drastic renovation in 1716 after it had been ravaged by "ye worms." In 1650 the first meeting house, erected only twenty years earlier, was so decrepit that it had to be replaced. And in 1690 it was necessary to demolish the stone schoolhouse on Dunster Street, built only sixteen years before.[22] This suggests that the early Cambridge housewrights had much to learn about the materials and methods of construction required in their new homeland.

The next major architectural undertaking at Harvard was the Indian College, described as a brick structure "strong and substantial, though not very capacious." Probably erected in 1655 just west of Harvard Hall I, it cost between three and four hundred pounds, funds for which were furnished by a charitable foundation in England, the Society for the Propagation of the Gospel in New England. Interested in missionary work among the Indians, this group incorporated in 1649 to collect funds and in 1653 instructed its commissioners in Massachusetts to erect "one Intyre Rome att the College for the Convenience of six hopeful Indian youths . . . which Rome may bee two stories high and built plaine but strong and durable." During the next year the size of the building caused considerable debate between the commissioners, who wished to authorize a 32-by-20-foot structure, and President Dunster, who envisioned one twice that size, a debate of a sort that would confront the college several times during the next century. The president prevailed: the building was described in 1698 as "a brick pile of two bayes" (two entries) and "large enough to receive and accommodate about twenty scholars with convenient lodgings and studies." That the commissioners' appraisal of the space needs of Indian students was more realistic is indicated by the proposal in 1656 that vacant rooms in the building be used for English students.[23] When the English students moved out in 1677 to newly completed Harvard Hall II, other uses were found for the Indian College. One function was to house the college printing press.[24] Here the famous 1200-page Indian Bible was printed between 1659 and 1663. With the closing of the press in 1692 the building stood empty, and a year later the Overseers voted its demolition. In May 1698 Samuel Sewell noted in his diary: "The Indian Colledge is pulled down to the ground, being sold to Mr. Willis [for] the building of Mr. Stoughton's colledge."

The description of the Indian College suggests a straightforward plan, which Shurtleff has convincingly reconstructed (fig. 8).[25] There were probably no gables, since there was no need for rooms in the attic. Although the building had no cellar and its bricks were reused for another structure, debris discovered in 1871 in the course of digging foundations for Matthews Hall was probably related to it.

With the completion of the Indian College in 1655 the prologue to this record of Harvard architecture comes to an end. By this time there were four main buildings: Harvard Hall I (1638), the president's house (built in 1644 as a replacement for Peyntree house and demolished in the 1670s), Goffe College (acquired in 1651), and the Indian College. In addition, there were several utilitarian structures about which we know only their names: a print house, two barns (one for the president), a brew house, a bake house, and, of course, privies (fig. 3).

Although the four main buildings stood near one another, each appears to have been located with regard to the boundaries of the narrow house lot on which it stood rather than with an eye to creating some kind of unity. As any respectable private dwelling should, both the president's house and Goffe College sat at the front of their respective lots close to the street (Braintree Street, now Massachusetts Avenue); their rear elevations faced back yards even though the principal college buildings were behind them. The latter could hardly have been seen from the street. This curious unrelatedness of the two pairs of buildings plus the gap between them precluded any sense of visual order in this first Harvard Yard. Furthermore, the rear portion of the Peyntree lot, on which Harvard Hall I was placed, had been surrounded by Professor Eaton sometime before 1639 with a barrier of $6^{1}/_{2}$-foot pales. The wide Hall set athwart a long, narrow lot enclosed by a stockade must have appeared crowded indeed. (The stockade was expensive: it cost £30, one-quarter as much as the framing of the first unit of the Hall.) But Eaton built the stockade — $2^{1}/_{2}$ feet higher than the fence required by law — at a time when the settlers' foothold on the new continent was still tenuous. Perhaps he found psychological satisfaction in surrounding himself with a barrier that kept out the boundless forests (as well as strays from the adjoining ox pasture). And possibly it was the paling and the thirty apple trees within that moved Edward Johnson in 1651 to see the situation of the college as "very pleasant, at the end of a spacious plain, and more like a bowling green than a Wilderness."

The acquisition of land by the college proceeded in a piecemeal fashion. By 1670 five parcels amounting to about nine acres had been accumulated in the western third of the present Harvard Yard, and it was there that the next phase of building would take place. There appears to have been no awareness on the part of sponsors or administrators of a need to secure land for future development, especially when funds were barely sufficient to keep the doors of the college open. But even if money had been plentiful, it is too much to expect that type of foresight in men surrounded by endless forest who lived at a time when ample tracts of land were available almost for the asking. Their concept of environmental control was Professor Eaton's stockade.

2 The Brick Quadrangles

Keeping the young college afloat was a continuing struggle. Money was drastically short, and the problem of balancing outlays for instructional purposes against building needs was difficult. The General Court of Massachusetts Bay Colony, which established Harvard College and long served as a sponsor, tried numerous methods of financing the school in the seventeenth century: a direct appropriation of £1400 when the school was founded; the annual rent from the Boston-Charlestown ferry; and a system known as "College Corn," whereby every family in New England was encouraged to set aside a bushel of corn for the benefit of the college (this worked for about fifteen years). Several campaigns were mounted in England as well as in the United Colonies to raise money for scholarships for the education of Indian youth or for some stated need such as the erection or repair of a building. Prominent citizens in each town were appointed by the Court to solicit contributions from their townsmen, and when this failed, an annual tax was levied for the specific benefit of Harvard. Although well-to-do settlers in the colony were slow to follow the generous example of John Harvard, several substantial gifts were eventually received. Notable among these were the Piscataqua Benevolence of £60 per year for seven years, which a group of wealthy Portsmouth merchants discharged with shipments to Boston of lumber to be sold for the benefit of the college, and the Eleuthera Donation of brazilwood from Puritans in the Bahamas in 1650. A few farms, houses, or entailments for the benefit of the college were received, but many of these lay at a distance from Cambridge and were therefore difficult to oversee. The Mowlson-Bridges fund, the college's only endowment for many years, was earmarked for scholarships.

Despite financial straits, especially during the early years under President Dunster and again in the 1670s, the president, Corporation, and Overseers persisted in their dream of providing an environment in which the educational process as they remembered it from England could flourish. It would have been much easier and less costly to make do with whatever facilities the village of Cambridge could provide: to use the meeting house for lectures and recitations, to rely on ministers from the local and neighboring churches to give the lectures, to let students room and board in whatever manner each could secure. Instead the college leaders persevered in efforts to create an environment in which students and teachers could eat, sleep, study, and converse together under one roof. An appeal written by the Overseers in 1671 to twenty patrons in England from whom they hoped to secure funds for the construction of the second Harvard Hall expressed it this way: "it is well known to your selves what advantage to Learning acrue's by the multitude of persons cohabiting for Scholastical communication, whereby to acuate the minds of one another."

The habitual shortage of money was exacerbated in the 1670s by King Philip's War, in which frontier communities were destroyed and about one-tenth of the male population of martial age killed, and the cost of which was estimated to equal the value of all personal property in the colony. As the generation of original Puritan leaders died off, questions began to be raised in some quarters about the need to maintain a college. Those drawn to a more fire-and-brimstone type of religion questioned whether preachers needed a college education to experience and interpret the burning spirit of the Gospel; some complained of the large proportion of Harvard-trained ministers (30 out of 122 by 1669) who returned to England; and still others doubted the worth of a college education for laymen given the time and money required. Support also diminished from wealthy Puritans in England, who had problems of their own now that the Stuarts had returned to power. Both financial support and enrollment dropped to alarming proportions. The number of graduating seniors declined from 12 in 1661 to zero in 1672; the enrollment, which had reached 57 in 1658, dropped to 25 in 1671 and only 3 in November 1674. For a few months in the spring of 1675 the college was actually closed. To make matters worse, the school lacked strong leadership following the death of President Chauncy in 1672. Under President Hoar (1672–1675), who proved unable to work with students or Overseers, college affairs ground to a standstill; from 1675 to 1707 the presidents served part time, giving the college only as much attention as they could spare from their churches in Boston. For four years (1688–1692) during his presidency, Increase Mather was in England. Had it not been for the devoted service of two tutors, William Brattle and John Leverett, who constituted the entire teaching staff, Harvard probably would have disappeared. Surprisingly, it was during this low period, in 1671–1677, that the college erected its next building, Harvard Hall II.

The second phase of Harvard building is inaugurated with a shift from the Peyntree and Goffe lots to the western edge of the present Harvard Yard. This was made possible by the acquisition in 1661 of the Betts lot, which rounded out college holdings in this area (fig. 9). The buildings erected here were located near the public road and grouped as quadrangles, a very different arrangement from that of the original Harvard Hall and the Indian College, which had been situated far back from the street on separate lots visually unrelated to one another. This attempt to create some order and relationship between buildings evidences a degree of sophistication in planning that was new to the colony; its origin can be found in English collegiate building of the preceding century. It also provided for a direct architectural relationship with Harvard Square.

Thanks to an engraved view of the college executed in 1726 by William Burgis, *A Prospect of the Colledges in Cambridge in New England*, we do not have to rely on conjectural restorations of the appearance of Harvard Hall II (fig. 10).[1] Despite its uncomfortable blend of Medieval and Renais-

9
Land parcels assembled to
make up Harvard Yard, with
the years they were acquired.

10
Harvard Hall II (1674–
1682). Detail from Burgis-
Price view (1726).

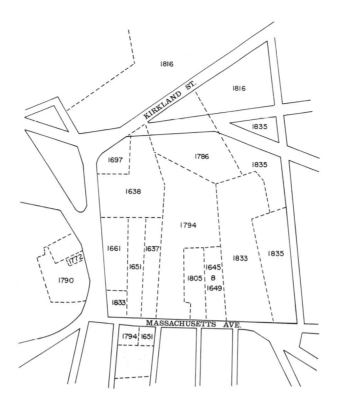

sance features, this building was a somewhat better conceived design than its predecessor. The geometric clarity of this large (42-by-97-foot) brick edifice was nullified by the complexity of its gambrel roof with fourteen gables (two end gables plus twelve cross gables) and ten dormers. The use of such closely spaced gables across the facade finds precedent in contemporary English collegiate building as well as in simpler New England domestic designs, but the scheme here is awkward and the roof appears not quite to fit, as though it belonged to a different building.[2] The fenestration was undoubtedly more regular than in the first hall, but the windows on the top two floors (in the gables and dormers) are of very different size and spacing from those below. The mullioned and diamond-paned casements are Medieval, but the rather extraneous brick cornices of the ground-floor windows supported on curious brackets topped with spheres, are a clear attempt at the Renaissance mode. Additional Classical (Jacobean) accents are the pilasters that frame both doors, the double belt courses between the first and second stories, and the water table, which was undoubtedly worked out in pressed brick. The same inspiration is responsible for the thin pilaster strips on the chimneys. The least successful aspect of the design resulted from an effort to force the bilateral composition into a centralized one as Renaissance taste demanded. To achieve this aim the belt courses over the two central bays of the main facade were slanted up, again in an uncomfortable Jacobean fashion, as if to produce some sort of pediment. The greater interval between the two center windows only heightens the tension between the divided halves of the composition, and it bears little relation to the axial placement of the octagonal lantern on the roof. The most recognizable Renaissance feature, the roof balustrade, was not added until 1691.

The Burgis Prospect in combination with early college housing records and a report in 1676 by Edward Randolph, an agent for the crown, enabled Harold Shurtleff to make a convincing reconstruction of the plan of the building (fig. 11). According to Randolph, "New-colledge, built at the publick charge, is a fair pile of brick building covered with tiles, by reason of the late Indian warre not yet finished. It contains 20 chambers for students, to [studies] in a chamber; a large hall, which serves for chappel; over that a convenient library."[3]

As at Harvard Hall I, all college activities, including instruction, were housed in this single building. This was possible because the method of teaching still stressed lecture and group recitation and because all members of a class followed an identical course of study. In the mid-eighteenth century, as the curriculum became slightly liberalized with the addition of a basic science course, space was obtained for the Philosophical Chamber by the removal of partitions that had divided the west end of the second floor into chambers and studies. This easy rearrangement provided room for storage and demonstrations. The hall, warmed by two fireplaces, was still conceived as a "great hall" with a parclose; but now this screen ran parallel to the front wall in order to connect the two stair halls and thus to shield the hall from cross traffic. Two sets of stairs made circulation easier than in Harvard Hall I. On the second level were the library and four chambers with attached studies, small and unheated as before, while the third floor contained six chambers and eighteen studies including the long chamber that served as a freshman dormitory. On the top floor were only three

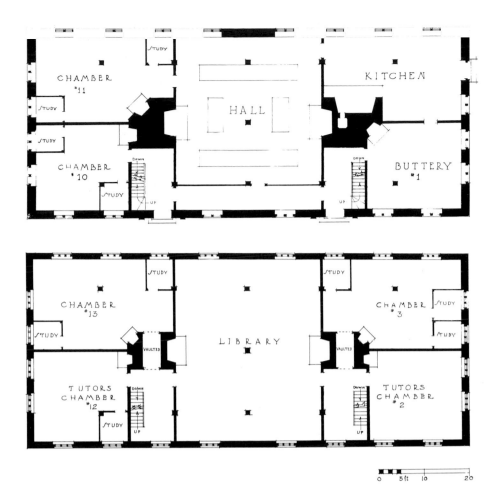

11

Harvard Hall II: reconstruction of first- and second-floor plans.

chambers with requisite studies, because the space here was so cut up by the construction of the roof. The enormous ten-foot-square chimney stacks had counterparts in contemporary Cambridge dwellings, such as the Lee-Nichols house (1686) at 159 Brattle Street.[4]

The most amateur aspect of the design was the roof. From the Burgis view it appears that the usual steeply sloped section of the gambrel roof did not extend out as far as the brick facades, and this necessitated adding a third slope of very low pitch at the bottom. This curious complication made for great inconvenience within and without. On the inside it could have required posts set in eight or ten feet from the exterior walls, which would have interrupted the interior space. On the exterior the pockets created between the cross gables and bottom slope of the roof caught rain and snow and invited decay—as any practical housewright could have predicted. It was the source of enough trouble that in 1712 the Overseers were advised that "the best way is to take off the roof and raise a third Story upright instead of the two Storys which are now under ye roof, with a flat roof well shingled; with a Coving or Mondillions on each Side of it, and a battlement of Brick at each Ende." Just such a change was made at the Lee-Nichols house when it was renovated in the 1740s, but the suggestion was not followed at Harvard Hall II even though such a remodeling would have provided an opportunity to "fancy up" the exterior with new Renaissance trim.[5]

19   *The Brick Quadrangles*

12

*The Burgis-Price view (1726)
shows Harvard's brick
quadrangle as it appeared
after Massachusetts Hall
(1718) replaced the President's
House across from Harvard
Hall II. Stoughton Hall I
(1698) faces the street.*

The committee to supervise the construction of Harvard Hall II consisted of Deputy Governor Leverett "along with Deacon John Cooper and Mr. William Manning of Cambridge, to be agent and Stewards to manage that work, both in hiring and paying workmen and Artificers, in procuring and purchasing materials and in doing all other matters and things referring to the building and finishing of said Colledge." The master builder was Samuel Andrew of Cambridge, "a master mariner and well skilled in mathematics." Although the new hall was undeniably needed, the struggle to pay for it was grim. Construction was authorized in 1671 and sufficient funds were subscribed, but collection proved difficult because of the dislocations caused by King Philip's War. Building materials were being assembled before the forced resignation of President Hoar in March 1675.[6] The frame was raised on August 7, 1674, but work had to be suspended a year later. In February 1677 the Council of Magistrates ordered "that the Stewards for the new brick Colledge doe forth with finish up the place appoynted for the Coll: library, that so they may be immediately secured therein," because by this time the library in old Harvard Hall was no longer usable. The books were transferred the following summer. By late May 1677 the project had been "brought so farr as that the outside worke is for the most part finished & the liberrary completely finished & one chamber, all the rest of the house, for the present useless, the most of the floores wants boards, 3 cases of holppacte stairs to bee made that will not be done with a little cost, & the greatest part of the house to plaister & siele withinside . . . And mens eyes upon us to get the new building finished, but we haue not wherewithall."[7]

By August 1677 Commencement could be held in the hall, but it was probably the following spring before the students moved in. Of the £3028 subscribed for the building only £1969 could be collected, though attempts to do so dragged on as late as 1678. The total cost came to about £2000, a reasonable charge for the largest and finest building in the English colonies prior to construction of William and Mary College in 1698. Harvard Hall II served until January 24, 1764, when it burned accidentally.

Next in order of construction was a house for President Oakes (1675–1681). This third shelter for Harvard presidents cost £280 and was put up speedily between July 1 and September 23, 1680. When in 1684 the college entered the era of part-time presidents who had residences elsewhere, this edifice was used to quarter students. No picture of it is known, but doubtless it also was a large, conventional, two-story, center-chimney dwelling.[8]

The location of the president's house on the present site of Massachusetts Hall and facing Harvard Hall II established the second side of a quadrangle and thus inaugurated a more formal concept of planning at the college. The third side of the open quadrangle was completed in 1698 when Old Stoughton Hall was constructed solely to house students, whose numbers increased significantly in the late 1680s (fig. 12). The hall was named for William Stoughton, Lieutenant Governor of Massachusetts and unrepentant judge in the Salem witchcraft trials, who donated £800 toward its construction. This gift is important as the first example in the long and important list of structures given to Harvard by individuals.[9] Four stories high and 23 by 100 square feet in area, it could house forty students. One can easily read the plan from the facade: two entries, each of which gave access to two chambers per floor; the locations of studies are indicated by the narrow windows. Though this building was more elaborately decorated, its plan must have been similar to that of the Indian College, and essentially the same arrangement would be used for subsequent Harvard dormitories until the construction of Holworthy in 1811 (and for dormitories at Yale, Brown, and Princeton as well). The orderly fenestration, the use of a clearly defined main cornice and dormer windows rather than gables in the gambrel roof, and the presence of pedimented door frames, quoins, string courses, and an inscription panel topped by a small pediment mark this clearly as a Georgian design. Here at the very end of the seventeenth century Harvard finally put the Medieval tradition behind.

Unfortunately, the construction of Old Stoughton was not as competent as its design. Built without a basement (though a small wine cellar was later dug), the structure was neither stable nor weathertight. In 1710 a shingle roof had to be substituted for one of slate that leaked. In 1721 the Overseers appointed a committee to arrange that a "Cross Wall or Walls (as by the Skilfull shal be found necessary) be built for the strengthening of Stoughton-College and that the said College be Clap-boarded on the East Side." But the skillful mason advised that the building was "so far bow'd that it could not be Secur'd as proposed . . . 'twas necessary to take it down." In 1755 a remarkable thing reportedly happened: the Lisbon earthquake, which was felt in Cambridge, shook the walls of Old Stoughton straight. The troops of the Continental Army who were quartered at Harvard during the Siege of Boston finished the rickety dormitory, however. In September 1779 the college faculty voted to demolish it and instructed "that the College Carpenters be directed to take way all the Boards & Timbers in Stoughton Hall, that may be removed with safety . . . & secure (them) in Holden Chapel, & then draw all the Nails that may be of Use, & reserve them for the Benefit of the College."[10] But as with Harvard Hall I a century earlier, nothing was done until a great part of one wall collapsed. Finally in 1781 a contract was given to Deacon Aaron Hill for the demolition, provided he pile the brick, save the stone, and remove the rubbish, for which labor he was allowed to keep half the brick.

Within a generation of the completion of Old Stoughton, the college was again in need of housing as enrollment expanded rapidly. The class of 1721, which entered in 1717, graduated 37 members; the average for the previous five classes was 18, that for the succeeding five classes 39. There were 124 students (undergraduate and graduate) enrolled in 1718, but accommodations existed for no more than 79 (40 in Stoughton and 39 in Harvard Hall II). One senses alarm in a memorandum addressed to the legislature: "the Numbers of ye Sons of ye Prophets are now so increas'd that the Place wherein they were wont to dwell is become Streight." Many lived in town, "so much & so far from . . . constant Inspection & ye Slender Authority ye College is capable of Exerting." Although the legislators were sympathetic, they cut the size of the proposed dormitory by half, but after a year of persistent appeals from President Leverett (1708–1725), they relented and increased the appropriation to the required £3500.[11] Begun in May 1719 and finished a year later, Massachusetts Hall is Harvard's oldest surviving building.

Occupying the site of the third presidential residence, the new dormitory formed an unequal counterpart to Harvard Hall II and with Old Stoughton created a small, well-defined courtyard (fig. 12), a concept easily traced to Cambridge and Oxford.[12] This new quadrangle opened to the west, toward the Common, with its back to the still shapeless area that would later become Harvard Yard. The three buildings were uncomfortably crowded; the distance between Old Stoughton and Massachusetts Hall was less than five feet and that between Old Stoughton and Harvard Hall II but slightly more. It seems strange to us that with ample acreage at their disposal the officials should have chosen so tight a scale for their buildings. Perhaps this small, rigidly conceived space, like Eaton's palisade, was an attempt to place restraints on nature, which elsewhere in early eighteenth-century America was so vast and overwhelming. But in failing to plan for future growth by turning its back on its extensive holdings to the east (which by 1718 included about one-third of the present Yard), the administration established a precedent that would unfortunately be followed for generations. Of course, there had to be a back yard of some kind in which to locate two privies, a brew house, and the fellows' barn. President Leverett may have seen to it that the college front yard with its brick fence was fairly orderly, but the back yard as late as the inauguration of President Kirkland in 1810 was "an unkept Sheep-commons, almost treeless."[13]

In plan Massachusetts Hall followed the two-entry scheme of Old

Stoughton with an important difference: it was twice as deep. This made room for 16 studies on each floor rather than eight. Theoretically, 64 students could be housed here, but in practice two chambers were reserved for tutors, and one of these was later set aside as the Apparatus Chamber, successor to the Philosophical Chamber and ancestor to Harvard's later scientific laboratories. Although this double-width arrangement housed more students per floor, it had the practical disadvantage of leaving four studies per floor (those on each side of the transverse dividing partition) without windows; these could have served no other purpose than for storage. A floor plan—possibly drawn by President Leverett, who took an active interest in the land and buildings owned by the college—survives in the Harvard Archives. It shows the studies as no more than closets about 4½ by 5 feet in size, symmetrically disposed on either side of a fireplace alcove, but there is no way of knowing if this scheme was followed.

The Early Georgian character of Massachusetts Hall marks a considerable advance over previous Harvard architecture. All traces of the Medieval tradition are gone, yet the facade lacks the elaborate decorative adjuncts that characterize High Georgian work. It possesses the simple dignity of a building in a provincial town where the budget was limited and sponsors were opposed to external show. Its aesthetic value depends on its proportions, minor differences in window height and spacing, and slight accents supplied by brick belt courses and water tables that mark floor levels but do not interrupt the continuity of the fine brick masonry. The twin paneled chimneys of the gable ends and the roof balustrade that disguises the upper slopes of the gambrel roof provided Harvard architects of the present century with a model that would be copied many times. The clock face in the west gable and the college bell were added in 1725. The most elaborate feature, as seen in the Burgis Prospect, was the hood, supported on generous scrolled brackets over each doorway. This element, the undersurface of which was hollowed in the shape of a scallop shell or half-dome, was popular in England during the reign of Queen Anne. Unfortunately, New England frugality determined that these rather delightful elements were too expensive to maintain, and they were removed by 1790.[14]

Later changes were more drastic. Since brick masonry was employed in the original structure only for peripheral walls and chimney stacks, the building lacked a transverse wall of brick to act as a fire barrier and a tie between the long facades. Thus moving interior partitions of wood involved no major structural change. In 1870, when the college was desperately short of classrooms, Massachusetts Hall was completely gutted to create four large spaces, each two stories high, which were used for lectures, laboratories, and examination rooms. After a fire in 1924 the interior was rebuilt as a dormitory, but in 1939 the first two floors were again remodeled, this time as administrative offices. Metal window sash were added in 1974, but the detailing of the new windows, designed in consultation with the Cambridge Historical Commission, is so accurate that the change is not apparent.

While serving as Harvard's president, John Leverett lived in his own house. (This property—originally owned by Thomas Shepard—was not acquired by Harvard until 1794.) Following the progressive Leverett administration, the provincial legislature celebrated the appointment of conservative President Benjamin Wadsworth (1725–1737) by building him

13
*Wadsworth House (1726)
served as the official residence
for Harvard's presidents for
over a century. The original
roof of Boylston Hall can be
seen on the right.*

an official residence. Befitting the dignity of its occupant, the house, which would serve as the presidential residence for more than a century, was planned on a generous scale (fig. 13). Indeed, Wadsworth House was one of the few large Cambridge residences at the time of the Revolution which had not been built by a Tory. From the outset the committee overseeing its construction ignored the legislature's authorization of £1000; in less than a year they spent more than the allotted amount, and the interior was only half finished. The final cost was almost twice that appropriated.[15]

Despite its function and the fact that it was located on college land, President Wadsworth's house was set apart from the college buildings like any private dwelling. Facing south toward Braintree Street (now Massachusetts Avenue), it was one of a row of large residences of substantial Cambridge citizens, including the parsonage. Like its neighbors, Wadsworth House had a barn, outhouses, and a pasture. The president's field comprised a good part of what is now the Old Yard; when this area was mowed, it was the responsibility of the freshman class to rake the hay. Between the house and the street in front was a pleasant garden with a paved courtyard. This was lost to successive enlargements of Braintree Street in 1797 and 1894.[16] Even today Wadsworth House maintains a certain independence from the Yard. It is the only wooden building within that area, a distinction emphasized by its traditional yellow paint and its position as the only structure not enclosed within the stately Memorial Fence.

Wadsworth House is one of the few good examples of Early Georgian domestic architecture remaining in Cambridge. The most distinctive feature of its five-bay facade is the gambrel roof with hip dormers. The eaves are boxed to form a cornice supported by curious small brackets, a local detail repeated in the William Brattle House erected one year later, and not unknown in Boston and elsewhere at the time. The clapboards that sheathe the facade are narrower and shorter than those employed today, and they are planed to a beaded edge. Lapping of the clapboards at the corner rather than using a mitre is awkward but not uncommon among eighteenth-century houses in Middlesex County.[17] Markedly different from the center-chimney and winding-stair plan of Colonial times is the Georgian center hall, used here with a straight run of stairs. The fenestration is symmetrical and substantially larger than in Colonial buildings, but the glass panes (twelve per sash) are smaller than those used half a century later. The placement of windows close under the eaves is characteristic of the early eighteenth century; indeed these are so close to the cornice that when shutters (a new feature in American architecture just after the Revolution) were added to the upstairs windows about 1820 their tops had to be cut off to enable them to swing, a detail obscured in recent renovation.

By the 1840s Wadsworth House must have seemed old-fashioned and inadequate to serve the president. In 1843 Isaiah Rogers produced plans and specifications for a large Greek Revival residence and for an even larger Italianate dwelling.[18] These of course were not realized. But Wadsworth House was soon adapted to other uses, and in the course of time it sustained several remodelings. After 1849 it was given over to student occupancy because President Sparks lived in his own house, after 1900 it was occupied by visiting and resident clergy, and in 1950 it was converted to university offices. Modifications of this building have been rather severe: an enlargement of the ground story in 1781–1783 added bays at each end of the house and probably the entrance porch. Characteristic of later Federal details, the thin dentil cornice used for the extensions as well as for the remodeled interiors is out of scale with the original heavy cornice. Other additions of this time are the brick kitchen wing and the two-story brick building that served as the office of the college steward and housed the college archives. This was attached in 1871 when the southwest corner of the Yard was reorganized to permit construction of Matthews Hall. Except for the stairway with its rather clumsy newel, little of the original interior trim of Wadsworth House remains.[19]

The building of Holden Chapel in 1742, giving Harvard its own legitimate religious structure, must have reassured many people in the Bay Colony that they had indeed created a college in the tradition of the great English universities. The need for a separate chapel was more psychological than practical, since students and faculty had always attended both Sunday services in the meetinghouse and had used the main college hall for daily prayers.[20] And in fact within less than a generation of its construction, Holden Chapel was abandoned for religious uses.

That the college fathers were now somewhat less narrow in their view of the world than their ancestors is suggested by the fact that they accepted the full Renaissance style of architecture, similar to an English college chapel (fig. 14), along with a ceremonial manner of organizing the new interior. Timothy Pickering described the chapel as he remembered it from his student days around 1763: "on either side of the middle aisle were ranges of seats with backs made wholly of oaken wood and rising one above the other to the side walls. The door was at the western end and the pulpit or raised seat for the President at the eastern."[21] This longitudinal organization of interior space with seats running parallel to the side walls, accen-

14
Holden Chapel: west front (John Smibert, 1742). This Baroque cartouche in the western pediment was duplicated on the unadorned eastern elevation after Harvard Yard turned inward in the nineteenth century. Richard Bond's Lawrence Scientific School (before its remodeling) appears to the left and Charles Bulfinch's Stoughton Hall II behind.

tuated by a vaulted ceiling, was in sharp contrast to the purposeful nonaxial arrangement of Puritan meetinghouses.

Holden Chapel was constructed with a gift of £400 from Mrs. Holden, the widow of a wealthy English Dissenter, member of Parliament, and director of the Bank of England. The construction of the new chapel inaugurated a second quadrangle to the north of Harvard Hall II, which also opened west to Cambridge Common. Despite its simple format — a small brick box, 32 by 40 feet, with a ridge roof — Holden achieved considerable dignity by reason of its proportions and well-placed architectonic accents: a water table that forms a base, paired pilasters with crisply detailed brownstone capitals and bases (omitted on the east elevation), a full wooden entablature (remaining now on the west elevation only), round-headed windows (originally shorter than at present), and in the tympanum of the pedimented gable (west front only) a handsomely carved coat of arms surrounded with florid scroll work. This design introduced Cambridge to a degree of sophistication that would not be seen again until the construction of the Vassall and Apthorp mansions and of Peter Harrison's Christ Church (1760).[22]

Even by Boston standards the design of Holden Chapel was revolutionary, though a year before, in 1740, a very similar scheme employing paired pilasters to frame round-headed openings was used at the original Faneuil Hall. Although that structure, of two stories with an open market at ground level, was considerably more complex, the profiles of the brownstone capitals and bases of the two buildings are strikingly similar. Given this close parallel, it hardly seems necessary to hypothesize a British origin for the design of Holden as some have done. More plausibly it has been suggested that the author of the two might have been John Smibert, a

British-trained portrait painter who was active in Boston after 1730.[23]

Important as Holden Chapel was to the image of the college, its use for religious services was short-lived. When Harvard Hall III was finished in 1766, morning and evening prayers were transferred to the larger chapel on its first floor.[24] When the Continental Army was billeted in Cambridge in 1775, Holden served first as a general utility room, then as a barracks, and was so roughly used that the next college records report it unfit. It was fit, however, to house the college fire engine; and in 1779 the faculty directed the carpenter to store there the lumber salvaged from Old Stoughton, which was to be demolished. In 1782 the chapel was fitted up as the first quarters of the newly formed Medical School, in which capacity it underwent numerous modifications. Most drastic was the insertion in 1800 of a mezzanine ten feet above the first floor and a cross-wall that cut the interior into east and west halves: the east used by the Medical School (physics and chemical laboratories on the ground floor, an anatomical lecture room above), the west end by the college for four recitation rooms. Access to the second story was gained through a new brick stair tower at the east end. After the Medical School moved to Boston in 1810, both floors of Holden were used for lectures or recitations. To provide adequate light two cone-shaped skylights were inserted above and the windows on the ground floor were lowered by two feet. Another major change occurred in 1850: the upper level was converted into a lecture hall with 150 seats arranged in curved tiers. With the addition of the second skylight, this area became the most popular lecture space in the university. Meanwhile the lower floor was used as a museum. The 1870s saw the lecture hall fitted with a stage and used for college musicals. The intermediate floor was removed in 1880, thus restoring the interior to its original condition. Since then the old chapel has been used for classes in music and elocution and for choir rehearsals.

The exterior of Holden Chapel has also seen its share of "improvement." Sometime after 1806 a vestibule capped with rectangular merlons was added to the west front and the original tall rectangular doorway (fig. 15) was replaced by one that was arched (fig. 14).[25] A brick stair tower had been added in 1800 to the east side to provide access to the second floor, but it was removed in 1850 when inside stairs were substituted. At that time the west vestibule was demolished and the present door frame added to the round-headed door. In 1880, in recognition of the fact that most users now approached from the Yard, a new main entrance was cut in the east elevation where the brick stair tower had been, and the original front door on the west was blocked up. Finally, in the 1920s, a duplicate Holden coat of arms was made for the pediment of the east (rear) facade. The irony of this is that the original builders had economized by omitting the stone capitals and bases on this rear (but now front) elevation. In terms of adaptive use at Harvard, Holden Chapel holds the record.

A period of prosperity and increased enrollment forced the administration to appeal again for a new dormitory in 1759. The justification was familiar: "inspection cannot be had of those who live in families in town as might be had if they resided within the walls of the College." In 1762 the legislature appropriated £2500 for a new dormitory, which was promptly erected by Master Builder Thomas Dawes, whose brother William was later to be a hero in the Revolution. The name, Hollis Hall, honored a family whose generosity for several generations had aided the college with endowments for the library, two professorships, and twelve scholarships.

Copying the two-entry plan of Massachusetts Hall, Hollis was also two suites deep and thus had some windowless studies. On the exterior it differs from Massachusetts Hall in just the way one expects a Middle or High Georgian design to differ from an Early Georgian one. Despite the use of two entrances, the composition of Hollis is divided into three parts, the center of which is treated as a pavilion capped by a pediment (fig. 15). The projection of this pavilion, however, is very slight, so slight indeed that the change in the facade plane is almost obscured by a downspout. So minute an enlargement of this section had no effect on the interior arrangement of rooms, and its only purpose was to provide a theoretical base for adding the gable, which could be treated as a Classical pediment. (Similar structural complication made solely for the sake of visual elaboration of a central frontispiece may be observed in the Longfellow House on Brattle Street, built three years earlier and in the Apthorp House of 1760, now Adams House.) In order to provide the required central axis for the rather arbitrary three-part design of Hollis Hall, a false entrance was placed on the ground floor. Inside the frames of this central "door" and the windows above it, there was always a division so that two small windows illuminated separate studies, but a brick fire wall was added in 1875. Other differences at Hollis are the hip roof (instead of a gambrel), the noticeably shorter windows of the top story, and the frames of the main entrances, elaborated with pilasters and a dentil course instead of the older, simple architrave moldings. Only one original door frame is preserved, that of the center false door of the west elevation, and even it lacks its original segmental pediment (fig. 16).[26] The frames of the west doors (the original front entrances) were removed in 1898 when bathrooms were installed and these entries were blocked. Entrances on the east (the only ones now functioning) are original, but they were always simpler because they were back doors, used by students en route to the college pump or privy.

With Holden Chapel and Harvard Hall, Hollis formed a second small, U-shaped courtyard (fig. 15). Inasmuch as the buildings were placed close together, the space of both the small yards was clearly defined. But because these areas remained open to the west in the direction of Cambridge Common, separated from it only by a low wall, their importance seems diminished; their vital, sharply controlled relationship appears to drain off into ill-defined and empty space. On the other hand one could — as John Coolidge has — read these open quadrangles as an expression of interaction with the city of Cambridge.

No sooner was Hollis finished than Harvard Hall II was destroyed by fire on January 24, 1764. At that time the General Court had transferred to Cambridge from Boston because of a smallpox epidemic. Along with the building, students' belongings, scientific apparatus, and the library of five thousand books were lost, including all but one of the books bequeathed to the college by John Harvard. Assuming responsibility for the loss, the legislature agreed to provide a replacement. Because a building containing all the activities housed in the old structure would have been prohibitively expensive, it was decided that the new one would accommodate only public functions; student quarters would have to be found elsewhere. Thus Harvard Hall III was the first college building in America devoted entirely

15
This view by du Simitière (1767) shows the second brick quadrangle, formed by Holden Chapel and adjacent Hollis Hall.

16
Hollis Hall: west door (Thomas Dawes, 1762). The central doorway of Hollis originally faced outward toward Cambridge Common, onto which its quadrangle opened; it has always been subdivided.

to academic uses. The understated exterior design appears to be a competent exercise of the sort that any amateur of the period with a taste for architecture and a few reference books might have produced—until one considers its early date. It was obligingly provided by Sir Francis Bernard, the Royal Governor, and erected by Thomas Dawes (fig. 17).[27] The center of the main facade and each of the end elevations of the 107-by-40-foot building is enlivened by a pavilion capped with a pediment to achieve a more impressive High Georgian appearance, but again the projections are so slight, that one is scarcely aware of their existence except when seen in a raking light, and certainly they do not affect the interior plan. Here the architect designed on paper without considering how the building would appear in three dimensions. Although the cornice was constructed of brownstone to minimize the risk of fire, it is too thin and light for the size of the building. Crowning all is a somewhat heavy cupola, which contained the college bell. Yet these very proportions augur the Federal style of the century's end.

Despite some discussion of locating it northwest of Hollis, the new Harvard Hall was placed on the same site as its predecessor. This was an unfortunate decision: Harvard and Hollis Halls continue to crowd one another, an unnecessary limitation in light of the extent of open college land. But the new building could not have been placed farther south, because Old Stoughton was still standing and the arrangement of the quadrangle would have been disturbed.[28]

The ground floor of Harvard Hall III contained two large areas on either side of the stair hall: a chapel on the west side, on the east a commons above a basement kitchen (fig. 18).[29] The west half of the second level housed the new library that was rapidly assembled from donations by alumni and friends; in the east was the Philosophical Chamber, where scientific instruments were stored and demonstrations mounted, plus smaller rooms known as the Hebrew School and the Mathematical School, in which these subjects were taught. The Philosophical Cabinet, as it was sometimes called, was also used for the storage of a miscellany of natural history objects. Sidney Willard, the college librarian from 1800 to 1805, commented on this progenitor of the vast University Museum that would be built a century later: "Another room was the museum, containing reptiles in alcohol, stuffed skins of beasts and birds, and miscellaneous curiosities which were a great attraction to the country census and a great weariness to the showman, the librarian."[30]

The rebuilders of Harvard Hall made an all-out effort to erect an edifice that would reflect credit on the school and its sponsors. The commons room was especially ornate, recalling the halls of English colleges with their carved woodwork and portraits. The east wall originally contained no windows, in order to leave space for a center fireplace and flanking bays in which were hung (if briefly) Copley's heroic portraits of George III and Queen Charlotte.[31] The library had rich woodwork (fig. 19) and brocade-covered walls. Even the Philosophical Chamber was no ordinary laboratory, for its walls were covered with flock wallpaper, fragments of which were discovered when the building was renovated in 1968. All in all, Harvard Hall III, incorporating paintings and interior design, was the most sophisticated American college building before Bulfinch, though its importance has been overlooked by architectural historians.

17
*Harvard Hall III (Gov.
Francis Bernard and Thomas
Dawes, 1764). Drawing by
du Simitière.*

18
*Plans of Harvard Hall III.
Drawing by du Simitière.*

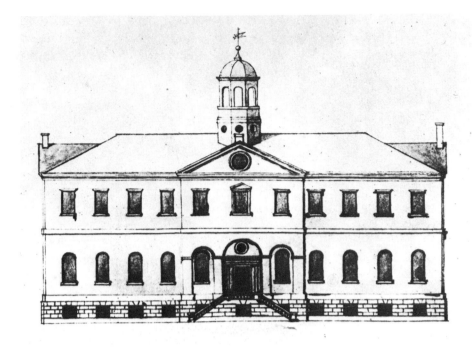

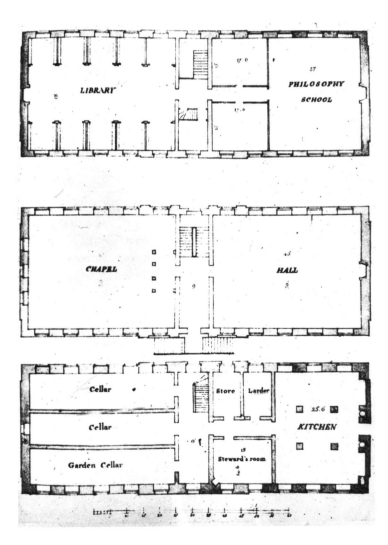

31   *The Brick Quadrangles*

19
Harvard Hall III: library, c.
1790. Conjectural restoration
by F. W. Bang (1939).

When the commons and the chapel were transferred to University Hall in
1815, the first floor of Harvard Hall III was converted into classrooms, a
mineralogical cabinet, and laboratories, while the entire second story
became the library. In 1842, responding to pressure from the Society of the
Alumni for a sufficiently large room to contain the annual Commencement
banquet, all partitions of the Hall's main floor were removed to create a
single space, even though this left the upper floor to be supported by a
forest of cast-iron columns. At the same time, a center pavilion designed by
Richard Bond was added to the front of the building (fig. 20), but Bond
made no attempt to match the size and texture of the old brick masonry or
the stone of the foundation. Although the addition crowds the original
fenestration and appears to pull away uncomfortably from the old facade,
Bond at least duplicated the pediment and the timid stone cornice of the
original design, and he left the end walls unchanged.

To meet an acute shortage of instructional space, Harvard Hall was
remodeled once again in 1870 to provide lecture, laboratory, and storage
space for the science department. The corners of the then T-shaped building
were filled in with one-story additions (fig. 21). This enlargement was done
with a sensitivity most extraordinary for the time. The new brickwork
(actually antique brick seems to have been used) as well as the brownstone
trim matches the original exactly, and granite blocks from the foundation
of the old facade were reset so carefully that it is impossible to detect a
break. The new fenestration repeats the old, round-headed design, including
three new windows opened in the east wall of the original building. On the
new south front, pilasters between the windows were desirable because of
the horizontal proportions of the one-story addition, but the profiles of the

20
Harvard Hall III: addition of a two-story porch by Richard Bond, 1842.

21
Harvard Hall III: enlargement by Ware and Van Brunt, 1870.

22

*Stoughton Hall II (1804). Here
Bulfinch duplicated the earlier
east elevation of Hollis Hall.*

23

*Plan of Harvard Yard
property, 1799.*

1. *Old Stoughton, 1699*
2. *Massachusetts Hall, 1718*
3. *Wadsworth House, 1726*
4. *Holden Chapel, 1742*
5. *Hollis Hall, 1762*
6. *Harvard Hall III, 1764*
7. *College House I (Wiswall's
   Den), acquired 1772*
8. *College House II (Webber
   House), acquired 1790*
9. *Kidder Estate,
   acquired 1791*
10. *Marrett Estate,
    acquired 1793*
11. *College House III
    (Bordman Estate),
    acquired 1794*
12. *Wigglesworth Estate,
    acquired 1794*
13. *Danforth Estate,
    acquired 1795*
A. *College Burying Place,
   date of acquisition
   unknown.*

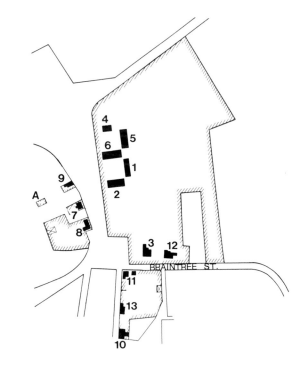

brownstone caps and bases were copied from those of Holden Chapel.

This 1870 reconstruction is certainly one of the most careful pieces of remodeling done at Harvard. The President's Report for 1869–70 records Ware and Van Brunt as the architects in charge. That firm was then at work on plans for Memorial and Weld Halls and also executed that year the restructuring of the interior of Massachusetts Hall into four two-story lecture halls while preserving the exterior. These two commissions plus the enlargement of Christ Church in 1857 appear to be the earliest instances in Greater Boston of Victorian architects conscientiously and sympathetically preserving a Georgian exterior. Along with Gridley J. F. Bryant in his work at Holden Chapel (1850), they laid early milestones in the Colonial Revival movement.

Following unimportant changes in the early twentieth century, Harvard Hall underwent a drastic interior rebuilding in 1968 in order to bring it up to fire-safety requirements. Ashley, Meyer, Smith Associates skillfully directed the work, in which the exterior was happily left unchanged.

The present Stoughton Hall was a belated replacement for the seventeenth-century dormitory of the same name, which had been demolished in 1781. Despite the completion of Hollis Hall in 1763, the housing situation was so tight by 1800 that nearly all freshmen were forced to room in private houses. Public money was too limited to finance a new building, so the Commonwealth authorized a lottery to raise the funds. Although this was held in 1795–1796, construction did not begin before 1804.

New Stoughton has two entrances, and is so similar to Hollis in its three-part composition, fenestration, and general massing as to look like a twin. Only the more elegant detailing and the use of recessed granite door frames remind us that the designer was Charles Bulfinch. Closer inspection also reveals that flush lintels of granite scored to resemble voussoirs have replaced the flat arches of brick at Hollis, and no belt courses interrupt the sheer wall surfaces. A particularly nice detail is the recessed casing of granite enframing the two entrances on the east facade (fig. 22). The present cornice and hip roof, which would be unconscionably heavy on a Federal building, date from repairs in 1879 following a fire. These adjacent early buildings, along with their neighbor Holworthy Hall built a few years later, do more than any other factor to establish the architectural character of the Old Yard.[32]

While Harvard College was erecting new edifices, it was also purchasing property on the south and west sides of Harvard Square. By 1800 the college controlled more than half the frontage between Holyoke Street and the Burying Ground (fig. 23). In 1772 and 1790 two dwellings known as Wiswall's Den and the Webber House, or College Houses I and II, had been acquired. The former, bought at a bargain because it reportedly was haunted, served as an auxiliary dormitory. College House II was leased to members of the faculty (Professor Samuel Webber lived there before he became president in 1806) or used to house students, and between 1817 and 1833 it was the home of the embryonic Law School. On the southeast corner of Dunster Street and Massachusetts Avenue stood a third Harvard dwelling known as College House III, purchased in 1794 from Andrew Bordman. The College House II lot, a large area on the west side of the Square at the present location of Church Street, served as the college woodlot for the storage of fuel. Harvard Square thus became almost as much a part of the campus as the quadrangles. This westward drift of the school was countered by the acquisition in 1786 and 1794 of the Appleton pasture and the Wigglesworth estate, located in the middle portion of the present Yard. But it would be another two decades before the school looked to this area as the logical place for expansion.[33]

The second phase of Harvard architectural growth extends well over a century, from 1671 through 1804. Although the degree of sophistication evidenced by the buildings is not particularly advanced, the area emerges as a handsome unit when viewed in the context of Harvard Yard today. The buildings achieved a certain harmony and dignity by adhering inadvertently to one building material and to the Georgian style of architecture. The harmony results not from a purist allegiance to a predetermined idiom but from a family resemblance attained through the use of brick, simple massing, and a restrained, familiar architectural vocabulary.[34] As George Santayana put it, "On the whole it was an architecture of sturdy poverty, looking through thrift in the direction of wealth. It well matched the early learning of New England, traditionally staunch and narrow, yet also thrifty and tending to positivism."[35]

The quadrangles seem to have been formed instinctively rather than as the result of conscious planning. By facing buildings toward the public road and away from the privies and pastures out back, the planners repeated the commonsense arrangement of President Wadsworth's or anyone's suburban house in New England. The scheme possessed a rudimentary order: the buildings were laid out on a rectilinear pattern (always aligned with coordinated axes), but there were no cross axes to relate the open spaces, no gateways, no covered passages. To walk from Massachusetts Hall to Holden Chapel required an awkward "end run" through cramped, unaligned gaps between buildings; the end elevations of the three buildings that projected toward the public road and the Common made no effort at architectural unity (fig. 15). Although a third quadrangle was begun with the erection of New Stoughton in 1804, the enclosure of this space was left incomplete until the building of Phillips Brooks House more than ninety years later. Despite such indeterminate qualities, however, a potential for order did exist, a potential that was realized much later with the fencing and filling in of the Yard with additional buildings.

3 The Early Nineteenth Century

The first two-thirds of the nineteenth century were a period of transition for Harvard College. The student body increased rapidly after a century of moderate growth; with financial support from the Massachusetts government no longer certain, the college was forced to find new sources of revenue; there was urgent need for new kinds of instructional buildings such as laboratories, museums, a botanical garden, an observatory, an expanded library, and facilities for athletics. It is not surprising that changes of such moment were reflected in the variety and the uncertain quality of architecture commissioned by the college.

Harvard College was governed by two bodies: the Corporation and the Board of Overseers. The Corporation consisted of the president, the treasurer, and five fellows; the fellows, it was at first expected, would be faculty members. But because the reservoir of teaching fellows was small in number and subject to rapid change as a result of poor salaries and because it developed that the responsibilities of the Corporation were largely financial, the fellows after 1784 were chosen from men of affairs. Except for financial transactions, the decisions of this group were subject to the approval of the Overseers. Established in 1642, the Board of Overseers consisted of the college president, the governor, the lieutenant governor, certain magistrates of the colony, and the ministers of Boston, Cambridge, and four adjacent towns. Until 1707, when they lost their veto power, the Overseers had final say in all decisions; thus church and state in this period had firm control of the college. It was only after 1865 that independent Overseers were selected from Harvard alumni.

For financial support the college depended on the good will of the legislature and of individuals, many of whom undoubtedly looked upon it with favor because of its role in inculcating the Puritan ethic and in training preachers. With the growing division between Unitarianism and Congregationalism in the early nineteenth century, part of such church support was alienated. And in the financial straits following the Revolution the Commonwealth found it increasingly difficult to aid Harvard with outright appropriations. Permission was granted for two lotteries (in 1793 and 1805) to raise funds for the construction of Houghton and Holworthy Halls, and in 1816 revenue from a tax on the Massachusetts Bank for ten years was granted to three colleges, Harvard, Bowdoin, and Williams. But aid for the construction of a much needed library was refused in 1833. At that point Harvard, definitively separated from both church and state, realized that in the future it would have to depend for support on friends and alumni.[1]

This changing financial situation in the early nineteenth century came at a time of marked numerical growth of the university population, as shown in the table.

	Undergraduate students	Graduate students	Total students	Faculty
1652	40	10	50	3
1670	17	—	—	—
1712	—	—	54	—
1718	—	—	124	5
1771	—	—	172	12
1809–10	—	—	188	12
1828–29	252	172	424	25
1869–70	563	534	1097	41

Relations between students and college officers were often strained in these years, undoubtedly partly because of the rigid system of education and the absence of a good athletic program to provide students with an outlet for youthful spirits. The faculty, generally only a few years beyond attainment of the B.A. degree, were charged with monitoring the students' conduct, while their teaching was limited to little more than rote instruction. The tension between students and faculty was aggravated by a stringent system of grading, instituted in 1825, in which daily recitation was given a numerical rating. Infringements of college rules also had numerical equivalents, which were deducted from the academic total to determine the student's rank in each class. During his administration President Kirkland attempted to move away from this rote-learning and recitation method toward the European university system with lectures and individual study; unfortunately his reforms met with much opposition from the faculty.

It is convenient in an overview of Harvard history to consider the sixty-odd years prior to the Eliot administration as a unit. Yet the eighteen-year presidency of John Kirkland (1810–1828) requires special note. The Kirkland administration invites comparison with that of President Eliot, for it foreshadows on a smaller scale some of Eliot's innovations in the academic realm and improvements in the physical plant. Kirkland was the first president to attempt to break with the classical education that had remained almost unchanged since Harvard's founding. He liberalized the curriculum, including the introduction of modern languages, and established two professional schools (law and divinity). He more than doubled the size of the faculty (creating 15 new professorships for a total of 25) and increased faculty salaries. He also moved the college in the direction of graduate work, establishing the status of Resident Graduate, in which a student with a B.A. could attend lectures and use the library. This was one of the reforms opposed by the faculty, however, and real graduate study at Harvard had to await the arrival of President Eliot in 1869.[2]

As was often the case with enterprising presidents, Kirkland was also a builder. He improved the Yard by planting elm trees and laying out paths; he sponsored the erection of three important buildings (Holworthy, University, and Divinity Halls); and with an eye to the future needs of the university, he purchased the large Shady Hill estate north of Kirkland Street, a portion of which would become the North Yard. But the changes he attempted required greater resources than he was able to obtain, although he succeeded in raising something like $400,000. The total budget for the year 1809–10, just before he became president, was $35,000, but annual expenditures more than doubled in the next decade to $83,000.

In the mid-1820s Kirkland's vision for progress was checked by an acute crisis in college finances, the causes of which lay both within and without the school: a severe economic depression gripped New England in the wake of the Jefferson Embargo and the War of 1812; the value of "college stock" (endowment) dropped alarmingly from $149,000 to $67,000 between 1810 and 1821;[3] enrollment declined because of hard times and because of conservative Calvinist disapproval of Harvard's too-liberal position. Poor financial management compounded the problems: the college had come to depend on a temporary yearly bank tax of $10,000 that expired in 1826; it had established new professorships without procuring endowments to support them; and it had diverted funds from investments to construct buildings and to purchase land at a time when the college was dependent on the endowment for 21 percent of the operating budget.

The crisis was met by the appointment as college treasurer of Nathaniel Bowditch, a hard-headed businessman who insisted on drastic fiscal reforms.[4] The college sloop, the *Harvard*, which had transported firewood for college use, was sold, as was the printing press; land not producing income was disposed of (especially interesting to us are the five large lots on Kirkland Street known as Professors' Row, which extended from the present Science Center to Divinity Avenue); and professors' salaries, which amounted to two-thirds of the budget, were slashed. In 1826 Bowditch also produced the first Treasurer's Report. Under such stringent management the college clearly would not be allowed to engage in more building for some time.

Before President Kirkland took control in 1810 the Corporation had made a significant move in acquiring the land that now constitutes the middle third of Harvard Yard. This property, amounting to 8½ acres, was made up of three parcels: the Appleton pasture (bought in 1786), the Wigglesworth property including the old Ox Pasture (1794), and the Sewall lot (1805). These became the sites of many structures erected in the pre-Eliot era. Somewhat later three more important acquisitions, amounting to 8¼ acres, secured the eastern edge of the Yard. They were the extensive plot on which stood the seventeenth-century parsonage, bought in 1833, and the Dana and Bigelow estates, acquired two years later. Since this last area was not then needed for academic buildings, it was used for five residences, which were rented to professors or used to house other college activities.[5]

In the sixty-odd years following the completion of the new Stoughton Hall by Charles Bulfinch in 1804, the college erected seventeen major structures and ten minor ones,[6] but these were distributed almost at random. No consistency can be observed in the choice of materials or the

24
*Holworthy Hall (Loammi
Baldwin, 1811) formed the
northern boundary of the Yard.*

architectural style selected for these buildings, even for those erected within
a few years of one another. Seven major structures were erected in Harvard
Yard, all but one of them situated in its middle third (see fig. 51). The siting
of the two earliest of these, Holworthy (1811) and University (1813) Halls,
had a close visual connection with the eighteenth-century quadrangles to
the west, and with them helped to establish the boundaries of what would
become the Old Yard. A generation later in 1862 Grays Hall was added as
a counterpart to Holworthy at the south end of the same area. But if there
were logical reasons for the location of the other four structures erected in
these years — Dane Hall (1832), Gore Hall (1838), Appleton Chapel (1856),
and Boylston Hall (1857) — we fail to understand them today. It is not
unfair to say that the impressive unity that now pervades Harvard Yard was
achieved in spite of the mid-nineteenth-century administrators and architects who expanded it.

Holworthy Hall, designed by Loammi Baldwin in 1811, was the first
structure erected east of the brick quadrangles (fig. 24).[7] Its facade, placed
at right angles to the rear elevations of Hollis and the new Stoughton,
forms the northern boundary of the Old Yard. It was the first dormitory to
abandon the Medieval tradition of individual closet-sized studies opening
off the bedchamber; instead this design employed suites consisting of a
study with a southern exposure and two bedrooms on the north, an
arrangement that provided better light and cross-ventilation. Holworthy has
three stairways rather than two as in earlier dormitories, so the center
doorway is functional, and all three entrances have handsome frames made
of rusticated granite blocks. Initially the top story was lower than it is

today; the eave line was raised by two feet when the dormitories in the Yard were refurbished in 1871 as part of President Eliot's campaign of improvement.

University Hall, begun in 1813 from designs by Charles Bulfinch, is one of Harvard's most famous buildings and occupies a critical position in the evolution of Harvard Yard. The concept of the Old Yard as a public space rather than simply a back yard was first mentioned in 1804 when New Stoughton was built and inaugurated with the erection of Holworthy,[8] but it was Bulfinch who established the scale of the Yard and gave it visual coherence by the siting of University Hall. Instead of opening outward toward public roadways and the Common, the college now began to develop a spacious academic precinct facing inward with Bulfinch's building as its core.

In an era before there were such practical things as sanitary sewers and motorized trash collection, a back yard was a necessary adjunct for the location of privies and the like. So before the new University Hall could be constructed, the old privies and brewhouse that had stood behind (east of) Old Stoughton and Hollis Halls had to be demolished and a new privy (known as the University Minor) constructed. The location east of the new hall was originally screened by a row of pines, at about the place where the large and sole surviving pine tree now stands. Adjacent to the privy and near enough to the dining halls and kitchen for convenient disposal of scraps was built a pig pen, which soon attracted a colony of large rats.[9]

Oblivious to the necessity for such facilities, Bulfinch at first envisioned his new hall in the center of a large ellipse of trees rather resembling a racetrack (fig. 25). Though the building as designed would not have been large enough to dominate so extensive a space as indicated in this proposal,

25
"Racetrack" plan of Harvard Yard by Charles Bulfinch, 1812–1813. Bulfinch's concept of University Hall as fulcrum introduced the idea of an inward orientation for Harvard Yard.

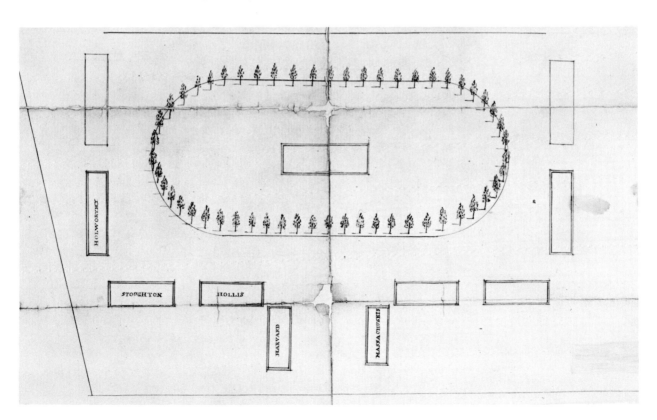

26
University Hall: west facade (Charles Bulfinch, 1813). The awkward spacing of the windows was determined by the central chapel on the second floor.

the scheme possessed a certain logic.[10] Since the structure was to house such public spaces as the chapel, four dining halls, six classrooms, and the president's office, it was appropriate for Bulfinch to differentiate it from older structures of more ordinary usage by isolating it and by constructing it of newly available Chelmsford granite instead of traditional brick.[11] Construction was begun on the strength of the promise of $10,000 per year from the bank tax; the building cost $65,000, of which $40,000 came from the tax and the rest was drawn from university funds.

The balanced, compartmented design of University Hall is traditional: end wings of three stories framing a center unit with larger fenestration, full entablature, and roof balustrade; the central section is further subdivided into a middle unit of six bays and end bays furnished with pilasters (fig. 26). The composition is accented by large, round-headed windows in the center but stabilized by the squared fenestration in the ground story, which is repeated in the end wings. Although the detailing of the pilasters and capitals is robust for Federal work, the building's date is indicated by the low pitch of the roof.

As an academic performance the design suffers from the even number of bays of the middle zone and wider interval between windows at the exact center of the building, a fundamental defect by Classical standards. This flaw arose from the need to provide space for chimney flues for fireplaces in the chapel above and dining halls below. The pairing of dining halls required an even number of windows in the center section, but it is surprising that Bulfinch did not devise a less awkward scheme. It is gratifying to discover that the clumsy one-story porch seen in old prints extending across the west facade (removed in 1842) was added at the Corporation's insistence after construction had begun.[12] The original design included a cupola that was never built.

University Hall provides one of the few instances at Harvard in which officials and designer anticipated future architectural requirements. Even though when University Hall was constructed its eastern front opened toward the college privy, this facade was given the same pilasters and handsome granite surface (if not the present granite stairways) as the western elevation. As a result, the building now faces Tercentenary Quadrangle to the east with the same dignity with which it fronts the Old Yard. Aided by equally splendid elevations on both fronts, University Hall functions as a pivot and link between the university's two most important spaces.

The building has fortunately suffered few external modifications, though the interior has been remodeled repeatedly. Changing uses of the first floor have not required major structural alterations. Originally planned as four separate dining halls, one for each class, the rooms on this floor were connected with large round openings, undoubtedly in the hope of fostering interchange and camaraderie between classes. Unfortunately what was often exchanged through the openings was insults, morsels of food, even crockery, and the occuli were soon filled in. One hall was fitted as a gymnasium in 1826, and fourteen years later the university commons was terminated when the remaining halls and basement kitchen were needed for instructional purposes.[13] After religious services were transferred to Appleton Chapel, University Hall's large second-floor chapel with balconies at either end was divided horizontally and vertically into four classrooms (1869), and dormer windows were installed to illuminate and ventilate the upper rooms. In 1896 these rooms were removed and the old chapel was restored by Pierre la Rose as the meeting room for the Faculty of Arts and Sciences. The granite steps on the east front were added in 1917; the statue of John Harvard (1882) by Daniel Chester French was placed in its present position in front of the hall in the spring of 1924; and the president's office located on the second floor south was transferred to Massachusetts Hall in 1939.[14]

Within a very short time the idea of the Bulfinch "racetrack" appears to have been discarded and the eighteenth-century system of forming small quadrangles along the western edge of the Yard reinstated. Such a relapse is indicated by the construction in 1832 of a building to house the Law School, Dane Hall, to the south of Massachusetts Hall with its axis parallel to Massachusetts Hall (figs. 27, 51). The new brick building was provided with an Ionic portico on the end facing Harvard Square, but the end toward the Bulfinch quadrangle was left plain. Here was added in 1844 a brick wing to contain the growing law library.[15] When the time came in 1871 to add a building on the third side of the projected quadrangle (between Dane and Massachusetts Halls), the large size of the proposed structure, Matthews Hall, required that Dane be moved seventy feet south, to the present site of Lehman Hall. By 1883 the Law School had so outgrown Dane that a new building, Austin Hall, was constructed. Dane Hall burned in 1918. This initial growth of the Law School, which corresponded with the appointment in 1829 of Joseph Story as the first Dane Professor of Law,[16] also required the construction and repeated enlargement of the dormitory for law students, Graduates' Hall (later called College House), on the west side of Harvard Square.

Neither the Bulfinch plan for developing the Yard nor any other formal scheme guided the authorities in the location of the next major building, Gore Hall, the college library erected in 1838. Occupying a portion of the

27
The Greek Revival portico of Dane Hall (1832) faced outward toward Harvard Square. This was the first Law School building.

present site of Widener Library, the new building faced Massachusetts Avenue and ignored the other Harvard buildings as though they belonged to a different institution (figs. 28, 51). The only way it did relate to them was in maintaining their system of coordinate axes. The location chosen was too close to University Hall to fit the Bulfinch ellipse yet too far away to function with that building in forming the present Old Yard. Indeed, the library appears to have been deliberately placed apart from other buildings so that it would have as ample a sylvan setting as possible. Also noticeable here is a decidedly different system of paths, which encircle the building in sweeping curves, entirely unlike the prim, efficient walkways of the earlier campus. As this apparently deviant planning indicates, by the 1830s, sylvan concepts—exemplified at nearby Mount Auburn cemetery—had modified eighteenth-century landscaping ideals. These concepts would have far-reaching influence in establishing picturesque standards in American landscape design.[17]

Gore Hall, distinctly Gothic in style, was designed by Richard Bond and constructed of granite purchased from President Quincy's quarry.[18] Its cost was $273,500, twice the original estimate. Cast in the shape of a cross with rather irrelevant transepts, it had small octagonal towers which enframed large traceried windows located in each end of the main block and in the transepts as well. Although he was aware of King's College Chapel in Cambridge and may have seen the designs of New York University, Bond was unable to make his Gothic forms convincing, as can be seen today from the clumsy finials preserved on either side of the south, ground-level entrance to Widener Library. That Gore Hall was much admired in its day, however, is indicated by the fact that it was chosen as the dominant design element for the city seal when Cambridge was constituted a city in 1846.[19]

Gore Hall was no more distinguished for the way it functioned than for its visual qualities. The nave of the Gothic edifice served as the main reading room, and books were grouped in alcoves located in the narrow side aisles (fig. 29). The designer tried to minimize the danger of fire by using iron roof trusses and floor supports, but there was still some wood trim to remove in 1895 when the building was thoroughly fireproofed. The original installation included a steam heating system, which, though it did not function well, attracted attention at the time. President Eliot remembered: "The original heating apparatus . . . was a memorable piece of pioneer work in a subject which has since received a tremendous development. It was a low-pressure steam heat system, the radiators for which were very tall and large, and built of large copper tubes soldered together. The tubes, however, were apt to leak steam, in consequence of which the atmosphere of the library became charged with aqueous vapor, and this vapor condensed not only on the windows . . . but on the books themselves."[20]

In the course of its life this building underwent various changes and enlargements. About 1850 the octagonal corner towers, which rose to 83 feet, were reduced for structural reasons. But lack of space presented a more urgent and never-ending problem. After losing all but 400 of its books in the Harvard Hall fire of 1764, the college library made a remarkable comeback in spite of the fact that as late as 1857 the annual budget for purchasing books was only $500. Friends and alumni donated books, and the libraries of confiscated Tory estates were later added. Between 1832 and 1902 the collection doubled in size, and when moved out of Gore Hall in 1913 it numbered 645,000 volumes.[21] Having failed to find a donor for a new building, the college in 1876 appropriated money from general funds for a sizable stack wing to be built on the east side. The design of this addition was considerably more successful than that of the original building, and the project has some historical importance because of the experimental method of shelving, in which the weight of each tier of books was transferred to the foundations through steel book stacks rather than through the frame of the building (fig. 30). The stack design was worked out in 1874 by Ware and Van Brunt, John Sibley (the college librarian), and Sibley's successor, Justin Winsor.[22]

In 1895 the building was again remodeled, this time by subdividing the old reading room in the nave into three tiers of stacks plus a reading room on the top level. Electric lights had been installed in 1891, a year before they were put into other college buildings. Up to this time the library had depended solely on daylight for illumination, because candles and even illuminating gas were considered a fire hazard; when it became too dark to read, the library simply closed, sometimes in winter as early as 4:00 P.M. A two-story administrative wing was added in 1906. Since the location of Gore was clearly the proper place for the college library, the old building had to be demolished in 1913 before Widener could be begun, and the collection had to be moved to temporary storage during the two years of building. Thirteen depositories were needed to accommodate the half-mil-

28

Gore Hall (Richard Bond, 1838–1841). This romantic vision of the Gothic edifice in the landscape embodies the picturesque ideals of mid-nineteenth-century design.

lion books; the largest part of the collection was stored in Randall Hall (on the present site of William James Hall), which had been built in 1898 as a students' dining hall.

Harvard's next buildings were two large structures designed by the same architect, Paul Schulze, but totally unrelated in style, material, or location. In 1856 Appleton Chapel took the place of the chapel in University Hall (fig. 31). For its construction $200,000 was donated by the trustees of the estate of Samuel Appleton, a wealthy Boston industrialist. In what appears to have been an architectural competition in 1855 (though there is no reference to a competition in the minutes of the Harvard Corporation), Edward Cabot, Jonathan Preston, Arthur Gilman, and Paul Schulze submitted drawings.[23] Those of Schulze were used.[24]

It is impossible to say what determined the location of the chapel. Placed with its long axis at right angles to University and Gore Halls, it defined one side of the large open space that eventually would become the Tercentenary Quadrangle in a way that Gore Hall opposite it failed to do; but it had little effect on the Old Yard because it was placed too far to the east behind University Hall; and although its major axis aligned with the earlier Holden Chapel, its tower was pushed off center in a way that rendered the Holden axis meaningless (fig. 51).

Visually Appleton Chapel stood apart from other buildings in the Yard by reason of its light Nova Scotia sandstone, which differed from the granite of University and Gore Halls and from the brick employed elsewhere. Its architectural style was an ungainly mixture of Classical and Romanesque, an ambivalence that caused some to observe that "it had no style." The design of its staged bell tower forms an interesting if heavy addition to the sequence of Harvard towers extending from the "Turrett" of Harvard Hall I to Lowell House finished almost three centuries later. In

29

29
The majestic Gothic interior
of Gore Hall was remodeled
repeatedly and eventually
subdivided into three levels.

30
Gore Library demolition,
showing the metal stack wing,
an innovative design when it
was added in 1876 by Ware
and Van Brunt.

31
Appleton Chapel (Paul Schultze, 1856), of light sandstone, stood for eighty years in the Yard before it was replaced by the brick Memorial Church.

32
Appleton Chapel interior. Exposed metal columns and stenciling of this kind became anathema to the Colonial vision of the early twentieth-century planners.

33
Boylston Hall as remodeled in 1959 (Paul Schultze and Schoen, 1857; Peabody and Stearns, 1871; TAC, 1959).

1872 the deplorable acoustics of the chapel were improved and the seating capacity increased to nine hundred with the addition of a gallery by architects Peabody and Stearns (fig. 32).[25] The chapel replaced Isaiah Rogers' First Parish Church as the locus of Commencement exercises from 1872 until Sanders Theatre was readied in 1876. Two more interior remodelings (in 1886 and 1919) took place before the chapel was demolished in 1931 to make way for Memorial Church.

Schulze's second work, Boylston Hall (1857), was more successful in design, and, in spite of the fact that its siting also appears to have been somewhat random, has served as an anchor for brilliant planning by subsequent designers. The west wall of Boylston was aligned visually if not metrically with the west facade of University Hall, and the main entrance faced the core of the Yard instead of facing Massachusetts Avenue as did Gore Hall. The failure to center Boylston axially with University Hall makes clear that the authorities had abandoned all thought of University Hall as the center of the Bulfinch ellipse.

Constructed of stone in accordance with Ward Nicholas Boylston's bequest, the new hall was closely related in design to contemporary mercantile buildings of granite in Boston (fig. 33).[26] The size of the blocks and the textural contrast of the quarry-faced surfaces remind one of buildings by Gridley J. F. Bryant, at that time Boston's most prolific architect.[27] Boylston Hall originally housed a chemistry laboratory (it was probably the first space built specifically for this purpose in America; the laboratory had formerly been in University Hall, where it was inadequate and unsafe), an anatomical museum, and a collection of mineralogical specimens; in the

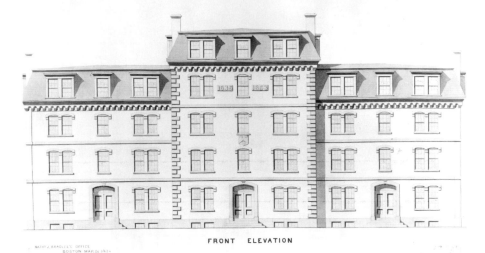

34
Grays Hall: drawing of north elevation (N. J. Bradlee, 1862). Grays was considered notable because it had water closets (in the basement).

35
College House (1832–1870) combined student housing and ground-level stores.

course of time it has served many other purposes. It is one of the few Harvard buildings that have been improved by later alterations: in 1871 a third-floor laboratory was created by the addition of a mansard story by Peabody and Stearns, but best of all was the thorough rehandling in 1959 under the direction of The Architects Collaborative (fig. 33). At that time the interior was gutted and entirely rearranged, and the arched windows, formerly divided by clumsy wooden mullions, were filled with undivided plates of glass.[28] Now the contrast between the rough Rockport granite and the polished glass is brilliant, and the detailing of other new elements, such as the arched metal vestibule at the main entrance, enhances the sense of strength conveyed by the granite masonry.

Immediately west of Boylston Hall, a dormitory was erected in 1862 from plans by N. J. Bradlee.[29] It was called Grays Hall, after three graduates in whose honor it was donated.[30] This building resembles Holworthy in plan, but its appearance is strikingly different because of its vertical proportions, paired windows, heavy granite trim, and mansard roof (fig. 34). It is fortunate that this structure was situated in the southern end of the Yard, near Boylston, rather than near Hollis, Stoughton, and Holworthy Halls. The mass of Grays Hall, which rises five stories, is sufficiently great to delimit as a quadrangle the vast space of the Old Yard.[31]

Harvard also erected buildings outside the Yard in this period. One focus of activity was Harvard Square, where the college owned most of the west side. Wiswall's Den and Webber House (College Houses I and II) were demolished to make way for a three-story brick edifice built in 1832, which combined student rooms and ground-level stores. Known first as Graduates' Hall because of the law students who were quartered here, then as College House, the structure eventually extended as far as Church Street, with floor levels somewhat elevated because of the rise in terrain (fig. 35).[32] The building was thrice enlarged, the last time in 1870 by the addition of mansard roofs and a four-story center pavilion. Ownership of this property continued in university hands until 1916 (when it was traded with the Randolph Trust for Apthorp House, Randolph Hall, and other property on Linden Street).[33]

A fascinating but now almost forgotten building from this period was constructed in 1843 to house the Panorama of Athens, a large cityscape of ancient Greece painted by Barker and Binford that President Everett had persuaded Theodore Lyman, Jr., to purchase for Harvard in 1819. Similar to but evidently smaller than the later Cyclorama in Boston, this painting might be termed an early visual teaching aid and perhaps represents the college's first recognition of the legitimate role of the visual arts in formal education. The circular building that housed the panorama stood in back of College House and was not replaced after it burned in 1845.[34]

Peripheral in a physical sense to the center of the college was the Harvard Botanic Garden, opened in 1807 near the corner of Garden and Linnaean Streets. The 7½-acre garden occupied land that had been part of the West End Field, distributed to new settlers who arrived in Cambridge in 1633–34 with the Reverend Thomas Hooker. The first structure of importance here was the Garden House (1810), built by the college and long occupied by the botanist Asa Gray (fig. 36).[35] This fine Federal building is the first known work of Ithiel Town, who later became a leader in the development of nineteenth-century American architecture in New Haven and New York

City.[36] Originally occupying the present site of Kittredge Hall, the house was enlarged in 1848 and moved in 1910 to its present location on the west side of Garden Street. A brick herbarium was erected in 1864 immediately east of the dwelling.[37] Donated by Nathaniel Thayer and designed by Ryder and Harris, this utilitarian building was enlarged by the addition of a laboratory and an auditorium in 1870 and a library in 1879. It was replaced in four building campaigns between 1909 and 1915 by attached fireproof structures; the resulting building, known as Kittredge Hall, has housed Harvard University Press since July 1956.[38]

Acquisition of land on the north side of Kirkland Street, the area now known as the North Yard, began during the expansive administration of President Kirkland with the purchase in 1816 of Shady Hill, a 64-acre estate, which had been a showplace in Cambridge for a century (fig. 37).[39] Almost immediately Harvard sold the east half, including the mansion, to Professor Henry Ware; the west half it kept, though a decade later it sold five large house lots fronting Kirkland Street to faculty members, whose homes there gave the area the name Professors' Row.[40] A third holding of ten acres belonging to the Frost and then Ware families did not come under Harvard control, though later the college acquired several parcels of it. Most of Shady Hill lying to the north behind Professors' Row and the Frost-Ware estate was retained by the university, and access was provided by Divinity Avenue. Here in 1825 was erected Divinity Hall, the first Harvard building located outside the Yard.

The new building for the Divinity School was commissioned and paid for by an independent group, the Society for Promoting Theological Education in Harvard College. Designed by Solomon Willard but adapted by Thomas Sumner, who took charge of the commission at an early stage, the building

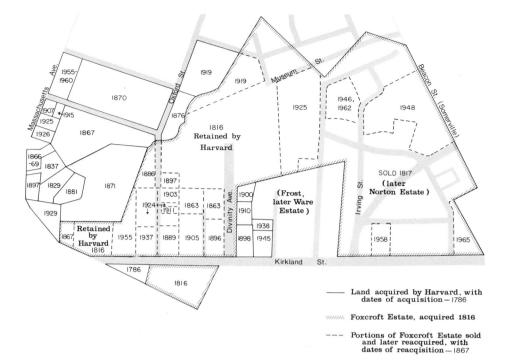

37
Land acquisition in the North Yard.

——— Land acquired by Harvard, with dates of acquisition — 1786

///// Foxcroft Estate, acquired 1816

- - - Portions of Foxcroft Estate sold and later reacquired, with dates of reacqisition — 1867

38
Divinity Hall (design by Solomon Willard, 1825, adapted by Thomas Sumner). The tall arched windows in the central portion mark the chapel.

39
Harvard Observatory (Isaiah Rogers, 1843–1851), isolated on its hillside site north of the Yard. Many structures now surround and obscure the original octagonal observatory.

is related to the Bulfinch tradition but with stylistic indications of the approaching Greek Revival (fig. 38).[41] It has in common with University Hall the use of twin entrances separated by a middle portion whose long, round-headed windows contrast with smaller rectangular fenestration elsewhere, as well as variation in floor levels and a chapel as the prominent center space. Quite dissimilar to University Hall, however, is the manner in which the pedimented center of Divinity Hall breaks free of the block. The arched windows illuminate a chapel whose interior was completely refitted by A. W. Longfellow in 1904 with golden oak paneling that is ill-suited to the exterior.[42] As the result of later developments within the North Yard, Divinity Hall has become the focus around which some of the most adroit site planning at Harvard has been done.

North of Harvard Square but some distance from the North Yard is the Harvard Observatory. A temporary observatory had been improvised in the Dana-Palmer house in 1839 after President Quincy persuaded William C. Bond to bring his equipment and become "Astronomical Observer to the University," but it was four years later before the president, taking advantage of a swell of interest in astronomy caused by the Comet of 1843, was able to procure funds to build a permanent observatory.[43] The new building, begun from designs by Isaiah Rogers, followed a familiar Palladian scheme with a central section and end pavilions connected by low wings (fig. 39).[44] The geometric formality of the design with its early and important octagonal dome was enhanced by broadly overhanging cornices. Such compartmentation suited a building serving varied activities. Clearly expressing its purpose by the dome set on a low attic above the pediment, the central block of brick housed the observatory; the east wing of wood was the residence of Professor Bond; and its counterpart on the west, added in 1851, contained classrooms and library. Located at the crest of Observatory Hill, near the site of the old summer pavilion on the estate of the flamboyant Tory John Vassall and some fifty feet above the general level of Cambridge, the building with its three pediments and formal mass must have originally presented a striking visual composition. Unfortunately, both wings were later removed to permit enlargements, the one on the east in 1954 and the other in 1960. The old observatory, which was the scene of numerous important discoveries, is now so hedged in by later buildings that it is difficult to find.

Lawrence Hall (1847), the early home of the Scientific School, endowed by Abbott Lawrence, was another mid-century work by Richard Bond (fig. 40).[45] Planned as a five-part composition like the observatory, this building was never brought to completion by the addition of a west wing to balance the professor's residence. A comparison of the upright proportions and active geometric shapes of this building with those of Divinity Hall show how much American architecture had changed in twenty years. The full-blown Italianate style of Lawrence, with broad cornices supported by heavy brackets, was not used for any other Harvard building. Lawrence Hall faced directly onto Kirkland Street, bearing no relation to buildings in Harvard Yard, while its back was turned to the extensive but then undeveloped area that would become the North Yard. Its independent design and placement well illustrate the administrative status of the Lawrence Scientific School, for its curriculum, student body, and financial structure were initially quasi-independent of Harvard College. (Only gradually did the two grow together, until in 1890 they were united as the Faculty of Arts and Sciences.)[46] But the pattern begun here and followed by other donors and administrators has made it impossible for later architects to mold the North Yard into an integrated space. The hall was radically remodeled in 1871 by Ware and Van Brunt. The architects were freer in modifying this exterior

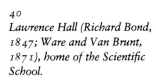

40
Lawrence Hall (Richard Bond, 1847; Ware and Van Brunt, 1871), home of the Scientific School.

41
Thayer Commons railroad station (1849). The octagonal station adjacent to the home of Oliver Wendell Holmes served the Harvard Branch Railroad line. It became a commons in 1865.

than those of older college buildings on which they worked in the same period: they added a low third story and removed the impressive central door. Nevertheless they worked within the style and reproduced the original pediment. In 1970, when scheduled for demolition to make way for the Undergraduate Science Center, Lawrence Hall was gutted by fire.

Another factor that contributed to the chaotic development of the North Yard was the Harvard Branch Railroad, incorporated in 1848 by Cambridge citizens in the hope of promoting the town as a commuter suburb of Boston. Beginning at a wooden railroad station constructed in 1849 facing the Little Common (the area in front of the present Littauer Center),[47] the tracks followed the northwest edge of the old Shady Hill estate to beyond the Somerville boundary, where they joined the main line of the Fitchburg Railroad. After the road failed and service was discontinued, the station was renovated by Nathaniel Thayer in 1865 for use as a cooperative dining hall to provide Harvard students with inexpensive meals. A simple, interesting building with a centralized plan and a triple arched entrance porch (fig. 41), it was demolished in 1883 after the construction of Austin Hall.

One other structure that contributed to the architectural variety and uncoordinated planning of the North Yard was the University Museum. Begun in 1859, this immense structure was not completed until 1913; because most of its actual construction as well as the prodigious growth of its collections came during the Eliot administration, discussion of it will be deferred to the next chapter.

Inconceivable as it would be for a modern college, athletics were almost entirely lacking at Harvard for almost two centuries. For one thing, the school day was so tightly structured as to leave virtually no time for recreation, unless one includes in that category putting up hay for the president. The Spencer orchard, acquired in 1697 and designated the "play place" or the "playing pasture" in 1712, was enlarged twenty-five years later by the addition of the President's Field.[48] Still larger was the two-acre "Delta" acquired in 1816 – the area where Memorial Hall now stands — where an unstructured, informal sort of football was played between class teams as early as 1820. The first athletic building was a bathhouse constructed in 1800 on the bank of the Charles at the foot of Ash Street near the site of a seventeenth-century windmill and later the gas works. But bathing was probably valued more for reasons of hygiene than for exercise or recreation. Other bathhouses were constructed in 1813 and 1841, the latter on the college wharf.[49]

A second athletic activity, gymnastics, was introduced when Charles Follen, a German professor seeking political asylum, came to teach history and language at Harvard in 1825. It appears that at his instigation one of the dining rooms in University Hall was fitted up with limited gymnastic equipment.[50] Professor Follen introduced jogging as well, and led enthusiastic runners cross country to Prospect Hill in Somerville. Gymnastic apparatus was also set up in the Delta, and this was followed a generation later by the construction of the first gymnasium. Built in 1859 and designed by E. C. Cabot, this was an unimposing octagonal building 74 feet across (fig. 42). Mainly used for gymnastic exercise (though it did have two bowling alleys), it contained neither showers nor toilets, an indication of the rudimentary nature of buildings and hygienic ideals in that period (fig. 43). The structure stood on the triangle of Cambridge Street, Broadway, and Quincy Street. After the original Hemenway Gymnasium was finished in 1878, the old building, renamed Rogers Hall, was used first by the Engineering School and later by the Germanic Museum.[51] In 1928 Harvard exchanged that triangle for the Little Common; the building was demolished and replaced, in 1933, by the city fire station designed by R. Clipston Sturgis.

There was no rowing at Harvard until 1844, but once introduced it stimulated the construction of a series of wooden boathouses. The first built was primitive, accessible to the water only at high tide, and was constructed by a private entrepreneur and rented to the four student clubs that had purchased boats. Next came a floating structure, which was destroyed by ice during its first winter, 1856–57. A third house stood on piles a safe distance from the main channel and connected with it by a lateral canal that had to be dredged. The fourth boathouse, put up in 1879–80, had a floating dock; it was demolished in 1894 to make way for the new river parkway.[52] These early structures were located downstream from the site of the Weld boathouse (built in 1890), between Dunster House and Peabody Terrace, because the area near Boylston (now J. F. Kennedy) Street was occupied by a coalyard and a planing mill.

When the twentieth-century critic reviews the physical growth of Harvard during this period of sixty years from 1804 to 1864, the expansion undoubtedly seems random, unstructured, inconsistent, unbusinesslike. The variety in architectural style may not bother us so much. It is disconcerting, but we have come to understand the nineteenth century as a period of change and variety, one in which the old classical architectural precepts — beautiful (and repetitive) as they were — gave way to experimentation and individualism. It is harder for us to understand what appears to be an

42
Old Rogers Gymnasium (E. C. Cabot, 1859), another octagonal mid-century building, stood on the triangle where Cambridge Street meets Broadway.

43
Rogers Gymnasium interior.

absence of planning of the grounds, a lack of provision for the addition of buildings in the future as well as a lack of foresight in acquiring land for expansion.

But these strictures need some qualification. The college administration at that time had problems enough without worrying about a land bank for future needs, and the concepts of good planning held by the nineteenth century were not those of today, or those of the eighteenth century. One has only to recall the range of problems that faced nineteenth-century Harvard administrators, from the Unitarian-Congregationalist rift to student riots, educational reform, and short finances. The college generally operated with a small surplus in this period, but resources were still slender. Substantial gifts—bequests of $50,000 to $100,000—were beginning to come in, but Harvard was still dependent on Boston philanthropy; the "big" money did not begin until after 1900, when financial support became nationwide.[53] For such limited resources there appeared to be better uses than to buy land for some undetermined time and need, especially when that commodity was abundant. In the 1840s so much unused space remained within Harvard Yard itself that it was considered expedient to erect three suburban villas there, each set in its own ample yard. And outside, empty land abounded: large stretches east of Cambridge Street were devoted to truck gardens and nurseries; numerous fields along North Avenue (the earlier name for the north-south stretch of Massachusetts Avenue) remained from colonial farms; and east of that street and north of Kirkland the Pine Swamp seemed to go on forever. Here the university already owned considerable amounts of land, leftovers from the Shady Hill purchase that no one had wanted to buy. Furthermore, at that time a college paid taxes on unimproved land as did any other corporation.

As to the location of the buildings it erected, nineteenth-century Harvard undoubtedly deserves criticism if judged from a modern vantage point. When building jostles building, as is the case today, development has to be orderly, neighbors have to consider one another, the whole must control the individual part. But that was not the condition of Harvard in 1830. Instead of fitting buildings together, the ideal of that era was to fit them into nature. This was the period when the most admired attraction in Cambridge, indeed in all of Boston, was Mount Auburn Cemetery. Although Harvard Yard lacked the strikingly irregular topography of that much visited locality, it possessed sufficient room to place its Gothic library and towered chapel in an informal, picturesque setting, to surround them with trees, to approach them by winding paths. This was, after all, the era of the Hudson River painters and of the landscape gardener Alexander Jackson Downing.[54] When we criticize these planners of Harvard's Romantic era for making things so difficult for modern architects, who are faced with a very different set of problems, we must at least remember that they placed their buildings where they did not because they were careless but because they wanted them there.

4 President Eliot and the Harvard Yard

The importance of Charles W. Eliot to Harvard cannot be overstated. It was his vision and determined leadership that transformed a provincial nineteenth-century college into a cosmopolitan university. Because his accomplishments have been thoroughly chronicled, suffice it here to mention the number of avenues along which he moved simultaneously: educational reform (revolution is a more accurate word for what he achieved); administrative reorganization; redefinition of the role of the American college teacher; cultivation of financial support from the alumni; more construction in forty years than had been accomplished during the college's previous two hundred years; and a manifold increase in its real estate holdings.[1]

As Morison reminds us, in the middle decades of the nineteenth century Harvard was not prosperous, despite its seniority among American institutions of higher learning, and was challenged on many sides by competitors. Yale had exceeded Harvard in enrollment; tuition and expenses at Williams, Amherst, and Bowdoin were substantially less and the education not very different; conservative Calvinist parents preferred to send their children to Princeton or Brown, which were less threatening to their beliefs; and Johns Hopkins, though a new school, had seized the leadership in graduate training.[2] Furthermore, the student body at Harvard was sometimes rebellious, the faculty routinized, and responsibility for financial support of the school uncertain. Nevertheless, within twenty-five years of Eliot's selection as president Harvard emerged unmistakably as the preeminent American university, the first to stand as a peer among leading institutions in Europe.

President Eliot's concept of education was very different from that which had prevailed during Harvard's first two centuries, especially before the Kirkland reforms. In the old view an education was mastery of a specific but limited body of information—ancient languages, certain classical philosophers and writers, and such Christian theology as was acceptable to the Puritan (or later the Unitarian) view. Attendance at Sunday worship and daily prayers were a part of the curriculum, and the faculty was as much concerned with the theological beliefs and moral conduct of the students as with their intellectual progress. Mathematics and natural science were neglected until well into the eighteenth century, and history as well as modern languages and literature remained so even longer. Learning at this time was "transplanted" by means of patient study and absorption of a few standard books (or summaries thereof) that were prescribed for each subject, and by means of hours of oral drill—recitation, as it was called. To become educated, a student merely memorized the required facts. Although such a background provided a certain commonality among men, it did little to sharpen students' creative abilities or to extend their understanding of man or the universe.

Until the mid-nineteenth century there was a fixed curriculum. Each year all members of a class followed an identical course of study with one tutor who taught all subjects; the class moved along at the pace of a convoy, some days studying a single subject. Since independent study and wide-ranging intellectual exploration were not encouraged, there was little need for or use made of the library. The role of the teacher, as practical-minded President Josiah Quincy (1829–1845) saw it, was "to see that the boys got their lessons," to assign a numerical grade to each and every recitation, and to maintain discipline and keep track of demerits.[3] It is not surprising, therefore, that an adversary relation developed between faculty and students. Furthermore, the system was a crushing burden in terms of hours required of the faculty each day, so that professors had little opportunity to work on their own or to share their discoveries with pupils.

President Eliot, who had tasted the exhilarating intellectual freedom and challenge of German university life, envisioned a different Harvard from the one he had experienced as a student and young instructor. He realized that the sum of human knowledge had grown beyond the tight package of ideas the ancients (as reinterpreted by the Middle Ages and the Renaissance) had identified. He believed the student should be exposed to the whole spectrum of information and experience gathered by man and be allowed to inquire into and explore it as curiosity and ability dictated. The faculty should function to guide and stimulate the student rather than merely to oversee the "furnishing of his mind" with prescribed bits of information. Whereas President Quincy had regarded college education as a "thorough drilling," a discipline for which ancient languages, classical philosophy and literature, and mathematics were useful vehicles, President Eliot viewed education as a process of discovery in which all branches of learning not purely vocational were of equal importance and for the mastery of which self-discipline was necessary. Rather than reverentially guarding a fixed body of knowledge that had been identified long ago, the university, in Eliot's opinion, should be a reservoir for all the experience and information accumulated by man. But more than that, it should be a place where the expansion of this store of knowledge was encouraged and where it was turned to man's benefit.

As soon as he was elected president in 1869, Eliot set to work to liberalize the curriculum, though this had to be done gradually and often over the opposition of various members of his faculty. Step by step between 1869 and 1884 the old requirements were relaxed (made optional) and students were given increasing choice as to which subjects they would study—that is, the elective system was introduced.[4] By 1880 old-fashioned recitations were done away with except in courses like mathematics and beginning language where drill was indispensable, and honors were granted by 1887. In place of recitations lectures were given by professors who were expert in specific fields, and students were encouraged to ask questions rather than memorize. Equally important was the institution of a graduate curriculum, in which professors pursuing research were expected to share their methods and discoveries with students. Encouraging this kind of interchange helped to dispel the antagonisms between faculty and students that had characterized Harvard during the early nineteenth century.

It would be wrong to think that the transformation was accomplished overnight or that Eliot did it single-handed. The presidency of John Kirkland in the 1820s, in a sort of false dawn, had pointed toward some of the same goals, and the need for educational change and modernization of the curriculum had been discussed by faculty and Overseers in the 1850s and 1860s. In 1857 written examinations were required for the first time. Under President Walker, in the 1850s, Harvard had also attracted a remarkable faculty.[5] Indeed, the introduction of some degree of choice of studies and other reforms were already under way before Eliot assumed office. Thus Eliot had a foundation on which to build. But his role of reformer was neither easy nor always popular. Many members of the faculty were threatened by innovation. By the 1890s, however, Eliot's elective system had been successfully put into effect, and his graduate program, established in 1872, was acknowledged as preeminent in America.

Such changes were terribly expensive. They required more faculty, library resources, equipment, and buildings to accommodate both the greatly expanded educational activities and specialization. All of these needs resulted in serious yearly deficits, from which Eliot did not shrink, since he was good at finding money among friends of the college who realized the importance of his objectives. But deficit spending is never popular with trustees and fiscal officers of an institution, and Eliot had his share of trouble with the Corporation and college treasurer.[6]

Eliot knew his Harvard: his grandfather had endowed a chair of Greek literature, his father had been treasurer for the college from 1842 to 1853, and the young son had shared the father's interests. Young Eliot had taught at Harvard for four years and had helped President Walker to prepare the agenda for Corporation meetings. And he had gained an objective view of Harvard during his four years of teaching at the Massachusetts Institute of Technology. Therefore as a new president he did not have to waste time in appraising the situation or getting acclimated. His first year began with a burst of activity: pay raises for and enlargement of the faculty, curriculum reform, land purchases, and a building program — urgencies all.[7]

In the 233 years preceding Eliot's election, Harvard had erected or purchased something like 34 substantial structures (15 of them still standing in 1984); during Eliot's 40-year term, 35 new structures or major enlargements were created.[8] The imprint Eliot left on the physical environment of Harvard can be appreciated by a comparison of two site plans: the "Design of the Buildings, Paths, and Trees in the College Yard" prepared by students under Eliot's direction in 1856–57, when he was tutor in sophomore mathematics, and a map of the university in 1909 at the end of his administration (figs. 44, 45).

When President Eliot assumed office, Harvard faced acute shortages of both dormitories and classrooms. Instructional space he could find (at least for the time being) by remodeling four of the old buildings. These changes we have already discussed while tracing the histories of Massachusetts, Harvard, and University Halls and the Lawrence Scientific School. But the

44
*Map of Harvard Yard
(1856–1857). The irregular
distribution of buildings
defied attempts to create an
axial plan, and the irregularity
of walkways lacked rational
organization.*

45
*Plan of Harvard, 1909. By
the end of Eliot's tenure, the
Sever quadrangle on Quincy
Street and other construction
had set the stage for the Yard
as we know it today.
Memorial Hall, north of the
Delta, was Harvard's largest
building.*

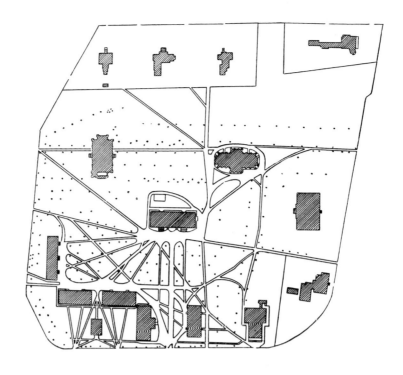

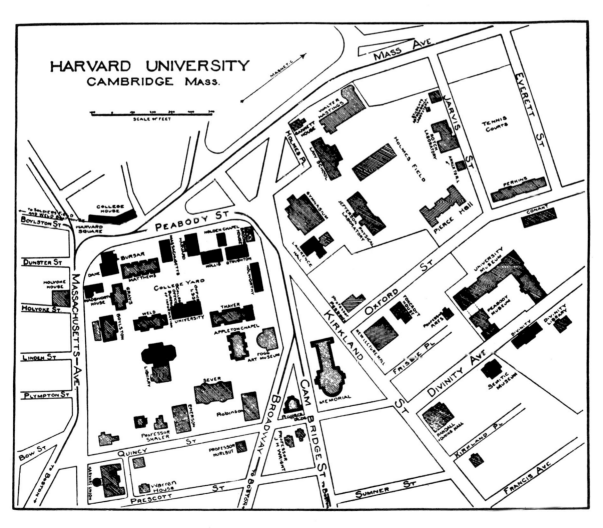

63   *President Eliot and the Harvard Yard*

problem of finding housing for the rapidly growing body of students could not be solved by such measures. Even before Eliot was elected the need for housing was critical. For a student body of about one thousand in 1867, the college halls offered accommodation for only 330. The Commonwealth of Massachusetts had long since made it clear that Harvard could expect no further public aid; no generous donors had come forth with offers of help; and the college treasurer, Nathan Silsbee, forthrightly opposed the withdrawal of capital from the endowment to build dormitories. His reasoning was sound: the budget had been in the red since 1866; using capital would deprive the college of badly needed dividend income; and even if rents were derived from a new dormitory, the income would be so small and uncertain as to constitute a poor investment.[9] Eliot solved this problem of dormitories, but before we see how he did so a word must be said about our approach to the complicated story of all his buildings.

A survey of the buildings could be organized in any of three ways: chronological, stylistic, or topographical. Each method has advantages. A chronological treatment would be systematic and would demonstrate that construction came in waves in which certain types of building predominated. For example, the first buildings ministered to undergraduate needs for dormitories, a commons, and classrooms. After that Eliot turned away from undergraduate dormitories; influenced to some extent by continental educational models, he believed that private interests were supplying all the new space that was necessary. In the 1880s he shifted to buildings (including dormitories) for graduate students in the fields of law, divinity, and science. After 1900 assistance went to classrooms and laboratories like Lowell Lecture Hall, Emerson Hall, Pierce Hall; to structures for art and architecture, Hunt and Robinson Halls; to the Medical and Law Schools; and to such community facilities as the stadium, field and boat houses, Phillips Brooks House, the Semitic Museum, and the Harvard Union.

Another method of surveying the building of this era would be according to architectural style, though such an approach would probably have had little meaning for President Eliot. A man of culture, sound judgment, and great administrative ability, he was, as his writings indicate and as Harvard historians have observed, simply not architectural. To him a handsome building was one that was soundly constructed and effectively planned to accommodate a useful occupation. To paraphrase comments he made in a lecture in 1905, noble public buildings are those which house useful occupations; they provide inspiration through the abstract beauty of good proportions, but most of all perhaps through the beneficent motives that produced them.[10] His one excursion into architectural design was a double house for his bride and his parents at 59-61 Kirkland Street, a compact, fairly institutional mansard design of 1858. But as an administrator he kept himself minutely informed about all that went on in the college, including the planning and construction of new buildings.

In contrast, some benefactors of the college or their architects did not shrink from expressing strong design preferences, often with great independence. The university appears to have allowed considerable latitude in this matter, and the resulting styles of architecture during this era varied enormously. Some buildings were large and plain, striving for useful space at the least possible cost; the best example of this is the University Museum. John Coolidge refers to such structures as Industrial Harvard. Picturesque

Harvard, according to Coolidge's categorization, is almost domestic in vocabulary, with emphasis on decoration and variations in architectural style—from Weld Hall (1870) to Weld Boathouse (1907). Imperial Harvard begins with the first Fogg Museum, Hunt Hall (1893), and ends long after Eliot at Littauer Center (1938), Widener Library being the most imperial of all. The Imperial manner, which parallels a national cultural trend that began in the 1890s, relies on imposing classical shapes and formal planning.[11]

The drawback to a strictly chronological or stylistic approach is that buildings so discussed do not fall into the topographical groupings one experiences in an actual inspection. And since an objective of this book is to observe the process by which the present Harvard environment emerged, we must proceed in a topographical manner. Thus let us begin with Harvard Yard, move to peripheral areas, and finally focus on the North Yard and the Soldiers Field athletic facilities.

Much of Harvard Yard as we now know it took form under President Eliot: the last of the brick quadrangles on the west was largely completed; the scale of Tercentenary Quadrangle east of University Hall, which had been only suggested by the locations of Gore Hall and Appleton Chapel, was established with the erection of Sever Hall (1878), Widener Library (1913), and Memorial Church (c. 1930); the eastern third of the Yard along Quincy Street was incorporated into the planning of the total unit; and the whole was enclosed within its monumental fence. The new president turned initially to the problem of living space for students. Within two years four large dormitories were constructed, another (College House) was enlarged, and three others (Hollis, Holworthy, and Stoughton) were remodeled. Aside from construction of Grays Hall, nothing in presidential reports or corporation minutes prior to Eliot indicates that the previous administration had laid the groundwork for this sudden burst of construction.

Thayer Hall, the first of the group, was built in 1869 through the generosity of Nathaniel Thayer, who had previously sponsored the Herbarium and Thayer Commons. A letter from President Eliot to Thayer's biographer in 1883 indicates what minimal control the university exercised over the design of certain buildings and helps to explain the resulting architectural variety: "A few weeks after I became President, Mr. Thayer told me . . . that he thought the College ought to have another dormitory, the rents of which should be applicable to any college use . . . and that he meant to see that it was shortly built . . . Mr. Thayer selected as architect Mr. Edward D. Harris, junior member of the firm of Ryder and Harris, of Boston, and son of Thaddeus W. Harris, a former Librarian of the University. In making his choice Mr. Thayer told me he was influenced by early friendship for the Harris family . . . The main object which Mr. Thayer had in view was to secure a solid and durable building (almost all the interior partitions are brick) with a considerable rental and accommodations for a large number of students. He deliberately preferred a plain building to an ornate but smaller one . . . At the start the corporation expected to pay part of the cost of the Hall, but before the plans and specifications were complete, it became perfectly understood that Mr. Thayer meant to pay the whole cost. He made all the contracts and paid all the bills himself . . . I never knew the exact cost of the whole work."[12]

Four stories high with a five-story central pavilion (fig. 46), Thayer Hall supplied rooms for 117 students and 3 proctors. Despite its elephantine

46
Thayer Hall (Ryder and Harris, 1869) separates the Old Yard from what later became the Tercentennial Quadrangle.

size, it fits nicely into the Yard; one large building in its location defines the spatial limits of the Old Yard more effectively than two smaller ones would have done. The placement of the building, well behind the facade of University Hall, admirably allows the older building to maintain its preeminence despite its smaller bulk. This, however, was not the reason for Thayer's positioning: it was pushed back to the east to allow a view of Memorial Hall from the Old Yard, even though it crowded Appleton Chapel considerably.[13] Although the design of Thayer makes no attempt to copy Georgian or Federal forms, its stolid composition, academic detailing, and use of brick ensure compatibility with the three earlier dormitories at the north end of the Yard. It is fortunate that Harris did not use rough granite trim as Bradlee had done seven years earlier at Grays, for that would have made the already large building too distracting to stand comfortably next to University Hall. The emphasis on the rusticated sandstone frames of the entrances and the windows above them is restrained, if heavy, but the detailing of this Italianate building is not incompatible with that of its Georgian neighbors.

The shortage of rooms, Nathaniel Thayer's example, and undoubtedly Eliot's persuasiveness inspired the gift of two other dormitories, Weld and Matthews. That they were located together at the south end of the Old Yard is salutory, because their complex massing, irregular silhouettes, and active fenestration would have been disturbing in proximity to the earlier Georgian dormitories. Although there were already four buildings in the south end of the Yard (Boylston, Dane, Gore, and Grays), none except Boylston influenced the location of the new dormitories. The entrance of Boylston provided an axis for Weld, a formal decision that had the beneficial result of placing the main (west) facade of the new dormitory about thirty feet behind (east) of the facade of University Hall. As in the similar situation of Thayer, this solution left the center of attention clearly upon Bulfinch's early granite building. In order to get enough room in which to place Matthews Hall, the old brick law building, Dane Hall, had to be moved 70 feet to the south.[14]

The architectural styles of the two dormitories are very different (figs. 47, 48). At Weld Hall (1870), Ware and Van Brunt employed stepped gables and strapwork reminiscent of Renaissance Flanders or Elizabethan England and the English Queen Anne manner which would soon become so prevalent in America; in contrast, the sharp gables and pointed arches of Matthews Hall (1871) by Peabody and Stearns are close to Ruskin's version of the Gothic and carry the earliest foliate stone carving in Harvard Yard.[15] Yet the two designs are similar in their vertical emphasis and restless massing punctuated by pavilions with bay and oriel windows. Both also use intricate Panel Brick designs, although the color of brick in the two structures is not the same. The most inspired elements of Weld are the twin towers with clerestory windows which light the stair halls below (now unfortunately ceiled off as a fire precaution). Deeply recessed entrance vestibules mark the design of the main facade and align it with Thayer.[16] Matthews, in contrast, was provided with identical Gothic porches on both facades in order to present polite fronts to both the Old Yard and Harvard Square. Although Matthews is gabled and picturesque, its symmetrical plan and its subdivision into bays conform to the context of the Old Yard.

47
Weld Hall (Ware and Van Brunt, 1870). Weld's height, elaborate Flemish gables, and Jacobean ornament introduced the picturesque silhouette considered essential in later nineteenth-century design. A spire of Gore Library can be seen just to the right.

48
Matthews Hall: architects' sketch (Peabody and Stearns, 1871). Matthews Hall introduced carved stone sculpture in the Gothic style. Massachusetts Hall appears to the right.

49

Holyoke House (Edward Harris, of Ryder and Harris, 1870). In the nineteenth century Harvard dormitories, including this one on Massachusetts Avenue, filled in the Square.

A fourth dormitory, Holyoke House, located just across Massachusetts Avenue and therefore outside the Yard, was an integral part of this campaign of dormitory construction. Built during the first year of the new administration, it was demolished almost a century later, in 1961, to make way for Holyoke Center. Holyoke House was also designed by Edward Harris, architect for Thayer Hall. Like College House, the older university dormitory on Harvard Square, Holyoke House was provided with stores in the ground story; space at the rear was reserved for a public restaurant (fig. 49). On the floors above were suites, each consisting of a study, two bedrooms, and a bath. Though the public areas (stores, stair halls, and corridors) had central heat, each suite was dependent on its own coal grate. The use of a mansard roof on Holyoke House was prompted as much by economy as by fashion: it was cheaper to construct a wooden roof covered with slate than to carry up masonry walls for another story. The design had a certain public role to play because it faced Massachusetts Avenue, and for many years the stores on the ground floor set a standard of magnificence to which still-provincial Cambridge was quite unaccustomed.[17] These four dormitories, totally different in appearance yet erected within the space of three years, illustrate the architectural inconsistency of the Eliot administration and of America itself in these years.

Dormitory building drew attention to sanitation problems in the Yard and to a need for improvements now that the city provided a water main and a sewer line along Massachusetts Avenue. But the change from eighteenth-century hand pumps and privies to modern plumbing came slowly. The first dormitory to be equipped with cold running water was Grays Hall (1862), but it had no inside toilets. "Water-trough privies," according to the President's Report of 1870, were first installed in the south basement of University Hall and the west basement of Holworthy Hall. It was 1880 before waterclosets existed in all basements; not until 1898 were bathrooms with hot and cold water installed in all residential buildings in the Yard.[18]

Central heating was provided in a few of the nonresidential buildings, including Gore, Boylston, and Sever Halls at the time of construction, but this luxury appeared only gradually in dormitories, where fireplaces were long relied upon. (Several books of reminiscences by alumni refer to the tradition of warming a dormitory chamber by heating an iron cannonball in the fireplace until it was red hot, then placing it in a skillet in the center of the room.) Heating apparatus was not installed in Memorial Hall until it was decided to open the commons there in 1874; University and Matthews Halls and two-thirds of Thayer had steam heat in 1887 (the rest of Thayer not until years later). Before a new steam system was substituted in 1898, Harvard and Massachusetts Halls had been for many years minimally heated by hot air furnaces. Grays Hall lacked any form of central heating until 1908.[19]

It is likewise sobering to realize how tardily artificial illumination made its appearance. In 1855, three years after a plant was established in Cambridge, gas lighting was installed in recitation rooms and as an experiment in Holworthy.[20] But electricity was not introduced until the summer of 1891. To do this the college had to maintain its own dynamo. Lights were placed in Gore Library, Sever Hall, Memorial Hall, Hemenway Gymnasium, and the reading rooms of several departmental libraries. The installation of electricity in Gore was especially welcome because it meant that the main library, which had prohibited candles and gas lights for fear of fire, could now stay open at night.[21]

The removal of the privy from Tercentenary Quadrangle led to thoughts about the improvement of that area. In his annual message of 1871 President Eliot reported the expenditure of $4000 for landscaping, but even more important, he outlined a plan for the future growth of the Yard: "The rectangle between Holworthy and Grays Halls is considered to be now completed; unless at some future date it should be thought best to put a building with a wide archway between the eastern ends of Harvard and Massachusetts Halls in the position of the Old Stoughton Hall. For the rest of the Yard, the Corporation are proceeding upon the plan of keeping the space between the Library, the Chapel, and University Hall forever open. A building may be placed on the eastern side of the avenue which leads to the southern door of the Library to match Boylston Hall on the western side, and a continuous, or nearly continuous structure may stretch along Quincy Street, from Harvard Street to Broadway. The building along Quincy Street, from Harvard Street to Broadway, should be imposing and a unit of design . . . University Hall, the Chapel, Boylston Hall, and the Library being of stone, it is desirable that all future buildings to the eastward of them should also be of stone." The concept expressed in this statement is illustrated by a map preserved in the Harvard Archives, which anticipates Eliot's later planning activities such as the Memorial Fence (fig. 50).

Despite this resolve, the proposal to build in stone had been forgotten by the late 1870s when a bequest from James Warren Sever and his wife, Mrs. Anne Sever, made it possible to construct an urgently needed building containing classrooms, a need that had been met only temporarily in 1870

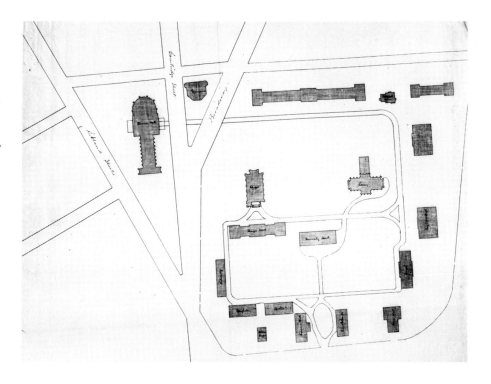

50
Harvard Yard: plan of 1870 (Charles W. Eliot). In the later nineteenth century various attempts were made to organize Harvard Yard despite the irregular placement of the chapel and library. This proposal advocated a long building as eastern terminus.

51
Bird's-eye view of Harvard Yard proposing Sever Hall (office of H. H. Richardson).

71   *President Eliot and the Harvard Yard*

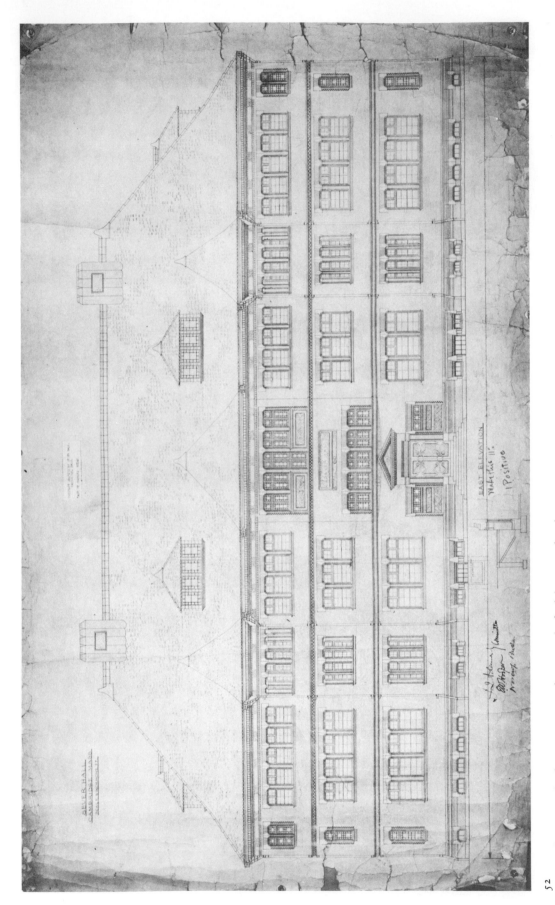

52
*Sever Hall (H. H. Richardson, 1878): east elevation. The final design employed
a Georgian doorway, relating the building to earlier precedents at Harvard.*

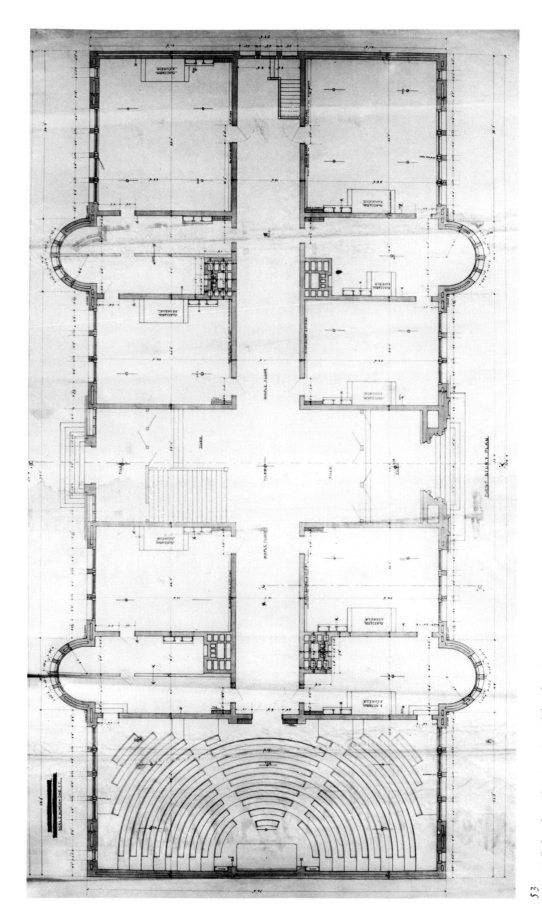

53
Sever Hall: first-floor plan. Sever's modular plan gives equal importance to east and west elevations.

by the remodeling of older structures. The Corporation appointed a building committee to employ an architect and to oversee the undertaking. H. H. Richardson was selected in October 1878, construction began the following spring, and the building was ready for use in September 1880.[22]

The new structure provided 24 classrooms varying in capacity from 40 to 350 seats. There were in addition 12 preparatory rooms which could be used by the faculty or for small classes; these were placed between classrooms to form suites of three rooms which could be assigned to academic departments. Space allocated to the fine arts in the north half of the third floor included a 300-seat lecture room and two exhibition galleries. An examination room of 70 by 52 feet was placed in the attic, but this seems to have been something of an afterthought, because the long shed dormer needed to light it does not appear in early studies for the building; in later years this room was used for a fine arts museum and studio.

Sever Hall was the first important academic building erected in the eastern third of the Yard. It was located too close to Quincy Street to permit placement in front of it of the long building hypothesized in the president's plan of 1870. That the plan had not been entirely forgotten, however, is proved by a watercolor sketch (fig. 51), a bird's-eye view of the Yard, which may have been drawn in Richardson's office as an enticement to potential donors. It shows Sever Hall in some detail in the foreground while other buildings appear more sketchily. Instead of a long, continuous structure along Quincy Street, three detached buildings are shown with a wide gap in front of Sever; this is the first suggestion of the present Sever Quadrangle. The sketch must have been drawn during the winter of 1878–79, because it shows the east facade of the proposed building in a slightly different form from what was actually built.[23]

The east-west orientation of Sever astride an old property line seems to have been influenced by the location of Gore Hall, now enlarged by the addition of a bookstack wing. But Sever was not aligned with any single building. To have placed it exactly opposite University Hall would have emphasized the sharp differences in architectural style and material between the two buildings—for symmetry invites comparisons—and it would have crowded Gore. As a practical matter, it was desirable to place it so as to dislocate only one of the university's three rental properties facing Quincy Street, number 31, the Pierce house. After much historical puzzling to explain the placement of Sever, it now appears that its location was probably determined empirically by staking out several positions and trying to envision which would look best within the spatial context of the Yard.[24]

In Sever Hall Richardson combined lavish ornamentation with monumentality in a way that no other nineteenth-century designer (save his admirer Louis Sullivan) could (figs. 52, 53). The contained outline of the building and its substantial mass clearly define the open spaces upon which it fronts, and Sever Hall takes its place among the other structures of the Yard with an authority that enhances the whole area. Its position is basically parallel to that of Bulfinch's University Hall, which is also an elongated rectangular shape. Furthermore, the use of red brick at Sever carries the color of the building materials of the Old Yard into the Tercentenary Quadrangle, where brick has wisely been continued in later buildings. The eastern doorway, the style of which is unique in Richardson's work, recreates in cut brickwork the design of a High Georgian entrance, relating the building nicely to the Old Yard. The balance of proportion between the doorway and the mass of the building, along with its detail in brick, are clearly influenced by the colonial surroundings of the Yard. Although retaining his individualism and using lavish ornamentation, Richardson did not allow the design to become too complex. He achieved this goal in part by restricting the material to brick. No matter how profuse or intricate the detail, it is made of brick, and as such it reads as masonry. Only when viewed from very close range does his extraordinarily rich and inventive decoration emerge.

The color of this brick is neither that of Thayer nor that of the eighteenth-century buildings, yet its hue blends well with both. Richardson used a great deal of cut brick and molded brick ornamentation; newspaper accounts say that sixty different brick shapes were used in the design. The brickyard that produced the best cut work and molded brick ornamentation was located in Northwest Cambridge and operated by J. L. Sands and Sons. Clay from the Sands pits, which were not exploited before 1863, burned a different color from that which had been used earlier.[25] The choice of brick for Sever appears to have established that material for use in subsequent buildings in the eastern part of the Yard, and we hear no more of stone construction for that area.

Fenestration is the other factor that unifies the facades of Sever. A modular window runs throughout the design, used singly or grouped and carried into the tower-like bay windows. Multiplication of the module in long banks provides maximum light for the interior without diminishing the apparent strength of the building as perforating it with many holes would have done. The low arch of the west entrance is Richardson's primary concession to his characteristic Romanesque manner, and the pediment above the roofline projects outward, associating the classical theme of the eastern entrance with the inner elevation. To have used such arches elsewhere would have complicated the design and reduced the area devoted to windows. The towered bay windows, however, and the strong horizontal silhouette express the different interior function of the preparation rooms. As the late Dean Joseph Hudnut of the Graduate School of Design put it, "Sever Hall is the most American of our buildings — and our most important one."

Between 1878 and 1905 Harvard Yard was filled out to both the north and the east and surrounded with Charles McKim's magnificent Memorial Fence. The structures that followed Sever established a new stylistic direction toward an imperial and larger-scale image based on European architectural models rather than relating to the American colonial context of the Yard. The first of these, Hunt Hall (figs. 54, 55), was designed in 1893 by the New York architect Richard Morris Hunt as the original Fogg Museum. Less skillfully sited than Sever Hall, Hunt Hall was never considered a success; it was criticized as unfunctional by the first faculty members to use it, and it moved the visiting committee of 1894 to call for consultation with faculty in the planning of all future building. In later years the structure proved no more adaptable to the needs of the Graduate School of Design. The earliest of Harvard's imperial buildings, executed in limestone and with studied elegance in its classical European forms, Hunt Hall was oblivious of everything else in Harvard Yard.[26] The building was placed so close to the street that it defied enclosure within the Memorial Fence and turned its

54
Hunt Hall (Richard Morris Hunt, 1893), the first Fogg Museum, faced north, turning its back on the Yard.

55
Hunt Hall interior. Next to the axial symmetry of a divided grand staircase, ancient sculpture was displayed for study.

*56
Robinson Hall (Charles
McKim, 1904), built to house
the School of Architecture,
forms the northern side of
Sever quadrangle. The clock
tower of Memorial Hall
appears beyond.*

57

*Emerson Hall: west facade
(Guy Lowell, 1900). Emerson
was originally designed as a
stone building; its sculpture
and dressings were ultimately
executed in terra cotta, the
only use of this material in
Harvard Yard.*

back on Appleton Chapel and Thayer Hall. Because it functioned badly and
made poor use of valuable space, its demolition in 1973 to make way for a
dormitory (Canaday Hall) was generally approved.

The northeast corner of the Yard was completed a decade later by the
addition of Emerson Hall (1900) by Guy Lowell and Robinson Hall (1904)
by McKim, Mead and White. Robinson (fig. 56) was constructed to house
the Department of Architecture, founded in 1894. It reflected the axial
symmetry and organized parti or plan that characterized designs from the
Ecole des Beaux Arts in Paris. Indeed these French theories, popularized by
McKim in his own work, dominated the teaching methods of the Department. The ornamental program for Robinson incorporated eclectically
derived classical bas-reliefs on either side of the entrance, while plaques
celebrating the names of architects, sculptors, and philosophers were placed
below the upper windows. The hard, crisp detail and machine-like quality
of Robinson are rescued by the concession McKim made in using brick
rather than his customary stone for the low-lying and symmetrical elevation.[27]

Emerson Hall (fig. 57) housed the Department of Philosophy, then in a
golden hour with professors William James, Josiah Royce, and George
Santayana. Its architect Guy Lowell initially planned a stone building, but
even on a lower budget provided an imperial image with his characteristic
baroque panache in the raised attic and the giant engaged columns of brick

58
*Emerson Hall: north facade.
Emerson faced Robinson to
form the southern side of the
Sever quadrangle. A common
use of brick and simple
rectangular shapes combined
with good scale and spacing
unify these three buildings of
disparate style.*

79   *President Eliot and the Harvard Yard*

59
Architect's sketch for Phillips Brooks House (A. W. Longfellow, Jr., 1898), the first Colonial Revival building in Harvard Yard.

60
Phillips Brooks House: south facade.

61
*Phillips Brooks House:
staircase hall.*

on the northern elevation facing Robinson (fig. 58). Lowell's design for
Emerson Hall was the first at Harvard since Hemenway gym to utilize terra
cotta for its richly displayed ornament. It reflects a Parisian sophistication
which, while softer in execution than the ornament of Robinson, is also
directly derived from large-scale European models.[28] Placing the new
buildings as counterparts flanking the eastern elevation of Sever Hall retained the solution if not the picturesque style suggested in the Richardson
watercolor (fig. 51). The calm, rectangular massing of these new brick
buildings, placed at right angles to Sever, complement it and each other
admirably. The sense of enclosure of the new quadrangle was enhanced later
by the construction of the Memorial Fence and the location of the new
Fogg Museum (1925) on the other side of Quincy Street.

The last free space in the northwest corner of the Yard was taken by
A. W. Longfellow's Phillips Brooks House (1898). Expertly sited, this
building filled what had been an empty and awkward corner and created a
new quadrangle to balance the one on the other side of Holden Chapel.
Facing both the small new quadrangle and Kirkland Street, Phillips Brooks
House has no rear elevation: both fronts contain handsome entrances (figs.

59, 60). In the south facade Longfellow transposed the Palladian window from the north elevation of Harvard Hall III to a position above the doorway, and the recessed arches in the walls retain their vigor adjacent to the robust forms of Hollis Hall to the east. The oak-sheathed hall of Phillips Brooks emulates closely that of the Jeremiah Lee House in Marblehead (1769), with a broad staircase and elaborately turned newel and balusters (fig. 61). Thus on both exterior and interior Longfellow utilized passages from colonial models rather than drawing upon more general sources of inspiration from the past. The massing, choice of materials, and detailing of the new building harmonized with its eighteenth- and early nineteenth-century neighbors, establishing for the Yard the precedent that was followed later by Charles Coolidge when he completed the small quadrangles with Lionel and Mower Halls toward the Square.[29]

Phillips Brooks House, it should be noted, came into being as an outgrowth of changing religious activities at Harvard. When students in 1885 protested compulsory chapel, the administration and Overseers agreed to a proposal to establish a Department of Religion with a staff to hold voluntary daily services. In 1890 this staff sent out an appeal for funds to build a center that would provide space for the University Preacher and various religious activities (missionary, charitable, and social). The center was named after—and partly furnished with objects that had belonged to—Phillips Brooks, rector of Trinity Church in Boston, who had died in 1893.[30]

The Memorial Fence, connecting several existing gateways and enclosing the Yard, was begun in 1901 from designs by McKim, Mead and White but was not completed until the mid-1930s. It is an unusually fine combination of wrought iron sections separated by brick and limestone piers. It followed a succession of earlier fences: the earliest was the six-foot stockade around the Peyntree lot ordered by Professor Eaton in 1638. The next of which we have visual record is the low, presumably brick wall stretching along the western edge of the college and pictured in the 1726 Burgis view (fig. 12). This construction is said to have been demolished by troops of the Continental Army who were quartered at Harvard in 1775. A more elaborate barrier, apparently with a masonry base, pickets, and handsome pilastered gateposts surmounted by globes, is recorded in drawings dating between 1790 and 1828. This elaborate fencing only extended along the western edge of the yard, from a point north of Holden Chapel to one south of Massachusetts Hall. Beyond those points the enclosure appears to have been simpler, with granite posts carrying two wooden rails (a design still used for the fence around Cambridge Common). A photograph of Wadsworth House dating from about 1860 shows fencing of the same height but of solid boarding set vertically (fig. 13). The familiar two-rail fence in front of the main college buildings first appears in a view of 1830.[31]

The substantial cost of Memorial Fence was defrayed by various classes whose dates are worked into the iron ornamentation. It is punctuated by nine major gates and several minor ones, likewise donated by classes, clubs, or individuals.[32] The first and most elaborate of these is the Johnston Gate (1890), by McKim, Mead and White, at the main entrance to the Yard (fig. 246). This first commission of Charles McKim at Harvard augured his major contribution to the creation of an axial and organized plan for Harvard Yard. As the Johnston Gate established the western access to the Yard, McKim's Robinson Hall finished off the Sever Quadrangle, which

62
Harvard Union (Charles McKim, 1902).

was opposite Johnston Gate on the east and where McKim also designed a gate. Thus McKim, particularly in his work at Harvard before 1900, was, like Richardson and Bulfinch before him, thinking in terms of the pre-existing structures in Harvard Yard as the ambience of his own design. The Johnston Gate was the first university structure to use what later became known as Harvard Brick, hand made and wood burned to resemble brick used in the early buildings.[33]

In addition to filling the Yard with new structures, President Eliot's administration engaged in real estate exchanges and building activity on all sides of Harvard Yard: to the south and west near Harvard Square, to the east beyond Quincy Street, and to the north on the Delta and in the North Yard. The university had acquired considerable property in the area of Harvard Square by 1800, and in 1870 was erecting or expanding two large dormitories there. But despite these investments Harvard tended to sell rather than purchase Harvard Square property. Sales included parcels on Dunster Street, where a horse-car barn and stores known as Little's Block were later constructed, as well as the rear portion of the Holyoke House lot, which was sold in 1898. The university did, however, retain the old college wharf waterfront property, where a bathhouse was built.[34] In the absence of university involvement south of Massachusetts Avenue, many private dormitories and clubs, known as the Gold Coast, were erected in this period.

On the east side of Quincy Street Harvard obtained a bridgehead in the form of the Harvard Union (fig. 62), which was erected in 1900–1902 with a gift of $150,000 from Major Henry Lee Higginson.[35] To make room for the new building, Warren House (1833) was moved back from its position on Harvard Street to its present location. The handsome Union, the work of McKim, Mead and White, was intended by its donor to provide an attractive gathering place for students not wealthy enough to afford the luxuries of a Gold Coast club. It was thus envisioned as an attempt to encourage an esprit de corps among the rank and file of students. With its red brick walls and white stone trim, the Union is probably the most authoritative of the several Georgian Revival designs constructed at Harvard near the turn of the century, being more closely related to late nineteenth-century English Georgian than to American Colonial prototypes. The Union interiors, incorporating sculpture, painting, and carved heraldic paneling, provide an extension of the English image envisioned by Ware and Van Brunt at Memorial Hall and recreated later by Charles Coolidge and his associates in the River Houses of the 1930s. But Colonial models were also invoked, in Perkins and Conant Halls (1893) and Phillips Brooks House (1898); the use of such models continues far into the twentieth century with the new Fogg Museum and the Harvard Faculty Club on Quincy Street, both of which are of provincial style and scale. The Union was augmented in 1911 by the Varsity Club, a structure of comparably good design by Thomas Mott Shaw.[36]

In contrast to his apparent indifference to the area south of Massachusetts Avenue, President Eliot actively extended Harvard's holdings north of Kirkland Street, where an impressive number of new buildings or sizable additions to old ones were constructed. When Mr. Eliot assumed control, this area, which came to be known as the North Yard, was far from the topographical unit it is today. The terrain was uneven, some of it swampy, and it was cut off from Harvard Yard by three streets that intersected at awkward angles.[37] University ownership in the area was spotty, confined to unsold sections of the Shady Hill estate, a portion of the Jarvis estate, and several parcels near the Little Common (fig. 37). It was to this area that President Eliot turned his attention after satisfying the needs for dormitories and classrooms in the yard. First came the acquisition of parcels between Massachusetts Avenue and Oxford Street: Jarvis and Holmes Fields were acquired in 1870 and 1871 and frontage on Holmes Place increased. He next considered property fronting Oxford Street that Harvard had once owned, noting with satisfaction that this could now be "bought back at prices less than ['with compound interest at 5% compounded thereon'] those for which it was sold by the college." But to make these purchases Eliot was forced to draw on the college endowment, for which he was criticized. The process of repurchasing land in this area continued until 1955, by which time twenty parcels had been reassembled.

Access to a good portion of this land was restricted, except for Divinity Avenue, because the university had sold most of the frontage of Kirkland Street, but this problem was somewhat alleviated by the acquisition of several parcels facing Oxford Street between 1886 and 1924. In the long run this isolation may have proved advantageous, for large portions of the area are not now traversed by streets or disturbed by through traffic.[38] But because the area was so ample (approximately twenty acres) and the buildings set so far apart, early builders were not forced to consider the relationships among structures as they had to do in Harvard Yard, where space was limited. Thus the North Yard suffered a careless dispersal of buildings.

63
*Memorial Hall (Ware and
Van Brunt, 1866 – 1878). The
soaring polychromatic exterior
of Memorial Hall evoked
Ruskin's version of Gothic
design.*

64
Memorial Hall: tower with clock, which was destroyed by fire in 1956.

The most important building to be erected under Eliot in the area north of the Yard, and indeed one of the three or four most significant structures erected by Harvard throughout its history, is Memorial Hall.[39] As it was designed and remained during most of its first century, Memorial Hall stood apart (fig. 63). Only with the closing of Kirkland Street and other changes resulting from the construction of the Cambridge Street underpass in 1966–1968 has it been brought into an orderly integral relationship with the North Yard. As a memorial it was originally intended to be seen alone, to stand as a conspicuous and constant reminder of alumni who had fought and died in the Civil War. For this reason a location separate from Harvard Yard was desired. The Delta was the obvious choice, but this site was used as a playing field, and the administration refused to relinquish it except in exchange for a comparable field for athletics. To meet this requirement the committee of alumni in charge of the memorial purchased the Jarvis Field and presented it to Harvard in 1870 in exchange for the Delta.

The construction of Memorial Hall stands as a milestone both for Harvard and for American architecture. The building, designed by Henry Van Brunt, is a textbook example of Ruskin Gothic design, that phase of Victorian architecture which reached its peak of popularity in England in the 1860s.[40] Characteristic of the movement are a dynamic silhouette and assertive massing, inventive use of the Gothic precedent, polychromatic surfaces of varied and contrasting materials, and well-crafted detail.[41] In design and execution Memorial Hall is comparable to contemporary work in Great Britain, and the extravagant admiration it evoked at home when it was built was comparable to that inspired by the Carpenter Center almost a century later. That two generations after its erection Memorial Hall suffered a decline in popular esteem is only to be expected, for such is the history of taste: every old building — even those venerable Georgian piles in Harvard's brick quadrangles — has passed through a valley of disfavor and enjoyed rediscovery. The low period for Memorial Hall began with the Georgian Revival about 1900 and reached rock bottom with the arrival of Functionalism in the late 1930s. For a time it even seemed that the structure was being deliberately neglected so that it would become unstable and require demolition. Fortunately the tide has turned: a younger generation sees Memorial Hall with new eyes and responds to its surging energy, even in its present state of mutilation.

As a Harvard milestone Memorial Hall commemorates the almost religious sincerity with which the alumni regarded the justness of the Civil War and the sanctity of the sacrifices that had been made. As such it was the occasion of the first large-scale fundraising program undertaken by Harvard alumni. By the time the building was completed in 1878, $368,980.90 had been contributed, a figure representing approximately one-twelfth of the total endowment of the college (at that time about $4.48 million). Although there was little disagreement about the appropriateness of honoring Harvard's Civil War dead in a signal manner, the cost of the edifice seemed extravagant at the time, the more so because of the financial straits that developed throughout the nation halfway through the fundraising campaign. That Memorial Hall was completed without drastically compromising the original scheme and in the face of great obstacles is indicative of the importance leading alumni attached to this undertaking.[42]

The idea of a war memorial was first discussed in 1863, and by 1865 a Committee of Fifty had been formed to realize the project. An architectural competition was announced for the design, and from an unknown number of submissions, that of Ware and Van Brunt was chosen.[43] Plans were ready by 1866, although they were modified in important details in 1868 and again in 1871. Work began in the fall of 1870; Alumni Hall and Memorial Transept beneath the tower were ready by June 1874; Sanders Theatre was substantially completed by May 1875 but not used until Commencement exercises the following year; the tower was finished in 1877. In 1878, when the structure was finally adjudged complete, it was formally turned over to the university. The great clock in the tower was added in 1897, a gift from the Class of 1872 (fig. 64). During World War II the iron cresting of the

65
Memorial Hall: final plan.

66
Memorial Hall: drawing of first design. In the several earlier designs, smaller than the final architectural solution, the paired towers of the transept porch and the rounded shape of Sanders Theatre had not yet been developed.

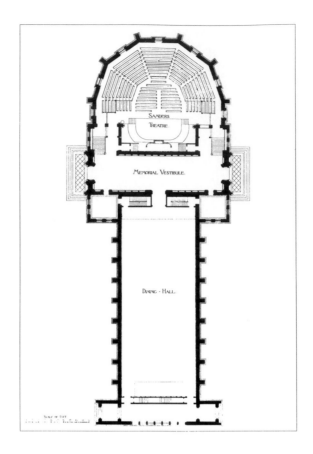

67
Memorial Hall: Memorial Transept, its Gothic vault executed in wood. The Martin Brimmer Memorial Window was designed by Sarah Wyman Whitman.

tower was removed (and given to the war effort) and the building suffered neglect; it was being restored in September 1956 when workmen accidentally ignited the wooden substructure of the tower roof, which burned. For almost two decades repairs were minimal, but in 1976 the multicolored slate roofs were restored and the iron cresting was replaced on the peaks of the four subsidiary towers. The roof of the tower, along with the clock and the iron cresting, which are essential to the monumental appearance of the building, have yet to be replaced.

Memorial Hall is really three buildings: a memorial chamber, a banqueting hall, and a theatre (fig. 65). The design expresses these separate functions clearly, yet integrates them. It is unfortunate that the building looks so much like a cathedral, for it has led some to suppose that the architects started with a preconceived shape into which the separate functions were forced. This seems not to have been the case, however, for the first studies placed the memorial at the west end rather than its final location under the

68
Memorial Hall: dining hall looking east. The iron columns of the staircase rose against a stenciled terra-cotta red wall.

69
Memorial Hall. Sanders Theatre is based on Wren's Sheldonian Theatre at Oxford. To the right of the stage is William Wetmore Story's statue of Justice Story.

central tower. Though the first sketch had a less ecclesiastical appearance, its plan was inferior (fig. 66). The successful design of the tower was arrived at after the architects had lived with the project for almost six years and worked through no fewer than four recorded solutions (many modern architects would be grateful for similar opportunities to correct and refine an early design). The final solution, resolved in 1871, unifies the original concept in a great pyramidal shape, culminating in the tower. Before the roof burned, the building was best seen from an angle in which the roof slopes of the projecting arms repeated the outlines of the tower roof. A view from that position is now forced on the visitor as the result of the construction of the underpass.

Located under the tower, Memorial Transept is appropriately somber: sepulchral light filters through stained glass windows, the walls are sheathed in white marble bearing memorial inscriptions, the floor is paved with marble, and the wood of the vaulting is lusterless (fig. 67). The "correctness" of these vaults and the appropriateness of simulating vaults in wood — both topics of heated debate at one time — undoubtedly interest modern critics less than the imaginative way in which the volumes of the hall fuse with those of the large stairwells that provide access to the balconies of the adjacent theatre. From a modern point of view it is felicitous that a commemorative space finds so vital and lively a function as a lobby for a concert hall and a dining hall.

In addition to establishing the memorial area, a principal objective of the alumni was to provide an appropriate space where all Harvard graduates attending Commencement could sit down together for the traditional banquet. This was an honored college custom and one for which numerous dining halls had been devised, each to be abandoned as it became too small.[44] As this annual feast took place in June and was arranged through caterers, central heating and extensive kitchens were not necessary. Use of the hall as a student commons had not been part of the original plan, but with the success of Thayer Commons, which was then overflowing the limited quarters in the remodeled railroad station, it was decided in October 1874 to provide a student-directed commons in the recently completed hall. This entailed installing a basement kitchen, a heating system, and later (1908) adding a serving pantry on the north side. These improvements, along with furniture and equipment, cost about $40,000, which was met with a loan from the university and the understanding that the student organization directing the commons would repay the debt with interest.

The inspiration for the great hammerbeam trussed ceiling of Alumni Hall (fig. 68) lay in the Medieval halls of the colleges of Cambridge and Oxford. The 59-foot width of the dining hall is not much less than the 68-foot span of Westminster Hall (1399) in London, the largest wood-truss interior surviving from the Middle Ages. In further emulation of British prototypes (a continual tendency in Harvard architecture until World War II), the university in the summer of 1874 adorned the hall with a collection of tapestries, portraits, and marble busts. A dado of walnut paneling, stained glass windows, and a stenciled ceiling enhanced the interior.[45] If much of this embellishment is so inhibited by tradition as to be a bit dull, elements like the balcony at the east end of the hall with the sequence of stair flights leading to the upper levels of the tower are splendidly imaginative. The use of the same polychromatic brick surfaces on the interior walls as on the exterior unifies the complex decorative program.[46] Another good feature is the outside porch that extends across the west front of Alumni Hall. This element is a residue of the ungainly memorial plaque, rather resembling an oversized tombstone, that was featured in the first design. Now providing a memorial to President Walker (1853–1860), the arcaded porch has good scale, and it diminishes the ecclesiastical appearance of the building considerably. The handsome wrought iron gates of the Walker porch were acquired with a special bequest of $500 made in 1876.

The greatest achievement of Memorial Hall is Sanders Theatre (fig. 69). Its woodwork is lustrous, its carving and colors sympathetic, its acoustics and sightlines magnificent. The spatial configuration is so good that the auditorium, although seating twelve hundred spectators, conveys a feeling of intimacy. The theatre was built with a bequest of $50,000 from Charles Sanders, the college bursar, for "the erection of a large and substantial hall of simple architecture." Although he did not specify Wren's Sheldonian Theatre (1664–1668) at Oxford, that building was obviously in the minds of the university officials and architects who planned Sanders Theatre. The five-sided plan of Sanders translates Wren's Baroque design into Gothic Revival terms without sacrifice of function. The west balcony over the stage, designed to accommodate overflow crowds, is an acoustical aid whose coved soffit, along with the many different surfaces of roof, walls, and trusses, breaks the reflected sound waves to make the acoustics almost perfect. Roof trusses of wood conceal iron tension rods, a subterfuge for which the architects were much criticized by their contemporaries.[47]

The pious determination of the alumni to memorialize their fallen classmates is best expressed by the tower, which soars 195 feet. The highest construction for miles around, it was for generations the focus of Harvard life, its bell calling and dismissing classes, its dining hall providing food for over half the student body. Even the townspeople were beholden, for anyone who lived within a quarter mile could see the face of one of the clocks and hear the tolling of the quarter hour. When the tower roof, clock, and cresting have been replaced, Memorial Hall in century-old splendor will resume its pivotal visual role in the world of Harvard.

5 The North Yard and Soldiers Field

When President Eliot took office in 1869 there were only three college buildings north of Kirkland Street: Divinity Hall (1825), the Lawrence Scientific School (1847), and the first unit of the University Museum (1859). The location of Lawrence Hall bore no relation to the other two structures, which were situated at the far end of Divinity Avenue, a cul-de-sac off Kirkland Street. Placed on opposite sides of the street, the museum and Divinity Hall had the aloof air of mansions of none-too-friendly millionaires attempting to ignore each other. It is hard to say whether the first architect for the museum had any plan to relate his design to Divinity Hall, because he was building at the far end of what was envisioned as a much larger structure. Not until the scale of the new complex was established by the construction of the opposite wing, the Peabody Museum (1876), did it become clear that the new architects would ignore Divinity Hall. Still one of the largest buildings at Harvard, the University Museum is a self-contained giant, seemingly set down at random in the central North Yard. In fairness to the university administration, however, one must remember that the design of both Divinity Hall and the museum was under the control of outside corporations.[1] It was not until the 1930s that the two buildings were brought into a unified spatial relation with each other through brilliant planning by subsequent architects (see Chapters 8 and 11).

The museum, whose construction stretched from 1859 to 1913, was conceived by Professor Louis Agassiz first as a great collection of comparative zoology, the American counterpart of the Jardin des Plantes in Paris, but eventually as a center dedicated to nothing less than the study of the earth and life on the earth. This vast scheme, whose realization was due to the founder's irrepressible energy and dedication, brought together under one roof such diverse studies as zoology, mineralogy, botany, and anthropology. To house these, an enormous six-level, U-shaped building, 364 by 269 feet, was eventually erected—but as the diagram in figure 70 indicates, it did not grow systematically from a single center. Though there are slight differences in detail between one part and another, a high degree of architectural unity was maintained through the simple, "industrial" character of the design. Nevertheless the consistency of both material and style is remarkable, considering that the building was constructed in eleven stages

70

The University Museum as it
grew over the years.

1. *1859, Henry Greenough
and George Snell*
2. *1871, Henry Greenough
and George Snell*
3. *1876, Robert H. Slack*
4. *1876, Robert H. Slack*
5. *1880, George R. Shaw*
6. *1888, Stone, Carpenter
and Co.*
7. *1888–89, architect
unknown*
8. *1889, architect
unknown*
9. *1900, Shaw and
Hunnewell*
10. *1906, architect unknown*
11. *1913, Walter S. Burke*

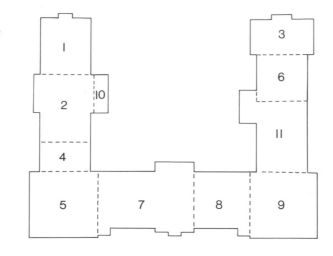

71
*University Museum: first
section (Henry Greenough and
George Snell, 1859).*

72
*University Museum. The
second section was attached to
the first in 1871, and at that
time a mansard roof was
added to the first section.*

under the direction of at least seven architectural firms over a period of
fifty-five years.

The first section of the museum, devoted to comparative zoology,[2] was
designed by Henry Greenough and George Snell and constructed in 1859
(fig. 71).[3] This unit has a spare, clean-cut quality, whose rectangular mass
depends on a projecting entrance pavilion (rebuilt on a larger scale in 1895
and 1906) and on variations in the height of windows emphasized by
brownstone lintels. Although functionally far superior, such a timid academic scheme makes an instructive stylistic comparison with the dynamic
Gothic carving and iron-and-glass interior of the Oxford Museum of
Natural History in England, designed by Deane and Woodward, of contemporaneous date and identical function.[4] The Harvard building was composed of three horizontal divisions: a high basement with windows and two
principal zones, each divided into a main story and a gallery or mezzanine.
The differentiation between a principal floor and a mezzanine reflected
organization of the interior, where each exhibition gallery was divided into
a main floor and a balcony surrounding a high central space. Several such
interiors can still be seen in the comparative zoology wing of the museum.

The original design underwent some modifications. One change in the
early 1870s, when the second section was built, added a mansard roof to
the original wing in order to accommodate an additional floor of offices
(fig. 72). On the Peabody Museum wing, built in 1876 to Robert H. Slack's
design, a continuous story of brick arched windows was substituted for the
mansard dormers so as to create a full attic story; in 1884 this attic scheme

replaced the mansard roof on the original wing to make it more fireproof and to bring it into conformity with the rest of the building. Another modification increased the height of all windows, especially those of the mezzanines, thus changing the latter into regular floors and diminishing the amount of room for display and storage. The 1859 wing, however, retains its original square mezzanine openings. Also in 1884, flush lintels of stone, and later segmental arches of brick, were substituted for the earlier lintels of academic design capped with a crown molding. A small amount of Panel Brick decoration was incorporated in the Peabody Museum pavilion as well as in those at each corner of the main (west) facade; and finally in 1889 another gabled pavilion, filled with a large arch enclosing a bank of windows, was added to the west facade to provide a principal entrance, even though each unit of the museum continued to have its own entrance. Despite these accents, there is a businesslike directness about the design; essentially the museum is a warehouse for the storage and display of vast collections. Its giant interiors have allowed flexibility for much remodeling. The floor supports were originally exposed, and the utilitarian character of the structure is indicated by the exposure of iron stairs and cast-iron columns and by the use of simple brick for interior wall surfaces.

Long before the museum was completed, three more large buildings were added to the North Yard: Hemenway Gymnasium (1876), Austin Hall (1881), and Jefferson Physical Laboratory (1884). Although built within an eight-year span and situated hardly more than fifty yards apart, their styles of architecture and choices of materials were completely different, and they were not even located on the same system of coordinates. To judge from an unofficial plan that survives from about 1880, the university administrators may have dreamed briefly of the new area as a quadrangle centered in Holmes Field with buildings facing inward as in the Old Yard. But even in the short run this comprehensive approach was put aside so that two of the new buildings could enjoy maximum public exposure on important streets (Kirkland Street in the case of Hemenway, the now vanished Holmes Place in the case of Austin Hall). Jefferson Laboratory, coming last, after the prime frontage had been allocated, was placed in Holmes Field, its axes related to Kirkland and Oxford Streets. Whereas Jefferson became an anchor for future orderly building in the North Yard, Hemenway and Austin, set at odds, their angles determined by the streets on which they faced, created problems that modern planners have been unable to solve.

Athletics at Harvard had been housed during the early nineteenth century in Bulfinch's granite University Hall. The importance of physical training had been gaining recognition at the university since Professor Charles Follen's initiatives in the mid 1820s. By 1859 E. C. Cabot had designed the octagonal old Rogers Gymnasium, which served for a quarter-century for exercising and drill programs of the Swedish and German systems then in vogue. In June 1876 the Corporation received a letter from Augustus Hemenway of Boston asking that a lot be assigned on which he might build a new college gymnasium. He informed the Corporation that plans had already been prepared by Robert Peabody. When the building was completed two years later, Harvard had the largest gymnasium in America and the first one to be equipped with special rooms devoted to such activities as rowing, baseball, and fencing (fig. 73).[5] The construction of this elaborate building led the way in the rapid upswing of college sports that followed the Civil War.

73
*Hemenway Gymnasium
(Peabody and Stearns, 1878),
center of athletic activities
until the development of
Soldiers Field.*

When construction of the Hemenway Gym began, President Eliot invited Dr. Dudley Allen Sargent to come to Harvard as its director. Sargent (1848–1924), born in Belfast, Maine, had lifelong athletic ambitions, beginning with a three-year stint as a professional acrobat for a traveling circus following the Civil War. Between 1869 and 1875, while still an undergraduate, he directed the athletic program at Bowdoin College. In 1878, just prior to coming to Harvard, he obtained a medical degree at Yale. It was Dr. Sargent, more than any other individual, who was responsible for achieving a scientific rationale, long-range curricular continuity, and eventual acceptance for college athletics in America.[6] He advocated the Greek ideal of a sound mind in a sound body, and he believed physical education could improve the scholarly as well as the athletic capabilities of students. He had already introduced in New York City a new system of gymnastic equipment that could be adjusted to the strength of the gymnast. Hemenway was soon fitted out with Sargent's apparatus (fig. 74), presenting a different picture from the stark interior of old Rogers Gymnasium.

Harvard's Hemenway Gym under Sargent, assisted by colleagues such as George L. Meylan and Tait McKenzie (both also medical doctors), was the cradle of physical education in America. Here were trained also the leaders of the summer camping movement that developed in these years at the turn of the century when Theodore Roosevelt was president. At Radcliffe Sargent established a separate gymnasium for women, which, ironically enough, served as one of the closest curricular links between that institution and Harvard.[7]

The original Hemenway Gymnasium was animated by an assortment of gables, wings, dormers, chimneys, and cupolas, to say nothing of an entrance porch that looked like a porte cochere. The highly picturesque mass was encrusted by quantities of architectural terra cotta sculpture of more or less Renaissance derivation, a rich, free mixing of traditions and motifs that made it the best Cambridge example of the Free Classic brand of the Queen Anne style of architecture and the most ornamental building at Harvard. It was also the earliest and most lavish display in Boston of American-made terra cotta, the building material that made sculpture on this scale possible. The large arched window framed by rusticated voussoirs on the main gable resembled that used later by an undocumented architect (perhaps Peabody and Stearns) over the principal entrance of the University Museum.[8]

The situation of Hemenway, facing Kirkland Street at the corner of Holmes Place (on the present site of Littauer Center), also recalls that the college athletic area was once in the north campus around Holmes and Jarvis playing fields. Jarvis Street was the location of the low-lying Carey Athletic (later Rotch) Building (1889), by A. W. Longfellow (fig. 75). This shingled, Richardsonian design, so different from Hemenway although built only a decade later, documents the swift stylistic change of American architecture between 1870 and 1890. Harvard's athletic activity did not shift to the Charles River until the acquisition of Soldiers Field in 1890. After the Indoor Athletic Building (1929), by Coolidge, Shepley, Bulfinch and Abbott, became the center of undergraduate athletics for the river houses, Hemenway was replaced in 1938 by a smaller gymnasium of the same name, also by this firm, for use by law students and other graduate students living in the North Yard. The Rotch Building, replaced as an athletic facility by the Carey Cage at Soldiers Field, housed the School of

74
Hemenway Gymnasium interior with Sargent apparatus.

75
The Carey Athletic Building (A. W. Longfellow, Jr., 1889), in Holmes Field, which provided for overflow activities from Hemenway Gym.

99   *The North Yard and Soldiers Field*

76
Gannett House (1838) was later turned ninety degrees to the east. It is Harvard's only remaining academic building of the Greek Revival.

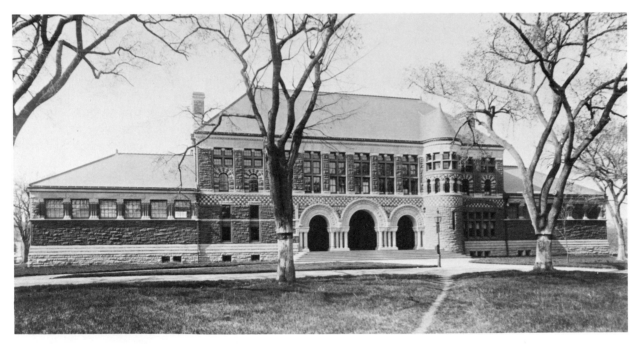

77
Austin Hall (H. H. Richardson, 1881–1884).

Architecture from 1897 to 1904 and was destroyed after Langdell Hall was erected.

The commission to design a building west of the gym for the Law School came to H. H. Richardson from the donor rather than from the administration. Edward Austin, a merchant who had made a fortune in the China trade, gave the building in memory of his brother Samuel. Austin seems to have been as autocratic in planning his hall as had Nathaniel Thayer. The new building memorializes the invigoration of the Law School as it moved toward the revolutionary case-study approach propounded by its new dean, C. C. Langdell. Under Langdell's leadership the enrollment had swelled after 1875, and for years President Eliot had appealed for a new building for the school. Although the commission came to the Richardson office in February 1881, the first reference to the building in Corporation records was in April of the following year, by which time the complete design had been approved by Austin. There must have been consultation with the faculty as the program for the building was developed. Nevertheless, a note in the minutes for April 24, 1882, confirmed officially that "no modification of the outside of the building . . . [is] to be made without Mr. Austin's consent." The administration also guaranteed that no building would ever be erected within sixty feet of the hall. Given this kind of deference to a donor, it was hardly more likely that architectural consistency could be obtained on the campus than on a street of suburban villas.[9]

The situation of Austin Hall, today facing nowhere in particular, is explained by reference to the former street called Holmes Place. This was an L-shaped passage bordering two sides of a small triangular park known as the Little Common, then owned by the city and once part of the Cambridge Common (see fig. 45). The north arm of Holmes Place unfortunately did not quite parallel Kirkland Street; hence the lack of alignment between Austin Hall, which faced the former, and Hemenway Gymnasium, which fronted the latter. Besides these university buildings, there were two residences here: Gannett House (1838), which then faced south rather than east as today (fig. 76), and the important early-eighteenth-century Holmes house. When his hall was finished in 1884, Edward Austin paid $3000 more to have the historic Holmes residence demolished in order that the view of his building might be unimpeded.[10]

While Austin Hall turned its handsome facade toward an ambiguous front yard, it completely ignored what was behind it, a field then used for athletics but since transformed into one of the most interesting outdoor spaces at Harvard. So disdainful of this field were architect and donor that not even a back door provided access to the area, an omission that caused no little inconvenience to later generations of law students shuttling between classes in Langdell and Austin Halls. Only very recently has this back yard been reclaimed and given definition by the construction of the International Legal Studies Center and especially by Benjamin Thompson's two handsome office buildings for the law faculty (see Chapter 11).

The face of Austin Hall (fig. 77) is picturesquely asymmetrical without sacrificing order, for despite the tower and unequal arches of the entrance loggia, the composition is stabilized by its compact geometry and the unbroken stretch of the string course connecting the cornices of the balancing wings.[11] Minor variations in fenestration express differences of internal use, as for book stacks, offices, and lounges, but constant window

78
Austin Hall plan. The irregular fenestration masks an axially aligned interior, which focuses on the lecture room.

79
Austin Hall: interior stair hall, a powerful Richardsonian connecting space.

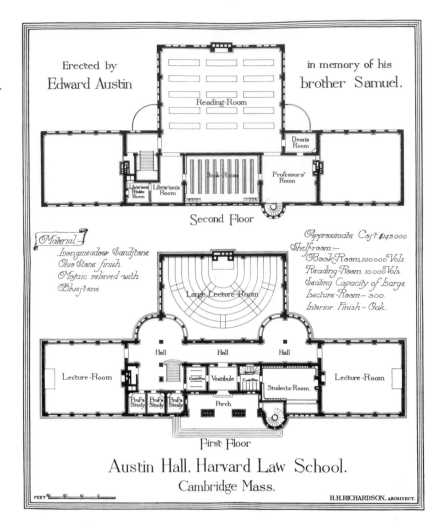

Erected by
Edward Austin
in memory of his
brother Samuel.

Reading-Room

Dean's Room

Librarian's Private Room | Librarian's Room | Book-Room | Professors' Room

Second Floor

Material:—
Longmeadow Sandstone.
Ohio Stone finish.
Mosaic relieved with
Bluestone.

Approximate Cost $145,000
Shelfroom:—
Book-Room 100,000 Vols.
Reading-Room 10,000 Vols.
Seating Capacity of Large
Lecture-Room — 300.
Interior Finish — Oak.

Large Lecture-Room

Hall | Hall | Hall

Lecture-Room

Coat Room | Vestibule | Coat Room

Prof's Study | Prof's Study | Prof's Study

Students' Room.

Lecture-Room

Porch

First Floor

Austin Hall, Harvard Law School.
Cambridge Mass.

FEET

H.H.RICHARDSON, ARCHITECT.

80
*Jefferson Physics Laboratory
(Shaw and Hunnewell, 1882)
with Lyman and Cruft
Laboratories. Behind is the
east facade of Langdell.*

height and spacing prevent these differences from becoming distracting. The building's most striking element is its broad expanses of masonry, which combine pink granite and two shades of sandstone. The quarry-faced stone generates a feeling of enormous strength, a sensation augmented by skillful contrasts of smooth surfaces with intricate carved decoration. Clear massing, consistency in fenestration, contrasting textures, and exquisite detailing make this a textbook example of Richardson's mature Romanesque design. One might question, however, whether the polychromatic masonry, whose contrasts must have been startling when the building was new, did not then diminish the sense of integrity of the masonry. A little grime may be a good thing.

As in many Richardson buildings, the rigorously symmetrical *parti* of the Austin Hall plan (fig. 78) belies the asymmetry of its fenestration. Facilities for the Law School were centered on a large lecture room that dominated the northern elevation and separated the building decisively from its surroundings. The law students enjoyed generous quarters with lecture rooms and a students' room. Spectacular staircases, one of which is expressed on the exterior, connect the three floors and provide for Harvard one of Richardson's most creative spaces (fig. 79). The great reading room with a hooded fireplace has a roof of hammerbeam trusses similar to the interior of Richardson's earlier Trinity Church, Boston (1872–1877). But it is in the corridors and connecting spaces of Austin Hall that recessive ornament and characteristic monumental proportions best reveal Richardson's genius.

Quite unlike picturesque Hemenway Gym and Austin Hall is the neighboring Jefferson Physics Laboratory (fig. 80). This building, the gift of T. Jefferson Coolidge in 1882, was designed by Shaw and Hunnewell. In his memoirs the donor expresses satisfaction with its simplicity but says nothing of his role in its design. He does mention that the building, one of the first in America constructed specifically as a physics laboratory, had an

independent system of internal piers to support instruments that might have been affected by building vibrations.[12] There is an element of academic discipline in the way the facade is organized into bays framed by brick pilasters carried on a high base; but the designer did not hesitate to sacrifice symmetry when a section of blank wall and an entrance vestibule were required by the large lecture hall. This hall, whose interior brick walls repeat the pilastered treatment without, is one of the handsomest classroom spaces in the university; and the use of exposed brick for interior walls in corridors, offices, and laboratories began here a tradition that would be followed in scientific and engineering buildings at Harvard down to World War II. Because the north side of the laboratory faced Holmes Field, no entrance was provided there, although the pilastered wall treatment was continued. Once again a Harvard back yard is today a handsome tree-filled quadrangle, but to it Jefferson Laboratory has no access.

Sixteen years later Shaw and Hunnewell's next commission, Pierce Hall (1900), was placed facing Oxford Street at right angles to Jefferson Laboratory but with no connecting tie (fig. 81). A twin-entry plan similar to that of Jefferson Laboratory was followed, though the white limestone and Classical detail differ. The facades of Pierce Hall incorporate more elaborate stone sculpture than any earlier building at Harvard.[13] Whether from the particular foundation conditions in that area or because the system had proved practical at the University Museum, where the same architects were currently designing one of the additions, the floor levels of Jefferson were maintained at Pierce. This meant that the subsequent linking of the two buildings by placing Cruft and Lyman Laboratories between them could be achieved with visual harmony and a minimum of inconvenience to users. Indeed, the design of Lyman Laboratory in 1930 by Coolidge, Shepley, Bulfinch and Abbott is one of the finest pieces of "supplementary architecture" to be found at Harvard. Rather than attempt an independent masterpiece, the designer was content to subordinate Lyman to the role of a unifying link incorporating features of all its neighbors: brownstone trim, dark brick, and single fenestration from Jefferson, cornice height and design format from Cruft and Pierce (fig. 80).

The physical expansion of Harvard's present complex for physics and chemistry without having to discard older facilities in the process was possible because sufficient space had been left around Jefferson and Pierce Halls. This was done, as far as we can tell, for quite different reasons than that of providing for future expansion: each donor wanted an ample setting to show his building to the best advantage; and leaving plenty of room between structures minimized the danger of a spreading fire. (Harvard had lost $300,000 in real estate in the Boston Fire of 1872, and there had been two serious dormitory fires in the late 1870s.) President Eliot also had a strong interest in landscaping and believed Harvard had a responsibility to the citizens of Cambridge, in exchange for relief from taxation, to provide handsome and well-tended grounds. Only in the twentieth century did Harvard begin to follow the two principles of leaving open area surrounding a building to allow for future expansion and of grouping together departments with a community of interest so they could share space and equipment.[14]

A new surge of dormitory building, for graduate students and centered in the North Yard, occurred around 1890. With the aid of a quarter-million-

84
*Langdell Hall (Shepley, Rutan
and Coolidge, 1906). In color
and style the Law School's
new building in Holmes Field
related to nothing around it.
Carey Cage, later Carey Rotch
Building, at the far right, was
remodeled by Langford
Warren to house the Architectural School until Robinson
Hall was finished.*

83
Perkins Hall: architects'
sketch (Shepley, Rutan and
Coolidge, 1893). This was the
first Colonial Revival design
for Harvard by the architects
who later developed the South
Yard.

dollar bequest the university erected a graduate dormitory, Walter Hastings Hall (1888), designed by Cabot and Chandler (fig. 82). Like Austin Hall, this building has a handsome facade on a main street that totally disregards neighboring buildings. While careful to respect the sixty-foot "territorial waters" around Austin Hall, the new structure, which was planned to house law students, makes the most of the Massachusetts Avenue frontage with an almost too ornate collection of gables and bay windows and a lawn enclosed by an elaborate wrought-iron fence. By contrast, the rear (east) elevation is barren, the result of many small bathroom windows. The tawny brick, terra cotta, and brownstone trim are harmonious in themselves, but they contrast unpleasantly with the materials used at Austin Hall and with the richly ornamented red brick and terra cotta at the Hemenway Gymnasium.[15]

Two dormitories, Perkins and Conant Halls, designed by Shepley, Rutan and Coolidge, were constructed across Oxford Street from one another in 1893. Placed close to the street, they form a kind of northern gateway to the North Yard, which establishes a boundary for the spacious green park in front of the University Museum and forms a satisfactory terminus for the vista up Oxford Street. These buildings, together with the remodeling of Fay House at Radcliffe (1890) by A. W. Longfellow, Jr., mark a new epoch in Harvard architecture as the earliest examples of the Georgian Revival style that was to dominate university building for the next fifty years. The extraordinarily fine detail, the brick belt courses and other ornament, of Perkins Hall (fig. 83) are far more accurate and restrained than those Longfellow was using at the time and refer directly to the earlier architecture of Harvard Yard. In contrast to nearby Pierce Hall, which is similar in scale and massing, Perkins and Conant have very little carved stone ornament. These buildings were the first of many commissions of the Coolidge firm, which would monopolize Harvard building between the wars.

Completing the building program at the Law School during Eliot's term was Langdell Hall (fig. 84), begun in 1906 by Shepley, Rutan and Coolidge. During the last two decades of Eliot's tenure this firm invoked the imperial image of Charles McKim, returning only later under President Lowell to the Colonial inspiration first suggested in Perkins and Conant Halls. The Law School had grown from 180 students in 1886 to 684 by 1908. A new building was clearly needed, and because all the sites in this area facing streets were occupied there was nothing to do but to build in Holmes Field. Inasmuch as each of the four large structures on the periphery of the field faced outward and there was no possibility of effecting a visual connection with them, the designer of Langdell simply ignored them. The new building was placed on the west side of the field, parallel to Massachusetts Avenue and Oxford Street. It is ironic that the two structures that posed the biggest obstacles to securing an adequate environment for Langdell were also part of the Law School. The imperial porticos of Langdell open upon no formal axes, and the principal walkway by which one approaches the building forms so sharp an angle with the facade that it is impossible to comprehend the composition as a whole or to appreciate its hierarchical sequence of pavilions, colonnades, and wings. Furthermore, its white limestone surface and Classical forms were foreign to the Harvard campus (with the exception of an errant precedent at Hunt Hall in the Yard). The choice of white limestone shows how completely and promptly

85
*Randall Hall Commons
(Wheelwright and Haven,
1898). Vigorous English
Baroque forms defined the
corner of Kirkland Street and
Divinity Avenue for fifty years.*

the dark color and picturesque forms of Richardson's era were discarded for the imperial mood of the new Classicism. Langdell Hall would have been at home on the campus of McKim's Columbia University, and its style resembles that of the Harvard Medical School in Boston, designed a year earlier by the same firm. (Only the south half of Langdell was constructed in 1906; the remainder was completed in 1928.)

A few other buildings were erected on lots repurchased from the once extensive Shady Hill estate. One was Lowell Lecture Hall (1902), on the corner of Oxford and Kirkland Streets, the gift of the president-to-be and designed with incomparable assurance by his cousin Guy Lowell. This building, Harvard's first Paris-inspired effort after Hunt Hall, characterizes Guy Lowell's impeccable Classical style. Its red brick walls (unlike those of Langdell) preserve some continuity with its surroundings, and robust, heavy-handed sculpture enables Lowell to hold its own adjacent to the powerful forms of Memorial Hall. The Lecture Hall, seating almost a thousand, was a monument to Eliot's elective system, which encouraged survey courses with large enrollments and to which, ironically enough, the building's donor was somewhat opposed.[16] An interesting sidelight on this building is that it was designed with no specific site in mind. Both the donor and the architect hoped that it might be located inside the Yard, but the Corporation decided otherwise. Nevertheless, the building's brick and limestone walls and Baroque ornamentation ensured that it would harmonize with the monumental scale of other buildings then being erected.

On Divinity Avenue, Randall Hall (1898), by Wheelwright and Haven (fig. 85), was built as a dining place for economy-minded students. The building's richly articulated skyline and robust forms, executed in red brick, incorporated details from English Baroque models, which Charles Coolidge would use again at the river houses, particularly Gore and Standish Halls. Although Randall was rectangular in plan and raised on a rusticated basement, its siting was admirable, with the curved walls of its entrance projecting to define the intersection of Kirkland Street and Divinity Avenue. (The architect, E. M. Wheelwright, also used such a solution for site planning for the *Lampoon* Building on Mount Auburn Street, his best-known and best-loved work at Harvard.[17]) Randall Hall was requisitioned in 1912 to store part of the university library while Widener was under construction. It subsequently served as the university printing plant until it was demolished in the early 1960s to make way for William James Hall.

The Semitic Museum up the street (fig. 86), a Georgian Revival design of 1902, shares many characteristics with Randall Hall. It was the first of three buildings executed in this area by A. W. Longfellow; the others — the Gibbs (1911) and Jefferson Coolidge (1912) Laboratories — were constructed in the next administration. All these had been envisioned as part of a larger scheme, never executed, for chemistry laboratories by Longfellow (fig. 87). This grand plan, heavily influenced by the ideas of McKim, whom Longfellow much admired and with whom he had worked at Radcliffe Yard, is of considerable interest. Had it been implemented, as was Guy Lowell's contemporaneous quadrangle plan for Radcliffe, the informal integrity of the Harvard campus would never have been achieved. The central structure of this elaborate proposal served as an axial focus for the plan, in which all the other buildings were essentially similar. Longfellow's Semitic Museum and the laboratories that followed remain as vestiges of the huge *parti,* which was defiled by later building.

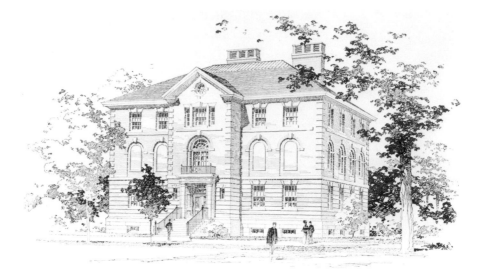

86
Semitic Museum (A. W.
Longfellow, Jr., 1902).

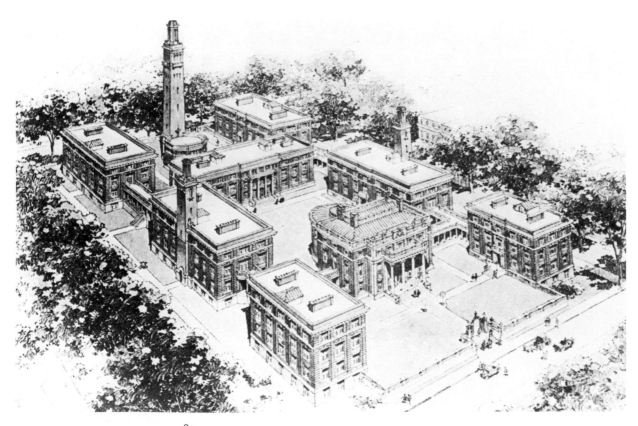

87
Chemistry Laboratories:
unexecuted project (A. W.
Longfellow, Jr., 1911).

88

*Harvard Divinity School
Library (Peabody and Stearns,
1910). This building, now the
Farlow Herbarium, has been
incorporated into the biological sciences complex;
it can be seen in fig. 144, to
the left of Divinity Hall.*

In the meantime the Divinity School was growing in the northeastern corner of the North Yard. In this area stands one of Harvard's most picturesque buildings, the former theological library, now known as the Farlow Herbarium (fig. 88). Designed in 1886 by Peabody and Stearns, the many-gabled, two-story brick building looks rather like a large residence. It is an example of what good work Peabody and Stearns often did, and stylistically it continues the Gothic manner they used in 1871 at Matthews Hall in the Old Yard (fig. 48).[18] Though the library was set close to Divinity Hall, there was originally no architectural relation between the two. Not until the area was reshaped by the erection of the Biological Laboratories in 1930 were the two theological structures brought into a meaningful unity.

Andover Hall (fig. 89), built in 1910 by Allen and Collens, a firm specializing in church architecture, was not a regular Harvard commission. It was erected by Andover Theological Seminary, which moved from Andover, Massachusetts, in 1908 to be affiliated with Harvard Divinity School. The building's distinctive architecture and isolated site reveal this institutional differentiation. Turning its back upon the straggling Harvard outbuildings and playing fields that then occupied this corner of the North Yard, Andover faces Francis Avenue and a neighborhood of fine Shady Hill residences. The granite building follows the collegiate neo-Gothic manner popularized so successfully by Boston's Ralph Adams Cram on other

89
*Andover Hall, Harvard
Divinity School (Allen and
Collens, 1910), Harvard's
only example of the collegiate
Neo-Gothic style.*

campuses of this era but otherwise absent at Harvard.[19] The design does not quite succeed. Its symmetry is forced, because two stories of dormitories do not comfortably balance a high-ceilinged chapel with the traceried windows of the library. But to a generation before World War I this hall better evoked the image of an ecclesiastical school than did simple old Divinity Hall, which was soon thereafter transformed into dormitories.[20]

Beyond the two yards Harvard did some additional building in these years. The reconstruction of the old Gray Herbarium at the Botanic Garden into the present Kittredge Hall, now used for Harvard University Press, was accomplished in four stages between 1909 and 1915, as portions were replaced by new fireproof structures.[21] The resulting straightforward design, by William Mowll, has been called Harvard's first "functional"— that is, unadorned—building (fig. 90). The Stillman Infirmary (1900), another work of Charles Coolidge's office, with its circular porch was close in style to McKim's contemporaneous Harvard Union. This three-story brick and limestone building (fig. 91) (enlarged a year later) occupied the site of the present tower apartments at 1010 Memorial Drive (1963) on the banks of the Charles.

Mention should also be made of the Medical School's new campus, begun in 1906 on Longwood Avenue in Boston—though the history of the facilities used by the medical faculty and the recent growth of the Boston complex constitute a separate story for another book. The school was founded in 1782 as the Medical Institution of Harvard University, with a staff of three professors who had worked together during the Revolutionary

90
Kittredge Hall and Observatory Hill. Kittredge, to the lower right, was a gradual reconstruction of the Gray Herbarium at the Botanic Garden. Early Cambridge residences, since replaced by the Radcliffe Quadrangle, appear to the left along Garden Street; the Observatory is above.

91
Stillman Infirmary (Shepley, Rutan and Coolidge, 1900). By the turn of the century a common Georgian statement began to develop for Harvard buildings by different architects.

92
Harvard Medical School's fifth home (Van Brunt and Howe, 1881–1883), on Boylston Street in Boston, subsequently razed for the Boston Public Library addition.

93
Harvard Medical School: Administrative Building (Shepley, Rutan and Coolidge, 1906).

War. Instruction began in October 1783 in slightly remodeled quarters in Holden Chapel, which since the war had served as a storage building. The school was financed entirely by fees of students who attended lectures. In 1810 it transferred to rented quarters on Washington Street in Boston to be closer to hospitals and to the offices of the medical faculty, most of whom largely supported themselves by private practice.

In 1814 the Corporation authorized $18,000, derived from the same bank tax that had paid for the construction of University Hall, for a new Medical School on Mason Street, near the Boston Common. The selection of the site, preparation of plans, and oversight of construction were left to the faculty. Domestic in scale and appearance except for three conical skylights, the building contained two lecture rooms, two dissecting rooms, an anatomical theater, an anatomical museum, a chemical laboratory, and a library (as well as one of the first hot air furnaces in Boston). This building served for thirty years (1816–1846), after which it was sold. The fourth home of the school, used from 1846 to 1883, stood on Grove Street near Massachusetts General Hospital. It was financed from the sale of the former building plus a $14,000 loan from the Corporation, which the medical faculty agreed to repay with interest. It was enlarged in the 1870s with two large laboratories after President Eliot had increased the curriculum to three years and instituted rigorous examinations. The fifth building (fig. 92), a handsome five-story brick structure with large windows, designed by Henry Van Brunt and much publicized for its careful planning and elaborate equipment, was opened in 1883 on Boylston Street on the present site of the Boston Public Library annex. It was sold to Boston University in 1906 when the Medical School moved to its sixth and present location.[22]

As the result of a successful fundraising campaign in the early years of this century, an entirely new campus for the Medical School was erected on 26 acres in the recently improved Fenway neighborhood. Since the budget was generous ($2.7 million) and no existing buildings had to be considered in the layout, the architects, Shepley, Rutan and Coolidge, were free to reach for the ideal solution—than which no more difficult architectural assignment exists. Arranged to look as large and impressive as the site would permit, their design follows the imperial aesthetic precepts of the time, with long vistas and a symmetrical and hierarchical disposition of comparable building units about a dominant focal point. Here the four large, white marble buildings—each one an imposing monument—are identical in design despite differences in internal function. The administrative building, dignified with a giant portico, elevated on a terrace, and approached by flights of steps, clearly controls the group (fig. 93) This is the grand and formal planning that the École des Beaux-Arts taught and which the Massachusetts Institute of Technology, among countless other educational institutions, would choose for its Charles River site four years later. It is undoubtedly what the architects and sponsors at Harvard during this period would have preferred for the two yards in Cambridge had they not been restricted by the legacy of older structures.

This formal scheme makes a profound first impression as it invites the visitor to take in the essentials of the imposing group, to verify the consistency of the architectural ensemble, to test its symmetry, and to stride the full 500-foot length of the court of honor in order to experience its

94
*Harvard Medical School. This
aerial view shows its grand
axial plan.*

monumental size (fig. 94). But the first impression is the best, and each
succeeding encounter becomes less rewarding. Eventually, no matter by
which route one approaches that quadrangle, it is comprehensible only as
the same inflexible space. Such formality seems stiff and dull to us today,
and it minimizes opportunities for modification and remodeling. Subsequent
construction of hospitals, dormitories, the Countway Library of Medicine
(1963–1965), and a building for the School of Dentistry (1909) have had to
proceed with little reference to the original medical campus (see Chapter 10).

In 1890, through the generosity of Henry Wadsworth Longfellow, his
family, and Henry Lee Higginson, Harvard acquired Soldiers Field, an
undeveloped piece of land opposite the university on the south bank of the
Charles. There in 1897 the Carey Cage (figs. 95, 96) was built to designs of
H. Langford Warren, Dean of the School of Architecture, and L. J. Johnson, professor of civil engineering. The cage was surrounded by a great iron
fence with piers of concrete, an experimental material in which Johnson
and Ira Hollis, professor of mechanical engineering, were extremely interested. The combination of concrete with brick made an attractive surfacing
material for both the gatelodge (fig. 97) and Carey Cage. The pleasing
monumental character of the gate and gatelodge, executed in concrete
accented with brick and with a dark exposed aggregate, was a unifying ele-

95
*Aerial view of Soldiers Field.
The concrete stadium (1902)
and athletic facilities
developed to the west of the
Boylston Street bridge, and the
new Business School campus
(1926) to the east, across from
the River Houses.*

ment in all these early Soldiers Field designs. The profile of the roofs of
Carey Cage was inspired by Japan's influential exhibition at the World's
Columbian Exposition in Chicago four years earlier. With its half-timbered
walls, Carey Cage was the first permanent structure at Soldiers Field, the
first three of which were of concrete. This Carey Cage replaced a building
of the same name (by Longfellow) in Holmes Field; the vacated cage then
housed the School of Architecture until the erection of Robinson Hall in
1904. With Carey Cage, for the first time, faculty from the School of
Architecture were involved in the design of Harvard buildings.

In 1899 the athletic cluster was augmented by construction of the slated
Newell Boathouse (fig. 98), the first permanent structure for such use, built
on the south bank of the Charles to designs by Robert Peabody of Peabody
and Stearns, who in his days at Harvard College had been captain of the
crew. (Peabody had also been involved with President Eliot during the late
1890s in earlier unexecuted plans for development of the Yard and of
Soldiers Field.) The complex profile of the Boathouse, closely resembling
that of Carey Cage reflected in the Charles in the early morning, has made
it a landmark on the river.

The Harvard Stadium was erected at Soldiers Field in 1902–1903 (fig.
99). Although the stadium was planned amid controversy regarding com-

96
*Carey Cage, Soldiers Field (H.
Langford Warren, 1897).*

97
*Fence and gatelodge,
Soldiers Field (Ira N. Hollis
with H. Langford Warren,
1897–1900).*

98
Newell Boathouse (Peabody and Stearns, 1900). The first permanent boathouse replaced a long series of lesser wooden structures.

petitive athletics, a convergence of interests from various unforeseen directions provoked a momentum for this commission that equaled that of Memorial Hall. This unity of thought, rarely reached in the generating conditions of any building, produced a masterpiece for Harvard. The stadium is functionally almost perfect, structurally innovative, and aesthetically advanced.

When the determination that the temporary bleachers of wood and iron in Soldiers Field were unsafe forced a decision to build a permanent facility, divergent forces miraculously converged. Ira Hollis, who in 1899 had spoken against athletics, became a champion of reinforced concrete construction, while Langford Warren invoked the analogies of Greek amphitheaters and Roman stadia to connect the erection of a Harvard stadium with the Classics. The involvement of Warren did much for the cause of the stadium. He had been influenced by Charles Eliot Norton and was devoted to the history of architecture, which he incorporated heavily into the curriculum of the graduate architectural program. He was also a practicing architect and capable of working well with the engineers.[23] The professors of mechanical and civil engineering produced a system of construction so innovative that it required continual modification in the process of the pour and erection of the ferroconcrete slabs, piers, and girders (fig. 100). Charles McKim, who had already shown affinities for imperial Roman design, was taken on with an associate, George Bruno de Gersdorff, to integrate a Classical proportional system into the enormous design. (While de Gersdorff actually did the drawings for the stadium, McKim and Daniel Burnham came up with its Classical proportions and the brilliant concept of

99
Harvard Stadium. The stadium (1902) combined the design of a Roman circus and Greek amphitheater with raised concrete seating. The open end was later closed with temporary bleachers.

orienting the structure with its open end toward the Charles, thus providing one of its chief aesthetic attractions.)

The Harvard Stadium was the largest ferroconcrete structure in the world at that time, and enthusiasm for the endeavor was unparalleled. A whole issue of the *Harvard Engineering Journal* in 1904 and 1905 was dedicated to articles by faculty members who had been involved in the planning and building of the stadium. The U-shaped stadium was shorter and wider than a Roman circus and yet, unlike a Greek amphitheater, was artificially formed through raised seating of reinforced concrete.[24] The elegance and power of the resulting building, opened in 1903, proved conclusively the aesthetic viability of massive ferroconcrete — the material that Frank Lloyd Wright would use two years later at Unity Temple in Chicago.[25]

The advanced engineering of the stadium had not, however, obscured the Classical symbolism of athletics, and the champions of physical education were understandably happy to capitalize on an association with antiquity. In 1906 the ascendant Classics department presented Aeschylus' *Agamemnon* in the stadium with a specially built temple, chariots, and live horses (fig. 101).[26]

The complex at Soldiers Field was enlarged within the next few years. In 1906 the aging Peabody designed the Weld Boathouse (fig. 102) adjacent to Wheelwright's Anderson Bridge. Of concrete with brick dressings, the

100
Harvard Stadium under construction. Precast concrete seating was laid on steel trusses for the stands. The unbroken exterior arcade was the largest massive poured concrete structure in the world when it was built.

101
Stadium with performance of Aeschylus' Agamemnon in 1906.

122　The North Yard and Soldiers Field

boathouse carried to the northern bank of the Charles a design similar to that of the Soldiers Field fence and gate. Its simple forms, while more ornamental than those of the stadium, have that functional quality which differentiates these athletic structures from other Harvard buildings. Even Guy Lowell's Briggs Cage (1926), placed on an axis with the open end of the stadium, was of concrete ornamented with brick dressings. Its original walls and ornate door were subservient to the geometry of its sleek slate hipped roof, the focus of the view to the river from the stadium. This simple design (one of Lowell's best), influenced by the stadium, far outdistances in quality the later Colonial Revival design of Dillon Field House (1930) and the Indoor Athletic Building (1929) across the river. Dillon Field House, one of the more standard designs by Coolidge, Shepley, Bulfinch and Abbott, introduced brick to the athletic complex—the start of a downward trend. While the elegant exterior of the Indoor Athletic Building (fig. 103), contemporary with the River Houses, works well on its site, Dillon Field House has always seemed misplaced and routine against the powerful forms of the stadium and the Briggs Cage. Later construction at Soldiers Field has been poorly planned and disparate, abandoning the simple concrete surfacing of the original structures.[27]

This impressive record of building under Eliot, achieved in the face of a constant shortage of institutional funds, would have been impossible if the president had not been able to call on individual donors and semi-independent committees formed to raise funds for special buildings.[28] Of Eliot's thirty-five buildings, twenty-two were the gifts of individuals and six were financed by special drives (Memorial Hall and Phillips Brooks House are examples). Only three (Holyoke House, the addition to Gore Library, and part of the 1888 addition to the University Museum) were built with university funds, though small deficits in other projects were also made up by the university. Some of the donors, such as Thayer and Austin, seem to have exercised almost patronal rights in selecting the architects and sites of their buildings; other gifts, such as the legacy from the Sever estate, were spent under direct supervision by the university.

This situation naturally led to substantial diversity among the architects retained. In the forty years of Eliot's presidency, thirteen architectural firms worked for Harvard. Peabody and Stearns with A. W. Longfellow, Jr., led the list with seven commissions (remodelings not included). Two firms had five commissions each: McKim, Mead and White; and Shepley, Rutan and Coolidge. Ware and Van Brunt received three plus three important remodelings; Shaw and Hunnewell and Ryder and Harris, three; and the firms of H. H. Richardson and Guy Lowell did two buildings each. As to which firm exercised a dominant influence, it may be observed that Ware and Van Brunt were important in the late 1860s and early 1870s when Memorial Hall, Harvard's most important undertaking of the century, was under way; but despite this achievement and their remarkably sensitive remodeling of several earlier buildings, they received no commissions after 1876. They appear to have been replaced as the dominant Harvard architects by Peabody and Stearns (Robert S. Peabody was President Eliot's brother-in-law), who enjoyed the most consistent patronage, with commissions extending from 1871 to 1907. Charles McKim's influence was paramount between 1890 and 1903 in establishing an imperial image. This new style

102
Weld Boathouse (Robert Peabody, 1906–1907). Peabody's second boathouse was built across the river from Soldiers Field.

103
Indoor Athletic Building (Coolidge, Shepley, Bulfinch and Abbott, 1929). With the erection of the River Houses, a new gymnasium, which echoed their style, was provided in the South Yard.

and scale of Eliot's late years were simultaneously extended at Harvard by the Baroque designs of Paris-trained Guy Lowell. A. W. Longfellow, Jr., in contrast, began producing a distinguished series of intimate, Colonial Revival structures in 1890 with his remodeling of Fay House at Radcliffe (see Chapter 6). He established a Georgian image for the university, which was later taken up by President Lowell. The office of Charles A. Coolidge (at first Shepley, Rutan and Coolidge and today after several changes known as Shepley, Bulfinch, Richardson and Abbott), which was to hold a virtual monopoly on Harvard work under President Lowell, did not obtain its first commission until 1893 (Perkins and Conant Halls). If this firm did not in the long run follow H. H. Richardson's style, it did succeed to his architectural practice; the partners were trained in Richardson's office, and one of them, George F. Shepley, married Richardson's daughter. At Harvard the firm was influenced initially by McKim's imperial mode but ultimately extended Longfellow's Colonial image into the twentieth century to create almost singlehandedly the present visual integrity of Harvard.

In relation to land acquisition, President Eliot showed great foresight. It must have been clear to him that the suburban character of Cambridge was changing as comfortable old estates around Harvard were subdivided, and even the marshy woodlots east of North Avenue (now Massachusetts Avenue) beyond the North Yard, heretofore avoided, were attracting attention. Eliot could see that if Harvard was to continue growing it must act quickly to acquire contiguous land before this was used for other purposes. In this he was encouraged by an important tax decision reached by the courts in 1869, namely that a municipality could not tax the undeveloped real estate held by a charitable or educational institution. Eliot also must have found a businessman's pleasure in a good investment, for often in his annual reports he noted specific amounts paid for various parcels of Cambridge land. The President's Report for 1896 was a very useful summary of land purchased for college use from the very beginning and of real estate transactions between the college and the city of Cambridge.[29]

Desirable as it was to procure land for future institutional needs, Eliot experienced considerable opposition in doing so, especially from the college treasurer, Nathan Silsbee, who pointed out that in the four years previous to October 1871 the college had dipped heavily into endowment to purchase twenty acres of non-income-producing land; the cost of this land, if invested at 7 percent, would have been producing income of $5600 yearly. The president was further admonished that he might be acting illegally by using for potential future benefit capital entrusted to the Corporation for the present benefit of the college. Silsbee reminded the president that as college treasurer in 1850 Eliot's own father had opposed the extension of the Observatory grounds for the same reason.

If the acquisition of land was a positive aspect of Eliot's administration, planning for its use was not, though this matter was much discussed in the decades after 1890. The president's son, landscape architect Charles Eliot, after three years of supervising the grounds (1887–1890), criticized the Corporation for not adopting a definite scheme for physical development: "This permitting donors of buildings and gates to choose their sites is fatal to general effect. Outside the quadrangle the Yard is already a jumble of badly placed buildings and roads." The same note echoed in Charles McKim's exasperated comment to the treasurer that "some plan is woefully

104
*Harvard Overseers Plan
(1896). One of numerous attempts to create an axial
arrangement for the Harvard
campus. Here a grand portico
is attached to the south of
Gore Library, Sever Hall doubled in size, and a boulevard
cut through the South Yard to
the river.*

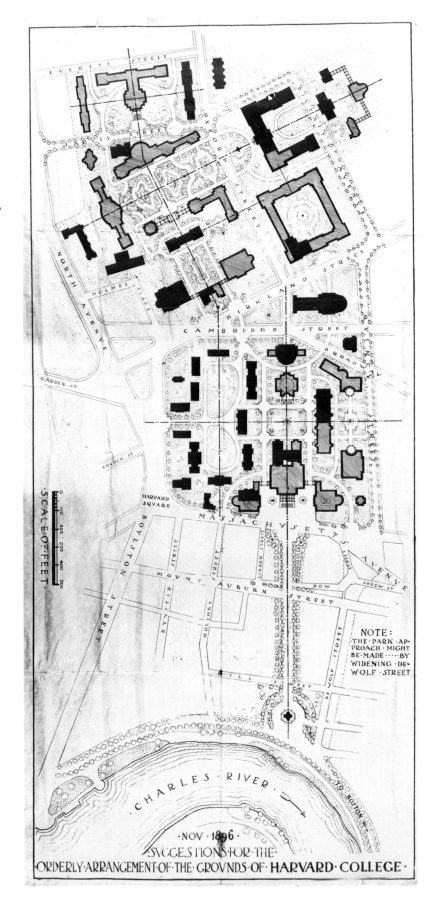

needed at Harvard." A resolution passed by the Board of Overseers in 1894 pointed out the need for a plan for the future development of college property.[30] Overseers also recommended the appointment of an advisory committee of competent professional men, selected by members of the university's governing boards, to approve all plans for future building.

The President and Fellows did not seem to think such plans for future development or the appointment of an advisory committee necessary.[31] They did, however, commission a series of plans by Aspinwall and Lincoln (1895) showing the boundaries of college real estate in Cambridge and the locations of existing buildings, with notes concerning restrictions and conditions governing placement of buildings on the various parcels. Apparently the Overseers did not consider this satisfactory, for a subcommittee of the Board (Robert Peabody, Augustus Hemenway, and George Shattuck) commissioned and paid for a study of their own entitled "Suggestions for the Orderly Arrangement of the Grounds of Harvard College." This they submitted to the Corporation in November 1896. Probably prepared by Olmsted, Olmsted and Eliot, the drawing that accompanies this report (fig. 104) concentrates on the Harvard and North Yards and illustrates the desire for breadth and for the long vistas that were so popular at that time. This plan attempts to patch together a sequence of axes and symmetrically arranged buildings that look more orderly on paper than it would have appeared in actuality. Interestingly, the 1896 plan anticipates a library as large as Widener but ignores Harvard Yard in its design by tacking a huge addition onto the south side of Gore Hall with a great porticoed facade facing Massachusetts Avenue. From there a processional way leads to the river, where the city was planning to create a parkway.[32]

Though the Corporation was obdurate for the time being, the widespread criticism of its failure to formulate a long-term plan or to seek professional advice appears to have had some effect in the early 1900s. In 1902 three architects were asked to consider the design and location of a proposed building for the Law School, and this experiment proved satisfactory.[33] The following year the Corporation asked the Overseers to appoint a committee of three to work with two Fellows to review plans and locations for each new building, but the record reveals nothing of such a committee's activities.

The Olmsted proposal was characteristic of several others—none of them acted upon—that followed during the remainder of Eliot's administration. In response to a report by the Visiting Committee on Fine Arts and Architecture in 1905, the treasurer of the Corporation, Charles Francis Adams, wrote that building during the previous sixty years had been "a disgrace, and I imagine that Eliot's long administration will hereafter be judged by it." However, the ideas contained in the various proposals did inspire a group of loyal alumni to lay the groundwork for future expansion toward the river (see Chapter 8).

The laissez-faire attitude of the Eliot administration to the planning of Harvard's grounds and the design of its buildings can hardly be explained as a matter of lack of interest on the part of the president. After all, Eliot's own son was a talented and articulate landscape architect, his brother-in-law was a prominent architect, his annual reports make frequent reference to landscaping the grounds, and he had even tried his own hand at house design and directed students in the 1859 survey of Harvard Yard. Although he never expressed the idea, Eliot may have believed the same latitude of choice was due to a donor or an architect designing a building as to a student selecting a course, a concept for which he had worked so diligently. And as a man trained as a chemist and skilled in administration, perhaps he was used to working with the world as he found it. Responding belatedly to criticism that he should have done more to direct the physical expansion of Harvard, he wrote in 1912: "growth is not initiative but responsive. Even in regard to the layout of grounds and buildings it has proved impossible at Harvard and every other growing university to make a layout for years to come and adhere to it. Three layouts were made for the Harvard territory in Cambridge by as many good architects in my time, but the Corporation found it impossible to adhere to any one of them except in a general way. In a few years unimagined needs, new resources, and changes in public taste will make any such layout obsolete except in its broadest features."[34]

6 Buildings for Radcliffe College

In December 1878 historian Arthur Gilman proposed to President Eliot the foundation of a college for women. Such an educational endeavor was hardly a new idea. A call for an establishment of this sort had been made in 1849 by the Reverend William H. Stearns of the Prospect Street Church in Cambridge, and in the ensuing thirty years Vassar (1861), Smith (1871), and Wellesley (1875) colleges for women had been established. None of these, however, was in so close a curricular relationship to a men's college as Radcliffe turned out to be. Yet Gilman initially envisioned Radcliffe as completely separate, with its own board of trustees. The only connection with Harvard he foresaw was that Harvard professors might be permitted to teach courses at Radcliffe without jeopardizing their positions at the older institution. To this President Eliot assented, and a committee of seven Cambridge women was nominated to make plans for the college.[1]

After indications of willingness to participate in instruction had been secured from several professors, the "Private Collegiate Institution for Women" was publicly announced in February 1879; in September entrance examinations were held in rooms leased for the school at 6 Appian Way (fig. 105). During the first term there were twenty-seven students. As enrollment increased, space had to be rented in nearby houses for classrooms, a laboratory, and a library. In October 1882 the managers became a corporation under Massachusetts law as The Society for the Collegiate Instruction of Women, though the school was popularly known as the Harvard Annex. The institution became officially associated with Harvard only in 1893, and the following year it was incorporated as Radcliffe College, the name derived from Lady Ann (Radcliffe) Moulson, who in 1643 had presented Harvard College with its first scholarship fund.[2] (President Eliot had suggested naming the women's institution Longfellow College after the poet, but Alice Longfellow, one of the founding committee, protested that it should surely be named after someone more concerned about the education of women than her father.)[3]

The seven women who founded Radcliffe were unusual by any standard, and each in her own way contributed substantially to the successful establishment of the institution. The leadership of Elizabeth Cary Agassiz was crucial in the implementation of the plan for the college during these early

105
Founders House, 6 Appian Way, the only Radcliffe building from 1879 to 1885. This house and others on Appian Way were demolished around 1970 for construction of the new School of Education buildings.

years. Her intellectual commitment was not that of an amateur but of one skilled in scientific documentation and research. She had worked closely with her husband, Louis Agassiz, recording, organizing, and editing his lectures; her contributions were largely responsible for the usefulness of his intellectual legacy.[4] Widowed at fifty-one, Mrs. Agassiz was well prepared by the time of the founding of the college to pour her enthusiasm and capabilities into the development of Radcliffe. It was largely because of her personal contacts and political expertise that—despite a storm of controversy—the association of Radcliffe College with Harvard was achieved.[5] At her memorial service in 1907 President Eliot stated, "There never was in this community a more influential woman, and in this case it appeared most clearly that her influence was the strongest with common men. That is as it should be. I am sure those men said to themselves as they listened to her . . . 'I will vote for the establishment of any college of which this woman is to be the head. I will vote for the establishment of any college which is going to give this woman an opportunity to bring up some women like her.'"[6]

Gilman selected the other members of the founding group for Radcliffe because of what each could personally contribute to the enterprise but also because they advocated no special cause (such as coeducation) and were already closely connected by marriage or family to Harvard. The institutional development of Radcliffe was frankly based on a familial network. Stella S. Gilman, Arthur Gilman's wife, was involved from the beginning in this implementation of an idea to give women the education available at Harvard for men. Ellen Hooper Gurney was the wife of Ephraim Whitman Gurney, historian and Dean of Harvard College, and the sister of Edward

N. Hooper, the treasurer of Harvard.[7] The Gurney home was often the site of receptions and gatherings for Radcliffe in the years before the college acquired buildings of its own. Mary Batty Greenough, wife of James B. Greenough, professor of Latin at Harvard, was chosen to create, with Ellen Gurney, a bridge between the women's educational endeavor and the humanities departments at Harvard. Access to the science faculty was provided by Mary Cooke, wife of Josiah Parsons Cooke of Harvard's chemistry department, and by Lillian Horsford, whose father, Elihu Norton Horsford, had taught applied science and had been dean of the Lawrence Scientific School. Radcliffe's aim of curricular strength in the sciences as well as the humanities, reflected in the connections of the founding committee, is noteworthy. It helped the fledgling college to gain intellectual respect from the Harvard faculty.

A particularly important member of the Radcliffe Seven was Alice Mary Longfellow. The only one of Henry Wadsworth Longfellow's daughters to remain unmarried, "Grave Alice" lived in the historic Craigie House on Brattle Street where she was born. Like the Gurney home, Craigie House was opened over the years for Radcliffe College events such as Commencement, since in the early years no college building could accommodate more than half of the student body. Alice Longfellow supplied both the books and the funds for the first Radcliffe Library, and she enlisted her cousin Alexander Wadsworth Longfellow, Jr., to design Radcliffe's earliest major buildings. A direct architectural connection was thus established with contemporaneous building programs at Harvard. It was A. W. Longfellow who first introduced the neo-Colonial concept to Harvard Yard in 1899 at Phillips Brooks House.

The first structure owned by the new college was Fay House (1806), one of the earliest brick houses in Cambridge, a handsome federal mansion on the Common, which had been erected in 1807 for Nathaniel Ireland (fig. 106). It had two swelling elliptical bays of a type that began to appear in American architecture in the 1790s and that was developed in Boston by Charles Bulfinch. The original entrance of Fay House faced north toward Mason Street. An oval drawing room in one elliptical bay at the southeastern corner of the house overlooked the garden. The original staircase was located in an adjoining eastern bay, which rose the full height of the Garden Street elevation. Stephen Higginson, a subsequent owner, removed these stairs when he relocated the entrance into this bay. The first substantial architectural alteration to the exterior was the addition of a mansard roof in 1870 while Fay House was rented to Harvard chemistry professor Wolcott Gibbs.[8] In 1876 Maria Denny Fay, who had been traveling in Europe, moved back into the family home, where she lived until 1885, when she sold it to the women's college, which for six years had been housed in temporary quarters.

By 1890 Fay House had become crowded, and Alice Longfellow provided funds to remove the mansard roof and replace it with a handsome third-floor library (figs. 107, 108). A. W. Longfellow, Jr., was selected as architect. He had recently designed the Cambridge City Hall (1888) and the Edwin Abbott House on Follen Street, both inspired by Richardson's Medieval style, but at Radcliffe his designs respected the red brick of Fay House as well as its style.[9] He made a large addition to the south side of Fay House, more than doubling its space, and reoriented the entrance inward. Another

106
Fay House, 10 Garden Street (built for Nathaniel Ireland, 1806; altered for Walcott Gibbs, c. 1870). The original entrance has already been moved to face Garden Street and a mansard roof has been added.

107
Fay House as altered (A. W. Longfellow, Jr., 1890). After acquiring the house Radcliffe replaced the mansard with a full third floor to house the library and added extensions to the north and west for an auditorium and classrooms.

108
Fay House: top-lit library on
the third floor.

109
Fay House hallway. As part of
the alterations by A. W.
Longfellow, Jr., a new
"Colonial" staircase and other
woodwork were added to the
interior.

108
*Fay House: top-lit library on
the third floor.*

109
*Fay House hallway. As part of
the alterations by A. W.
Longfellow, Jr., a new
"Colonial" staircase and other
woodwork were added to the
interior.*

110

The northwestern buildings cloistering the Radcliffe Yard (right to left): western extension of Fay House, Hemenway Gymnasium (Charles McKim, 1898), Agassiz House (A. W. Longfellow, Jr., 1904), Radcliffe Library (Winslow and Bigelow, 1907).

extension two years later on the north provided a small auditorium, a fine arts room, and classrooms. Typical of Longfellow's elegant reinterpretation are the brickwork of the additions, the exterior moldings, and the oval windows, which became favorite devices in American domestic design of the following decades. Despite these changes, something of the chaste character of the Federal manner is preserved on the Garden Street facade. The interior was also augmented with a handsome new staircase (fig. 109), Federal Revival woodwork, and arched moldings, which enhanced the decorative quality of the interior where the original staircase had been removed.

In 1887 Radcliffe began to purchase the rest of the block that now constitutes its Yard, a process that involved assembling eighteen small parcels over a thirty-year period. The northwest end was consolidated first, and construction of the college buildings began with McKim's Hemenway Gymnasium (1898), followed by Longfellow's Agassiz House (1904) and Winslow and Bigelow's Radcliffe Library (1907), the structure that now contains the Schlesinger Library and the Bunting Institute (fig. 110). Acquisition of the southeastern half of the block (except for one corner lot) was completed in 1917.

The scheme for surrounding the property with buildings was in fact envisioned by the landscape architect Arthur Shurtleff in 1906: "The plot of land bounded by Garden, Mason and Brattle Streets, and Appian Way is well adapted to the site of a college quadrangle. The contour of the ground is excellent, the orientation of the plot is perfect and its size is ample. Moreover, the greater portion of the adjoining property is either controlled by Radcliffe or by churches and parks. Fortunately the two permanent buildings already erected upon the land are admirably placed to form the beginnings of a quadrangular group." Shurtleff also apparently submitted a plan (which has not yet come to light) recommending "a group of eight large buildings arranged about the borders of the plot without crowding, to form a quadrangle. All the buildings are normal [rectangular] in shape and require no elaborate colonnades or oblique facades to adapt them to one another or to the bordering streets . . . I must tell you that I believe its realization would make an architectural unit unapproached in attractiveness and convenience by any other group of buildings about Boston."[10]

It was also Shurtleff who convinced Radcliffe that the library should be kept in the Yard rather than erected separately across Brattle Street and that the Yard plan should be informal. He drew comparisons with other colleges and Harvard Yard as well: "our American colleges have lost in cost of maintenance and in visual charm by scattering their buildings about their grounds in such a way that they do not count as a visual whole. The difficulty in this country has always been that plenty of land has been available for buildings, and the temptation to choose isolated sites, therefore, has been overcomingly great. In England, on the contrary, where college lands are relatively small, considerations of economy have made the closer nestling of buildings necessary, and it is upon this association of one building with another that the charm of the English colleges largely depends. The success of the old Harvard Yard depended upon a determined adherence to this principle covering over two and one half centuries." The remarkable architectural synthesis at Radcliffe was thus attained despite the differing authorship of the buildings in the original quadrangle. Its coherence was greater than that of any other woman's college campus at the time. Shurtleff's concepts also served as the model for Charles Coolidge in the 1920s when he "cloistered" Harvard Yard with Lionel, Mower, Lehman, and Wigglesworth Halls.[11]

A scheme for future placement of buildings on Radcliffe's Yard, as well as on the college's purchases south of Brattle Street, was indicated in a "Master Plan for Radcliffe" (1926) by Perry, Shaw and Hepburn. An accompanying perspective showed neo-Georgian brick architecture (fig. 111). To complete the enclosure of the Yard, this plan called for a laboratory east of Fay House, a chapel and lecture hall along Appian Way, another laboratory at the southeastern corner, and an eastern extension to the library along Brattle—all to be oriented inward to the center of the block. Of these only Longfellow Hall was built (1929); Byerly Hall (1931) follows the plan in location but not in massing.

It is fortunate that this plan was never carried to completion. Today there remain three plots within the Yard where additional structures could be located, but only with loss to the ambience. A unique flavor is imparted to Radcliffe Yard and to Brattle Street by Putnam and Buckingham Houses and the open space between them (fig. 112); both these houses were slated for demolition in the 1926 plan. The landscaping and intimate scale of the flower garden and terrace at the southeastern corner of the Yard, where Appian Way joins Garden Street, offer an effective counterpart to the lawn of the quadrangle. The domestic scale of the remaining houses facing Cambridge Common on Garden Street was skillfully respected in the design of the two-story wing of Byerly Hall. The third free location is the last

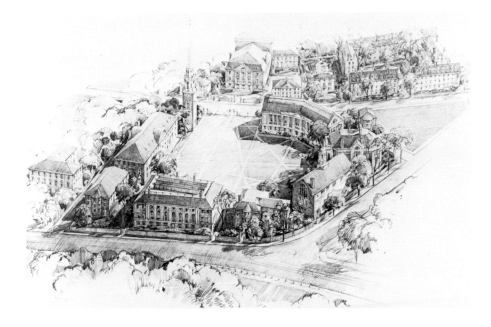

111

This unexecuted master plan for Radcliffe (Perry, Shaw and Hepburn, 1926) would have eliminated the small wooden houses on Brattle Street. This perspective is from Garden Street looking toward Brattle.

112

Aerial view of Radcliffe Yard. Buckingham House (1821) and Putnam House (1838), 77 and 69 Brattle Street, can be seen to the right of the library.

135   *Buildings for Radcliffe College*

113
Agassiz House (A. W. Longfellow, Jr., 1904): second-floor living room.

114
Agassiz House: theater auditorium.

115
*Radcliffe Library (Winslow
and Bigelow, 1907): Whitman
Room, c. 1938. The stained
glass is by Sarah Wyman
Whitman.*

piece of the block acquired by Radcliffe (1949), at the corner of Appian
Way and Brattle Street. Now used as a parking lot, it is so hedged by
arborvitae that it reads as a pleasant enclosed space.

The four buildings at the northwest end of Radcliffe Yard compose a
harmonious group, despite differences in detail and usage (fig. 110). Though
not axially placed, the Ionic portico of Agassiz House (1904), by A. W.
Longfellow, forms the focal point of the quadrangle. The height of its
cornice was established by the first building erected here in 1898, the gymnasium, by McKim, Mead and White, and the same height was maintained
by Winslow and Bigelow in 1907 for the library. Because of this consistency and the basic similarity in mass of the three new structures and Fay
House, variation in fenestration occasioned by very different uses does not
destroy the prevailing unity. The south extension of Fay House has little
architectural interest in itself, but its brick walls and massing enable it to fit
into the group with perfect harmony. These four structures, connected by a
colonnade, close the west end of the quadrangle effectively but informally.
It is this informality that allows the clapboarded Buckingham House (1821)
and Putnam House (1838) to the west to combine so naturally today with
the larger brick buildings and to act as a transitional link with the domestic
scale of Brattle Street.

McKim's Radcliffe Gymnasium is compatible in scale with Longfellow's
enlarged Fay House, and its red brick and white trim screen the Yard to the
north. More delicate and mannerly than McKim's contemporaneous design
for the Harvard Union, the Radcliffe Gymnasium established a finely scaled
detailing that was continued throughout the subsequent buildings of the

138   *Buildings for Radcliffe College*

116
Longfellow Hall (1929): north elevation. As a screen from Appian Way, Perry, Shaw and Hepburn provided a red brick transcription of Bulfinch's University Hall for Radcliffe Yard.

117
Byerly Hall (Coolidge and Carlson, 1931).

Yard. The light, airy interior of the gym with less equipment than that used by Sargent at Harvard, was innovative when it opened in 1899.

Agassiz House was given to Radcliffe in 1903 by alumnae and friends in honor of the eightieth birthday of President Agassiz, who was then pleading to retire from her position. She had long wished to establish a students' building at the college. Agassiz House, completed in 1904, contained classroom areas on the first floor, a lunchroom in the basement, and on the second floor a large living room (fig. 113) that provided the college's first space to hold large meetings in the Yard. The interior of this living room, with its dark woodwork, monumental columns, paneling, and raised balcony, is equal to those of Divinity Hall and Phillips Brooks House, designed by the same architect. With the Agassiz living room, interior space began to become more substantial and more architecturally significant than it had been in many of the university's earlier buildings. The second floor of Agassiz House also held Agassiz Theater, a gem of Cambridge architecture and one of Longfellow's best designs (fig. 114). In this auditorium five hundred people (the full Radcliffe constituency) could be seated in one room, a space that was acoustically excellent and had superb sight lines.[12] The exterior portico of Agassiz was intended from the start to form the central focus of the Radcliffe Yard, and its great columns serve that purpose much as those of the Memorial Church later focused the plan of the Tercentenary Theater in Harvard Yard. Subsequent architecture, such as the Radcliffe Library by Winslow and Bigelow, is purposely more recessive and innocuous, designed to echo the shape of the gymnasium and to leave the bombast to Agassiz. Yet all are of high-quality construction. On the staircase in Agassiz, Longfellow's interior designs for woodwork were combined with decorative stained glass, like that in Winslow and Bigelow's Whitman Room in the Radcliffe Library (fig. 115). Lighting fixtures, tapestries, and other such furnishings were selected in consultation with Sarah Wyman Whitman, a Boston artist and a close friend of President Agassiz, who was active with Longfellow in the Boston Society of Arts and Crafts, which had been founded in 1897.[13]

Longfellow Hall (1929), by Perry, Shaw and Hepburn, is a brick neo-Georgian version of Harvard's University Hall, with paired entrances framed with pilasters and round-headed windows in the central block (fig. 116). Longfellow Hall was named not after the poet but after Alice Longfellow, in honor of her many contributions to Radcliffe. Forming a barrier between the Yard and Appian Way, the building completes Shurtleff's vision of a cloistered plan for the college.[14]

The most elegant building in Radcliffe Yard is Byerly Hall (1931), by Coolidge and Carlson, named after William Byerly, a professor of mathematics and a member of Radcliffe's Governing Boards.[15] The creative plan of Byerly performs the same dual role in Radcliffe Yard as does Memorial Church in Harvard Yard. Byerly is actually two buildings, each scaled and sited to meet the requirements of the area it faces (fig. 117). In keeping with other structures on the Yard, the southern half of Byerly is three stories tall. The central third of the facade — treated as a pavilion capped by a pediment — has analogies with Hollis and Stoughton Halls, though here the proportions and detailing are lighter and more graceful. The northern half of the building, kept to two stories, is set on a slightly different axis so as to accommodate the line of Garden Street. Handsome architectural features of both Byerly and Longfellow Halls are the numerous pairs of bulky chimneystacks used as fresh-air intakes. The architects of Larsen Hall (fig. 218), across Appian Way, later seized upon these striking vertical masses as an important motif in their design.

Beginning in 1905, Radcliffe acquired several important dwellings along Brattle Street. The largest and earliest of these was the Greenleaf House, which has been used since 1913 as the president's residence (fig. 118). It had been the home of Mary Longfellow Greenleaf, sister of the poet and the aunt of Alice Longfellow. While the interior has been modified over the years, the blocky exterior anchors all of this area of Brattle Street. The red brick walls of the quoined house were originally stuccoed, and its robust balustrades were painted in natural earth colors. With its concave mansard roof still intact, Greenleaf House stands today in ample grounds, unlike so many other Cambridge houses of this period, and is admirably located adjacent to Radcliffe Yard.

The 1926 master plan placed a graduate center and a fine arts building on either side of Greenleaf House. The former was projected at that time to face on Brattle Street. Several of the designs suggested then would have maintained the domestic scale of Brattle Street established by the Buckingham and Putnam Houses. When Cronkhite Graduate Center (fig. 119) was eventually built, in 1955 and 1959 by Perry, Shaw and Hepburn, it faced the large side yard on Ash Street to the west. Although its interior is pleasant and light, opening from a sheltered courtyard, Cronkhite is the least successful of all Radcliffe buildings as urban design. It reflects the architectural schizophrenia of the 1950s by intruding Williamsburg red brick walls into an earth-colored nineteenth-century environment and by breaking out of the inward-facing arrangement of the Radcliffe Yard, which had been so skillfully defined by Shurtleff. Its isolation from the Yard is "inexplicable on aesthetic grounds," as Shurtleff had predicted a building on this site would be. Cronkhite's isolation became more marked as later Radcliffe development concentrated on the dormitory quadrangle to the north on Garden Street. The fine arts building, planned as a companion for the graduate center, was never built; its site was sold to Harvard for the Loeb Drama Center.

Most of the land on Shepard Street now occupied by the Radcliffe Quadrangle (fig. 120) was acquired in 1900 with the purchase of the Willard Phillips estate. The Phillips mansion (called Trowbridge House) was used for a time as a dormitory and then for housing for Radcliffe employees, and the old stable served as a field house until the playing field was covered with residential halls. The axially aligned quadrangle was laid out in 1902 by Guy Lowell.[16] The nine halls (South and North Houses) were designed by five firms over a 56-year period: Bertram (1901) and Eliot Halls (1907) by A. W. Longfellow, Jr.; Barnard (1911) and Whitman (1912) by Kilham and Hopkins; Briggs (1923) by Elwell and Blackell; Cabot (1936) by Ames and Dodge; and three sections of North House (1947–1957) by Maginnis and Walsh. Each of a somewhat different design but comparable in mass, material, fenestration, and style, these buildings face inward to share the open area. Reduplicating the sense of closure already developed in the original Radcliffe Yard, the Colonial Revival design of the Radcliffe Quadrangle creates, on a grand scale, a world unto itself. Indeed an entrance arcade by Bremer W. Pond between Bertram and Eliot Halls, completing

118
Greenleaf House, 76 Brattle Street (1859). The stucco home of Henry Wadsworth Longfellow's sister, across Brattle Street from Radcliffe Yard (in foreground of fig. 112), was acquired by the college for the President's House. Since this early photograph its exterior has been scraped to reveal red brick walls, and its porches and woodwork have been removed.

119
Cronkhite Graduate Center: unexecuted project drawing (Perry, Shaw and Hepburn, 1926). Early plans for the graduate center were of more domestic scale than the large red brick building finally executed in the 1950s.

120

*The Radcliffe Quadrangle,
Garden Street between
Shepard and Linnaean
Streets. Moors Hall, with a
large portico and cupola, faces
Bertram and Eliot Halls
(1901, 1907), lower right.
Briggs (1923) and Barnard
(1911) are to its right, across
from Cabot (1936) and
Whitman (1912). The houses
on Garden Street to the left
were removed for the
construction of Hilles Library
and Currier and Daniels Halls.*

the southern edge of the quadrangle, was once contemplated to emphasize this closure (fig. 121).

In the Quadrangle, the designs of the exteriors are sympathetic overall, but they differ widely in quality. Longfellow made creative use of the elegantly executed Colonial idiom in Bertram and Eliot Halls. The proportions of their exteriors and the quality of workmanship of the finely laid red brick and carved stone dressings (fig. 122) illustrate the finest sort of collegiate design being produced in New England before World War I. Bertram and Eliot Halls continued the stylistic premises of Radcliffe Yard in the Quadrangle. But the rectangular disposition of both buildings masks interiors that are no longer subdivided into box-like compartments as eighteenth-century precedents would have suggested. Instead, interior space flows easily from room to room. In Bertram a staircase with twisted newels (similar to that in Phillips Brooks House), based closely on prerevolutionary models, rises from a broad light hallway and public rooms that are warm with the afterglow of the Colonial image in their rich details of finish (fig. 123). Even the bedrooms in these houses have fine paneling and amenities such as fireplaces and window seats that would have been unheard of in spartan dormitories such as Grays or Thayer in Harvard Yard.

121

Radcliffe Quadrangle: unexecuted project drawing by Bremer W. Pond of entrance arcade joining Bertram and Eliot Halls.

122

Bertram Hall (A. W. Longfellow, 1906). The rich marble and carved stone of Bertram and Eliot were replaced with simpler wooden trim and sparse detailing in later buildings in the Quadrangle.

123
*Bertram Hall: dining room.
Broad hallways and fine detail
distinguished Radcliffe's early
interiors, most of which were
designed by A. W. Longfellow,
Jr. The bedrooms in Bertram
had window seats and
fireplaces.*

The well-proportioned and impressive facade of Moors Hall forms a
focus for the Quadrangle, but by the time Moors was built, in 1947, the
quality of construction had fallen. While the motley details of Cabot (1936)
have little architectural rationale, they serve as a continuation of familiar
building materials and colors. Variation in detail from one building to
another is welcome, counteracting an impersonal, barracks-like appearance,
but differences in choice of materials chronicle changing building conditions and labor costs. Thus there is a shift from the marble trim and granite
foundations of Bertram and Eliot to the wooden trim and concrete foundations of the three sections of North House. The difference between the
amount of space allowed in a private apartment and in a dormitory can be
seen in a comparison of Wolback Hall with the other halls that make up
North House; Wolback, which was built in 1938 as an apartment house and
acquired by the college in 1962, has lower ceilings and smaller rooms, as
indicated by the fenestration. Jordan House (1960), by Carleton Granberg,
on the east side of Walker Street, looks more like a private apartment
complex than a college building. It was Radcliffe's first break with neo-
Colonialism.

Each of the three original dormitories of North House was designed with
its own dining room, but all three were supplied from a central kitchen

placed in the center of the complex. Such an arrangement forces the entrance and reception rooms of each dormitory to face outward, away from one another. Holmes Hall (1951) faces west to the pleasant new drive-walkway leading from Linnaean Street to the main quadrangle, and the pilastered facade of Moors Hall with its cupola fronts directly on the Quadrangle, providing it with a focal point. Comstock Hall (1957) is in a corner by itself facing east on Walker Street, cut off from the Quadrangle by the service drive leading to the North House kitchen. A successful recent addition to North House is Faculty Row (1971) facing Linnaean Street, designed by Gourley and Richardson. Of excellent contemporary design, fragmented rather than monumental, these buildings provide a pleasant limit to the dormitory precinct and contribute to the urban quality of Linnaean Street.[17]

For many years the Radcliffe dormitories occupied only three-fifths of the large block bounded by Shepard, Linnaean, Walker, and Garden Streets, for six large houses fronted Garden Street (fig. 120). Three of these houses were removed in 1964 to make room for Hilles Library, one in 1965 for Daniels Dormitory, and two more, including the old Warner House (1855) designed by Henry Greenough, in 1969 to make way for Currier House.[18] The new buildings were designed by Harrison and Abramovitz. Radcliffe was particularly fortunate in the timing of the design and construction of these buildings, which coincided with the accession of biologist Mary Ingraham Bunting to the presidency. By the mid-1960s the last throes of serious colonial revivalism, which produced such designs as the Cronkhite Graduate Center and North House, had definitively subsided, along with the monumental concepts of urban renewal that had produced the most destructive urban planning of the century. An early acceptance of modern design and a move toward the articulated exteriors of the late 1960s had appeared, but the aggressive demands of the New Brutalism and the articulation of function in concrete walling had not yet been fully formulated. Thus the mannerly quality and intricacy of the Radcliffe buildings of the 1960s represent a positive architectural moment, and they blend nicely with the extant structures of both the Quadrangle and Garden Street without having the overbearing qualities of large buildings erected only two or three years later, such as the Boston City Hall by Kallmann and McKinnell.[19]

Currier House comprises a group of four pavilions intricately related by courtyards, terraces, or low buildings containing lobbies and public rooms (fig. 124). The two central pavilions are situated on the main terrace, thus appearing to be somewhat more than five stories in height; the other two, with the same number of floors, rise from sunken gardens to four stories above the street. Daniels is effectively isolated from the street and the paved mall by a series of sunken courts so that it can be approached by only a limited number of entries, thus ensuring privacy for the inhabitants. Because many of the barriers are below ground, the feeling is anything but cloistered; indeed much of the protective garden area can also be enjoyed from the outside. The presence of pleasant, usable spaces at the lower level of the courts also permitted the dining rooms and kitchen to be placed there, thereby avoiding the mistake made earlier at North House.

The handling of levels is equally masterful at Hilles Library (fig. 125). One approaches the elevated courtyard core of the library through a series

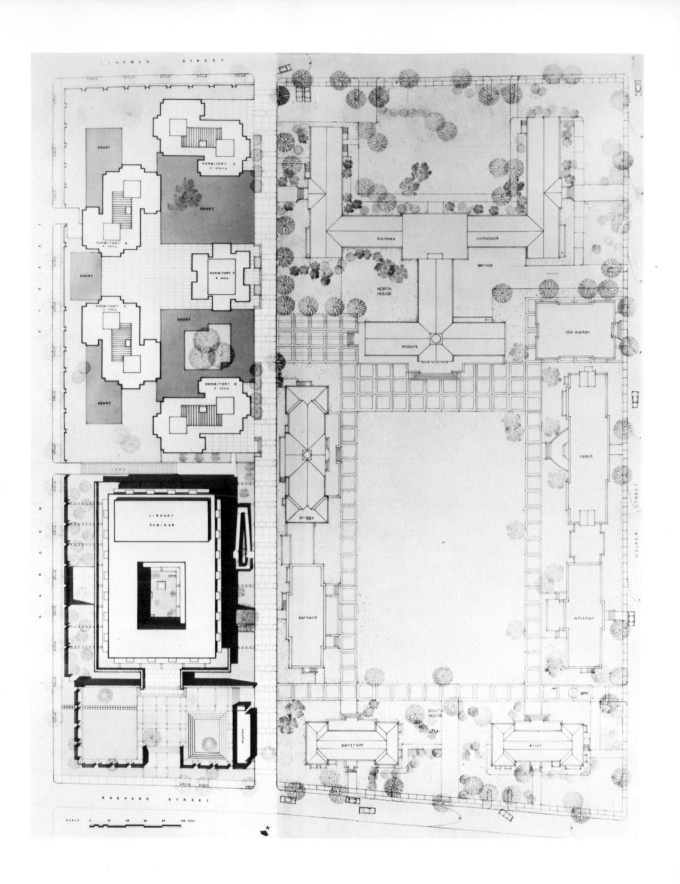

125
Hilles Library (Harrison and
Abramovitz, 1965).

◄124
Plan of Hilles Library and
dormitories making up
Currier House (Harrison and
Abramovitz, 1965). Articula-
tion of the exterior walls of
Hilles reflects individual study
carrels on the second floor.

126
*Hilles Library. The central
courtyard lights the surrounding library interiors.*

of terraces, finding oneself there almost before being aware of it, because
the rise from one level to the next is so gentle and the arcade through
which one penetrates to the courtyard looks very similar to other bays on
the ground story filled with plates of glass (fig. 126). Another paved terrace,
which can be entered only from the library interior, surrounds the building
on three sides. Despite this feeling of openness, the library stands isolated
in a deep garden moat; this moat controls entrance to the building and
provides rooms in the basement with almost as much light from outdoors
as those above. Here, as at Currier House, imaginative landscaping by Zion
and Breen of New York does much to unify the different levels.

In elevation Hilles Library is somewhat restless, with many small elements
working against each other. The reason for the alternate projecting bays is
to create individual carrels with side light, to provide spaces that are
pleasant, private, and conducive to study. The elevations may appear a little
too complicated until one realizes that the upper floors are divided into
12-foot bays to provide alternate carrels and light sources; on the main floor
these combine into 24-foot bays, the transition being made by large T-

shaped piers. All the Abramovitz buildings maintain an admirable human scale, and their striking visual qualities are arrived at by way of practical humanistic considerations, not as rationalized visual symbols.

New construction at Radcliffe has for the most part enhanced the architectural quality of earlier buildings of the college and preserved that remarkable integrity which is its primary characteristic. This approach has persisted in the design of the Athletic Center (1978) at Garden and Bond Streets. Even the scale and style of Hilles Library reveal a sensitivity to site and setting that is noticeably absent to the south on Quincy Street, where a new generation of assertive and aggressive structures compete vainly for attention while continuing to be overpowered by the vertical vigor of Memorial Hall.

7 Academic Architecture under President Lowell

During his twenty-five years in office (1909–1933), President A. Lawrence Lowell gave of himself and his fortune to Harvard with single-minded dedication. His effects on the school are as evident in the physical as in the educational realm, and much of the architectural character of Harvard as we know it today was formed under his untiring direction. Although the new president was in sympathy with and able to build upon the solid educational and administrative foundations laid by Eliot, he nevertheless was aware of areas where improvement was needed, including the academic curriculum, control of the physical expansion of the university, and housing for undergraduates.

The first matter does not directly affect this book but should be briefly noted. The Eliot elective system, of which Lowell basically approved and which he retained in a modified form, had often fostered superficiality, allowing students to take a disparate array of introductory courses without developing competence in any one area. In 1898 under President Eliot more than half the students elected only elementary courses. One disturbing consequence was a loss of pride in intellectual achievement. To correct this President Lowell added the requirement that an individual choose one field of concentration in which he must pass a comprehensive examination—his famous Concentration and Distribution Plan. His other major reforms included requiring examinations in French and German at the end of the sophomore year, inaugurating the tutorial system and divisional examinations, and instituting reading period.

Control of and planning for the physical expansion of the university were necessarily of major concern to President Lowell. Harvard erected more buildings during his administration than in all previous administrations combined. Within four years of his election, Lowell and his advisers sought to establish a policy of land use and acquisition. Undoubtedly the most important aspect of this was the decision to develop a new campus—the South Yard—in the heretofore neglected area near the Charles River. Soon after that an official style of architecture was adopted, the Georgian Revival manner, to be constructed of red brick in harmony with the school's oldest surviving buildings, and a single architectural firm was retained for most university work. As the result of this attitude toward design and planning, and also because so much building was accomplished in a relatively short span of time, a new architectural order emerged throughout the extended Harvard campus. Building on such a scale was made possible by a phenomenal outpouring of gifts from alumni and friends. In the course of a single decade, 1922–1932, 35 million pre-inflation dollars were donated for Harvard buildings.[1]

But there is more to it than that. Friends and colleagues of President Lowell recall his personal enthusiasm for building and for architecture. He was intimately involved in the planning of the undergraduate houses; he spent hours scrutinizing and checking plans, working with room arrangements to see whether he could discover a more efficient use of space; he made daily — sometimes twice daily — inspections of buildings under construction. Julian Coolidge reports that Lowell was convinced that only one architect, Charles A. Coolidge, could understand Harvard's architectural needs, and that he almost resented the intrusion of outside firms.[2] Architect Coolidge for his part is reported to have observed that the president "could tuck more into a given ground line than he could."[3] Such mutual respect and agreement upon what is needed between client and architect are important prerequisites for good design. To this relationship was added, in Edward S. Harkness, the ideal patron, who satisfied himself that goals had been properly and clearly defined and then left the working out of the design to the architect and the president. Harkness was a very different kind of sponsor from Edward Austin, Augustus Hemenway, Nathaniel Thayer, or, as we shall see, Mrs. Widener. It is not surprising that the architectural achievement of this harmonious triumvirate was both impressive and congruent.

Fortunately the Lowell administration also recognized the need for comprehensive planning. Vacant university land was rapidly being occupied, and the school was beginning to encroach on the town; no longer was it possible to treat each new structure as a self-sufficient entity, to allot it independent frontage on a major street, to concede to the donor decisions that rightly belonged to the university. In formulating plans Harvard also began to recognize its responsibilities to Cambridge. In 1912 Harvard Square businessmen, through the mayor of Cambridge, requested that the university assist them in improving the appearance of Harvard Square by drawing plans to guide future development. The resulting plan and perspective, prepared in 1913 by E. J. A. Duquesne of the architectural faculty, dealt more with commercial property than with university-owned structures, but among numerous recommendations it proposed that Prescott Street and Appian Way be the east and west limits of Harvard's expansion, and it called for fostering architectural unity by emphasizing the Georgian tradition.[4] Little was done with this document because of the cessation of building caused by World War I. It was not until 1922, twelve years after his election, that Lowell activated a committee to supervise the planning of grounds and buildings and charged it with formulating a working plan — though not a mold — for Harvard's development in the next fifty to one hundred years.[5] The result was the "Study for the Future Grouping of Buildings," begun by Coolidge and Shattuck in 1922 and later carried through several stages by the successor firm Coolidge, Shepley, Bulfinch and Abbott. Because in both firms Charles Coolidge was the partner in charge of these plans, they are referred to as the Coolidge Plans.

Although these plans, drawings for three of which are preserved in the office of Shepley, Bulfinch, Richardson and Abbott, differ in details, they all seek to form a series of orderly quadrangles of differing size and shape in all three yards.[6] It appears that the designers were consciously attempting to project into all parts of the extended campus the system already successfully worked out in the old brick quadrangles, the Old Yard, and Sever Quadrangle. In the North Yard five such nodes or self-sufficient open spaces occur. The plans also proposed the cloistering of Harvard Yard, the completion of Sever Quadrangle with the construction of the new Fogg Museum, and considerable expansion of the South Yard. The location and shape of the structures for the South Yard vary from one map to another, but by 1922 the general outlines of Lowell and Dunster (if not Eliot) Houses appear to have been established, as well as the location of the Indoor Athletic Building.

During the Lowell years Harvard Yard pretty much took on its present form. A decisive change, which created Tercentenary Quadrangle between University and Sever Halls, now the visual as well as the educational core of the university, was the construction of Widener Library and Memorial Church. These buildings are sufficiently monumental and the space of the quadrangle is commanding enough to dominate the widely dispersed yards. The new library, which in scale and style was an extension of the Imperial Harvard of the late Eliot years, was the largest and most important building the university had yet undertaken. It filled a desperate need; repeated remodeling and two additions to old Gore Hall had failed to produce a library adequate to the university's growing requirements. Besides the 3,200,000 books in Widener itself, there are today approximately one hundred departmental branches in Cambridge alone, some, such as the law library, themselves of formidable size.[7]

As the heart and matter of a university, a library should be imposing in mass and design. Though often criticized as elephantine, Widener fulfills this visual function; its imperious colonnade and flight of steps across the main facade do not shrink from announcing that it (with its subsidiaries) houses the third largest collection of books in America (figs. 127, 128). In addition, the facade forms an admirable sounding board for the daily activity that centers in the quadrangle, and its huge bulk stabilizes the diverse architectural forms that surround it. Erected in 1913 as a memorial to Harry Elkins Widener of Philadelphia, the building was designed as a condition of gift by Horace Trumbauer, an architect of the same city. In fact, however, the fundamental design had already been established in 1911 by a committee of three university architects who had determined the approximate size and plan and also the fact that the library would face the Yard rather than Massachusetts Avenue.[8]

In his annual report for 1911–12, President Lowell announced: "Mrs. Widener generously determined to build . . . the library on the general interior plan worked out by our committee of architects a year ago with the additional room for her son's books as part of the open court." But privately, in a letter to Charles Coolidge on October 3, 1912, he complained: "Mrs. Widener does not give the university the money to build the library, but has offered to build a library satisfactory in external appearance to herself. She accepted the plans of the former committee of architects as far as the size of the building and its interior arrangements were concerned,

127
Widener Library steps with Weld Hall. This romantic drawing by Louis Orr shows the Flemish gables and picturesque silhouette of Weld Hall adjacent to Imperial steps of Widener.

128
Widener Library (Horace Trumbauer, 1913).

153   *Academic Architecture under President Lowell*

except for the Memorial Hall and place for the collections of her son's
books; but the exterior was her own choice, and she has decided architectural opinions."

Construction began in February 1913. One virtue of Widener's design is
the reorientation of the entrance to face inward toward Tercentenary
Quadrangle rather than outward toward Massachusetts Avenue, as had the
old library as well as the 1896 plan suggested by the Board of Overseers
(fig. 104). Without this change the Tercentenary Quadrangle could never
have emerged as the heart of the university. Because of the library's great size
— it has ten floors of stacks — its massing and design had to be straightforward lest the building overwhelm its environment. Its proportions based on
the theater at Arles, Widener is clearly Imperial and Classical rather than
Georgian, but the use of brick is compatible with other buildings in the
Yard and the white stone columns and trim relate to the adjacent granite of
University Hall. The marble-clad interior staircase with mural paintings by
John Singer Sargent (fig. 129) and the Widener Memorial Room are fitting
preliminaries to the enormous reading room, which extends the entire
breadth of the building and is the most ostentatious interior space at
Harvard (fig. 130).[9]

130
*Widener Library: reading
room. Widener's imposing interior was of a scale unprece-
dented at Harvard.*

155   *Academic Architecture under President Lowell*

131
*Memorial Church (Coolidge,
Shepley, Bulfinch and Abbott,
1931). The massive south
portico, facing Widener's
steps, defines the north side of
the Tercentennial Quadrangle.*

132
Memorial Church interior:
view east toward Appleton
Chapel.

Although mid-eighteenth-century designers had envisioned royal portraits
by Copley and rich paneling for the library interior of Harvard Hall III,
such elaboration had not subsequently been customary at Harvard. Appleton Chapel and Gore Hall, for example, had been well-articulated public
spaces, but no university structure save Memorial Hall had generated a real
program for the decorative arts. Only recently at Phillips Brooks House,
Agassiz House, and the other turn-of-the-century Radcliffe buildings had
the architectural interior been of such central concern.

Whereas Widener dominates Tercentenary Quadrangle and Harvard Yard
by sheer bulk, the slender, soaring spire of Memorial Church serves as a
beacon at the university's center (fig. 131). Designed in 1931 by Coolidge,
Shepley, Bulfinch and Abbott, this building conforms to the Georgian
precedents that Lowell and Coolidge preferred to invoke. The 170-foot bell
tower is inspired by (though five feet lower than) the spire Bulfinch rebuilt
in 1806 on the Old North Church in Boston. But, as so often happens with
revival architecture, the designer, seeking to surpass his model, added
additional features—in this case a Classical portico. The enormous Doric
temple front of the south elevation has the heavy feel of the Greek Revival
and is somewhat incongruous with the light Federal detailing of the Bulfinch spire; it was deliberately scaled to the ponderous colonnade of

Widener.[10] Rather disturbingly, the tower seems to rise from the portico without visual support, while the presence of a second temple front at the west end of the building confuses the visitor as to which portico contains the actual entrance. The chancel of the church, architecturally more elaborate than the auditorium, is known as Appleton Chapel to commemorate the earlier building that stood on the site (fig. 132). Provided with a separate entrance and sheathed with carved woodwork in the manner of Grinling Gibbons (who provided such work for Sir Christopher Wren), it is designed to be used independently for small services. The room under the tower serves as a separate memorial chamber to Harvard soldiers who fought in World War I, and extensive marble inscriptions on the wall of the church proper commemorate those who died in the second world war. The multiple functions of this building are somewhat similar to but less well integrated than those of Memorial Hall.[11]

If Memorial Church is somewhat confusing as a building, its role in the organization of the space of Harvard Yard is brilliant. The spire provides a striking focal point, and the tower base with its portico, located on an axis with Widener, defines the limits of the quadrangle. Together the two buildings form the *skene* and *cavea* of a great unroofed theater in which Commencement exercises are held, an arrangement that gives rise to the name Tercentenary Theater.

The other stroke of genius that fostered a sense of unity within Harvard Yard was the decision to cloister the area with a series of seven buildings bordering Massachusetts Avenue in order to screen out the noise and visual disarray of that thoroughfare and of Harvard Square (fig. 133). Already in 1923 traffic was sufficiently disturbing to inspire administrators and architects to consider ways of shutting it out.[12] The goal was to give Harvard Yard that sense of scholarly seclusion which the sponsors so much admired in the gardens and quadrangles of Cambridge and Oxford. The cloistering screen, built between 1924 and 1930 by Charles Coolidge, consisted of six dormitories and Lehman Hall (originally the bursar's office).

To the northwest, Mower and Lionel Halls (1924) not only function as screens but also form the fourth sides of two small quadrangles. This completion makes the space of each quadrangle more self-sufficient than when it was "drained" into the much larger space of Cambridge Common. The new dormitories are kept to two stories in deference to the small scale of Holden Chapel, which stands between them. The four entrances of these halls duplicate in style the original main doorways of Hollis Hall. Farther south, Straus Hall (1926) rises to three stories in response to the taller Massachusetts and Matthews Halls, and appropriately the quadrangle between these halls is somewhat larger than those completed by Mower and Lionel. The intimate scale of these three courtyards provides a nice foil for the spacious proportions of the Old Yard.

Lehman Hall was built (with funds from the Business School) to house the bursar's office, and its public function is announced by an architectural frontispiece of giant pilasters and arched windows repeated on both major elevations (fig. 134). The building's mass also is sufficient to announce its official role and to define the triangular open space on its east side, although the pilasters are out of scale with other buildings in the Yard. Because this area is close to Harvard Square, the heaviest pedestrian traffic in the Yard converges here. Planted with beech trees and paved with a combination of

133
*Straus (left) and Lehman Halls
help to cloister the Yard,
screening it from Harvard
Square. The clock tower of
Memorial Hall can be seen
above the gables of Matthews
Hall. The landmark kiosk
dates from 1910.*

brick and asphalt walkways, the space is skillfully defined. Its landscaping
acts as a directional guide to users. Until recently the space was accented as
well by a contemporary sculpture by Henry Moore.

Wigglesworth Hall (1930) has eleven entries, strung along the southern
perimeter of the Yard in three buildings of similar style (fig. 135). Because
of proximity to Wadsworth House, where the only interruption in the
fence and cloister occurs, and because of the restricted area between some
of the units and Boylston Hall, the height of these dormitories was held to
two stories. A half-basement-level laboratory wing of wood that had been
added to the south side of Boylston Hall was demolished by 1900 to make
room for Wigglesworth.

A less important change than this cloistering screen of buildings was the
construction within the Yard of a new residence for the president, designed
in 1911 by Lowell's cousin Guy Lowell. The ornamental interior of this
Federal brick house incorporated a processional staircase based on eighteenth-century precedents such as the Hancock House in Boston; its
exterior, which resembles work of Bulfinch, announced the full-blown
arrival of the Colonial image for official Harvard design on the east side of
the Yard (fig. 136).[13] Like the previous (fifth) President's House, now
demolished, and the earlier eighteenth-century Wadsworth House, the new
one held aloof from the Yard as a private residence should. Situated about
fifty feet northeast of its predecessor, the building was isolated from the
Yard by a broad zone of planting and turned its facade to Quincy Street, as

134
Lehman Hall seen from the Yard.

135
Wigglesworth Hall (Coolidge, Shepley, Bulfinch and Abbott, 1930), facing inward, cloisters the Yard on the south; the Colonial details work well with adjacent Wadsworth House.

*17 Quincy Street (Guy
Lowell, 1911). The sixth
President's House emulated
Bulfinch's Federal houses on
Beacon Hill. Like earlier
residences in the Yard, it faces
outward to the street.*

had a number of handsome neighboring residences, now demolished. Three
of these on the east side of Quincy Street disappeared during Lowell's
presidency to make way for new Harvard buildings. In 1925 the new Fogg
Museum rose on the sites of two of them, one formerly belonging to the
Agassiz family; the third made way for the Faculty Club and the last for the
Carpenter Center.

Set on an embankment across Quincy Street from the Yard, the sizable
mass of the new Fogg Museum does not dwarf Robinson and Emerson
Halls as it would were it not separated from them by Memorial Fence and
the width of Quincy Street. The exterior architectural ornamentation of the
Fogg, which derives from such impeccable sources as the balcony consoles
and pilastered window frames of the Old State House in Boston, is one of
its notable features (fig. 137). Indeed, one of the great merits of all these
Coolidge buildings of the 1920s is the high quality of the exterior and
interior wooden trim. The main entrance of the Fogg (fig. 138) is derived
from Westover, the Byrd Mansion in Virginia. It is robust and convincing,
done at a time before economic conditions had restricted architects to
those timid stock moldings which have rendered most recent efforts to re-
create Georgian forms so contemptible. But planning for the interaction of
the many and complex simultaneous functions to be contained within this
building (galleries, storage, offices, classrooms, studies, library, and a public
lecture hall) was inadequate, a failure that produced confusion on the
exterior, with its two entrances, as well as in the floor plan (fig. 139).
Despite the 1967 enlargement, which moved most of the books to a new
underground wing on the east, a relocation of the Fine Arts Library and the
installation of an elevator to serve the entire museum have resulted in

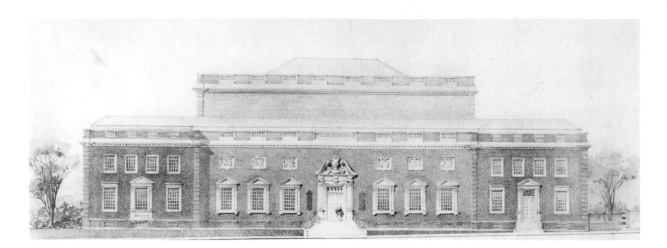

137
*The new Fogg Museum of Art
(Coolidge, Shepley, Bulfinch
and Abbott, 1925). Drawing
by Herman Voss.*

138
Fogg Museum entrance.

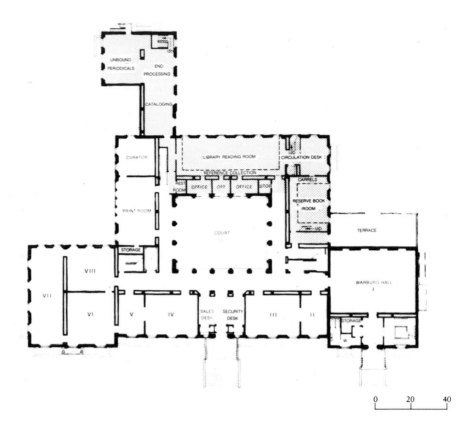

139
Fogg Museum: first-floor plan.

insurmountable problems of noise control and traffic, while access to the large public lecture hall is now exasperatingly congested and roundabout.

Contrasting with the Georgian design of its exterior, the Fogg's interior is dominated by a top-lit enclosed courtyard. Executed in splendid travertine (fig. 140), it is a four-fifths-scale replica of the famous Sangallo loggia at San Biagio, Montepulciano (1518–1534), measured drawings of which were made by Coolidge's partner Henry R. Shepley.[14] The large-scale courtyard (56 by 42 feet), located directly opposite the entrance of the Fogg, bears no relation to the exterior, and is flanked by a vaulted cloister on the first floor that is equally unrelated to it in style. A French sixteenth-century carved oak ceiling was brought from Dijon for two-story Warburg Hall, the largest exhibition space in the museum (fig. 141).[15]

In 1931 seventeenth-century English woodwork was reassembled for the Naumburg Rooms (fig. 142) in an ell attached to the northeast corner of the building. Used for private functions, these rooms were erected as a condition of the Naumburg bequest, which contained a number of fine seventeenth-century paintings the Fogg was anxious to acquire. In an age dedicated to authenticity and to connoisseurship, the Naumburgs wanted their paintings displayed in a seventeenth-century environment. Hence the rich tapestry, English paneling, and furniture of the period. Even the light in the room is filtered through stained glass of Swiss, German, and Flemish sixteenth- and early seventeenth-century origins.[16]

More than any other building at Harvard, the Fogg embodies the learned eclecticism that characterized American architecture of the first quarter of the twentieth century. European or American Colonial standards were no

140
*Fogg Museum: interior
courtyard.*

141
*Fogg Museum: Warburg
Room.*

longer sought through free copying of detail (such as that of Henry Van Brunt at Memorial Hall); instead, reassembly of actual fragments and heavy use of measured drawings provided the tools for design. No interior could have better symbolized the then-current system for study of the history of art and architecture than the fabric of the Fogg Museum.

The Harvard Faculty Club (1930) produced another change in this Quincy Street neighborhood (fig. 143). It occupies the site of the residence of Henry James, Sr., which had been remodeled as the Colonial Club, an early service club for townspeople and faculty. With its narrow end turned to Quincy Street, the new Faculty Club did not disturb the dominance of trees and side yards over buildings. But what had been a neighborhood of comfortable, wooden Victorian houses was now transformed into a street

143
*The Faculty Club: architects'
drawing (Coolidge, Shepley,
Bulfinch and Abbott, 1930).*

of harmonious neo-Georgian buildings of brick. In 1933 the Cambridge
Fire Station, an ornate Georgian Revival design by Sturgis Associates, was
built just north of the Fogg Museum on the triangular site of Harvard's first
Rogers Gymnasium.[17] The city had obtained the land from Harvard in
exchange for the small park at the southeast corner of the Cambridge
Common known as the Little Common. Though the Quincy Street area is
not physically a part of Harvard Yard, its spatial character and the compatibility of its buildings make it an intimate extension of that area. This feeling
of unity will be further enhanced if the university's wish to close Quincy
Street to traffic is realized.[18]

The unity of Harvard Yard as we know it coalesced during the Lowell
years with the construction of a dozen buildings that were sited and
designed with extraordinary skill. Many essentials of that larger order were
already extant — the early brick quadrangles, the Old Yard, Sever Quadrangle, the Memorial Fence — but the periphery of the Yard was ragged in
some areas despite the fence, and Tercentenary Quadrangle did not yet exist
to give the Yard an integrating link at the center. It required only the
addition of a few discretely placed buildings to precipitate a sense of order.
The order that was finally achieved in Harvard Yard — that grew organically over the generations — derives from more than half a dozen spatial
units, which key together in lively, unpredictable ways. The visitor cannot
stand in one place or walk along an axis and "read" the spatial organization
of the Yard; it must be explored unit by unit, by one who moves through
the area unable to predict the shape or size of the space that will emerge
beyond the next two buildings. Unexpected pockets of order appear, each
with a character of its own, yet all these fit together to form a coherent
pattern. Such a varied, individualistic environment, offering choices in its

variety, is appropriate for a university that encourages each student to pursue his own interests and to develop his own particular talents.

A good way to appreciate the genius of Harvard Yard is to compare it with a campus laid out in conformity with Baroque principles as interpreted in the early years of this century by the Ecole des Beaux-Arts in Paris, where so many American architects studied. For such a comparison one need only turn to another Harvard complex, the campus of the Medical School in Boston, which was designed in 1906 by Shepley, Rutan and Coolidge. The buildings of the Medical School are deliberately grand and imposing, and they are grouped to look as large and impressive as the size of the lot would permit (figs. 93, 94). The absence in Harvard Yard of such formality and of great axial vistas drew criticism at the turn of the century. A search for it is detectable in the unrealistic axes in the Overseers Plan of 1896 (fig. 104) or in the Duquesne Plan of 1912. Even the usually perceptive architectural critic Montgomery Schuyler, in his essay on Harvard architecture in the October 1909 issue of the *Architectural Record,* found the Yard confused and suggested that the judicious moving of a few buildings could create suitable vistas: an east-west axis terminating in the Memorial Hall tower and a north-south mall between Peabody and Quincy Streets. But Charles Coolidge, who was required to utilize the architectural legacy of Harvard, found better ways of dealing with the problems. He appreciated that legacy, and he made the most of it.

In the North Yard the obstacles to unity were even more complex, perhaps insurmountable. Nevertheless, Coolidge and his office drew up several plans in an attempt to give the area some degree of order. All the drawings identify five nodes or centers of order, though these vary in shape from one scheme to another: (1) a chemistry quadrangle east of what is now Mallinckrodt Laboratory; (2) a large quadrangle formed by the University Museum and the Biological Laboratories; (3) a long mall running between Oxford Street and the Common; (4) and (5) quadrangles on both east and west fronts of the Law School. Significantly, only one of these, the second, was fully implemented, while the last two were realized only in altered form in very recent times (fig. 144).

Two rather small and unimpressive chemistry buildings, the Wolcott Gibbs Laboratory and the T. Jefferson Coolidge Laboratory, stood on Divinity Avenue. These were designed in 1911 and 1912 by A. W. Longfellow as part of a cluster of chemistry laboratories focusing on a tower near Mallinckrodt Laboratory (fig. 87).[19] Some of these, such as the Coolidge Laboratory, were to be reserved for research and therefore did not have to be large. The rationale for separate buildings was apparently to combine maximum light and protection from fire with minimum interference to the research activities within, but the scheme was abandoned because of the cost of duplicating services to the buildings. Many of the functions of these buildings were eventually subsumed in the enormous Science Center. Jefferson Coolidge was demolished in 1979; the larger Sherman Fairchild Biochemistry Building was constructed on the site.

Across Divinity Avenue is the Semitic Museum (1900), also designed by Longfellow. Somewhat isolated and at loose ends, it is an adequate Georgian Revival design whose straightforward character contrasts with its suave neighbor at 2 Divinity Avenue, designed in 1930 by Horace Trumbauer for the Institute of Geographical Exploration. Concerning the refined proportions, detailing, and elegant marble trim of the Trumbauer design, one might observe—in the words of Edward Johnson, that critic of seventeenth-century Harvard—that it is "too gorgeous for a Wilderness" like Divinity Avenue. When the building was enlarged in 1957 to house the Harvard-Yenching Institute, a satisfactory addition at the rear by Shepley, Bulfinch, Richardson and Abbott, conforming in scale and material to both the original unit and the adjacent Semitic Museum, did much to alleviate this visual disparity.

But an architectural wilderness Divinity Avenue clearly is. Every structure from the Busch-Reisinger Museum and William James Hall at one end to the University Herbarium at the other is of different form and in competition with its neighbors. If all of Harvard were like this, it would be indistinguishable from the usual American college campus.

Although an interesting design in its own right, the Busch-Reisinger Museum (known in the early years as the Germanic Museum) is a German pre–World War I building plunked down out of context in Cambridge (fig. 145). With its enclosed garden the museum constitutes a self-sufficient unit, and it succeeds in its avowed purpose to inform Americans of the achievements of German culture.[20] Like its contents, the design for the building was imported from the Old World; the plans by Professor German Bestelmeyer of Dresden were adapted for Yankee construction by Professor H. Langford Warren of the Harvard architectural faculty.[21] Although the collection of art objects given by Kaiser Wilhelm had been displayed as early as 1900 in the Rogers Gymnasium on the triangle, the opening of the new building was delayed, for reasons of security, until 1921. Each of the three exhibition halls was designed to contain full-scale reproductions of important monuments from one of the three greatest periods of German history: Romanesque, Gothic, and Renaissance.[22] Although the museum is handsome in its own right, little can be done to integrate its stucco walls into these surroundings; but despite this isolation, the building disrupts the environment less than the skyscraper format of its newer neighbor, William James Hall (1963).

At the north end of Divinity Avenue lies one of the most important architectural complexes at Harvard: the enormous compound formed by the University Museum and the Biological Laboratory (fig. 144). Of the additional quadrangles envisioned in the Coolidge plans, this was the only one to be more or less fully realized. The spatial organization of this complex would never have been arrived at by a designer sitting at a drafting table dreaming of an ideal form. It is not a lucid space, with classic proportions and clear accents; it is a space that is impossible to understand as a whole, that reveals itself part by part, in a fascinating series of visual relationships.

The museum and laboratory, huge, U-shaped structures whose arms project toward each other, form a vast quadrangle two hundred by five hundred feet. Like Harvard Yard, this is an organic space that developed in stages over a century and a half. The first building in the compound was Divinity Hall (1825; fig. 38). The process of enclosure began with the museum (1859–1913; figs. 70–72) and was completed by the Biology Laboratory in 1930 and the University Herbarium in 1953. A final jewel for the setting, Tozzer Library, a counterpart of Divinity Hall, was added in 1974.

144
*The enormous University
Museum facing Oxford Street
forms a quadrangle with the
Biological Laboratories east of
Divinity Avenue. To the right
along Divinity Avenue are the
Semitic Museum and the
Institute of Geographical Ex-
ploration (Horace Trumbauer,
1930). Lowell Lecture Hall
(Guy Lowell, 1902) is at the
lower right on the corner of
Oxford and Kirkland Streets.*

145
*Busch-Reisinger Museum
(German Bestelmeyer and
H. Langford Warren, 1914):
architectural model.*

146
*Biology Laboratories:
architects' drawing (Coolidge,
Shepley, Bulfinch and Abbott,
1930).*

147
*Biology Laboratory entrance.
The brick relief and other
sculpture is by Katharine
Ward Lane.*

Divinity Hall and the University Museum were discussed earlier. The Biology Laboratory is one of Harvard's largest structures (214,000 square feet); it is also one of the most significant ones, for both educational and architectural reasons. It brought together four departments that had been scattered in seven buildings, each with its own collections, laboratories, and library, to constitute the Division of Biology. One more example of Industrial Harvard (fig. 146), it was designed in 1930 by Coolidge, Shepley, Bulfinch and Abbott. Its style is surprising from the firm that was concurrently designing Lyman Laboratory and the Harvard houses along the river. Though executed in Harvard Brick and described by some critics of the time as Modern Georgian, the building is unmistakably "WPA Modern" or "stripped classic," similar to such contemporary Cambridge buildings as Rindge Technical High School and the Central Square Post Office, both built in 1932.[23] The courtyard facades are composed of vertical stacks of factory windows separated by brick pylons. Although the composition lacks Classical decorative details, its basic form, with alternating walls and windows plus a windowless top story, conceptually recalls a colonnade and entablature. On the rear elevations, however, where top-story windows were permitted, the utilitarian nature of the building—which here contains ventilating equipment and a skylighted greenhouse—is unabashedly revealed.

The simple, straightforward facades are animated by an engaging series of reliefs, depicting birds, animals, and fish, incised in the blank walls of the top story (fig. 147). The placement of these vignettes is determined by the fenestration below. The crisp outlines of the carving are all the more effective because surfaces elsewhere are simple. Like the splendid bronze rhinoceroses at the entrance, the reliefs are the work of Katherine Ward Lane, and they constitute magnificent architectural sculpture. The way in which this brick ornament counts first as masonry and then as decoration suggests comparison with the earlier Panel Brick work of Weld Hall (fig. 47) and with the splendid cut brick ornamentation used by Richardson at Sever Hall (fig. 52).[24]

While the architectural design is good and the brick relief very good, the genius of the laboratory is the way it organizes space and pulls together a cluster of diverse structures at the far end of Divinity Avenue. Beginning with the old theological library of 1886 (now Farlow Herbarium) as an appendage to one arm, the new laboratory wraps itself around three sides of Divinity Hall to create a large open court (some 200 by 240 feet), but its projecting wings also respond to those of the earlier University Museum. Since old Divinity Hall occupies most of the frontage on the avenue and stands on a terrace, it somewhat isolates and reinforces the independent spatial character of the biology courtyard, which thus appears to be lower than the street. Because the hall does not center with the laboratory, the two entrances to the court differ in character: one is very narrow, the other broad and terraced. Inside the courtyard, however, the sufficiency of the space as well as a spatial flow from the avenue becomes apparent. While the museum and the laboratory are comparable in massing and shape, their architecture and brickwork are quite different. But this discrepancy, most happily, is partially screened by Divinity Hall, which minimizes differences in detail without obscuring the larger relationship of the mass. Thus the university was well advised not to demolish Divinity Hall as architect Coolidge proposed in 1922.

148
Tozzer Library (Johnson and Hodvelt, 1974). Asymmetrical fenestration and subtle massing relate this building well to the simple forms of Divinity Hall to the east.

The most recent addition to these quadrangles is Tozzer Library, designed in 1974 by Johnson and Hodvelt for the Division of Anthropology (fig. 148). The new building screens the museum courtyard much as Divinity Hall screens that of biology. The frequent breaks in massing and the intricate fenestration of this small building differentiate it from the huge mass and workaday facades of the museum. At the same time, the plum color of the Tozzer brick blends beautifully with that of Robert Slack's Peabody wing of the museum (1876). Although Tozzer is very different in architectural style from old Divinity Hall across the street, the two buildings are elegantly compatible in size and in the way they function in the setting. This complex is one of the clearest demonstrations on the extended Harvard campus that buildings of different architectural styles can coexist harmoniously if scale, material, and massing are handled with skill.

The University Herbarium was erected in 1953, long after Lowell's time, as a connecting link between the University Museum and Farlow Herbarium. The use of brick and the way the mass of this building fused the museum with the laboratory are to be commended, but the fenestration of the new herbarium was grossly at odds with that of its neighbors (fig. 149). Nothing in the related structures suggested the narrow strip windows of the upper stories or the scaleless sheets of plate glass surrounding the entrance; indeed, the pattern of isolated windows employed on the rear (north) elevation, dull though it is, would have been a far better design for the facade. It is almost as if the designer had gone out of his way to compete with rather than complement neighboring structures. Surprisingly he belonged to the same architectural office that twenty years earlier had produced the Biological Laboratory and Lyman Laboratory, each of which is so marvelously suited to its architectural setting. The Herbarium's facade was thoroughly revised by the addition opened in 1980.

The most chaotic part of the extended Harvard campus is the area lying between the new Hemenway Gymnasium and Oxford Street. Between 1922

and 1929 three of the Coolidge Plans attempted to bring some order to this area by establishing a long east-west mall running from Mallinckrodt Laboratory almost to the Cambridge Common. Foci at opposite ends of the quadrangle were to be provided by the two-story porticos of Mallinckrodt (fig. 151) and Gannett House (fig. 76); to achieve this, south-facing Gannett House, Harvard's only remaining Greek Revival academic building, was rotated to its present position facing east. The width of the proposed mall was to be determined by the interval between Jefferson Laboratory and Paine Hall, and two new buildings were projected to enclose the east end of the area. Inevitably, however, a hole remained at the southwest corner, where there was insufficient space to erect another building. It is fortunate that the attempt to forge this quadrangle was abandoned, because the component parts were patently incompatible. Though both Mallinckrodt and Gannett had porticos, the scale of these was so discrepant that their forced visual association would have been ludicrous. The Music Building (Paine Hall) and the laboratory are likewise totally unrelated in scale, building material, and architectural style, and their center axes do not quite correspond. To have paired them in so formal a manner would only have accentuated these differences. If that were not difficulty enough, Austin Hall — that Narcissus — sat at just enough of an angle from the others to have disrupted the attempted order. Finally, the rear elevation of old Hemenway Gymnasium was of yet another architectural style and did not align with either Paine or Austin, a discrepancy that was aggravated in 1938 when the old gym was replaced by Littauer Center (figs. 179, 180), a structure located with respect to the streets it faced rather than the quadrangle behind it.[25]

The Music Building, with Paine Hall, was designed in 1913 by John Mead Howells. This competent, delicately detailed Federal Revival building (fig. 150) has much in common stylistically with Trumbauer's later Institute of Geographical Exploration on Divinity Avenue. Its unfortunate siting, however, represents one of the few planning blunders of the Lowell years. (It is significant that this decision was made early in the administration, before the establishment of the Committee on Plans for the Future Development of Harvard.) The position of Paine Hall was affected by the fact that Harvard did not yet own the lot to the east, which would have been needed to place it on an axis with Jefferson Laboratory.[26] In contrast to the big scale and heavy detailing of the laboratory, Paine Hall appears almost frivolous. The difference between the brick used for the two buildings is distinctly unpleasant, a discrepancy exacerbated more recently by the use of yet another shape and color of brick when the Fanny Mason wing was added in 1970.

The idea of the mall from Cambridge Common to Oxford Street had obviously been abandoned by 1930, when the Lyman Laboratory was constructed. Instead of being placed along one side of the mall as shown in the 1922 plans, the new laboratory was set at right angles to it and attached to Jefferson Laboratory so as to link it with Cruft Laboratory. The design of Lyman was modulated with unusual care to relate it to its two neighbors. With the concept of the mall long abandoned, no question arose in 1951 about placing Gordon McKay Laboratory parallel to Oxford Street, directly athwart the proposed mall.

The Coolidge Plans show two more quadrangles on the east and west sides of the Law School. Langdell Hall was not extended to its present length until 1928, and several different treatments for the (east) Law Quadrangle were proposed in 1922. But the awkward angle between the axis of Langdell and Jarvis Street and the Rotch Building posed a problem that could not then be resolved. The futility of the grandiose Langdell facade, which looked out at the rear elevations of four scientific laboratories, has already been noted; there was nothing to do but enjoy the isolation of the cul-de-sac location until the construction twenty years later of the Graduate Center (1949–1952) removed both Jarvis Street and the Rotch Building, which had nestled uncomfortably close to Langdell with complete stylistic incongruity, and opened up another fine quadrangle beyond.

Similarly, the area west of Langdell Hall could not be arranged in a conventional, symmetrical manner. For example, the Coolidge Plans proposed adding a second L-shaped dormitory facing Massachusetts Avenue as a counterpart to Walter Hastings Hall, a move that would have established a neat quadrangle between these two halls and Langdell. Unfortunately for this solution, the lot needed for the expansion was already occupied by the Harvard Epworth Methodist Church (1891). Thus the area remained at loose ends until the construction in 1968 of Benjamin Thompson's two asymmetrical office buildings for the law faculty.

The only open area in the north campus that the Coolidge Plans of 1922 did not try to encircle with symmetrically disposed buildings was the park, traversed by Oxford Street, that lies between the University Museum and Pierce Hall. In 1927, however, the lower stretch of Oxford Street was transformed by the construction of Mallinckrodt Laboratory (fig. 151), designed by Coolidge, Shepley, Bulfinch and Abbott. Of deceptively large scale (the windows that seem to be of domestic size are roughly nine feet high), Mallinckrodt is placed close to the street; its enormous mass establishes a visual limit to the clearly defined street corridor and helps to create a vista toward its end and the facade of Memorial Hall. This compelling

150
Music Building and Paine Hall (John Mead Howells and Stokes, 1913).

151
Mallinckrodt Laboratory, Oxford Street facade, looking toward Memorial Hall (Coolidge, Shepley, Bulfinch and Abbott, 1927). The giant portico of Mallinckrodt was intended as part of an unrealized mall.

175   *Academic Architecture under President Lowell*

view, framed by the portico of Mallinckrodt, McKay Laboratory, and the new Science Center, is one of the most memorable at Harvard. The Mallinckrodt portico is a simplified version of that of Bulfinch's Massachusetts General Hospital, its cupola an enriched version of that on Harvard Hall but almost double in scale. Otherwise the laboratory has little ornamental relief except for the contrasting smooth ("repressed"), salmon colored brick used for quoins, window heads, and the like.[27] If not a masterpiece in its own right, Mallinckrodt is good supporting architecture. Immediately to the east is Converse Laboratory (1927), devoted to organic chemistry and containing the chemistry library. Constructed of the same material and at the same scale as Mallinckrodt, Converse is simpler in design because it does not face a major street.

These two laboratories are the successors of A. W. Longfellow's proposed chemistry quadrangles, discussed earlier in this chapter. The sequence of chemistry laboratories — beginning in 1850 with one room at the north end of University Hall, moving in 1858 to a single laboratory in Boylston Hall (a building originally tied to a proposed School of Mines), expanding to larger quarters when the mansard roof was added to that building in 1875, and beginning expansion in the North Yard with the two special research laboratories (Gibbs and Coolidge) in 1911–1912 — reflects an enormous expansion in teaching and research facilities for the sciences within only eighty years. This growth would accelerate during the tenure of President Conant, a chemist, with much additional construction for the sciences in the North Yard.

8 The River Houses and the South Yard

If President Lowell had only to augment the flow of academic building begun in the Eliot administration, in the matter of constructing student housing he had to reverse the current. Following the surge of dormitory building at the outset of his administration, President Eliot was not much interested in housing for undergraduates, and although the number of students increased rapidly, the university did nothing to provide for their accommodation. The size of the freshman class grew from about two hundred students in 1877 to seven hundred in 1914. Of these an ever smaller proportion could find space in college halls. In 1867, just before the dormitory building campaign of 1869–1871, 59 percent of the students were housed in college halls; by 1900 this figure had fallen to 27 percent.[1]

The administration was also slow to improve the existing undergraduate dormitories. For example, not until 1894 did Hollis and Stoughton Halls receive basement water closets or steam heat in their entries (even then the studies continued to be heated by coal grates).[2] The excuse for such deliberation was that expenditures for modernization forced up room rents. This, of course, was true, but as a result the university offered some of the most minimal housing in Cambridge, and certain dormitories became a kind of ghetto. The growing body of students who were unable to find rooms in university buildings, or preferred not to live in them, turned to private accommodations. These were of two sorts: roominghouses and luxurious quarters that cost much more than Harvard's. While the cheapest rooms in College House and the Yard cost but $30 and $50, in 1893 rooms in private houses generally cost more than $100; by 1904 a rich student wishing to cut a social figure could spend as much as $700 a year for his rooms.[3] Such extremes indicate the extent to which a caste system based on wealth had developed at Harvard before Lowell became president. Less visible if more numerous than the luxury quarters were the roominghouses, many of which were undoubtedly satisfactory. It was common for widows who had children to educate to lease a house near Harvard and rent rooms to students or take them in as boarders. An increasing number of students lived at home, many commuting from Boston, especially after electric trolleys began service in 1894.[4] An obvious result of this situation was a deep social cleavage in the student body.

Harvard did somewhat better at seeing that students were properly fed. Two university-sponsored but student-managed dining halls existed: one at Memorial Hall, established in 1874; another in Randall Hall, a building especially constructed for this purpose in 1898 (fig. 85). By 1900 the commons in Memorial Hall provided meals for 1150 students at $4 per week; economy fare at Randall was available for 800 students at $2.50; board in private houses or clubs could be had for $5 to $8.[5] Since students were free to shop around for sustenance, the managers of the university commons were kept on their toes. This was particularly true at Memorial Hall, where a certain volume had to be maintained in order to amortize the debt incurred in fitting out the kitchen and hall in 1874.

In the last decades of his administration President Eliot appears to have been satisfied with the existing housing situation. He looked with favor on the investment of private capital in dormitories, since this released university funds for other uses that he considered more important. He was more and more concerned with the graduate program, and he assumed that students would make their own arrangements for accommodations as did their counterparts in Europe. In this he was correct as far as club men were concerned or the increasingly large proportion of students (77 percent in 1890) who entered Harvard from preparatory schools with an established circle of friends. Many of this group lived in luxury halls or in final clubs, which now began to erect houses of their own.[6]

Although many less affluent students managed perfectly well, especially after their first year, some entering freshmen found it difficult to get to know their classmates. It became harder as the size of the entering class increased. At the same time, the growing number of courses and the overwhelming size of some introductory courses made it difficult for students to get acquainted by studying together.[7] Class spirit—that most cherished part of the Harvard education in the mid-nineteenth century, which had developed spontaneously when a graduating class numbered less than one hundred and when every student more or less followed the same basic course of study—was disappearing rapidly. (As late as 1856, for example, 40 percent of the curriculum was composed of Greek and Latin subjects.) About the only thing that countered this centrifugal dispersion was athletics, the rapid growth of which at this time may be explained in part by the students' instinctive need for some sort of shared activity. The lack of social cohesion was all too evident to many concerned observers. A journalist for the New York *Evening Post* in 1896 even referred to Harvard as a "social orphan asylum." It was in order to provide students with a common meeting place that Colonel Henry Lee Higginson contributed $150,000 in 1900 for construction of the Harvard Union (fig. 62).

Long before he became president, A. Lawrence Lowell had determined that steps must be taken to rectify this situation. In his inaugural address in 1909 he announced: "we must construct a new solidarity to replace that which is gone. The task before us is to frame a system which, without sacrificing individual variation too much or neglecting the pursuit of different scholarly interests, shall produce an intellectual and social cohesion, at least among large groups of students, and points of contact among them all."

One of Lowell's ideas was to build residential halls with equally good accommodations for all.[8] These he thought would provide a common meeting ground where differences of wealth and origin would be minimized and where students could develop wider circles of friends. The scheme was not quickly realized. The process by which it was implemented can be followed in six steps: (1) acquisition by Harvard of land near the river (1902–1912); (2) construction of private dormitories on the so-called Gold Coast (1892–1903); (3) construction of freshman dormitories in the South Yard (1913); (4) acquisition of the Gold Coast dormitories by Harvard (1916–1920); (5) construction of additional dormitories when Harvard Yard was cloistered (1924–1930); and (6) construction and remodeling of the seven houses in the South Yard (1929–1931). Not every part of this development was planned (or even approved) by President Lowell, but each step was essential to the eventual realization of his goal.

The university acquired the land that would become the South Yard before Lowell became president.[9] This area, lying between Mount Auburn Street and the Charles River and known as Riverside, was not an attractive one in the late nineteenth century. It contained a mixture of modest residences and commercial buildings, and its riverfront was clogged with an assortment of wharfs, coalyards, storehouses, and a power plant (fig. 152). The extensive mud flats were malodorous when the tide was out, and the river was beginning to be contaminated. Of the irregular gridiron of streets laid out when Cambridge was founded in 1631, some parts near the river had fallen into disuse. Interest in the area quickened in the early 1890s with talk of construction of a tidal dam that would stabilize the water level in the Charles estuary and make improvements of the riverbank possible. Attention was increased by the establishment in 1893 of the Cambridge Park Department, a component of the Metropolitan Park Commission. Although work on the dam did not begin until 1903 (and was not finished until 1910), construction of a carriageway along the river extending from Boylston Street to Flagg Street was started in 1895 and completed seven years later. Boston had already reclaimed the Back Bay, so the citizens knew what could be accomplished.[10]

Harvard was slow to take an interest in the area. As late as 1898 it was disposing of property south of Massachusetts Avenue instead of acquiring it, and when alumni began to discuss the possibilities of improving the area for the benefit of the school, President Eliot made it clear that Harvard had no funds for such projects. Anything accomplished here, he said, would have to be done with outside financing.[11] He also opined that an expression of university interest in such a project would cause land prices to soar. Nevertheless his son, landscape architect Charles Eliot, Jr., had already (in about 1894) proposed the improvement of university land in Brighton that bordered the river, the Longfellow meadows and Soldiers Field.

After 1900 discussion of creating a boulevard to connect Harvard Yard with the river gave way to a more significant scheme to acquire the entire area between Mount Auburn Street and the river and to develop it along the lines of the Thames riverfront in Oxford.[12] The chief proponent of this ambitious project was recent alumnus Edward Waldo Forbes, who proposed to purchase the numerous small properties, hold them until Harvard needed the area, and then offer them to the university at a reduced figure. In 1902 Forbes established the Harvard Riverside Associates, and this organization shortly raised $300,000, which was used as a sort of revolving fund. Working through various real estate firms, the group bought property outright or purchased options.[13] Forbes also arranged a five-year mortgage with the Mutual Life Insurance Company of New York City: the company agreed to lend six-tenths of the value of each parcel acquired, said amount then to be used for additional purchases. In this way the group acquired about 7½ acres. In 1906 Harvard agreed to assume a $300,000 mortgage on this land and Forbes raised another $130,000 to meet the insurance company mortgage of $485,000. Thus Harvard for its mortgage received property worth $800,000. The Associates turned the land over to Harvard as needed, the first section in 1913 for the construction of freshman dormitories. The group's only requirement was that it be consulted in planning the area to ensure optimum use of the riverside location.

Planning the South Yard was a challenge, for the Riverside neighborhood was not very attractive (fig. 152). Mud flats bordered the river, land usage was mixed, and upkeep of the modest existing structures had been indifferent. The irregular gridiron pattern of streets laid out in 1631, when Cambridge was founded, was still clearly evident. Beginning in the 1890s, various schemes were proposed for the improvement of the area. By the time actual construction began a few years later, practical aesthetic considerations had altered initial ideas of what was wanted. Similarly, objectives have changed at each stage of development as new factors have had to be reckoned with: higher property values, political and sociological pressures, the automobile, larger numbers of students to be accommodated, and an enlargement of the area to be planned. Rather than representing a gradual implementation of a single scheme, the present form of the South Yard has resulted from a series of linked decisions.

The initial schemes for the improvement of Riverside were theoretical, drawn to demonstrate that the area could be made attractive. Indeed the very first plan of 1896, done for the architectural committee of the Board of Overseers, was commissioned for the sole purpose of educating the President and Fellows of Harvard College to the need for a master plan for the university (fig. 104). In this plan a wide boulevard slashes through the Riverside neighborhood without regard for the existing street pattern. In good Baroque fashion, this avenue terminates at imposing focal points: a fountain or monument near the river and a colossal portico on the facade of an enlarged college library in the Yard. So overwhelming an entrance facing Massachusetts Avenue would have demoted Harvard Yard to a mere appendage, and it is fortunate that so arrogant a concept was not implemented.

The other early plans were simpler, concerned only with the design of a carriageway to connect Harvard Yard and the river while leaving the district unchanged. Three plans dated June 12, 1897, by the Olmsted brothers propose alternate approaches to the Yard along wide, tree-lined streets.[14] These were conceived more as part of the system of boulevards being built throughout metropolitan Boston than as a neighborhood improvement. This scheme as slightly revised in 1901 shows DeWolfe Street as graceful and undulating rather than straight; it is really an extension of the river parkway into Quincy Square, where it terminates with a view of the formal Class of 1880 gate at the foot of the Dana-Palmer terrace. That so much attention is given to this gateway recalls the fact that the Memorial Fence and gates were being constructed at just this time.

152
Cambridge Riverside about 1896. Wooden boathouses, coalyards, and small wooden houses filled the waterfront that was to become the site of the River Houses.

Plans of slightly later date, which consider Riverside as a neighborhood rather than merely as an area through which runs a major street, have greater interest for us because they contain the germ of the present South Yard. The principal feature in these plans is a dormitory precinct of considerable size, though the boulevard to link Harvard Yard with the river is also present. Here, however, the purpose of the boulevard differs from that of the parkways of the earlier plans; it is for the benefit of Harvard students going to the dormitories and the riverside recreation area rather than for visitors driving to Harvard Square by carriage. Unfortunately, the linking corridor was lost sight of as the South Yard evolved over the years.

A striking component of some of these plans is their gross scale and formality, so unlike that of Harvard Yard or of what eventually was built in the South Yard. A 1909 plan by Charles Wetmore, of the New York firm of Warren and Wetmore, proposed to clear the whole section south of Mount Auburn Street and to create a formal park surrounded by a series of uniformly monumental buildings. He also provided a wide processional way more or less in line with Holyoke Street leading through the dormitory quadrangle and across a monumental bridge to the stadium on the far side of the river. Perfectly representative of Beaux-Arts Baroque planning of the time as exemplified by the Columbia University campus in New York (1894), such a scheme strikes us today as grandiloquent.[15]

Other plans of 1903, while also formal and axial, had more spatial interest. This is particularly true of one by "V,"[16] which retains the bridge and the Holyoke Street axis without widening that thoroughfare, and

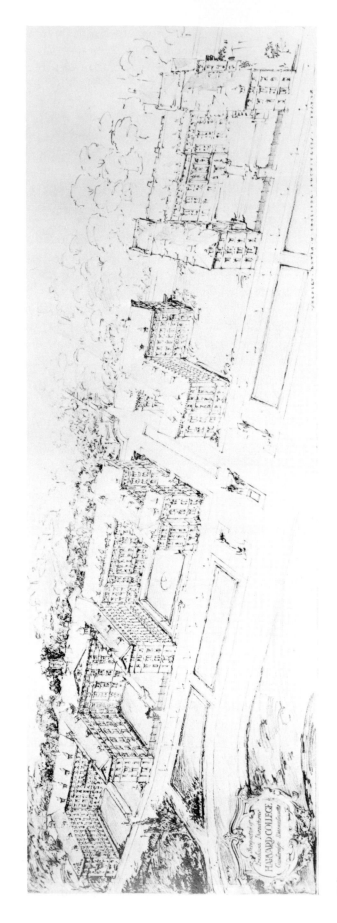

153
Plan for freshman dormitories along the river (Charles Coolidge, 1910).

which organizes the proposed campus into a series of interlocking quadrangles that vary in shape and size. Best of all, the buildings conform to the scale of those in the Yard. A plan of October 1903 by the Olmsted brothers is a less successful compromise. It retains the DeWolfe Street carriageway, which is too far to one side to serve pedestrians going between Harvard Yard and the dormitories. Nevertheless it is inventive in its use of buildings to break up the new campus into several informal courtyards, a feature that anticipates the South Yard as it came to be built.

If a plan comparable to the above group was made by Shepley, Rutan and Coolidge in 1903, it has not survived, but it was that firm, always favored by President Lowell, that received the commission to design the dormitories. By 1910 the firm had provided a carefully delineated plan for the buildings, which the president undoubtedly used for purposes of fundraising (fig. 153). A letter from Coolidge demonstrates that by the spring of 1912 the program for the freshman dormitories had been clearly formulated: (1) the new buildings would be recognizable as part of Harvard College; (2) though they would be larger in size, their style of architecture would recall that of the old buildings in Harvard Yard; and (3) in placement as well as in design the first structures built in the area would allow views through to the river for those to come after them.[17]

So much for designs on paper. When it came time in 1912–13 to build the freshman dormitories, their exact locations were subject to certain practical considerations: ownership of land, income from rented structures, the existing pattern of streets, and the availability of funds for new construction. The Riverside Associates had not quite succeeded in acquiring all of the parcels (22 were missing out of approximately 115) in the target area.[18] Thus, for example, a dormitory could not be located on the important riverfront corner of Plympton Street. Also, there was the matter of how much land should be cleared to make room for the first dormitories; it was important to retain rents from as many buildings as possible to cover mortgage payments.[19] Fortunately, the area closest to the river, where the dormitories were to be constructed, contained the fewest buildings. To make room for the three freshman dormitories, only fourteen residential buildings had to be demolished, along with miscellaneous structures pertaining to a planing mill and a coal wharf that the university already owned.

A sketch was done in 1909 for a shallow dormitory; this apparently was an attempt to squeeze Gore and Standish into only half the block between the river and Mill Street. The more finished perspective of 1910 (fig. 153), which created an unbroken barrier close to the river, could not have satisfied the Riverside Associates' requirement that vistas and access to the river be retained. In January 1911 the Associates agreed to deed Harvard the land lying south of Mill Street. Final plans for the freshman dormitories were prepared in the autumn of 1912, construction began the following spring, and new housing was ready by the autumn of 1914 for the entering class of 1919.

The construction of three freshman dormitories in 1913 and a fourth in 1925 brought building in the Riverside area to an end for the time being. Yet members of the sophomore and junior classes remained without adequate housing. Although there was no immediate hope of big donations for additional dormitories, President Lowell continued to work toward the larger goal by purchasing, whenever they came on the market, parcels that the Associates had not already acquired. The future site of Dunster House (sixteen parcels on two irregular blocks) was bought between 1926 and 1929; the future site of Eliot House (then occupied by the power house of the West End Street Railway Company) in 1930. At the same time the boundaries of the area in which Harvard was interested expanded to Western Avenue and across the river to Soldiers Field.[20]

The second step toward achieving President Lowell's goal concerns the Gold Coast dormitories, those luxurious private halls located on Mount Auburn Street (fig. 154). Their construction also occurred before Lowell assumed office, and undoubtedly he would not have approved of it. President Eliot had encouraged private investment in student housing by promising that while he was president Harvard would not construct undergraduate dormitories of its own. But he could not bind future administrations to the same course, as Lowell would soon demonstrate.

Claverly Hall (1892) was the first of the luxurious dormitories on the Gold Coast. It contained fifty-five suites, each with a bath, and unlike quarters in the Yard the entire building was steam-heated; it did not have dining facilities because most inhabitants belonged to a final or a dining club. Claverly was financed by recent Harvard graduate Charles D. Wetmore, who would later become a prominent New York architect and suggest a formal plan for the South Yard that would have an impact on this Mount Auburn Street area. When Archibald Coolidge, also a graduate and later a history professor, proposed to construct the adjacent Randolph Hall on an even more luxurious scale, Wetmore suggested that he leave a ten-foot setback on Linden Street so as not to diminish the light in Claverly. Coolidge quite naturally rejected the idea and prepared to build his dormitory as planned. Wetmore then secretly purchased the small triangular block on the south side of Bow Street, opposite the proposed dormitory, and threatened to erect a ten-story structure that would put Randolph Hall in the shade. To prevent this Coolidge agreed to pull back his structure to the suggested setback and also to purchase the triangular lot (the present site of the *Lampoon* Building) at the exorbitant price that Wetmore had paid for it.[21]

Randolph Hall was erected in 1897 in the garden of Apthorp House (1760), one of the finest eighteenth-century mansions of Cambridge (fig. 155), through whose stately and well-proportioned doorway the young Charles Bulfinch visited his uncle East Apthorp, minister of Christ Church, in the years before the Revolution when Bulfinch was at Harvard. Randolph, with its Queen Anne turrets and red brick gables, is laid out around an open quadrangle in the manner of English colleges. It has much more light than Claverly, which crowds its lot like a New York apartment house. In 1906 Randolph Hall acquired an added attraction: private squash courts. Designed by the firm of Coolidge and Wright, Randolph contained fifty suites, which rented for $300 to $650 a year.[22]

By 1913 Lowell had been in office for four years and was ready to start construction of dormitories fronting the river. Because freshmen suffered most from the lack of adequate housing, the proposed dormitories were to be for them. Various advantages to the students were predicted. In an address delivered at Yale in 1907 Lowell had described the advantages of a residential college: "the obvious solution is to break the undergraduate body into groups like the English colleges, large enough to give each man a

154
Gold Coast Dormitories,
Mount Auburn Street, about
1910. The Harvard Lampoon
Building *(Edmund Wheel-*
wright, 1909) stands at the
fork, across from Randolph
Hall (Coolidge and Wright,
1897); Claverly Hall (George
Fogerty, 1892) is to the left of
Randolph.

155
Apthorp House (1760,
attributed to Peter Harrison;
photo c. 1885 – 1895), now
the Master's Residence for
Adams House.

185   *The River Houses and the South Yard*

chance to associate closely with a considerable number of his fellows, and not so large as to cause a division into exclusive cliques . . . In short, what we want is a group of colleges each of which will be national and democratic, a microcosm of the whole university." And in the President's Report for 1912–13 he referred to the freshman dormitories as providing "an opportunity for contact in cultured surroundings." Edward Forbes, in a letter apparently used in efforts to raise funds for the dormitories, expressed another aspect: "You will see that the President has two main ideas: the first one is to throw the whole freshman class together, making a unit of them as much as possible and giving the boys who come from places other than from the few great preparatory schools of New England and New York a better chance to know their fellow students; the second is to try to solve the problem of making a half-way house between the boy's life at school, where he has scarcely any freedom, and the college life into which he plunges with absolute freedom which he does not know how to use."[23]

To accommodate the entire freshman class, four dormitories were needed. For one building funds were on hand, bequeathed in 1902 by George Smith, an alumnus from St. Louis. Mrs. Russell Sage agreed to sponsor a second; with great effort Lowell found money for another (he and Mrs. Lowell themselves contributed $100,000); but the fourth had to be deferred.[24] The president was careful to reassure Forbes and the Associates that ample vistas were being kept open to the river and also to enlist their assistance in fundraising. Of the 705 entering freshmen in 1914, only 488 could be accommodated in the three new dormitories: 159 in Gore, 197 in Smith, and 132 in Standish. Of the rest, 22 found places in other college halls, 29 in private dormitories, and 17 in private homes; 149 freshmen lived at home.

Each of the dormitories was conceived as a separate architectural entity with its own lounges, library, and dining room, but all three shared a common kitchen (under Smith Hall). Rooms were arranged in suites, each with its own bath, individual bedrooms, a sitting room, and a fireplace, to house from one to six students. Instead of opening onto the long institutional corridors that had been used at Perkins and Conant Halls twenty years earlier, these suites were organized about entries in the early Harvard manner. Suites of single and multiple occupancy were placed next to one another in a deliberate effort to avoid enclaves of poor and wealthy students within any house. With the freshmen now taken care of and seniors living in Harvard Yard,[25] the two middle classes still had to shift for themselves; thus there was much yet to accomplish.

Step four, the acquisition of the Gold Coast dormitories, came soon after.[26] This task was not too difficult, because the dormitories had not proved profitable. Privately financed buildings, which had to pay taxes and amortize a capital investment, could not compete with those built from legacies. Their position became even worse when the university's enrollment dropped sharply in 1917 — from 5,656 to 3,684 — as the result of World War I. In such a climate the university was able to purchase on advantageous terms seven dormitories and to exchange the old College House (fig. 35) facing Harvard Square for Randolph Hall along with its squash courts and Apthorp House.[27] The College House, the least modern and desirable of the school's dormitories but valuable for its location, was renovated as offices; and in 1926 a movie theater was added in space that had once served as the college woodyard. Now the owner of the majority of the private dormitories and most of the land between the river and Mount Auburn, DeWolfe, and Dunster Streets, the university could proceed, when finances should permit, with plans for housing the remaining undergraduates.

An intermediate step was the construction in 1925 of the fourth freshman dormitory on the river, McKinlock Hall, and of the several dormitories that cloistered Harvard Yard. The latter, of course, are not part of the development of the South Yard, but they were needed before the house system could be put into effect in 1930.

The climax of the development of the South Yard was the creation of the seven Harvard houses (since expanded to ten). This spectacular architectural program was made possible by a gift by Edward S. Harkness in 1929 of over $13 million.[28] Such munificent support of Harvard by an alumnus of Yale requires some explanation. Harkness had long been interested in education and in improving the learning experience of students in large schools. His opinions were sufficiently strong to prompt him to offer to build Yale a number of residential halls modeled on the colleges of Oxford and Cambridge. The Yale faculty engaged in considerable discussion as to how the proposed buildings could be used to create a challenging academic environment; when they did not act within the time set by Harkness, he turned to President Lowell. Fortunately for Harvard, the two men were personally congenial; both were independently wealthy, accustomed to commanding, and given to prompt, businesslike decisions.[29]

Harkness approved of Lowell's proposed honors program open to all serious students, which appeared to tie in nicely with the house system. It provided each student with a tutor to direct his preparation for the general examination in his major field that came at the end of his senior year. Tutors would be assigned to the new houses where they would live or at least have an office and take some meals. Equally conducive to Harkness's goodwill was the promptness with which Lowell and the faculty acted and the fact that Harvard already owned the land that would be needed for the expansion. Indeed, the president even had architectural sketches of the kind of buildings he would like to see erected. In November 1928 Harkness indicated his support for one or two residential dormitories; soon this was extended to include housing for all upperclassmen. Exactly three months after his first meeting with Lowell, Harkness signed a letter promising more than $11 million to carry out the house plan (the final gift was considerably more).

To describe the new dormitories, President Lowell insisted on the term "house" instead of "college" because he feared that the latter might imply to alumni that the new plan was somehow going to diminish the importance of Harvard College. Ground for the first new building was broken in early spring of 1929; by September 1930 two new houses, Lowell and Dunster, were inaugurated; a third, Eliot House, erected on the site of the former power plant for the West End Street Railway Company, was open in 1931. In the meantime the four freshman halls were remodeled and expanded to form three houses, and Adams House was created by combining two private dormitories, Randolph and Westmorely.

Some opposition to the house system was voiced, especially by the final clubs, who saw it as a threat; a vocal minority denounced it as a scheme to undermine student freedom by extending a boarding school control into

156
Perspective sketch of the River Houses (Coolidge, Shepley, Bulfinch and Abbott, 1928).
The final arrangement of the River Houses incorporated the earlier freshman dormitories.
Right to left: Dunster House; Leverett House; Gore and Standish Halls (Winthrop House)
on the river with Lowell House and the Indoor Athletic Building behind; the triangular
yard of Eliot House and Kirkland House behind it.

the university. The administration was careful not to force any individual or group into the new system. Yet in 1930, when the houses opened with a capacity for 1,713 students, only 9 seniors, 35 juniors, and 33 sophomores elected not to live in them. Residents of a house were not required to be present at meals as had been the practice of the nineteenth-century university commons, but inasmuch as they paid for meals even when missed, attendance was fairly regular. The main disadvantage of the house system was that the cost of board and the most modest room was more than poor students had previously had to pay, and there were no dormitory scholarships. In 1930, when Harkness again offered dormitories to Yale, two improvements were made over the Harvard arrangement. The colleges, as they were called at Yale, were made somewhat smaller than the Harvard houses (accommodating about 200 instead of 250–300 students), and a special endowment provided funds for the Bursary system, whereby pay from a meaningful job offered assistance to students needing financial support.[30]

The Harvard houses along the river form one of Greater Boston's most majestic sights (fig. 156). Looking more like palatial residences than college dormitories, the structures are set among trees which unite them as a group yet keep the individual buildings from competing visually. Several towers are discernible above the treetops but not so many as to clutter the scene, and the houses open toward the almost idyllic foreground of the riverfront—that is, if one can forget the automobile traffic on Memorial Drive. The remarkable element of the design is how harmonious yet individual are the five large brick structures facing the river. Each appears to have grown separately in response to its own set of requirements, yet because those requirements were similar, the buildings have visual unity. Indeed, there is so little repetition among them that it is surprising to discover that all were designed by one architectural firm within a seventeen-year period.

These houses represent a conscious effort by the administration to extend the atmosphere of old Harvard Yard to the new South Yard and thus to symbolize the continuity of Harvard's "collegiate way of life." There was a conscious imitation in the River Houses of the architectural style used in the Yard, although the new buildings were necessarily much larger in scale (to accommodate 250 students instead of 64). Each house was situated and designed as a distinct entity. No two plans are alike, and some of the houses are fitted to very irregular sites. The architectural ornamentation is subtly handled, with one dormitory using details from a particular historical model, another from a different one. Thus each of the houses achieves an identifiable individuality.

Kirkland House (fig. 157) is the only one of the River Houses to use the twin-chimneyed gable connected by a horizontal parapet found at Massachusetts Hall. The stepped gable, volutes, and paired oculus windows of McKinlock Hall (Leverett House) evoke the Old State House in Boston (fig. 158). Appropriately, the doorways of McKinlock imitate the original front entrance of Hollis Hall, with pilasters superimposed on rusticated jambs (fig. 16) (this design was also used earlier at Lionel and Mower Halls). The florid scrollwork from the tympanum of Holden Chapel (fig. 14) provides a model for larger embellishment in the gables of Dunster House, and the unusual gable ends of Harvard Hall (fig. 20), with a pediment superimposed on a hip roof, are repeated at Standish Hall (Winthrop House). Because

157
*Kirkland House (Coolidge,
Shepley, Bulfinch and Abbott,
1913): gable end.*

Standish is considerably larger than Harvard Hall, however, its cornice was made more three-dimensional than that of the original, which was rather thin and worked in brownstone. When the scale of a new house required a heavier, more elaborate architectural accent than colonial prototypes provided, the designer did not hesitate to turn to opulent English precedents, as at Gore Hall (fig. 159), which recalls Sir Christopher Wren's late-seventeenth-century garden facade of Hampton Court. Another detail used was the console-supported balcony and enframed window of the east facade of the Old State House, which stood just across the street from the architects' office in Boston. This famous detail, already replicated at the new Fogg Museum (1925), was repeated in simpler form and smaller scale on McKinlock Hall and Eliot House.

Beyond such differences of detail, each house has a distinct character.[31] The Smith quadrangle of Kirkland House may be the least interesting. Its ornament, typical of the early 1900s, is elaborate but somewhat dry, and the courtyard is confining as well as rather dull since it can be read at a glance (fig. 160). Much livelier is the long narrow court framed by the annex, Bryan Hall, which is separated from Dunster Street only by fencing and planting around the master's garden.[32] Hicks House (fig. 161), which serves as the Kirkland House library, was built of wood in 1762; it furnishes a

191   The River Houses and the South Yard

160
*Smith Hall Court, Kirkland
House (Coolidge, Shepley,
Bulfinch and Abbott, 1913).*

161
Hicks House (1762) perpetuates the small scale of the original riverfront area of Cambridge.

welcome relief in scale and material, and it represents Harvard's first effort to preserve an early Cambridge building other than its own.[33] Most significantly, the placement of Kirkland House effectively screens the quiet tree-filled South Yard from noisy John F. Kennedy (Boylston) Street.

Eliot House (1930) uses an irregular plot to great advantage and is one of the best house designs from an architectural point of view (fig. 162). A skillful control of taller and lower sections placed at angles around a polygonal courtyard keeps this composition from resembling a barracks. Most effective is the way the south side of the complex opens toward the river, thus augmenting the feeling of spaciousness in the inner court. Screened by an iron fence and a monumental gate, this riverside opening is adroitly connected to the four-story corner pavilions of the house by blocks of intermediate size. Another successful feature results from the way in which the important intersection of John F. Kennedy Street and Memorial Drive, an acute angle, is counteracted by the concave southwestern facade of Eliot House, accented by colossal pilasters and great round-headed windows, those favorite Harvard means of achieving architectural accent. This handsome facade provides a fitting introduction to the university for those who approach from the river. Less felicitous is the dense volume of dormitory rooms, as indicated by the fenestration, placed above

162
*Eliot House: courtyard
(Coolidge, Shepley, Bulfinch
and Abbott, 1930). The great
tower of Eliot House is
equivocally related to the
building from which it rises.*

163
*Winthrop House: dining hall
(Coolidge, Shepley, Bulfinch
and Abbott, 1913).*

the large, hollow volume containing public rooms. Another shortcoming is the bulky Eliot tower emerging uncertainly — without means of visual support — from the roof of the principal block. Objections like these, of course, are academic, based on an awareness of the structural difficulties such solutions would have imposed for eighteenth-century builders limited to wood and masonry construction.

Standish and Gore Halls, now combined to form Winthrop House, are smaller in size and simpler in massing, a welcome foil to the larger scale of Eliot and Dunster.[34] And it is fortunate that neither has a tower; were it otherwise, the riverfront would look more stereotyped. The way these buildings are linked by handsome wrought-iron fences is also visually commendable. Gore Hall is enough wider than Standish to allow a more elaborate facade. Seven bays of the center block constitute a frontispiece faced with limestone, of which the middle three units are accented by engaged columns. Less heavily ornamented, but also built of stone in contrast to the red brick used elsewhere, are the three central bays of the wings. Gore Hall is one of Harvard's handsomest buildings. The fenestration of both Gore and Standish is so regular that it is surprising to find in each interior a two-story dining hall (fig. 163), arranged by lowering the hall floor to basement level.

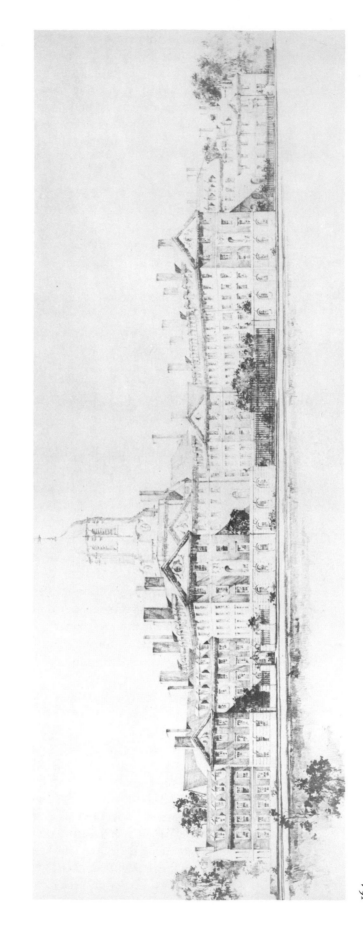

164
*Dunster House. Perspective drawing by Constantin Perzoff. Tom Tower at
Oxford provided inspiration for the tower of Dunster House, which rises above a
triangular segmented plan.*

Built twelve years later than Standish but of about the same size, McKinlock Hall (fig. 158) repeats the same basic U-shape. When it became Leverett House in 1930, a dining hall, including a penthouse residence for the house master, was added on the only accessible free land, a plot, unfortunately, that was much too small. Originally an additional section of Leverett called Mather Hall stood on the north side of Mill Street. One side of its rather cramped courtyard was formed by a line of squash courts, but when Mather Hall was transferred to Quincy House in 1958, these were demolished to open the court toward the yard of the new house of which it had become a part.

Ingenious planning made Dunster House (figs. 164, 165, 166) possible on a small triangular plot. Here the larger scale and heavy architectural trim are more reminiscent of English eighteenth-century Baroque prototypes than of American colonial buildings. The tower was inspired by Christopher Wren's Tom Tower (1681) at Christ Church, Oxford. The softer profile and integrated shapes of the Dunster tower retain the spirit of its model, while Charles Coolidge and his associates, with the freedom in manipulation of historic motifs that characterizes their best work, transposes its Gothic ornament to Classical form.

Adams House consists of an interesting assortment of structures ranging in date from 1760 to 1931, including an important eighteenth-century mansion, two former Gold Coast luxury dormitories (Randolph and Westmorely Halls), and a private squash court. Additional construction from the Lowell period consists of the upper and lower lounges and the dining hall (which recalls the pump room of an eighteenth-century British spa), as well as a five-story tower and Entry C (fig. 167).[35] The tower, capped by a hip roof with a cupola reminiscent of Harvard Hall, provides a focal point for these rather disparate elements. On the interior the lower lounge and main entrance hold surprises; only here, among all the Harkness houses, are there departures from the Georgian Revival tradition. In the lounge is a handsome antique Renaissance mantel from Italy (fig. 168), and the main entrance has an intricate Mudejar dome over the principal staircase (fig. 169), a vivacious Moor among so many well-bred Brahmins. This exotic stylistic deviation is suggested as well by the Flemish gables, oriels, and multiple chimneys of the courtyard (fig. 170).

The largest and perhaps the handsomest of the River Houses is Lowell House (figs. 171, 172, 173), erected upon the knoll where the first settlers of Cambridge had planned to build their fort.[36] Since Lowell House consists of two enclosed quadrangles, the result might have been as confining as at Smith Hall. Such a feeling is avoided by exploiting irregularities in the topography and varying the heights of units enclosing the courtyards. The entrance through the tower is uppermost in the elevation, and here also the building, which is four stories on a high basement with a raised cornice, reaches its greatest height (fig. 172). The dining hall and lounges facing one another on the south side of the court not only stand on lower ground but are just one story high. Thus one easily looks over them, and the quadrangle appears larger than it is. Building blocks on the east and west side of the main court are arranged at intermediate levels so that there is constant variation in floor heights, and the wing between the two courtyards is held to two stories. The courts are connected by interesting vaulted passageways with changing levels. The sense of space of these quadrangles is

165
*Dunster House: tower. The
wrought iron gates and
baroque cartouche in the
Dunster pediment relate it
stylistically to early buildings
in the Yard.*

166
Dunster House: the elaborately paneled walls of the dining room.

*167
Adams House: Entry C,
viewed along Bow Street; the
dinning hall is in the
foreground.*

168
Adams House: common room.

169
Adams House: interior stair.

170

Adams House: courtyard of Randolph Hall. The interior staircases are articulated in the picturesque elevation of this courtyard, punctuated with elaborate Flemish gables.

Lowell House (Coolidge, Shepley, Bulfinch and Abbott, 1929). Perspective drawing by Constantin Perzoff.

172
Lowell House: courtyard.

thus less static and restrictive than that of Smith Hall. The design would have been strengthened, however, had the base of the tower been more clearly differentiated from the walls of the facade and forecourt.

Large and imposing buildings can be monotonous if the neighborhood does not possess some variety in scale and spacing. The South Yard avoids monotony by means of the varied placement of the houses along the curving bank of the river and the irregular, tree-filled park at the foot of Dunster Street. Also essential to the noninstitutional feeling of the area is the continued presence of several dwellings, with yards and gardens, which introduce a nice visual rhythm to the streetscape. The cottage at 17 South Street is noteworthy, constructed on a bank supported by a rough stone retaining wall that recalls the way the district looked in the early nineteenth century.[37] Other early residences, all owned by the university, stand at 21 South, 41 Winthrop, and 53 and 69 Dunster Streets.

It is natural to compare the South Yard with the campus of the Business School on the opposite side of the Charles River. Dating from 1926, the Business School was built between the freshman dormitories of 1913 and the Harkness Houses of 1929. It benefited from the university fund drive of 1925, which also raised $15 million for the construction of chemistry laboratories and the new Fogg Museum. Construction was assured at the outset of the campaign when George Baker, a New York banker, subscribed the full $5 million estimated cost of the Business School complex. At his suggestion the design of the new campus was opened to competition, the winner of which was the venerable New York firm of McKim, Mead and White (fig. 174).[38] (By this time, however, Charles McKim, the most active of the original partners, had been dead sixteen years.) The winning design was unique in that its plan faced directly onto the river, ignoring a power station (later demolished and replaced by Eliot House) that stood on the

174
*Harvard Business School:
unexecuted competition
drawing (Coolidge, Shepley,
Bulfinch and Abbott, 1926).*

opposite side. All other entrants sited their plans west toward the stadium or diagonally to the west corner on the river. The correspondence between President Lowell and the architects has a distant and critical note that reminds us of Julian Coolidge's comment that Lowell believed only Charles Coolidge was suited to design buildings for Harvard.

As construction of the Business School progressed it became evident that the cost estimates had been low, and economies had to be effected; decorative features such as towers for some dormitory blocks were eliminated, cast concrete ornament was substituted for limestone, and the marble trim of Baker Library was reduced to a token. Despite these difficulties, the Business School is an impressive counterpart to the Harvard Houses. The main quadrangle, along with the riverbank parks, forms a great open mall between Baker Library and Eliot House across the river, each with its gilded cupola. In contrast to the openness and formality of the main quadrangle are a series of inner residential courtyards of different sizes, grouped symmetrically. Though smaller, the scheme somewhat recalls the plan of the Royal Naval Hospital at Greenwich or Gabriel's Ecole Militaire and J. H. Mansart's Les Invalides in Paris. The rigid symmetry is relieved by the cross-axis of Harvard Way, laid out as an arc corresponding to the bend of the river. The curving vista along this street is one of the most attractive aspects of the Business School's campus. The designer attempted to offset the institutional formality of the scheme by breaking the extensive dormitory blocks into units of more domestic scale: large three-story blocks are interspersed with freestanding two-story units covered with white stucco (fig. 175), and long stretches of facade are subdivided into sections with different wall surfacing and fenestration to relieve monotony. Variety is also achieved by interrupting the cornice with gables or pediments, for which there are three alternative designs. Such variations are somewhat mechanical,

175
Alumni Center, Harvard Business School (McKim, Mead and White, 1926).

and there is an awkward disparity between the domestic scale of the subdivided blocks and the grand formality of the overall scheme. Nevertheless, the library with its giant portico provides a dominant focus for the campus, and the great reading room that extends the entire length of the building on the second floor is a magnificent space (fig. 176). The subdivision of this room into three parts by huge Venetian arches echos the scheme for the remodeled picture galleries in the south wing of Versailles. In this room, at least, the tight budget did not preclude the use of fine materials.

Their riverside locations and similar architecture make comparisons inevitable between the Business School and the Harvard Houses. The plan of the Business School is big and mechanical; the units are so interchangeable that they lack individuality and identity. By contrast, the Houses appear to have grown naturally, each in its own way, each with a distinct character. The quality of the decorative trim and woodwork is superb in the Houses, where the budget was ample, but only passable in the Business School, where funds ran short. The difference between the Business School and the Houses is the difference between reasonably good and extraordinarily good Georgian Revival design. Indeed, the River Houses of Lowell and Harkness are among the finest examples of Georgian Revival architecture in America.[39]

Later work in this style at the Business School includes the Dean's Residence of 1929, another good, formal design by Coolidge, Shepley,

176
Baker Library reading room, Harvard Business School (McKim, Mead and White, 1926).

177
Cotting House, Harvard Business School (Robert Shaw Sturgis, 1965), the last Georgian Revival building at Harvard.

178
Cotting House interior.

Bulfinch and Abbott. More recently, the Cotting House (1966) by Robert Shaw Sturgis, fronting North Harvard Street, occupied the remaining site at the west end of the campus (fig. 177). It has the distinction of being the very last Georgian Revival edifice erected at Harvard. One is grateful that the material and massing of neighboring structures were thus respected. Yet Sturgis was faced with a formidable design task on a constricted site between the Business School campus and the muscular concrete stadium. The Georgian building, envisioned as a memorial by its donors, Mr. and Mrs. Charles Cotting, fulfills its purpose with elegance.[40] A central hall bisects the plan east to west, allowing for a formal facade on North Harvard Street while maintaining direct access to the Business School behind. The proportions of ornamental detail, moldings, woodwork, window casings, and returns were consciously enhanced throughout by Sturgis, designing in an age that no longer provided the craftsmanship and hand-finished structural components of Charles Coolidge's era (fig. 178). It is architecture derived stylistically from an earlier time, but this tough little building provides a worthy final chapter to the saga of Georgian design that has been the underlying historic theme of Harvard architecture.[41]

9

President Conant, Gropius,
and Modernism

Hampered first by the Depression and then by restrictions imposed by World War II, the administration of President James Bryant Conant (1933–1953) had comparatively little opportunity for building, and the university erected only fourteen structures during the Conant years.[1] World War II marked an abrupt change in the history of Harvard architecture, a shift from neo-Georgian forms to the International Style. While this phenomenon reflected Conant's egalitarian and scientific educational concepts and the new political and social internationalism that followed the war, much of the architectural change came about because of the appointment of Walter Gropius, pioneer of European functionalism, to the faculty of the Graduate School of Design in 1937. This appointment revolutionized architectural education and placed Harvard at its forefront in America.[2] The advent of Gropius was to influence American architecture more than did all of the buildings of Lowell's administration. Yet a surprised, even embarrassed Harvard constituency was slow to avail itself of his assistance, and he taught for twelve years before being invited to design a structure for the university.

At the same time President Conant, an internationally recognized chemist, was leading Harvard to a position of intellectual leadership in the sciences, and building during the Conant years reflected this commitment. The number of laboratories in the North Yard was increased during the war, and then in 1951 the construction of Allston Burr Lecture Hall embodied the spirit of Conant's General Studies Program, aimed at integrating the sciences into the curriculum for all university undergraduates.[3] President Conant's long-standing interest in German culture was also to prove significant for Harvard during his administration.[4]

The first portion of Conant's tenure, culminating with the celebration of the Harvard Tercentennial in 1936, extended the architectural momentum of the later Lowell years. Rising American nationalism provided a cornerstone for the Tercentennial celebration, which produced not only Samuel Eliot Morison's great research on Harvard's history but also the closing days of neo-Georgian architecture for the university. One of the most visible buildings of the Conant era, by reason of its striking facade and prominent location, is Littauer Center, for many years the home of the School of Government (fig. 179). Designed by Coolidge, Shepley, Bulfinch and Abbott in 1937, it stands on an embankment above the Cambridge Street underpass. Its formal facade establishes an impressive terminus at one end of the large public space that includes Harvard Square. No one driving north or east out of the Square can avoid confronting this grave and stately building, lacking in applied ornament as were many designs of its time. So striking a form in so prominent a location (as prescribed by Littauer himself) must earn the envy of those autocratic nineteenth-century donors, Austin and Hemenway, who demanded that their edifices be placed in conspicuous positions. This building, with its imposing six-columned Ionic portico, has a mausoleum-like grandeur, and its calm, enduring mien reminds us that there is no substitute for hard granite. The last Harvard building in the Imperial tradition, Littauer is a conscious adaptation by the Coolidge firm of Charles Bulfinch's design for Massachusetts General Hospital, and in monumentality it also parallels his visionary schemes for the development of the Old Yard (fig. 25).⁵ Littauer represents what one hopes will be the last attempt at Harvard to confine rooms of dissimilar function behind an arbitrarily balanced facade: in this case, the two levels of offices to the left of the entrance and the high-ceilinged library on the right.

The siting of Littauer is its least successful aspect. Erected on the site of old Hemenway Gymnasium, it was situated in the nineteenth-century manner with overriding concern for its appearance from the street. Its imposing facade and its axial relation to Peabody Street (a thoroughfare since subsumed by northbound traffic on Massachusetts Avenue) accent the fact that it conforms to the building line of Cambridge Street (a line that later, in 1970, controlled the siting of the Undergraduate Science Center). This south facade is fine; less successful is the way in which Littauer disregards the open space behind it to the north. Its plain rear elevation (fig. 180) establishes yet one more direction for the already confused angles of the building lines of Austin Hall, Jefferson Laboratory, and Paine Music Building.⁶ Because of its size and the crisp simplicity of its shape, it defines with distressing clarity one side of a park–cum–parking lot — surely the most awkward public space in all of Harvard. Probably the only way to tame such an area is to fill it with trees and thus obscure the buildings that define it. To have placed the building parallel to Austin or Jefferson and thus to have established a smaller but regular courtyard would not have detracted seriously from the formal vista, and the amount of space "wasted" in front of the structure would have been negligible. This planning blunder was committed by Charles Coolidge's firm, but he had been dead for a year by the time it happened.⁷

This corner of the North Yard was further jumbled by the construction of the present Hemenway Gymnasium (fig. 181) by the Coolidge firm a few months after Littauer. This smaller replacement for the old gymnasium of the same name was constructed for the benefit of law and other graduate students whose places of study and residence are in the North Yard. It introduces yet another scale, building material, and style of architecture to an already confused environment. The color and texture of its brick would have been good in almost any other place, and its design is unobtrusive; but a truly inspired building was required to improve the spatial order and harmonize the disparate architectural elements of this difficult location. The new Hemenway Gymnasium is simpler, duller, and less imaginative than Coolidge's great neo-Georgian designs of the 1920s.

Two libraries in Harvard Yard, Houghton and Lamont, one built just before the war, the other immediately after it, mark the start of architectural

181
Second Hemenway Gymnasium (Coolidge, Shepley, Bulfinch and Abbott, 1938).

change. About Houghton Library (1941) there is a refined, somewhat precious quality, appropriate for a structure housing rare books and manuscripts (fig. 182). The design and execution of this edifice are exquisite; no expense was spared to make it a safe and worthy storehouse for the treasures it was to contain. Most of the details of the building were designed by Richard Dean, then a new associate architect in the Perry, Shaw and Hepburn office. Dean was able to maintain the pristine rectangular plan of the structure (fig. 183) by placing most of the stacks below grade, an idea suggested by wartime measures for protection against bombing.

The tradition that began with the elaborate interior decoration of the library in Harvard Hall III in 1764 (fig. 19) and continued in both Widener and Baker libraries reached its apogee at Houghton. For example, in the great south gallery even the floor-to-ceiling walnut paneling is painted in correct eighteenth-century manner, despite the rich wood of which it is made. With its two fireplaces, twin brass chandeliers, and finely detailed woodwork, this is probably the most beautiful traditional room of domestic scale at Harvard (fig. 184). But less than forty years after completion, this room already appeared to belong to history: it seemed unlikely that anything further of its kind would be built in this country except by way of historic restoration. The building is an elegant coda to the Georgian Revival manner begun at Harvard fifty years earlier. To be accurate, however, one should refer to its style as Late Georgian or Federal Revival; its elongated proportions and delicate exterior window and door caps supported by consoles

213 *President Conant, Gropius, and Modernism*

182
Houghton Library (Perry, Shaw and Hepburn, 1941). Drawing by R. C. Dean.

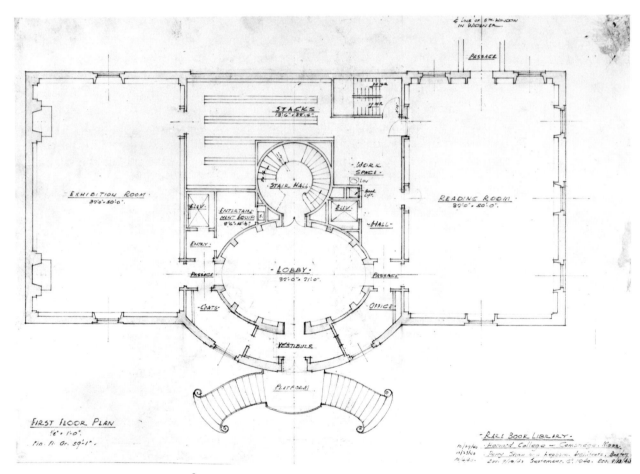

FIRST FLOOR PLAN

183
Houghton Library: first-floor plan. Drawing by R. C. Dean.

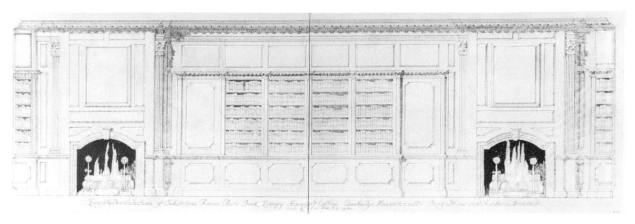

184
Houghton Library: south gallery. Drawing by R. C. Dean. The raised Georgian paneling, designed by the architects of Williamsburg, recalls the interior of Harvard's first library in Harvard Hall III (fig. 19).

derive from Bulfinch's third Harrison Gray Otis house (1806) on Beacon Street in Boston, and the intricate plan, with its oval entry hall and circular staircase, is based on Federal precedents.

Houghton Library was built at about the last moment in which it was possible to do such work. A few months later shortages of materials occasioned by the war would have made construction impossible; after the war the cost of materials and labor would have precluded such an undertaking for financial reasons alone. Today there are few designers and craftsmen capable of duplicating such work. And yet the same architects returned to design the oval Johnson Room (opened in 1977) in the unfinished attic space above the entry hall. Here they have applied the same high standards of quality, using original molds by the English architect Robert Adam (whose work inspired both Bulfinch and Samuel McIntire of Salem) for the elaborate plaster ceiling.

All the details at Houghton are wrought with scrupulous accuracy for historic precedent, a fact that is not surprising considering that its architects were the same firm entrusted with the restoration of Colonial Williamsburg in Virginia. Given their archaeological respect for precedent, it is interesting to note the creativity with which the designers employed an Early Georgian (c. 1740) style for the paneling in the main gallery but very Late Georgian or Federal (c. 1800) for the plan and the exterior (the dates are relative to Boston, not England). When Houghton was erected it must have appeared to be a rather small and esoteric building to place on the only side of Widener Library to which some future addition might have been attached, thus blocking future expansion into the only corner of the yard that was not already filled. This apparent impasse was avoided, however, by following the example of Houghton's underground stacks. The next generation of architects added two more libraries, one below ground level, the other on the knoll-top site of the old Dana-Palmer house, and connected them all by tunnels.[8]

The distinguished librarian Keyes Metcalf, brought to Harvard by President Conant in the 1930s, had worked closely with Dean on the plans for Houghton. Along with Conant, Metcalf assumed an even larger role in planning Lamont Library (1946), the first building undertaken in Harvard Yard after the war. Although it faced the same quadrangle as Houghton, the new design, by Coolidge, Shepley, Bulfinch and Abbott, discarded the

185
*Lamont Library (Coolidge,
Shepley, Bulfinch and Abbott,
1947).*

rarified Federal manner of its neighbor and became the first large building at Harvard designed in the contemporary idiom (fig. 185). Gone are the wooden, double-hung windows with muntins, the slate-covered pitched roofs with a multitude of dormers, the wooden gutter cornices with supporting modillions, and the elaborately molded doorframes. These changes were as much a matter of economy as of fashion, but in the enthusiasm of conversion to the new creed of functionalism, such design was hailed as honesty of expression. Despite this departure from the style that had become traditional at Harvard, Lamont does retain the customary color scheme of brick with white trim — though its windowframes are limestone, not wood trim painted white. The design is so restrained that it does not compete with Houghton or other traditional buildings nearby.

In the interior of Lamont, blond wood and reading rooms lighted by wide expanses of windows exemplify the International Style. An especially handsome example of this idiom is the second floor Poetry Room (fig. 186), which was designed by Alvar Aalto, whose Municipal Library in Viipuri, Finland (1933–1935), was known to Metcalf. At this time Aalto was designing Baker House Dormitory (1946–1949) at the Massachusetts Institute of Technology in collaboration with the Perry Dean office. Baker House was the most revolutionary architectural design in Boston at this time, and the poetry room at Lamont, with its recording and listening

186
Lamont Library: second-floor
Poetry Room, designed by
Alvar Aalto.

facilities, was the first such room in America. Lamont functions as the undergraduate noncirculating library, where stacks are open and where reserve books, popular periodicals, and microfilm are located. Placing these heavily used services in a separate building frees Widener to function as a scholars' library.

The irony of Gropius's unexploited presence at Harvard becomes clear in a comparison of the retardetaire modernism of the Lamont exterior with the degree to which the Art Deco, that streamlined early Moderne style, had already penetrated into Boston: by 1946 modern architecture, although less common than in New York, Miami, or Los Angeles, had made marked inroads into local design.[9] Even in 1937, the year Harvard erected the conservative Littauer Center, the same firm, Coolidge, Shepley, Bulfinch and Abbott, also designed the svelte B & B Chemical Company on the banks of the Charles. At B & B, as at the White Building at Massachusetts General Hospital, the firm used a glass brick central staircase, elegant signage, and glazed white brick—materials that were already familiar in Europe and other parts of the country but that would appear at Harvard only a decade later amid storms of controversy and criticism. Gropius thus found himself, when he arrived in late 1937, in a most curious milieu. Supported strongly by Dean Joseph Hudnut and President Conant, he would soon lead the most advanced architectural curriculum in America.

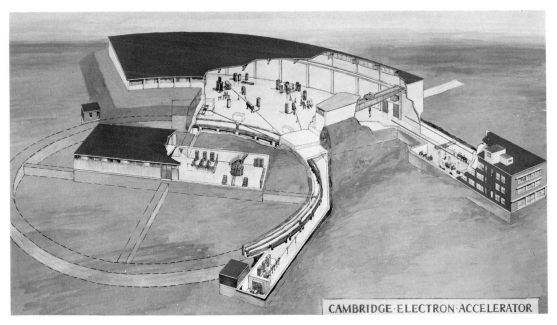

187
Nuclear Laboratory (Coolidge, Shepley, Bulfinch and Abbott, 1949).

188
Cyclotron, Cambridge Electron Accelerator (Charles T. Main, Engineers, 1946, 1957).

Conant, though he appears to have had comparatively little architectural interest, was conceptually a scientist, and the pseudoscientific rationale of the Bauhaus legacy must have had strong appeal.[10] And Conant's fundamental understanding of things German necessarily was a bond with Gropius. These predilections were underscored by the president's strong belief in the unique opportunity of universities such as Harvard to provide the matrix for great thinkers, of which in the late 1930s Gropius was fully acknowledged to be one.[11] Yet the colonial image of the Tercentennial, the afterglow of the neo-Georgian genius of Charles Coolidge, would take more than a decade to subside in the bricks and mortar of Harvard even while the intellectual momentum of modern functionalism flourished at the School of Design.

Most of the buildings erected during the Conant administration were constructed for scientific or engineering research and are located in sections of the North Yard where external appearance was not much considered. A cluster of two-story structures north of the University Museum was built to house electronic and nuclear laboratories. Consisting of two wings and located somewhat behind the others is the Nuclear Laboratory (1949) (fig. 187). In front of it stand the administrative offices and the former cyclotron building of the Cambridge Electron Accelerator, erected in 1946 by Coolidge, Shepley, Bulfinch and Abbott and extended in 1957 by Charles T. Main Engineers (fig. 188). The latter is a huge structure with a quarter-round shape, shielded on the outside with an earth embankment. The adjacent office building, now designated only as 42 Oxford Street, utilizes glass brick and strip windows with projecting metal sun shades and is a typical industrial building of the period. The Acoustic Research and Vanserg Laboratories, put up in 1942–43, were even simpler utilitarian structures of temporary construction. The Acoustic Laboratory, a wartime research laboratory attached to Cruft and containing an anechoic (echo-free) chamber, was demolished in 1971, but the wooden Vanserg Building behind the Biological Laboratory still stands.

Occupying the grounds of the old Botanic Garden, which had been discontinued during the war, the Botanic Garden Apartments by Des Granges and Steffian were erected in 1949, when housing for returning veterans was critically needed. The apartments were built at the insistence of the City of Cambridge, which otherwise was prepared to take possession of the land by eminent domain. Efficient if architecturally bland student housing of this caliber can be found at almost any land grant school in the country.

Immediately following the war, in 1946, Coolidge, Shepley, Bulfinch and Abbott began work on the Aiken Computation Center (fig. 189). Located in the northeast corner of Holmes Quadrangle, the computer center today is really two buildings, one deftly perched on top of the other. The lower was an economy-minded product of the war era, which used wooden sash (the only sort then available) placed contiguously to simulate the then-fashionable strip window. When expansion was required in 1964, the old structure was deemed inadequate to carry an additional story. A series of concrete piers was added just outside the perimeter of the old edifice, and these carry a system of girders to support the second building. The depth of the girders creates a dead space above the roof of the original building that is too low to be used as office or storage space; it is expressed on the

189
Aiken Computation Center
(Coolidge, Shepley, Bulfinch
and Abbott, 1946; expanded
1964). In 1964 a superstruc-
ture was added on piers above
the simple postwar building.

exterior by a bank of vertical louvers of wood. The rather tricky stair tower midway between Aiken and Pierce Halls, and connected to them by bridges, was constructed at the same time.

Other Conant buildings are the Gordon McKay Laboratory (1951) on Oxford Street (fig. 190) and the University Herbarium (1953), both by Coolidge, Shepley, Bulfinch and Abbott. The Herbarium, unsuccessful from a visual point of view, was discussed in Chapter 7 as a part of the large complex of museums and biological laboratories on Divinity Avenue. The detailing of the Gordon McKay Laboratory is not distinguished, yet its simple mass illustrates the positive environmental role that an auxiliary building, which does not aspire to be an architectural showpiece, can perform in blocking in an architectural space. Since the addition of two more stories in 1961 McKay is even more effective in defining the Oxford Street corridor.[12]

After Gropius's appointment in 1937 the architectural curriculum had been completely revised. Landscape architecture, design, and planning were brought under one all-inclusive umbrella. Architectural history was banished from the core curriculum to elective status; Kenneth Conant (no relation to the president), the sole instructor in architectural history, became more closely associated with the History of Art department at the Fogg Museum, while the Design School under Gropius developed its iconoclastic theories behind the neoclassical facade of Robinson Hall. Both Gropius and his students were ready to implement modern architecture at Harvard by 1949, when Gropius received his first commission for the

190
Gordon McKay Laboratory (Coolidge, Shepley, Bulfinch and Abbott, 1953).

191
Graduate Center: exterior elevation with World Tree *by Richard Lippold. Gropius' first commission from Harvard introduced the full-blown International Style.*

192
Graduate Center: Harkness Commons, concourse and ramp (Gropius and TAC, 1948–1952).

university: the Graduate Center, a counterpart for graduate students of Lowell's undergraduate houses. His success in obtaining the commission lay dually in the low budget quoted by Gropius for the job and the vigorous support of Paul Buck, Dean of Arts and Sciences and Provost of the university during the war years, who was shocked at Harvard's neglect of Gropius.

The Graduate Center was not only Gropius's first work for Harvard but also one of the first large commissions for TAC, The Architects Collaborative, an association of Gropius and several former students that has since become one of the largest and most influential architectural firms in the world.[13] When erected, the complex was one of the few examples of adequately understood International Style architecture in this country, and it generated great enthusiasm. But the perspective of a quarter-century makes it clear that it was epoch-making only in a limited frame of reference: it merely brought Harvard and New England abreast of European practice of about 1930.

The Graduate Center is, however, a more orthodox example of the International Style than Lamont Library, built three years earlier. Here are flat roofs, severe geometry, strip windows, and elimination of ornament (fig. 191). There is also a straightforward use of modular materials: brick and glass, iron for columns and window frames, concrete used in blocks and

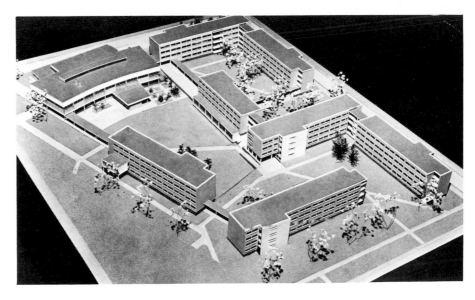

193
Graduate Center: Harkness Commons with mural by Joan Miró.

194
Model of the Graduate Center.

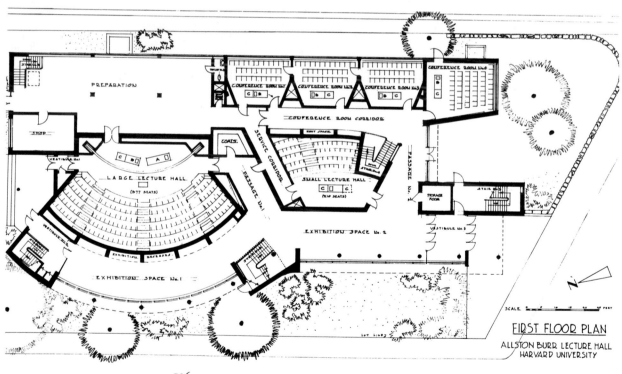

196
Allston Burr plan.

for columns but not yet for massive poured shapes. As at the contemporaneous Allston Burr Lecture Hall, a light-hued brick is used, in this case
cream-colored. The aesthetic impact of the complex comes from the informal but structured grouping of seven three-story residential blocks and
Harkness Commons ranged about two small quadrangles and a sunken mall.
The geometry is clean and sharp with some relief provided by overhangs,
retaining walls, and the sheathing of basement walls with dark brick. The
whole has a feeling of clarity and lightness, a quality enhanced by the thin
canopies that shelter walkways between dormitory pavilions. Interest is
focused on Harkness Commons (figs. 192, 193) by its more complex
geometry (a curved facade and an overhanging second story) and by its
location on the lower level of the mall. The Commons is also enlivened by
the World Tree, a large outdoor metal sculpture by Richard Lippold, and by
interior murals by Josef Albers and Joan Miró. A comparison of the Graduate Center with the buildings Harvard has erected since 1960 demonstrates
how far modern architecture has moved from the sparse, puritanical
functionalism of these early days.[14]

Of greater importance than innovation in design is the siting of Gropius's
building complex. A breakthrough in the organization of this portion of the
North Yard came when Harvard obtained permission to close Jarvis Street,
thereby making possible an extension of the Yard to include Jarvis Field.
This enlargement permitted a rectangular termination at the north end of
Holmes Quadrangle (previously precluded by the angle made by Jarvis
Street), and then the formation of the semi-independent Graduate Yard
beyond. The four-foot-lower graduate mall can be flooded in the winter for
ice skating — a legal requirement because the committee in charge of
building Memorial Hall had given this site to Harvard to use for athletics.
Aesthetically the sunken mall provides the Graduate Center with a core that
is distinct from Holmes Quadrangle (fig. 194).[15] Similarly, the covered
walkway between Harkness and Child Hall screens the graduate precincts
from Holmes Quadrangle. And yet the two areas relate easily to each other.
The south facade of Harkness Commons acts as a terminus for the long
walkway through the Quadrangle that parallels the east facade of Langdell
Hall, and the white limestone and blue glazed brick of the new building are
compatible with its venerable neighbor. A compromise was reached by
lowering the eastern wing, originally intended to obscure Perkins Hall
completely, but the one point on which TAC refused to conform with the
environment was in the choice of cream-colored brick. Today one questions
the rationale for this choice, and it is fortunate that this complex of light
brick structures is relegated to a corner of the larger campus. The same
group placed on the river near the older undergraduate houses would have
been offensive, more because of color than because of its flat roofs or style
of architecture.[16]

The university's other early modern building, Allston Burr Lecture Hall
(1951), stood just outside Harvard Yard on Quincy Street until it was
destroyed in 1983. Erected by Coolidge, Shepley, Bulfinch and Abbott
(with Jean Paul Carlhian as designing architect) in close approximation of
the International Style, it showed more verve and originality than the
contemporaneous Graduate Center.[17] Characteristic were bold, symmetrical
massing, the use of flat roofs and overhanging forms, emphasis on continuous strips of windows and horizontal lines, and a renunciation of applied

197
*Allston Burr: large lecture hall
interior.*

decoration (fig. 195). The high-budget building was a monument to President Conant's curricular vision: it was erected to provide large lecture rooms for science. This purpose was expressed on the exterior by two large fan-shaped masses that projected above the box-like shape of the remainder of the block filled with seminar rooms, offices, and lobbies (figs. 196, 197). These were designed with specified numbers of seats, sight lines to the podium, and other requirements deemed essential to the scientific teaching program for which the building was intended. They ultimately were responsible for the structure's demolition, for its interior, unlike the low-budget open space of the contemporaneous Gordon McKay Laboratory, could not be adapted to alternate use when the new Undergraduate Science Center was built in 1970.

The organization of strong geometric forms, reading the more clearly because of the light color of the brick masonry, provided the principal aesthetic interest of Allston Burr (fig. 198). This choice of brick was a departure from the white stucco that would have been used in the earlier stages of the movement in Europe, but it was justified here in terms of upkeep in the grimy atmosphere of Cambridge. This choice also avoided the

198
Allston Burr: west facade.

problem of articulation of the fenestration in a contrasting stone (such as that used at Lamont Library), which would have been required had red brick been used. The building's position, isolated by three heavily traveled streets, minimized its relation to Harvard Yard and thus the dissimilarity of its architectural style and materials. At the same time the Baroque undulation of its facade, enlivened by the shifting shadows of trees, was extraordinarily successful relative to the neighboring bombast of Memorial Hall.[18]

The intrusion into Charles Coolidge's red brick Harvard of the modern white brick of Allston Burr Lecture Hall and the Graduate Center was not accomplished without controversy. A strongly worded three-cornered debate evolved not only between modernists and traditionalists but also between the two modern factions, as Gropius's students, who had been involved with the austere plans for the Graduate Center, criticized the lavishness of Allston Burr. Opposition arose initially to the removal of 38 Quincy Street (1845), a charming frame house that had been the residence of several Harvard worthies. While furious letters filled the pages of the *Harvard Alumni Bulletin* attacking the site for Allston Burr because of the required demolition, the architect Stanley B. Parker dismantled the porch from the Quincy Street house for reuse as a gazebo at his summer home in Plymouth.[19] Other letter-writers invoked the stalwart and traditional qualities of Allston Burr himself and attacked as inappropriate the visual character of the building that was to bear his name.[20] Meanwhile, students in Gropius's Master's Class spoke vociferously against the high-budgeted Allston Burr Hall, which they considered to be in defiance of the puritanical principles of good modern architecture that they were attempting to implement in the low-cost and restrained design of the Graduate Center.

The modern design framework of the entire university building program was attacked head-on in October 1950 by the architect R. Clipston Sturgis (Harvard 1881), who had designed the Georgian Cambridge Fire Station opposite Memorial Hall and the wings of the Massachusetts State House and had restored the Old North Church in Boston in 1911. "*Time Magazine* of September 15," he wrote, "published a cut of the brutally ugly buildings designed by Gropius for Harvard and actually had the temerity to say 'the buildings are true to an old Harvard tradition' and added 'from Colonial to Bulfinch Federal, to Victorian Gothic, to nineteenth century Romanesque, Harvard has moved with the tides of U.S. architecture' . . . these new buildings show not a gleam of interest in Harvard's past nor any sense of value of beauty." To Sturgis the problem of the Graduate Center was secondary to that of Allston Burr Lecture Hall, which was nearer the Yard and opposite his fire station. In April 1951 he again wrote to the *Bulletin:* "It is an inexpressibly sad day for the architecture of Harvard when such unsightly buildings . . . become a part of the Harvard group . . . It is sad also to know that a firm which once included that great artist George Shepley, is now associated with and responsible for this degradation of architecture. No possible stretch of the imagination can see any sign of beauty in these structures. There is no excuse for such absolute disregard of Harvard's traditional right to have buildings that are at once functional, and, above all, beautiful."[21]

Gropius's Master's Class students responded to Sturgis in a letter to the *Bulletin* attacking his traditional position and laced with the new social concerns of architecture: "Must we take the word of our older alumni that ivory tower is the only true architecture? An ivory tower, to be sure, is a beautiful thing—ivory costs even more than marble. And a tower certainly is functional—it protects us from the sight of all the grubby creatures below. But Harvard, as she has on recent occasions reminded the world, prides herself, not on her ivory tower, but rather on her 'free marketplace of ideas' . . . Universal education, some say, is dangerous because people might learn "too much" and rebel against established authority. But imaginative authority checked by an informed electorate makes democracy unshakable. Similarly we feel that universal understanding of modern forces, human and technical, risking occasional mistakes, is the way to a new architecture as strong and as rich as any architecture of the past."[22]

When the Graduate Center finally opened, Gropius's remarks were brief at the dedication, and President Conant invoked the economy of the effort while avoiding matters of aesthetics. False birds perched that spring in Richard Lippold's steel *World Tree,* and a series of cartoons depicted it as a clothesline,[23] but Modernism had come to Harvard with splendid contentiousness. By the time President Conant stepped down in 1953 to become High Commissioner to Germany, a new age of Harvard architecture had begun. The virulence of the controversy surrounding the construction of Harvard's first modern buildings seems remote after a quarter-century, but its importance was profound. One of its effects was to separate art history from architecture. Kenneth Conant, affected by the antihistorical bias of the 1940s, gave up the practice of architecture for teaching and research and went on to publish his famous reconstructions of the Medieval monastery at Cluny.[24]

In 1953, a year before he was to retire, Walter Gropius resigned from the leadership of the School of Design in protest over Dean Hudnut's cancellation of his course "Design I." Gropius's theories of teaching, a philosophy of approach to architecture, were dominant in educating a generation of students. He always relied upon the collaborative method of design, and his ideas changed the monumental and monolithic traditional objectives of architecture to incorporate collaboration, social responsibility, and urban planning as legitimate elements of the architectural process. Yet Gropius's own work has been visually disappointing, an assessment which becomes increasingly apparent as the Graduate Center complex ages and the importance of his influence on twentieth-century architecture remains. Modern architecture in America was in its infancy at the time of Gropius's work at Harvard. The experimental nature of his own designs resulted in an achievement not so much in style as in liberating objectives.

10 President Pusey and the Program for Harvard College

Over the past century Harvard has experienced three periods of major building activity: 1876–1893 under President Eliot, 1924–1932 under Lowell, and 1958–1971 under Pusey. The buildings erected within these time frames are of course significantly different in architectural style and size and in the manner in which they are sited. But each provides an important visual image of its era. Certainly the architecture of the Pusey administration illustrates the changed condition of Harvard.

After World War II the university found itself substantially changed in a number of ways. The students were more numerous and independent, the instructional program had grown in size and variety, and the school was required to confront sociological problems of a kind it had not before had to face. The physical plant was seriously strained by rapid postwar growth. Harvard had much catching up to do. Two years after Nathan Pusey was elected president in 1953 he announced the Program for Harvard College, a bold plan for improvement of all phases of undergraduate education. The Plan called for raising a huge sum, about half of it for books (library endowment) and new professorships (especially in the social sciences), the other half for buildings and their upkeep. Under buildings were specified new housing for married students as well as undergraduates, classrooms and laboratories, a theater, art facilities, and a new health center and infirmary.

The $82.5 million goal for this ambitious program was raised over a two-year period, 1956–1958. Such a figure was staggering by comparison with previous Harvard fundraising attempts, to say nothing of those of most American colleges.[1] If the goal of $82.5 million seems high, so were all the other figures in this postwar period. Between 1939 and 1966 enrollment increased from 8,379 to 14,966, the endowment from approximately $117 million to $962 million. Yearly expenses climbed from $13 million in 1939 to $119 million in 1964. Whereas President Lowell spent $28 million on construction between 1923 and 1933, in the decade 1953–1963 Pusey spent or committed $70 million for buildings.

Like those of earlier administrations, Harvard buildings erected under President Pusey have a recognizable character. Yet this architecture, although entirely contemporary, is by no means uniform. There is a new repertoire of building materials, and structures are generally of larger scale than before. For the first time Harvard uses high-rise structures. There is also less of an overall order and plan in the placement of buildings than in Lowell's day. The reasons for such changes are not obscure. Open land was running out, and the school was encountering some opposition in attempts to acquire additional land. Building vertically was the only way to secure the space it needed. Increasing building costs were another factor: between 1913 and 1964 such costs are estimated to have risen 360 percent.[2] To perpetuate the elaborate wooden trim and complicated roof structure of Lowell's time, with towers and many dormer windows, was economically impossible. Buildings thus came to be constructed of prefabricated elements, and of poured and prestressed concrete, and careful thought was given to the matter of upkeep. The university also instituted a new policy of employing several architectural firms rather than a single one. In these years Harvard, along with Yale and some other universities, corporations, and governmental bodies, set out deliberately to commission work from architects of international repute, almost as a collector might acquire paintings by well-known artists. Whereas the buildings of the Lowell years bore at least a family resemblance, those built under Pusey are quite dissimilar—as dissimilar, indeed, as those erected during Eliot's administration. While Lowell's architect, Charles Coolidge, had been able to design several buildings in one area—the houses on the river or the buildings that cloister the Yard—designers in the 1960s created more fill-in work, single buildings in already established surroundings. But then some of the Pusey undertakings were large enough in scale to create their own milieu. As a result of all these factors, President Pusey's buildings convey less of a feeling of an orderly environment than do Lowell's.

The Pusey years saw the addition of no new buildings in Harvard Yard, but much meritorious renovation was accomplished there. Beginning in 1961 the dormitories were modernized, a process that focused primarily on interiors: plumbing and heating systems were replaced, fire hazards were reduced, plaster was scraped away to reveal some brick walls, and windows were refurbished with functioning inside shutters. This was done under the sensitive direction of TAC at a cost of $2.38 million. With the transfer of the university's business offices to the newly completed Holyoke Center, Lehman Hall (fig. 134) could be reconditioned in 1966 as Dudley House, the ninth undergraduate house, which serves as headquarters for commuting students. Changes here transformed the old main office, which rather resembled a bank lobby, into a handsome lounge and commons. Emerson Hall was also renovated and air conditioned. Harvard Hall underwent radical changes in 1968–69 to bring it up to safety standards: without disturbing the exterior, the interior was rebuilt, a system of inside fire exits provided, and lecture rooms fitted with sloping floors and up-to-date projection facilities. This renovation uncovered sections of eighteenth-century woodwork in the old Philosophical Chamber and with them traces of the flock wallpaper that John Hancock had presented to Harvard when the building was erected. The most remarkable change in the Yard in these years was the transformation in 1959 of the century-old Boylston Hall (fig. 33) from a gloomy monster to one of the most splendid buildings at Harvard. The interior was totally rebuilt, but nothing was allowed to interfere with the handsome granite masonry of the exterior. TAC, which carried out the renovation, is to be applauded.[3]

The Harvard administration appears to have learned that a policy of preservation and adaptation of its old buildings is good for economic reasons as well as to preserve the name and memory of early college benefactors. Seymour Harris, the chronicler of Harvard economic history, points out that while it costs the university about 3 percent of the replacement cost of a structure to maintain it each year, building costs have risen at $5^1/_2$ percent per year compounded, that is, an increase of 360 percent in the half-century 1913–1963.[4]

The success of the Program for Harvard College, along with large increases in enrollment and in research activity, produced a surge of new building in the 1960s. In a crescent-shaped zone adjacent to the Yard, five large and important buildings were constructed within a decade. Since their style of architecture and their scale are so different from anything the university had known before, it is fortunate that they were situated outside the Yard. Some are narcissistic and purposely disruptive of their surroundings, while others show remarkable responsiveness to the environment, though this awareness may be expressed in different ways. These buildings also are the visual results of the policy of collecting famous architects.

The Carpenter Center for the Visual Arts (figs. 199, 200) preempts the visitor's attention as it elbows two sedate Georgian Revival neighbors and confronts a third. Critical opinions about the Carpenter Center vary widely, depending upon whether the critic looks at it as a historical document, a work of art, or a component of an urban environment. Historically it has unquestionable importance as the only building in the United States designed by Le Corbusier. That master's career had begun forty years earlier, and this building of 1961 contains no ideas he had not previously explored, nor can it be considered a good representative of the International Style. Although criticism based on function is somewhat old-fashioned today, function was an important gauge of the success of an International Style building before World War II. By such a standard the ramp that curls up and through the Carpenter Center with such showmanship can hardly be justified; it conducts visitors from one corner of the lot, up one story, through the building, and down to the opposite corner without allowing them to enter. The real entrance to the main exhibition space is placed obscurely in the basement. It is also questionable whether the activities housed within the building require so many and such varied shapes as the exterior expresses (the needs of the department of visual studies were not yet defined when the structure was built). In the Cambridge climate surely little practical use can be made of the extensive roof gardens or the semi-subterranean loggias, which must have caused excessive complications in framing.[5]

Nevertheless the calisthenics of this design serve well to demonstrate the flexibility of reinforced concrete in meeting a variety of demands as well as the fact that massive walls are no longer essential to support a structure. The Carpenter Center also expresses the twentieth-century designer's freedom to create empty volumes as well as solid ones and to assemble or organize them as his creative will directs. Since the geometry of solids and voids can be so lively in itself, it is no longer necessary to rely on ornamentation for visual relief; the building itself is now sculpture. The design of the Carpenter Center is controlled by a fixed system of proportions based on a module, a matter with which Le Corbusier was much concerned.[6]

199
Carpenter Center for the
Visual Arts, the only building
in the United States designed
by Le Corbusier.

200
Carpenter Center (Le Corbusier, with Josep Luis Sert, 1961).

Here, however, such subtleties tend to be obscured by the frantic activity of the composition.

Looked at in purely visual terms, as a monument or a giant piece of sculpture with its own independent life, the Carpenter Center is forceful and dynamic. It is a different composition from every angle from which it is observed. The variety of shapes, openings, and angles is puzzling when taken bit by bit, but the composition holds together when grasped as a whole, as an equilibrium of opposing forces: solid and void, light and heavy, blunt and sharp, frenetic and static. These contrasts are resolved as the visitor abandons himself to the work of art, moves through it, explores it, becomes a part of it in the same way as he experiences a Baroque monument. Most students who work in the Carpenter Center approve of it; and while one may question whether it is a functional "machine for teaching," it is unquestionably a promethean symbol of creativity and of the mastery of technology.

The matter on which the Le Corbusier building cannot be condoned, however, is its intolerable disregard for environment. The building deliberately disassociates itself from its surroundings in choice of materials, restless composition, and the angle at which it is placed. It is said that Le Corbusier spent a weekend in Cambridge to view the site, at which time he somehow got the mistaken impression that an important line of march extended from Quincy Street northeast to Broadway—hence the useless ramp. It is ironic that one of the few times a Harvard building was provided with an adequate "back door," there was nothing for it to open into. Indeed, the university had no plans to expand in that direction and has agreed for the foreseeable future not to purchase property east of Ware Street.

Although no one would defend the Fogg Museum or the Faculty Club as architectural masterpieces that should have determined the character of the building erected between them, any structure placed there ought certainly to have taken them and the proximity of Harvard Yard into consideration. The fact that Le Corbusier was incapable of admiring this environment or of considering it when designing his building should not surprise anyone familiar with his work; the kind of design he produced was predictable. Therefore the blame for this ill-fitting building lies with university officials, who chose this architect to design a structure for this particular site. It was indeed a coup for Harvard to get a building by Le Corbusier, and he would seem to have been an ideal architect to design one for the creative arts. But an appropriate location should have been provided for him to produce his monument: a site, for example, like the top of Observatory Hill.

The architects of Holyoke Center on Harvard Square — Sert, Jackson and Gourley — had served as associates for the Carpenter Center. That is, they had adapted Le Corbusier's designs for construction by American workmen, just as in an earlier age Langford Warren had redrawn Professor Bestelmeyer's design for the Germanic Museum.[7] Sympathetic to and much influenced by Le Corbusier, Sert and his staff produced in Holyoke Center a better piece of urban architecture for Harvard than had the master. This building (a part of which occupies the old Bradish lot, owned by the college since 1654) houses many activities: the university business offices, the health services and infirmary, and several academic divisions, as well as numerous shops, a bank, and a parking garage. It was built in four stages, beginning in 1962 at the Mount Auburn Street end and finishing in 1967 with construction of the bank on Harvard Square. The architecture of Holyoke Center is an outgrowth of the International Style formula, but it gives more prominence to poured concrete, which is used in heavy, textured masses (figs. 201, 202).[8] Exposed concrete is far more acceptable on commercial Massachusetts Avenue than in the brick environment of Quincy Street.

The designers of Holyoke Center were concerned with maintaining variety within a system of standardized construction, as is evident in the punchcard fenestration with its exposed, reinforced concrete frames. In this respect the Massachusetts Avenue elevation is more successful than that on Mount Auburn Street (fig. 202), which is cluttered with shading devices because of the designer's rationalization that southern exposures require protection from the sun. Surprisingly, the module is wider (40 inches versus 26 inches) on the north facade than on the south. Visually and aesthetically, the projecting pavilion fronting Mount Auburn Street, with its own penthouse and a curious angle to its facade, although excelling as urban design, is also decidedly inferior to the bank pavilion on the north.

Holyoke Center's greatest success is the care with which it relates to and enhances its environment. Forbes Plaza on Massachusetts Avenue, with its benches and shade trees, is an eddy, a refuge of just the right size to relieve the crowded, narrow sidewalks and automobile-clogged streets of Harvard Square. The I-shaped mass of the upper floors allows ample light and air to penetrate the narrow side streets and keeps the building from looking heavy or overbearing. The grass mall on Mount Auburn Street is also pleasant but less vital to the environment. All in all, Holyoke Center is a brilliant planning device, the first step in Sert's concept of linking the three Harvard Yards.

Perhaps the most complex building, in terms of design, erected at Harvard in the 1960s was George Gund Hall (1969), which houses the Graduate

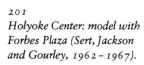
Holyoke Center: model with
Forbes Plaza (Sert, Jackson
and Gourley, 1962–1967).

202
Holyoke Center: view from
the southeast.

203
Gund Hall, Graduate School of Design (John Andrews with Anderson Baldwin, 1967–1969). The great trusses and exterior staircase of Gund were developed with thoughtful reference to Memorial Hall.

School of Design (fig. 203). The work of John Andrews, with Anderson and Baldwin, it is arrestingly original yet its massing and its siting show commendable awareness of the larger urban scene. As one looks east from the new underpass mall, it is quite clear where the "campus" ends. When it was built, the large, five-level Gund Hall, located on a strategic corner next to Allston Burr, established a kind of gateway on Cambridge Street and furnished a backdrop for Memorial Hall. The design draws on various elements from its surroundings to pull things together. Most laudable is the way it defers to Memorial Hall: the forward thrust of Gund, established by the giant "staircase" of its rear elevation, directs attention to its patriarchal neighbor; the angle of the overhang on Gund's facade reinforces the silhouette of Sanders Theatre as well as the pyramidal massing of all of Memorial Hall. Because Memorial Hall conveys a sense of direction, a feeling of focusing, even of reaching toward the west, it benefits from the strong shape of Gund, which seems to initiate and sustain this movement. On the south side of Gund a nice note was provided — until Allston Burr Hall was demolished — by the way the bottom edge of Gund's overhang picked up the roof line of Allston Burr, whose gray brick masonry seemed less intrusive than before. Gund's monumental colonnade, perhaps too short for its imposing depth and height, directs the eye northward toward William James Hall, a significant gesture indicating the presence of more Harvard buildings on Divinity Avenue beyond Langford Warren's little

204
Gund Hall interior.

Gothic Swedenborgian church, a jewel still allowed the space to glitter, and enhanced by its new setting.

The design of Gund Hall demonstrates how far the International Style has traveled since its classical stage (1920–1940). The manipulation of space, the structural dexterity bordering on exhibitionism, the fantastic complexity and originality of shapes at Gund suggest a Baroque frame of reference. And rather than sober function, which had been Gropius's expressive objective, the design now seeks an elaborate visual rationale. The controlling concept appears to be that the architectural disciplines using the building (originally Design, Landscape Architecture, and City Planning; now just the first two since City Planning moved to the School of Government) should share a common space as an expression of their mutual interests and objectives; each group is assigned part of the four identical tiers that make up the huge, glass-roofed drafting area (fig. 204). The tiers of drafting spaces step back like a colossal staircase and overhang the western facade to create the huge colonnade. The ground level is used for judging and exhibition space and as an informal lounge, while the basement is largely devoted to the storage of books and slides of the Frances Loeb library. The library itself is a two-story space opening to the west of the entrance. The enormous area underneath the staggered studios serves as public lobbies, a big reading room, and Piper auditorium; the remaining area is left open as a colonnade. Offices are contained in enclosed "balconies" overhanging the western colonnade and in a wing along the north side of the huge drafting space. Here, however, the design becomes indescribably complex, with most offices lighted by glazed "clerestories with pent roofs," which step down toward the ground until the lowest floor (which seems on the second level because of the large areaway) is continued outward to form a loggia. Each of the four facades is totally different, and any one by itself provides an incomplete idea of the building and what it contains. As with the Carpenter Center, only after deliberate and repeated exploration does the total form of the building begin to cohere as a visual unit.[9]

Whether this complexity impairs the building's usefulness or raised its cost unduly (it cost $10 million) is a question. Whether so large an undivided studio (the span of its truss is 134 feet) is desirable from the point of view of the students,[10] whether the glass roof will leak or admit too much light or heat,[11] or whether potentially usable area has been sacrificed to the gargantuan colonnade (fifty feet deep) seems almost beside the point. Yet these questions, which appear to have been secondary to expressive considerations for Andrews, would have been asked of earlier functionalists such as Gropius. The design of Gund Hall thus illustrates how radically the criteria of modern architecture had shifted in less than two decades.

The view along Quincy Street and past the colonnade of Gund Hall focuses on William James Hall (1963), a fifteen-story skyscraper designed by Minoru Yamasaki (fig. 205). Conceptually unrelated to its environment, it exemplifies yet another direction taken by modernism in the 1960s. This straightforward tower provides a library and lounge on the ground floor, a rather cramped observation terrace and faculty lounge on the top, and offices for behavioral scientists in between. Elevators and services are placed in a wing protruding from the north elevation. The system of framing creates four very large bays of forty by sixty feet, which are free of structural encumbrances so that inner partitions can be arranged at will. It also permits both main facades to be fitted with identical banks of windows spanning the intervals between the massive piers. About the five piers that sweep up each main face, diminishing in size as they rise, there is an undeniable grace. And yet the design makes no use of any local architectural characteristic or idiosyncrasy: such a building could just as well be erected in Los Angeles, Miami Beach, or Jersey City. And if the tower is satisfactory in itself, its siting is not. It is oblivious of any building or anything around it, and no structures of intermediate height placed around it form transitions to two-story neighbors. High-rise buildings do not have to stand out like sore thumbs, as we will see in Peabody Terrace, but William James Hall does so, all the more because of the vacant terraces, dry pools, and empty gardens that flank it on three sides.[12]

Before the university could start work on the Undergraduate Science Center, the last building in this arc of new construction near the Yard, arrangements had to be made for closing the west end of Kirkland Street. Legislation permitting this action was conditional on the construction of a large automobile underpass on Cambridge Street. This underpass, which conceals the awkward confluence of three streets, was implemented between 1966 and 1968. Its extensive covering provided a pedestrian crossing at grade level and fused for the first time the North Yard and Harvard Yard. It is surely the most important urban improvement in Cambridge since the construction of Memorial Drive in the 1890s. What

205
William James Hall (Minoru Yamasaki, 1963). A graceful tower, with no building of comparable height around it, the social sciences building ignores its environs. To the right is Langford Warren's Gothic Church of the New Jerusalem (1903).

had been an asphalt desert, as dangerous to limb as offensive to eye, is now a spacious pedestrian mall with ample grassed areas.

In a discussion of the topographical changes in the area around Memorial Hall, Harvard's preservation of the Jared Sparks House (1838) must be noted with appreciation. It was the home of the college's eighteenth president and one of the most important residences in Cambridge. The moving of this house in 1968 from 48 Quincy Street to its present location at 21 Kirkland Street to make way for Gund Hall demonstrated a shift in Harvard's architectural policy since the demolition in 1951 of 26 Quincy Street, which stood on the site needed for Allston Burr Hall.

The Undergraduate Science Center, another large and unusual building, was designed in 1970 by the Sert office and completed in 1972 (fig. 206). Although the Science Center is not entirely satisfactory from a visual standpoint, its siting is good. It integrates the building lines of three different streets, while its large mass defines the limits of the grassed mall that

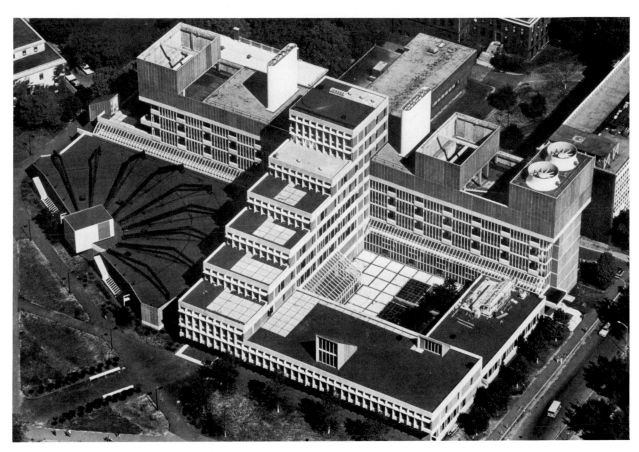

206
*Undergraduate Science Center
(Josep Lluis Sert, 1966–
1968). The Kirkland Street
overpass in the foreground
links the Yard and the North
Yard.*

overlays the underpass. In achieving this integration the design does much to resolve the dynamics of an environment that had earlier been chaotic. In various small but notable ways it also respects Memorial Hall.[13]

The limited space of the mall could easily have been overwhelmed by a tall building placed against it. The designer of the Science Center avoided this problem by shifting the bulk of his structure as far back (north) as the site would permit and restricting to a single story that portion adjacent to the mall. This unit, containing the lecture halls, is set parallel to the Memorial Fence. Projecting from the six-story spine of the building is a stepped pavilion with five setbacks, which mounts ultimately to a height of nine stories, a giant staircase forming a transition to the mall and a visual link to Gund Hall (fig. 207). Another wing of two stories, aligned with Kirkland Street, is large and simple enough to define the open space in front of it and to deflect a visitor's view toward Memorial Hall. Around the corner on its eastern elevation the science building picks up the building line of Gordon McKay Laboratory and thus reinforces the Oxford Street corridor. Although a more prominent facade might have made a better terminus for Kirkland Street, this could hardly have been provided without creating a form that competed with Memorial Hall. On the back side the new building simply drops off like a huge cliff, about the only remaining solution since the main block of the building is pushed back as far from the mall as possible. On the west there was no need to accommodate to neighboring Littauer Center, which is preoccupied with its own location commanding Harvard Square.

207
Undergraduate Science Center:
southeast elevation from
overpass.

208
Undergraduate Science Center:
central hallway with bas-relief
sculpture by Constantino
Nivola.

Less expert than the siting of the Science Center, its elevations are agitated and do not explain interior function as clearly as one might suppose. It is possible to read the identities of the two-story section along Kirkland Street as a library, the grand "staircase" as an area of offices, and the one-story polygonal area in the foreground as lecture hall space (it includes four lecture halls seating 500, 350, 250, and 150). The six-story backbone of the building as laboratory space is also comprehensible, but in fact the next-to-top story, which has windows equal in size to those of the floors below, is not occupied by laboratories at all but, together with the solid-walled area above it, provides an undivided space for air conditioning equipment. The giant boxes overhanging each end of the roof are water-cooling towers intended to service not only the Center itself but all buildings in the North Yard. The towers are connected with a gargantuan pump room in the basement, a magnificent Piranesi-like interior with the volume of Boston's Symphony Hall, one of the most impressive spaces in all of Harvard, which is in no way expressed on the exterior. The air conditioning boxes on the roof may appear grossly oversized; but two-fifths of the approximately $25 million cost of the structure was devoted to this equipment.

As is often true in Sert designs, the south elevation seems unnecessarily complicated. Both the fenestration and the precast panels are less interesting than those of Holyoke Center, and the silhouette is cluttered. This is particularly true when the building is observed from the Class of 1876 Gate, which leads from Harvard Yard to the underpass mall and is now the principal point of access to the North Yard. The main visual difficulty is created by the lecture hall area with its exposed roof girders — a giant tarantula — plus a box for mechanical equipment and glass bays that project from the facade to provide exits from the lecture halls. But the rest of the facade is equally agitated, with hit-or-miss fenestration plus a variety of wall textures, the staircase office wing, a frantic skyline that includes a silver observation dome, a giant white chimney that recalls (with Corbusian iconography) the stack of an ocean liner, several shed clerestory windows, and cooling towers overhanging each end of the building. Nevertheless, the new Undergraduate Science Center and the underpass mall clearly form the keystone of the extended Harvard Yards. The rising angular structure both defines the complex interaction of space with building that is the challenge of an urban environment today and echos the comparable function of Sert's Holyoke Center to the south.

Farther away from Harvard Yard a number of buildings were erected after World War II clustering about four older nuclei: the Divinity School; the North Yard; Observatory Hill off Garden Street; and Appian Way off Brattle Street. Because the existing structures in these areas had been spaced at generous intervals, it was possible to add new facilities without having to destroy the old.

Almost forming an independent campus are the three new buildings for the Harvard Divinity School that have grown up around Andover Hall. On the east side of Francis Avenue is the Center for the Study of World Religions (1959). Appropriate to its residential environment, the scale and appearance of this structure are domestic in feeling; it resembles an apartment complex, which in fact is its principal function (fig. 209). The Center

209
Center for the Study of World Religions (Josep Lluis Sert, 1959).

210
Andover Harvard Library (Shepley, Bulfinch, Richardson and Abbott, 1960). The slender oriel fenestration evokes the Gothic forms of the Divinity School's adjacent main building.

211
*Rockefeller Hall (Edward
Larabee Barnes, 1970).*

was the first Harvard commission of Josep Lluis Sert, whose own house
nearby at 64 Francis Avenue it somewhat resembles.[14]

The most interesting of these new Divinity School works is Andover
Harvard Library (1960), the exceptionally handsome two-story addition to
the older hall (with provision for two more stories, as indicated by the
completed elevator shaft) designed by Shepley, Bulfinch, Richardson and
Abbott (fig. 210).[15] Attached to the old hall of gray granite, the new section
is constructed of a slightly pinker shade of the same material. Although the
design makes no attempt to duplicate Collegiate Gothic shapes and details,
it complements them admirably by the scale and shape of its fenestration:
tall, narrow oriel windows of triangular projection. Furthermore, this
L-shaped wing on the southwest corner of Andover Hall forms a buffer
between the Hall and the extensive parking lots, creates a screen against the
ugly wooden Vanserg Building, and establishes as well a pleasant, sheltered
terrace.

Rockefeller Hall (1970), situated in a delightfully secluded corner at the
north end of Andover Hall, contains seminar rooms and apartments
(fig. 211). Designed by Edward Larabee Barnes, this building establishes no
rapport with its neighbors either in the way it is massed or in its choice of
material. Here, if anywhere at Harvard, a light-colored brick would have
been appropriate, to blend with the fine gray granite of Andover Hall, but a

plum-colored, almost black brick was selected. The massing is agitated, piled together without articulating the space between it and Andover and without realizing the possibilities inherent in the unusually attractive situation, while the strip windows and big plates of undivided glass are direct affronts to the elegant oriels and traceried casements of the other structures. A restless design lacking even the virtue of striking originality, Rockefeller Hall invites unfavorable comparison on several counts with contemporaneous new buildings for the Law School.[16]

Starting with the original insular placement of Langdell Hall in the middle of a former athletic area (Holmes Field), the campus for the Law School grew in seven increments between 1883 and 1968 into a surprisingly beautiful environment centered on a pair of secluded quadrangles a stone's throw from Massachusetts Avenue. The fine sense of order and enclosure that pervades the area did not emerge, however, until the two most recent structures by Benjamin Thompson Associates were erected: one containing faculty offices (1967), now called Griswold Hall, the other named the Roscoe Pound Building (1968).[17] Both buildings are sited with notable skill. Five stories were needed in the office building to provide the necessary accommodations. To keep from overshadowing adjacent Austin and Langdell Halls, an irregular bowl one story deep was hollowed out of the site and the building constructed in it. The massing of Roscoe Pound was even more difficult. The axes of Langdell and of the International Legal Studies Center (1957) by Shepley, Bulfinch, Richardson and Abbott, which (with Aiken Computation Center) had begun the definition of this space, were not parallel to Massachusetts Avenue, yet the Pound design had to respond to both while enclosing the northern quadrangle. The dilemma was solved by dividing the building into large, blocky units set on different planes, often overhanging or terraced, and sometimes projecting at a slight angle (fig. 212). So energetic a massing could have overpowered the environment had not the walls been sheathed in dark brick to minimize the complexity of the geometric composition. Simple but adequate relief from the dark brick and bronzed glass windows is provided by wide concrete lintels, which form continuous bands across the facade. The choice of materials is also appropriate in terms of the older buildings surrounding the quadrangles: the plum color of the dark brick combines admirably with the brownstone of Austin Hall, while the bush-hammered concrete recalls the limestone used for Langdell and the International Center. The admirable supportive quality of these designs is the more apparent when one compares them with Rockefeller Hall, which has certain superficial similarities. To achieve this splendid congruence the architect had to be willing to serve as an orchestrator rather than a virtuoso—a role too rarely accepted by designers in any generation. Together Roscoe Pound and Griswold Halls constitute the most adroit example of design for a given environment produced at Harvard since World War II, an achievement that equals Charles Coolidge's best work of the 1920s.

Unquestionably the best place at Harvard in which to observe the problems of adding to an existing structure is the University Museum. The building of that enormous complex in eleven increments was examined in Chapter 5, and its integration with the Biological Laboratories was discussed in Chapter 7. During the Pusey administration two more wings were added, and under President Bok yet another. The Hoffman Laboratory of Experi-

212
Roscoe Pound Building,
Harvard Law School
(Benjamin Thompson Asso-
ciates, 1968).

mental Geology (1962), by TAC, is successful both as an independent design and as an adjunct to an existing structure. Forming a wing of the museum but connected with it only by a glass-enclosed bridge, Hoffman is large enough that it might have been treated as an independent design, but the architects resisted the temptation to create an independent masterpiece. Instead they took important cues from the parent structure: the fenestration, though organized in an original way, retains the vertical shape and proportions of the museum windows, and the height of the projecting roof slab corresponds to the main cornice of the museum, whose attic and hip roof thus rise above it. One way in which the new design could have been better related to the parent museum is in the color of brick, a detail that was handled better with Tozzer Library (fig. 148).[18]

The more recent North Wing of the museum (1971), by the same architects, is less successful because it competes with the original building. Variations in bay widths, the expression of a stairway, one overhanging top story, and unpredictable fenestration produce a restless image; and though the wing employs the same combination of brick and concrete as does Hoffman, the balance is heavily in favor of concrete, whose textured surfaces further agitate the design. One is thankful that this building faces

213
Music Building: Eda Kuhn
Loeb Library Wing (Stanley B.
Parker, 1955). The first
addition to the music building
was related to the earlier
structure in form and style.

214
Music Building: Fanny Mason
Wing (James F. Clapp, Jr., for
Shepley, Bulfinch, Richardson
and Abbott, 1970). The
second addition ignores the
main structure (to the rear).

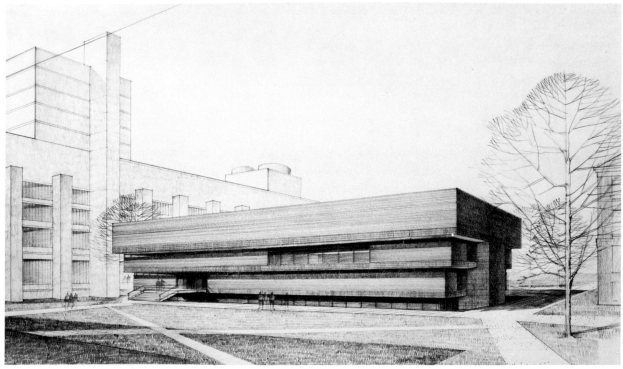

215
*Engineering Sciences
Laboratory (Minoru Yama-
saki, 1962).*

the architectural hinterland north of the museum, rather than the quadrangle on the west.

To the museum's generally successful sequence of enlargements, the two additions to the music building form a sobering contrast. To Paine Hall (1913) was appended in 1955 a wing for the Eda Kuhn Loeb Library (fig. 213), designed by Stanley Parker. It is a satisfactory design that follows the original in color of brick and general architectural style. Its detailing, if somewhat less ornate than that of Paine, is more refined in the manner of the Adam brothers and not unlike 2 Divinity Avenue (the Harvard-Yenching Institute), built twenty-five years earlier. The Loeb addition was the last neo-Georgian building erected by Harvard in Cambridge; there is a later one, Cotting House (1967), across the river at the Business School.[19]

The second addition to Paine Hall, the Fanny Mason wing (1970) by Shepley, Bulfinch, Richardson and Abbott, defies the original structure (fig. 214). Constructed of altogether different brick, the Mason wing is formed in three bands, each heavier in scale and overhanging the one below, separated by continuous strips of glass to form a dramatic, inverted, stepped pyramid. Such a design by itself is not without interest and reflects the then-fashionable manner of Kalmann and McKinnell's influential Boston City Hall (1967). But the scale of the addition is the same as that of the earlier sections of the music building, and rather than actually being a wing it is fused to them; these facts increase the disparity between the parts and discomfort that section of the North Yard in which the building stands.

Four engineering or scientific laboratories were built in the North Yard during the Pusey administration. The James Conant Research Laboratory (1958), used entirely for chemical research, is an integral part of the Mallinckrodt-Converse laboratory complex. A circumspect brick structure that lacks frontage on a public way, the building does not even have a main facade but is entered through the older laboratories. The other three are near the northern boundary of that area: the Electron Accelerator (1957), the building now designated the High Energy Physics Laboratory (1957), and the Engineering Sciences Laboratory (1962). The first of these has no architectural pretensions and lacks the innate sense of proportion and material that can raise a piece of engineering to the place of architecture. Fortunately the location of this structure is so remote that it has little effect on the university's architectural environment. The High Energy Laboratory is a routine design using glass brick, strip windows, and aluminum sunshades that can be duplicated by the dozens in industrial parks. Although the four-story Engineering Sciences Laboratory (fig. 215) was designed by a well-known architect, Minoru Yamasaki, it is stilted and pinched in feeling, and the ostentation of the fat golden entrance contrasts awkwardly with the squeezed, hooded windows. This building, of a glaringly white precast concrete, is as oblivious of its location as is the same architect's William James Hall.[20]

The Harvard Observatory on Garden Street is a world apart, atop its own hill and surrounded by tree-filled grounds (fig. 216). It is composed of seven connecting wings, each on a different level, strung together around the original observatory and creating in the process two irregular courtyards. Although the designer of each section appears to have ignored all that had gone before, a kind of organic growth is visually evident in the way the observatory expanded down the side of the hill, each unit larger and more imposing than its predecessor, and each of a different style of architecture. Of Isaiah Rogers's original 1843 observatory, only the central block, now called Sears Tower, remains. Crowned by a hemispherical observation turret, this small gray-painted building can barely be discerned among the confusion of later buildings and can be reached only from the rear (north) side. The original entry on the south, situated in a pedimented pavilion and enhanced by a heavy granite doorframe, is now inaccessible to the public because the traditional approach from the east has been blocked by recent additions. (The early additions were designed not by architects but by engineers.) The earliest surviving addition (1892), by G. Leslie Nichols, is a two-story edifice with a modest Panel Brick cornice, which once stood free of the original observatory. Lower on the slope to the northwest is a three-story wing in the familiar neo-Georgian manner of Coolidge, Shepley, Bulfinch and Abbott (1931). The meager wing by W. P. Hooper (1954) immediately west of the core replaces one arm (the original classroom and library) of the first building. Like the Nuclear Laboratory Building (1949) off Oxford Street, this unit was an early and inconclusive attempt to domesticate the International Style by using red brick and providing sunshades.

The space age and affiliation with the Smithsonian Observatory generated a burst of expansion beginning in the 1960s. The most interesting aspect of the complex consists of two sets of L-shaped buildings that enfold the early observatory tower. Their placement farther down the ter-

Sears Tower (Isaiah Rogers, 1843) and Harvard Observatory Additions (1892, 1931, 1954, 1960, 1970). The hillside site accommodated the growth of new structures at the Observatory as the space age dawned. The Perkin Building (Cambridge Seven Associates, 1970) is in the foreground.

raced hillside avoids any dwarfing of the original tower despite their larger size. The earlier of these wings, sheathed in red brick and comparable to the west wing, was built in 1960 by Griswold, Boyden, Wylde and Ames. Space was left between the wings for an ample paved court. The scale of the most recent addition, the Perkin Building (1970), by the Cambridge Seven Associates, is monumental, its facade articulated with massive posts and beams that resemble giant construction blocks. The huge corner utility towers surfaced with harrowed concrete are so rough that such a building could never have accommodated to a site in the Yard. Isolated in beautiful grounds, however, this brutal structure can afford to be impressive.

The Radcliffe Quad Recreational Facility by Hoskins, Scott and Taylor, added to the observatory grounds at the corner of Garden and Bond Streets in 1978, nestles into the profile of Observatory Hill. Thus having a minimal impact on the residential area around it, the building well illustrates a change of architectural philosophy at Harvard in the 1970s. The assertive qualities of earlier New Brutalist designs such as Perkin were replaced by mannerly design and thoughtful siting.[21]

One of the significant educational changes at Harvard in the postwar era has been its integration with Radcliffe. The architectural expression of this

217
*Loeb Drama Center (Hugh
Stubbins, 1959).*

gradual merger has been the invasion by Harvard buildings of former
Radcliffe territory on Appian Way, a trend underscored by the purchase in
1962 of Longfellow Hall (1929), which was originally a Radcliffe classroom
building, by Harvard's Graduate School of Education. The first new
Harvard construction in this neighborhood was the Loeb Drama Center
(fig. 217), a 1959 design by Hugh Stubbins Associates. Residents may still
think with nostalgia of the small Greek Revival dwellings that occupied the
site and recalled a more tranquil era on Brattle Street;[22] yet the new building with its pleasant garden is considerate of the environment. The combination of concrete and brick is appropriate to the neighborhood, and the
metal grilles keep the large plate glass windows from becoming too blank
and scaleless. The stagehouse is placed well back from the street so that its
profile does not appear uncomfortably high. Careful planning, the retention
of existing shade trees, and the use of brick sidewalks allow the building to
blend into its setting. Indeed, the substantial mass of Loeb creates a pleasant foil for the spacious garden of the Radcliffe President's House to the
west and helps somewhat to temper the sense of congestion caused by the
tall Elizabethan apartment house that crowds the opposite corner of
Hilliard Street.[23]

Both the Loeb Drama Center and the Carpenter Center for the Visual

Arts were constructed with funds collected by the Program for Harvard College. They symbolize the tardy admission of the performing arts to the heretofore strictly academic educational offerings of Harvard. The college had moved a long way from the fixed, restricted curriculum of the seventeenth and eighteenth centuries. First mathematics and modern languages were added, then history and chemistry; Eliot's elective system broadened the curriculum in general, especially in the social sciences, and even introduced some art. Charles Eliot Norton's classes in art history were popular. But it was the history and appreciation of art that were admitted to the curriculum, while the creative and performing arts were active on the periphery. Except for architecture, which had been established as a graduate professional course in 1893, the nonacademic performing aspect of art had to wait until after World War II to find a place among the legitimate (credit) courses offered by the university. The same can be said of drama, which earlier had been visible only with amateur theatricals or workshops sponsored by courses in literature or foreign language. The position of drama at Harvard is still somewhat tentative, but the Loeb Theatre is fully professional in its design and equipment and has some of the most elaborate facilities for staging that had been constructed in America up to its time.

The second Harvard building in the Appian Way neighborhood was Larsen Hall (1964), the administrative center of the Graduate School of Education, a division that has grown phenomenally in the last quarter-century. This building (fig. 218), by Caudill, Rowlett and Scott, has occasioned controversy.[24] Though Larsen is constructed of brick that blends nicely with the adjacent Radcliffe buildings, its towered mass and bellows-like windows disturb some critics. Actually, in this location a taller structure of restricted ground floor area is preferable to one of three or four stories covering the whole lot. A tower directly on Cambridge Common would have been a mistake; but placed as it is behind a fringe of houses, the new building does not upset the streetscape. Furthermore, this active, ingenious design is successful in its own right: slight variations in fenestration and well-controlled breaks in massing add vitality and surprise, elements that in moderation are welcome on a large structure. One exceptionally fine view of Larsen Hall, from Arsenal Square just north of the Common,[25] demonstrates the way in which the paired chimneys of the Radcliffe buildings, particularly Byerly Hall, are echoed in the thin, vertical alcoves of the Larsen tower. Larsen was the first Harvard building to be surrounded by wide areaways, somewhat resembling a moat. This solution allows for large windows in the basement, which thus becomes a fully usable work area, a system that has been adapted for several subsequent university buildings — most notably Hilles Library, the adjacent Radcliffe dormitories, and Pusey Library in the Yard. The success of Larsen emerges even more clearly in comparison with Harvard's other contemporaneous tall building, William James Hall.

The feeling of quiet amplitude present at the Loeb Theatre is also found in Gutman Library (1969), designed for the School of Education by Benjamin Thompson Associates (fig. 219).[26] The siting of the library is excellent, basically forming a diagonal leading back from the intersection of Brattle Street and Appian Way to the opposite corner of the property. Such a disposition was desirable as a way to enlarge as much as possible the remaining two corners of the lot, where space would have been cramped

218
Larsen Hall, School of Education (Caudill, Rowlett and Scott, 1964), viewed across a garden in Radcliffe Yard.

and wasted, and to provide visual linkage to Larsen Hall. Two small gardens were created where they are most appreciated, and occupants of the library and of adjacent buildings enjoy a maximum of natural light. Yet this diagonal placement was achieved while keeping the external walls parallel or at right angles to surrounding streets. Similarly, the apparent bulk of the structure is minimized by the pulling back of the walls of the ground floor, to leave the second and third stories overhanging newly created areaways. Gutman forms a good transition between the academic buildings of Appian Way and Radcliffe Yard and the commercial district a block away toward Harvard Square. This it accomplishes by combining the large plate glass windows and concrete construction of the stores with the setbacks and more ample spacing of academic building design.

Across the river in Boston, at the Business School and the Medical School, Harvard has also continued to build. Since the end of World War II the campus of the Harvard Business School has more than doubled in size. Two important buildings, Aldrich and Kresge Halls, both designed by Perry, Dean and Hepburn, were erected in 1953. Kresge, with its dining hall and lounges, occupies a prominent location at one end of Harvard Way,

219
*Gutman Library, School of
Education (Benjamin
Thompson, 1969), opposite
the Loeb Drama Center.*

the cross-axis of the campus plan, while Aldrich abuts Baker Library. Appropriately, both structures defer in some degree to the earlier architectural tradition, recalling the work of these architects at Houghton Library, and their modified Georgian Revival style serves as a transition between the old and the new. Buildings of completely contemporary design were the work of the late 1960s and the 1970s: Burden Hall, Baker Hall, McCollum Center, and the extensive Soldiers Field Apartments. For the most part these new buildings are well screened from the old campus by trees or placed at the rear of older buildings so that the differences in architectural style and construction are not disruptive.

Aldrich Hall, designed for classrooms, is of simplified Georgian Revival style (fig. 220). A deliberate lack of ornamentation places the burden of design on the clarity and proportions of the massing and fenestration. In this matter there is a certain resemblance to Regency work, but not an archaeological replication. The large half-cylindrical bays that rise through three levels and the simple circular fans above the entrances are memorable. Aldrich stands as a transition between the traditional earlier architecture and the stark geometry of buildings executed here since 1960. Kresge Hall's geometric clarity is similar to that of Aldrich but has a stronger archaeological flavor because of the addition of giant Federal pilasters across the facade (fig. 221). Given the handsome exteriors of these buildings, their interiors are disappointing.

Together Baker Hall and McCollum Center form a quasi-independent educational unit, where short specialized seminars for business executives are held (figs. 222, 223). Elevations of Baker Hall facing the river and the courtyard are arresting because of the contrast between the regular fenes-

tration and a number of large plate glass windows, expressing the organization of the dormitory into suites consisting of eight bedrooms and one two-story sitting room. McCollum contains seminar rooms, lounges, and a dining hall and makes extensive use of outdoor terraces with commanding views of the river. Both buildings employ broad lintels of rough-textured concrete on facades where there are windows. These and the varied fenestration provide the only relief to the otherwise unadorned dark red brick. Differences in architectural style between Baker Hall and the 1926 dormitories on the opposite side of the street are not disturbing, but when the two groups are observed from the riverbank the bold scale of Baker and especially the large two-story windows of the sitting rooms are overpowering in contrast to the weak and uncertain scale of the older buildings.

Burden Hall (1968) by Philip Johnson (fig. 224) and the Soldiers Field Apartments (1974) by Benjamin Thompson (fig. 225) are similar in their bold, cubistic massing and exclusive use of dark brick. This extensive complex avoids the barren feeling of ordinary large-scale housing through variations in the height and shape of the different buildings: heights are variously four, six, and nine stories; the customary regular disposition of blocks is relieved by placing some units on a forty-five degree angle; and the curve of the long four-story outer building responds to the bend in the river. Each open area in this complex has a distinct character; the largest contains a play area for the community nursery school, whose brightly colored play equipment doubles as outdoor sculpture. A five-story garage by Benjamin Thompson, sheathed with the same brick, at one end of the complex forms a decisive limit to the park and separates it from the vast area of surface parking that occupies the southern edge of the university property.

Farther away in Boston, the continuing growth of the Harvard Medical School has required the addition of several structures surrounding the rigorously aligned core campus laid out in 1906. Here a notable contrast with the contextual approach of new architecture at the Business School is provided by the Countway Library (1963), by Hugh Stubbins, a building of monumental proportions and frankly assertive design (fig. 226). Constructed in the curiously truncated space between the main pavilion of the Medical School and the Brigham and Women's Hospital on Huntington Avenue, the articulated exterior of Countway overpowers its neighbors. Even though it refuses to defer to the Classical ambience of its surroundings, the vigorous Countway Library relieves the dull, repetitive character of the quadrangles and is one of the most successful buildings erected in Boston in the 1960s. As usual with Stubbins' designs, the library's interior comprises beautiful spaces and provides dramatic lighting for a central staircase (fig. 227). Countway represents the best and most thoughtful application of the bombastic idiom of the late 1960s and early 1970s, which created such structures as the Boston City Hall and Sert's contemporaneous work at Harvard.[27]

Parallel with this impressive expansion of academic and laboratory facilities was the drive to provide living accommodations for increased numbers of students on the Cambridge campus. Freshman enrollment grew from 1,032 in 1932, to 1,491 in 1950, to 1,633 in 1976. The university met this change by constructing a freshman dormitory in Harvard Yard, two new undergraduate houses, and an apartment complex for married students, and

222
*Baker Hall, Harvard Business
School (Shepley, Bulfinch,
Richardson and Abbott, 1970).*

223
*McCollum Center, Harvard
Business School: view toward
the Charles River.*

224
*Burden Hall, Harvard
Business School (Philip
Johnson, 1968). Unrelieved
red brick has become
ubiquitous for new design at
Harvard.*

225
*Soldiers Field Apartments
(Benjamin Thompson, 1974).*

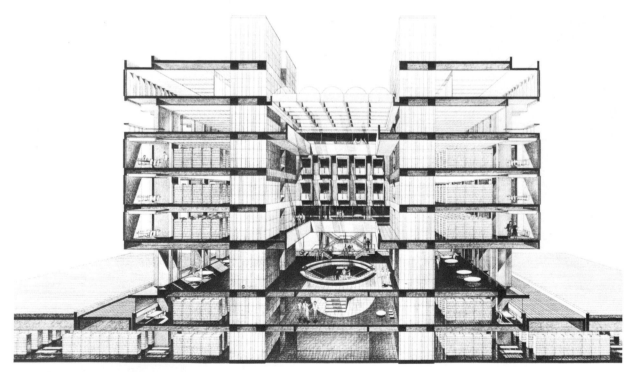

226
*Countway Library, Harvard
Medical School (Hugh
Stubbins, 1963).*

227
*Countway Library: curved
central staircase.*

by purchasing and converting three apartment buildings for freshman dormitories. Conversion came first, with the acquisition of Hurlbut and Greenough Halls on Prescott Street in 1956 followed two years later by Pennypacker Hall at 387 Harvard Street. Construction of married-student housing and enlargement of the house system in the South Yard took place in the 1960s, and finally during the summer of 1973 work began on the new dormitory, Canaday Hall, built within the Yard on the site of Hunt Hall (the first Fogg Museum).

The success of the Program for Harvard College made it possible to build more dormitories in the South Yard as well. This had high priority because the Harkness houses, now almost thirty years old, were filled to overflowing, with 3,971 students crowded into quarters designed for 2,670. The newly built Quincy House and Leverett Towers, with space for approximately 250 and 270 students, were both designed by Shepley, Bulfinch, Richardson and Abbott in the same year (1958) but in two very different styles. This greater latitude in design now allowed the architect highlights changes in the view of architectural symbolism since the Lowell presidency.

Quincy House (figs. 228, 229) represents a transition between Harvard's old and new architecture. In this its stylistic position somewhat resembles that of Lamont Library, designed a decade earlier: both show the efforts of designers to give the International Style an American form. One obvious concession to tradition in both was the substitution of textured Harvard brick for white stucco and the retention of limestone trim. Another was the attempt to relate the proportions of windows to those of earlier buildings: the proportions of the new steel casements match those of the openings (if not the structural subdivisions) of traditional wooden, double-hung sash. Such subtlety is almost obscured, however, by arresting variations in the shapes and sizes of the larger units of fenestration, which distinguish the different uses of the interior spaces they illuminate. Thus large plate glass expanses indicate the sitting rooms on every third floor, while casements signify bedrooms. Articulation of the ground story indicates yet a different occupancy — the residences of the tutors. Despite the complexity of the window system, the design module is repeated frequently enough without variation that the dormitory block reads as a unit. Architectural display is reserved for the commons and library pavilions, where more complex roofs with clerestories are provided and where the second story is visually emphasized to indicate the presence of important communal spaces.

Though different in obvious ways, the new house at least does not clash with the older ones in massing and in its effect on the neighborhood. Although seven stories high (as opposed to a maximum of five floors in the Harkness houses), Quincy does not rise much above the ridges of the gabled roofs of the older groups. The organization of the house plan around an ample courtyard is also traditional. Quincy is composed of four basic masses: a main dormitory block disposed along DeWolfe Street, a lower but more elaborate commons building paralleling Mount Auburn Street, a good-sized library, and a U-shaped Georgian Revival structure built in 1930 as part of Leverett House. The placement of the two larger buildings along streets carrying major traffic creates a quiet garden courtyard facing southwest. Since the library is on stilts and does not fill the entire corridor between the two dormitories, the vista here remains partly open, thereby extending the sense of space at the south end of the garden, a sense also

228
Quincy House: courtyard (Shepley, Bulfinch, Richardson and Abbott, 1958). The first new River Houses abandoned the Georgian image but perpetuated use of red brick, irregular courtyards, and limited height.

229
Quincy House: courtyard entrance with library.

263   *President Pusey and the Program for Harvard College*

230
Leverett House: perspective drawing of southwest elevation (Shepley, Bulfinch, Richardson and Abbott, 1958–1959).

231
Leverett House. The library presents its picturesque low elevation to the street with terraces and gardens.

enhanced by the changes in level of a terrace against the main building. This terrace provides a semiprivate precinct for the tutors' residences situated on the ground floor of the largest block. The top story of this building is a penthouse for the house master.[28]

The Leverett Towers (1958–1959), erected as an adjunct to Leverett House, were Harvard's first experiment with high-rise design, preceding Larsen and William James Halls. Given the relatively small available plot, the choice between a four-story walk-up covering most of the available space and twin twelve-story towers set in a garden was correctly made, both for the dormitory itself and for the neighborhood (figs. 230, 231). Because Dunster House is situated so close to Cowperthwaite Street and the commons of Leverett House so close to DeWolfe Street, the new building had to be set back from both to avoid unpleasant crowding. The asymmetrical location of the towers—facing in different directions—and the depressed level of the central plaza are successful. Paved with slate and marble slabs and ornamented by two splendid willow trees, the plaza provides an attractive focus for the complex, while screens of maple trees on one side and lindens on the other provide a certain privacy. A two-story gate pavilion serves as a transitional link between the new towers and older McKinlock Hall on the opposite side of DeWolfe Street. The textured limestone surface of the upper level of this pavilion and its ingenious but somewhat overdesigned clerestory of glass mark the house library situated above the gateway.

Designs hailed for originality at the time of their execution sometimes appear a generation later to have been merely novel and nonconforming. This appears to be the case with Leverett Towers. The landscaping and siting of the towers are the finest aspects of the design. The elevations are less successful. The design of the typical bay, a large square window flanked by small casements, lacks both scale and rationale. Surprisingly, both large and small windows light the same rooms, and there is no exterior differentiation between bedroom and sitting-room fenestration. The screen of restless polygonal panels crowning each tower calls attention to rooftop penthouses for mechanical equipment rather than disguising them. And the towers are not tall enough to soar, but only to compete. That is, they are just enough taller than the earlier towers of Dunster and the other houses to challenge their traditional supremacy, especially when the group is viewed from a distance. In contrast, the later Mather House, though much taller, is less competitive because it has a quite different dimension.[29]

Mather House (figs. 232, 233), also designed by Shepley, Bulfinch, Richardson and Abbott a decade later (1968), does not challenge adjacent Dunster House because its walls near the older dormitory are sheathed in brick; a consonance of building material is always more important than one of architectural style. Mather House illustrates the replacement of Gropius's architecture of function by an architecture of rationale. Visually the design expresses what goes on within by means of the materials employed for external surfaces. Thus a reddish-brown precast concrete indicates living space, white poured concrete signals public areas or structural support, and brick is used for the commons, the house master's entertaining pavilion, and the free-standing fire escape tower in the courtyard adjacent to Dunster House.

The complex consists of four elements: a twenty-one-story tower; a

232
*Mather House: tower
(Shepley, Bulfinch, Richardson and Abbott, 1968). To
the left are Weeks Bridge and
the River Houses.*

series of five-story wings that wrap around the main trapezoidal courtyard; the commons; and the relatively small house master's pavilion at the corner of Bowles and Flagg Streets. The visitor enters through one high colonnade and then passes through another on the opposite side of the courtyard, led to the commons building on the south edge of the property or to a second, smaller court in which rises the tower. The five-story wings surrounding the main court are of slightly different heights, but the top three levels of all sections are similar, labeled as dormitory areas by the red, precast curtain walls and by the fenestration (long fixed windows on the sitting-room floor, casements on the bedroom floors). White walls for the two lower levels indicate the presence of lobbies, the house library, tutors' offices or residences, and the business office. The tower, in a second court, draws the visitor toward it diagonally across the main quadrangle. The pylons of poured concrete at each end of the tower are structural, and the sharp vertical flute on the face of each both enhances the sculptural quality of the tower and contains the required outside fire escape. The fenestration system of the dormitory floors of the courtyard is continued in the tower, where there are fifteen levels of bedrooms and three of common rooms. This division into horizontal units—for each group of five floors of bedrooms there is a separate set of common rooms—is intended to break the large population of Mather House (about 425 students) into smaller, more intimate groups, similar to the entries in earlier housing.

233
*Mather House: dining hall.
Articulation with light and
form replaces the Georgian
paneling of the earlier dining
halls.*

The design of Mather House is undeniably dramatic. The building forms are large, harsh, and fundamental, and the open spaces have an abstract clarity (fig. 233). In contrast to the luxuriant sunken plaza at Leverett Towers, natural planting here plays a very limited role; many surfaces are paved, and even the bank of ivy below the windows of the tutors' houses on the east side of the main court is conceived abstractly as a geometric plane of uniform texture. The exterior courtyards and public interiors feel almost like a stage set, designed primarily to be photographed.[30]

Peabody Terrace (1963), a three-tower complex for married students, is one of the most successful contemporary buildings at Harvard and perhaps the best thing the Sert office has done (figs. 234, 235). Unfortunately, the least successful aspect of the design is seen from the riverfront and is the only view with which the general public is familiar. Here, as is so often true in Sert's designs, the combination of balconies and sunscreens makes the south elevation cluttered and overcomplicated. Nevertheless, the way the towers are varied by orienting suites on different floors in different directions is brilliant.

The most significant new concept at Peabody Terrace is the masterful way in which the three towers, twenty-one stories tall, are rooted to the site by intermediate structures three, five, and eight stories in height and the spaces between these elements are molded and shaped to form a sequence of engaging spaces. One never feels hedged in: in every space there are

234
*Peabody Terrace (Sert,
Gourley and Jackson, 1963).*

235
*Peabody Terrace. The size of
the married students' complex
is not apparent in its intimate
courts and gardens.*

236
*Canaday Hall (Ezra
Ehrenkrantz, 1973). The
demolition of Hunt Hall and
the erection of red brick
Canaday completed the link
between Harvard Yard and the
North Yard. Memorial Hall is
at left.*

visual exits that invite exploration, and variations in the height of structures surrounding the spaces keep these courtyards from being static or monotonous. Contrasts among open spaces of various sizes and building forms of different shapes and colors are handled so nicely that the design is never repetitious, never predictable. These towers avoid both the sterility of a public high-rise and the environmental defiance of William James Hall. Even the big garage with its tiers of ramps — not usually an architectural asset — is here turned to advantage in defining the space of the courtyards. All in all, Peabody Terrace is a pleasant, secure environment, one that allows a wide range of living styles and permits individuality among its residents. Anyone who believes that all high rise buildings must be antithetical to a humanistic environment should experience this building.[31]

The freshman dormitory added to the Yard in 1973, Canaday Hall (fig. 236), was designed by Ezra Ehrenkrantz. This building relates to its environment much better than did Hunt Hall, its predecessor in this location surrounded by Memorial Church, Thayer Hall, and the Memorial Fence. The required mass of the structure could have been disastrously aggressive had it not been subdivided into component parts: three units of varied shapes grouped about an open courtyard. This design creates the proper degree of architectural interest and activity — it is neither too complex nor too plain—to blend with other structures in the Yard without dominating them. The building is constructed of brick, and the lack of any sort of white trim effectively simplifies the design. The architectural features are muted: shed-roofed clerestories that keep the silhouette from being too bald and recall the pitched roofs used on neighboring buildings, and an interesting stepped design of the standard window unit, produced by combining a large fixed sash with a shorter casement. Though Canaday differs in appearance from the eighteenth-century dormitories, it resembles them in scale and in its division into entries, and it plays a role similar to theirs in defining spaces in the Yard. Canaday actually performs a dual visual role: it successfully provides a termination for the Yard and simultaneously (if less deftly) serves as a gateway to the overpass mall and the North Yard.

11 The New Harvard

The "wilderness" of Cambridge, which persisted beyond Bulfinch's time and into the later nineteenth century, has been transformed. Remaining green areas are no longer unused land but rather planned open space: the Cambridge Common from the seventeenth century; Mount Auburn Cemetery, a sculpture garden from before the Civil War; Memorial Drive to accent the Charles River; Longfellow Park to preserve the view of the river from Craigie House; and the Harvard and Radcliffe Yards and Quadrangles. As pressures for land have increased, careful planning has become ever more essential. Reflecting this need, the university's Planning Office in 1960 published *An Inventory for Planning,* outlining needs for future expansion. The potential for expansion of facilities within Harvard Yard was surveyed between 1968 and 1970 by Hugh Stubbins, who examined the 22-acre area closely and identified patterns of activity and circulation. One of his recommendations—the elimination of automobile traffic from the Yard—was implemented before the construction of Canaday in 1973.

Stubbins thus had reason to be sensitive to the environment of the Yard, and when he was commissioned in 1973 to design a new library, he demonstrated that sensitivity. His design for Nathan Marsh Pusey Library conceals most of the structure's mass underground and links it by tunnels to Widener, Houghton, and Lamont. The light and airy interiors of the semi-subterranean library, which opened in 1976, confirm the skill that has made Stubbins one of the most notable American architects of the twentieth century.[1] In the Loeb Drama Center he adjusted the mass of his design to the scale of the Brattle Street environment and initiated bold new use of the metal grille. At the Countway Library his towering construct carried off a difficult assignment with panache. At Pusey he abandoned an assertive posture entirely to produce an elegant contemporary building in Harvard Yard (fig. 237). Masterfully organized in this difficult space, the library achieves daylight illumination on the lower or middle level through a moat area around the building and a central lightwell. A staircase, walkway, and park cover the low octagonal mound of Pusey, allowing natural pedestrian circulation patterns to continue. This subterranean development barely disturbs the pristine facades of the President's House (1911) or Houghton Library (1937), yet utilizes the entire area between these buildings

(fig. 238). The open space and furnishings of the library interior, all of which were designed by the Stubbins firm, provide a serene area for researchers in the Harvard Archives and Theater Collection. Illuminated display cases form the walls of reading and assembly areas in the adjoining hallways to further a sense of space (fig. 239). While underground construction is not needed or desirable in every location, it was a brilliantly executed solution at Pusey Library. No other building has added so much to Harvard Yard yet disturbed its integrity so little.[2]

One of the most controversial architectural projects in recent Harvard history has been the building for the John F. Kennedy School of Government. The structure, begun in 1977 from designs by Architectural Resources Cambridge, Inc., represents a compromise arrived at after many years of negotiation, and like that of Pusey Library, its style has responded above all to considerations of planning. The original proposal was for a very large complex by I. M. Pei combining academic facilities with the John F. Kennedy Library, the design for which received national attention and

238
Pusey Library. Connected by underground tunnels to Widener and Houghton, the new library allowed traditional pedestrian patterns to persist.

239
Pusey Library interior. A surrounding moat, glass walls, spacious corridors with lounge areas, and lighted display cases for the Harvard Theater Collection add amenity to the subterranean interior.

273 *The New Harvard*

240
John F. Kennedy School of Government and Library: project model of unexecuted design (I. M. Pei, 1974).

241
John F. Kennedy School of Government (Architectural Resources Cambridge, Inc., 1977). This facade faces the river; Eliot House is across the street.

274   *The New Harvard*

242
John F. Kennedy School of
Government. The interior design accommodates small
conversation groups on
varying levels as well as large
lectures.

acclaim (fig. 240). This scheme had to be modified for two reasons. One was
neighborhood opposition: the Kennedy Library, with its memorabilia of the
late president, was certain to attract vast numbers of visitors, and Harvard
Square, which is ill adapted to handling automobile traffic, was already
congested. Secondly, the elaborate and highly original project had to be
simplified as the once ample capital fund dwindled because of sharp
increases in construction costs during the period between initial subscription and eventual construction, which began in 1977. The costly delay was
caused first by the time needed to acquire the site (the old MBTA rail yards
had first to be relocated) and then by extended negotiations with powerful
neighborhood and planning groups. The structure that was finally built
(figs. 241, 242) is far smaller and less spectacular than the Pei design, which
would have added a stunning gem to the architectural diadem of Harvard;
but it is more in keeping with academic building and undoubtedly represents
better environmental planning.[3]

Under the compromise the library and the academic activities were
separated. The John F. Kennedy Library was built adjacent to the University
of Massachusetts campus on Columbia Point in South Boston, a successful
siting of an excellent design. Meanwhile the John F. Kennedy School of

Government was assigned a portion of the site in Cambridge. The rest of the site was divided into a large park, to occupy the southern third of the tract near the river, and areas for parking and commercial and residential occupancy in the northern section nearer Harvard Square. The School of Government was the first part of the plan to be constructed, so it established the basis for the site planning and design of the other elements to follow.

The Kennedy School faces Boylston Street (renamed John F. Kennedy Street), a rather difficult design assignment because the Harvard buildings on the opposite side of the street provide few architectural cues with which to relate (though there is an obvious feature to be avoided: the large service areaway for the dormitory kitchens). Fortunately, the new school is set far enough back from the road to allow for a row of shade trees, which greatly enhances what had been a dull traffic way. The long south facade of the new building faces the park, which will always provide its view to the river and its position, with Eliot House, as the gateway to Harvard.

In appearance the school is simple and unobtrusive. Its visual interest derives from broken massing, the proportions of the fenestration and geometric units, and slight variations in the texture of the masonry. Sheathed entirely in brick, without white dressings, the new building follows in its unrelieved dark color recent Harvard practice as established at Larsen Hall and followed at Canaday Hall and Tozzer Library. The overall appearance of the structure, however, is somewhat confusing. At first glance the irregular massing of the silhouette caused by penthouses or clerestories suggests domestic purposes. Closer inspection reveals that the units are two or three times domestic scale, a discrepancy that recalls Mallinckrodt Laboratory.[4] Yet the scale of the building and its placement on the site work well when approached from the Larz Anderson Bridge. The abolition of the rail yards accompanying erection of the northern residential and commercial segment of the Kennedy School represents a final step in the reclamation of the riverfront area which began with the vision and first activities of the Riverside Associates three-quarters of a century earlier.

Meanwhile with the growth of the university art collections and expansion of the Art History department, the Fogg Museum had become hopelessly overcrowded. New conservation techniques and requirements for light filtration and humidity control made certain sections of the building obsolete. Finally a gift from Arthur M. Sackler made possible an addition to house the Asiatic and Classical collections and to provide much-needed faculty and administrative office space, exhibition galleries, and a lecture hall. With the Carpenter Center occupying the area to the south of the Fogg, the only other available site was that of Allston Burr Hall across Broadway from the Fogg. With streets on three sides, the site was problematic at best. The demolition of Allston Burr was a great loss, but the new Science Center had taken over the functions for which Allston Burr (the General Sciences Building) had been built, and Allston Burr's design did not lend itself easily to other uses. So in 1981, after extensive research and site inspection of museum buildings throughout the world, a committee chaired by Seymour Slive recommended that the commission be awarded to the British architect James Stirling from among 85 competitors. Stirling had already designed both museums and other buildings for Cambridge and Leicester Universities in England, and in this country for Rice University in Houston.[5]

243
Sackler Museum (James Stirling, 1981) from the north-west, looking toward the Fogg Museum. Pale orange and blue-gray striped walls curve around the corner of Broadway and Quincy Street.

The uninterrupted elevation of the Sackler Museum that curves around the northwest corner of Quincy Street and Broadway (fig. 243) is banded with slick orange and blue-gray brick. The syncopated placement of windows of varied width within the dark bands provides for optimum views outward from the offices within. These windows and also the shape of the building can be seen as alluding to familiar precedents in the work of H. H. Richardson (whose Sever Hall stands just out of view diagonally across Quincy Street within the Yard). At an earlier stage of the design, broad bands of black brick were planned at both the parapet and the sill of the building. These would have strengthened the Richardsonian allusion and prevented the present unfortunate evocation of dull British industrial architecture of the 1930s, which has no relevance here. The slick and unarticulated surface introduces to the area around the Yard yet another shade of red brick: this one a bald, pale orange glazed brick that no critical generosity can approve. Had it been of a more sensitive color and texture, or at least laid more three-dimensionally, this exterior might have worked well with the banded slate roof and rich polychromatic walls of Memorial Hall, its neighbor across the intersection of Cambridge and Quincy Streets.

The Sackler's exterior also suffers at present from the fact that the planned bridge linking it to the Fogg remains unexecuted (fig. 244). The scale and proportions of the entrance to the Sackler will become more

277 *The New Harvard*

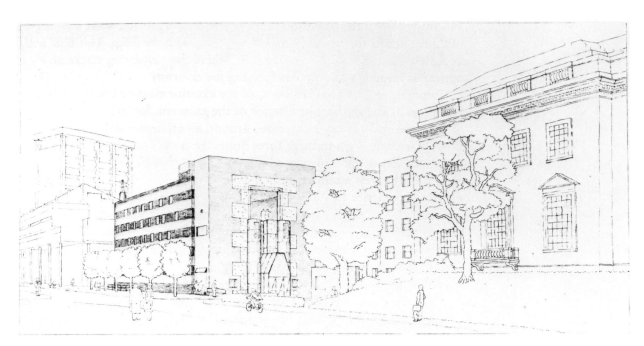

244
*Sackler Museum from the
southwest, looking toward
Gund Hall. The entrance was
designed to accommodate a
bridge across Broadway
connecting the Sackler and
Fogg buildings.*

245
*Sackler Museum: axonometric
drawing. The shape of the
gallery ceilings, like that at the
top of the seven-foot-wide
staircase, repeats the Egyptian
arch of the entrance.*

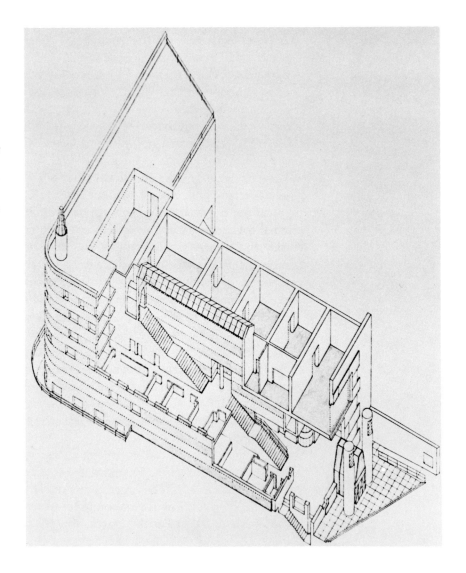

acceptable when the bridge is realized. The banding of the walls will continue across the bridge to join the Sackler with the Fogg. This link will complete the rationale of the entrance, where the ventilating stacks now appear as meaningless cylinders flanking the doorway.

Coloristic and textural criticisms of the exterior must be counterbalanced, however, by the spectacular interior of the museum, for this is an inward-looking design. Its plan is organized around an off-center staircase that flows grandly upward through three floors from the dominant postmodern entrance. The design provides a brilliant functional solution for the offices, ranged to the west around the curving exterior wall, and allows for ample exhibition galleries to the east of the stairs and a monumental space at the entrance. The entrance court echoes the interior organizational plan of the Fogg, thus linking the form of the two museums. The complex functions of the museum have been addressed thoughtfully within a limited budget, as indicated in the axonometric drawing (fig. 245).

Historical allusions and themes are introduced, for example, in the Egyptian arch of the glass-enclosed entrance vestibule, and implicitly echoed throughout in the treatment of volume and space. The enormous height of the flagstone entrance hall, lighted at night from behind its four megalithic columns, evokes the proportions of the Hypostyle Hall of the Temple at Karnak while eschewing its ornament. The toplit staircase repeats on the third floor (with perspective illusion) the Egyptian arch of the entrance and the horizontal exterior banding as well. On the staircase walls are embedded ancient sculptural reliefs from the Fogg collection. One of the most creative elements of the building, this staircase slashes up the full height of the structure at a width of only seven feet, producing a sense of compression and movement equal to that of the grand gallery leading to the King's Chamber in the Pyramid of Cheops at Gizeh. This avoidance of wide spans in the public spaces and openings of the Sackler provides visual delight for visitors, both those who do and those who do not identify these historic allusions to the collection it houses. Even the gallery ceilings repeat the shape of the Egyptian arched entrance. The Sackler interior abounds in original solutions for control of lighting, rich wooden flooring, and elegant display and lecture spaces. Despite its disdainful and arrogant elevations, Stirling has produced a masterpiece in this interior. Harvard has few other spaces of such quality.[6] Yet the exterior remains jarring and forbidding, unnecessarily out of context with its surroundings.

The small Gatelodge that ends this discussion of Harvard's buildings stands at the Johnston Gate, the main entrance to the Yard. This tiny new construction (fig. 246), designed by Graham Gund Associates in 1982, embodies, like the Sackler, the new architectural insouciance of the 1980s. Although the design was affected in its final form by too many committee decisions (which increased its price), it reflects the contextual competence that has distinguished much recent work of the Gund firm. Standing between Harvard Hall III and Massachusetts Hall, the wooden lodge, with the relief of its textured walls, provides a successful transition between the Yard and Harvard Square, which has focused for so many years on its subway kiosk of 1910. The lodge is intricately proportioned to synthesize the niches and panels of the elaborate Johnston Gate with the articulation of Isaiah Rogers' First Parish Church, which it reflects in both color and material.[7]

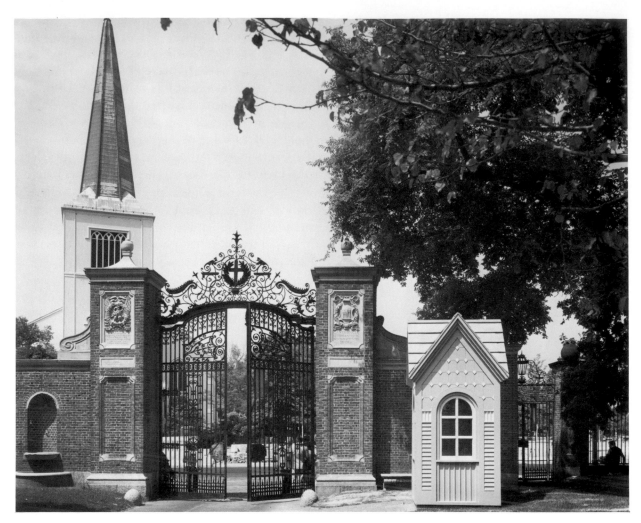

246
*The Gatelodge at the
Johnston Gate (Graham
Gund Associates, 1982).*

From a small wooden building on just over an acre at the northern fringe of
the seventeenth-century village, Harvard has grown to dominate not only
the site of the original village but most of eighteenth-century Cambridge as
well. The Harvard and Radcliffe academic areas in Cambridge alone now
cover something like 224 acres. Yet Harvard architects have been repeatedly
required to accommodate their designs not only to educational objectives
but also to earlier buildings of distinguished and distinctive design. Harvard's architecture represents a remarkably complete cross-section of
American architecture, yet manages in most areas of the campus to combine
it harmoniously despite the egos of architects of national importance such
as Bulfinch, Richardson, McKim, Gropius, and Le Corbusier. The brilliant
planning of Charles A. Coolidge in pulling together Harvard Yard and the
South Yard has combined with the innovative urbanism of Josep Lluis Sert,
who incorporated large complexes into the campus by introducing the mall
and welding to it the North Yard. The planning genius of Coolidge and Sert
have given Harvard today the visual unity that Montgomery Schuyler found
missing in 1909.[8]

The campus of Harvard, despite many attempts, has never been locked in
to an axial plan or an overall rigorous program such as the Business and

Medical Schools and most other American college campuses. Yet somehow, some persistence of the Puritan ethos of restraint has influenced the long list of Harvard architects as much as they have influenced its development. The early core of red brick building was so respected in the later nineteenth and early twentieth centuries that it has a life of its own which pervades the campus today. Those architects who most respected this ethos have been the most successful, for under this mandate both H. H. Richardson and Hugh Stubbins, for example, created some of their greatest designs. Despite changes in style and material, even Gropius, the iconoclast, bowed to the Harvard idiom in the planning of the Graduate Center. Today Harvard has one great heroic building in Memorial Hall, the fulcrum of the campus plan. The essence, the spirit, of Harvard's architecture lies elsewhere, in the unplanned and accidental continuum of its yards and great River Houses on the banks of the Charles. Like the intellectual spirit of Harvard, its architecture has been individual and yet coherent through three centuries.

Notes

1. Seventeenth-Century Harvard

1. The standard references on the history and the buildings of Harvard in the seventeenth century are by Samuel Eliot Morison: "A Conjectural Restoration of the Old College at Harvard," *Old Time New England* 23 (April 1933):131–158; *The Founding of Harvard College* (Cambridge: Harvard University Press, 1935); *Harvard College in the Seventeenth Century*, 2 vols. (Harvard University Press, 1936); *Three Centuries of Harvard University, 1636–1936* (Harvard University Press, 1936). In light of Professor Morison's virtual monopoly and exhaustive research on the subject, and because he uses many facts and quotations in more than one book, no attempt is made here to note each reference.

The primary sources of information are the College Books published by the Colonial Society of Massachusetts. College Book I, which covers the period under consideration in this chapter, was reproduced in the *Publications of the Colonial Society of Massachusetts* (hereafter cited as *PCSM*), *Collections, Harvard College Records*, Part I, vol. 15 (1925); Part II is published in vol. 16 (1925). Further references to early Harvard real estate are available in the files of the Cambridge Historical Commission, City Hall Annex, Cambridge, Massachusetts.

2. We do not know how Peyntree spelled his name. Robert Nylander has seen it spelled Peintre, Peintree, Peintry, Pentry, and Peyntree alternately in Cambridge town records. Comfort Starr may have owned the house in 1636 prior to its acquisition by the college.

3. Nathaniel Eaton (b. 1610), well born and well educated, who had been elected a scholar at Trinity College Cambridge in 1630, was dismissed from his post as head of the college for cruelty and beating of students. John Harvard, who later gave his library, a cash bequest, and his name to the college, migrated to America aboard the *Hector* in 1637 with Eaton. Harvard, a wealthy middle-class property owner from Southark, settled with his wife and family in Charlestown, Massachusetts, 1637–1638. He had been at Emanuel College Cambridge at the time when Eaton was at Trinity, but was never directly connected with the American college until his death in 1638. See Albert Bushnell Hart, "What Do We Know about John Harvard?" *Harvard Monthly* 2, no. 2 (April 1886):43–57.

4. W. C. Lane, "Foundations of Two Colonial Buildings," *PCSM* 13 (Jan. 1910):74.

5. No exact equivalence between seventeenth- and twentieth-century prices can be arrived at because the prices of commodities have increased at different rates. But Seymour Harris, in *The Economics of Harvard* (New York: McGraw-Hill, 1972), p. 199, judges that a small house would cost 170 times its seventeenth-century value, and estimates one New England pound as equivalent to about $3.30 in 1965 dollars.

Little is known about seventeenth-century urban house design. Robert Nylander points out that Cambridge inventories suggest some unusual plans, which frequently cite a "middle" room or chamber. Permits to "build and end" or mentioning a "leanto at the end" suggest that some urban houses were expanded lengthwise, rather than to the rear as in rural areas.

6. Bainbridge Bunting and Robert H. Nylander, *Old Cambridge,* Cambridge Historical Commission, Survey of Architectural History in Cambridge, Report 4 (Cambridge: M.I.T. Press, 1973), pp. 30–34.

7. Whereas ten thousand acres of land were promised an unrealized college in Virginia when it was projected in the seventeenth century and the state universities of California were each given one or two thousand acres in the nineteenth century, Harvard began life on a 1 1/8-acre plot plus a 2 1/4-acre pasture. All subsequent additions of land had to be purchased from the school's meager resources. Harris estimates that between 1636 and 1652 two-fifths of the operating budget was directed to capital improvements—land acquisition, construction of buildings, and their repair.

8. Cambridge Proprietor's Records, pp. 146, 165, indicate that Harvard owned three common rights in 1665 and 1683 (perhaps those belonging to the Peyntree House) and had bought two additional rights by 1703. Robert Nylander's study of the complex land history of Cambridge reveals that Harvard was allotted its proportion of land in every division of the Cambridge common lands through the last in 1724, except possibly that of 1645 where no acreage appears against its name. See Cambridge Town Records, p. 67.

9. President Eliot, summarizing in 1869 the school's land transactions with the city, revealed that Cambridge had given Harvard a total of 32 1/3 acres. Harris, *Economics of Harvard,* p. 329.

10. Letter from President Dunster, quoted in *PCSM* 15 (1925):lxxii. See also Benjamin Peirce, *History of Harvard University* (Cambridge: Brown, Shattuck & Co., 1833), pp. 2–18.

11. A bird's-eye view and plans of Harvard Hall I are published in Morison's *The Founding of Harvard College.* All of the Shurtleff drawings are filed in the Harvard Archives, UAI.15.25pf.

12. "His sizers studdy over ye porch off that Chamber," in "the studdies in Harvard College with their Incomes & quarterly Rents." *PCSM* 15 (1925):14. For an account of the Franquelin View of Harvard see Hamilton V. Bail, *Views of Harvard: A Pictorial Record to 1860* (Cambridge: Harvard University Press, 1949), pp. 10–16.

13. "The building called the Old Colledge, conteyning a Hall, Kitchen, Buttery, Cellar, Turrett & 5 Studyes & there 7 Chambers for Students in them, a Pantry & small corner Chamber. A library & Books therin, vallued at 400." *PCSM* 15 (1925):lxxiv.

14. College bills, according to Morison, were paid in service, commodities, and some silver. Wheat and malt were the most common media of payment; next was cattle on the hoof and then butter.

15. Unlike the British system of gradual amortization, however, the debt for finishing the study at Harvard was relayed from one occupant to the next without reduction until 1655, at which time the current occupant had to pay the whole charge.

16. Nathaniel Eaton, in settling the building accounts in October 1641 (by which time £301 had been spent), mentions both the "cost of frame, carriage, and setting up and digging cellar" at £150 and the "cost of additions to original frame plus unloading timber for the addition" at £113. This addition, which did not include a cellar, appears to have been almost the same size as the original unit. This suggests that the building as initially planned may have consisted either of the main rectangular block without the wings and low north chambers or of half the main block plus one wing. In either case the kitchen must have been planned for the western end of the building, since the cellar, which would undoubtedly have been adjacent to the kitchen, was included in the original scheme. Neither method of enlargement would have produced as formal a solution as Shurtleff proposes.

17. For a more fully documented recent study of seventeenth-century building practice, see Abbott L. Cummings, *The Framed Houses of Massachusetts Bay: 1625–1725* (Cambridge: Harvard University Press, 1979).

18. *Records of the Town of Cambridge*, Cambridge, p. 901, contain many permits to individuals to cut timber on the common lands for purposes of construction. The principal use for rough terrain such as Arlington Heights was as a woodlot.

19. *PCSM* 15 (1925):lxxiv.

20. Ibid., p. lxxiii.

21. Letter from President Dunster, quoted in ibid., p. lxxii.

22. Bunting and Nylander, *Old Cambridge*, pp. 75, 134, 143.

23. "The Indian College . . . cost between three or four hundred pounds . . . but not hitherto hath been much improved for the ends intended, by reason of the death and failing of Indian Scholars. It hath hitherto been principally for to accommodate English scholars and using a printing press belonging to the college." *PCSM* 15 (1925):lxxxiii. The windows were apparently glazed with paper (Robert Nylander).

24. The first printing press was brought to Harvard by Joseph Glover, whose widow married President Dunster. Beginning in 1646 it was installed in a ground-floor room of the second presidential abode. After Dunster's resignation, in 1655, it was moved to a small print house under construction. When a new, larger press arrived from England in 1659, both presses were installed in the Indian College, where two Dutch visitors observed them to be in a state of disuse.

25. Reconstruction drawings of the Indian College are filed in the Harvard Archives, UAI.15.25pf.

2. *The Brick Quadrangles*

1. William Burgis, " A Prospect of the Colledges in Cambridge in New England," 1726. The only known copy of this copperplate engraving (24 by 19 inches) is in the collection of the Massachusetts Historical Society. Probably of English origin, Burgis lived in Boston between 1722 and 1731 and drew several views of the city. The engraver of the plate is unknown, but it has been suggested that the printing was carried out in England.

2. Saint Catherine's Hall, Cambridge (1674) is one English precedent. Examples of New England parallels are the Ward house in Salem (1684) and the Cooper-Frost-Austin house in Cambridge (c. 1690; discussed in Bunting and Nylander, *Old Cambridge*, pp. 73–75).

3. *PCSM* 15 (1925):xc. Randolph's figure of twenty chambers, however, is disputed by university Chamber Settlement Lists from 1725, which never indicate more than thirteen chambers—a reminder of the inaccuracies in seventeenth-century records.

4. Bunting and Nylander, *Old Cambridge*, p. 75.

5. *PCSM* 15 (1925):xc. The Lee-Nichols House roof was done in two stages: front first, then rear. Robert Nylander has noted the similarities in complexity between Saint Michaels in Marblehead (1714), the McPhedris-Warner House (1716) in Portsmouth, and the construction of Harvard Hall II.

6. Leonard Hoar (A.B. 1650), who succeeded President Chauncy in 1672, had been in England following his Harvard graduation, only to be turned out of his Cromwellian living there in 1662. A man of medical and scientific interests, Hoar returned to America after having been made a doctor of medicine at Cambridge by Charles II. He came to Boston as minister of the Old South Church shortly before Chauncy's death and was elected president of the college. His most important proposal was the abortive establishment of a chemical laboratory and botanical garden at Harvard. Unfortunately his overbearing manner and temperamental unsuitability to administration created immediate difficulties, resulting in his resignation in 1675; he died shortly thereafter. Morison, *Three Centuries of Harvard*, pp. 40–42.

7. *PCSM* 15 (1925):lxxxviii. The meaning of "Holppacte" is not known; the term perhaps relates to "hollow newel'd," a three-run stair about a hollow core or well.

8. *PCSM* 15 (1925):cvii. The president's barn was constructed in 1681.
Urian Oakes (A.B. 1649), then minister to Cambridge, replaced President Hoar in 1675; he died six years later. Despite his considerable accomplishments as a man of learning and a Latin wit, Oakes presided over the upheavals of King Philip's War in a tenure of no great distinction. Morison, *Three Centuries of Harvard*, pp. 42–44.

9. Suggesting the importance of the gift to its donor, the facade of old Stoughton Hall is depicted in the background of the anonymous portrait of Lieutenant Governor Stoughton that hangs in the room of the Faculty of Arts and Sciences in University Hall.

10. *PCSM* 15 (1925):xcvii. The earthquake incident is reported (second hand) in Peirce, *History of Harvard*, p. 71. In a note the editor added that "the walls of Stoughton Hall had begun to settle and lean considerably; and that the shock of the earthquake restored them to their perpendicular direction."

11. An epoch of peace in the colony following the Treaty of Utrecht in 1713 allowed President John Leverett (1708–1724) to turn his attention to care of the college buildings and the erection of Massachusetts Hall. It was also under his vigorous administration that the Hollis professorship, Harvard's first chair, was established. See Morison, *Three Centuries of Harvard*, pp. 54–75.

12. For a discussion of the medieval origins of the quadrangles in England, see Paul Venable Turner, *Campus: An American Planning Tradition* (Cambridge: M.I.T. Press, 1984), pp. 9–16.

13. See Bail, *Views of Harvard*, plates 12, 18, 41.

14. The original hoods are clearly delineated in the Burgis engraving of 1726, the du Simitière watercolor of 1767–68, and a *Columbian Magazine* view of 1788 (the latter derived from Burgis). The hoods are missing, and capped by flattened pediments, in a *Massachusetts Magazine* engraving of 1790 and in gouaches by both Houdin and Story of 1795. All these pictures are reproduced in Bail's *Views of Harvard*.
A thorough renovation of Massachusetts Hall (new doors, door frames, windows) was carried out in 1812 under the direction of the engineer Loammi Baldwin. This was probably a delayed repair of damage sustained during the occupation by American troops in 1775. But the views reproduced by Bail indicate that the hoods had been removed before 1812. The remodeling contract and Baldwin's expense account are in the Harvard Archives, UAI.15.15 and UAI.15.15.2.

15. A record in the Butler's Book, 1722–1750 (along with the buttery accounts) shows that no fewer than thirty artisans were paid for work done or advice given. Some were Cambridge craftsmen: Prentice, Hicks, Hill, Wyeth. The framing was entrusted to Hunt and Chandler of Concord; the Coolidges of Watertown did most of the joinery; and the decorative detail and paving stones for the yard were supplied by William Burgis of Boston, the artist who drew the earliest picture of the college buildings. Harvard Archives, UAI.90.
President Benjamin Wadsworth, installed on Commencement Day in 1725, moved into his new house—which served as the presidential mansion for over a century—in January 1727. The decade of Wadsworth's presidency—marked by student and faculty upheavals—reflected his conciliatory and diplomatic personality.

16. Across the street from Wadsworth House, where Holyoke Center now stands, was another field owned by Harvard, the Bradish lot, where the freshmen also raked hay for the president's use. Octavius Pickering, *Life of Timothy Pickering* (Boston: Little, Brown, 1867), p. 11.

17. A number of contemporary dwellings in Concord used this curious lapped corner; an excellent example is the Heywood house of 1719 on the Lexington Road. This information, like so many other insights about colonial work, is from Robert Nylander.

18. Harvard Archives UAI.15.14pf (1843–1846). There are also plans for Edward Everett by George M. Dexter in the Dexter Drawings Collection, Boston Athenaeum,

dated Dec. 8, 1843. These are three years too early for Everett's presidency of Harvard (1846–1849). There may be some connection between their elaboration and a gift from Peter Chardon Brooks in 1843 of funds for a president's residence; Mr. Brooks was the father of Mrs. Everett.

19. Bunting and Nylander, *Old Cambridge,* p. 77; *PCSM* 15 (1925):cxxx; "Wadsworth House Clippings 1880–," Harvard Archives, HUV.187.3.2.

20. Having contributed to its construction, the college was part owner of the Cambridge meetinghouse, with rights to its use for commencement and exclusive regular use of one gallery. In 1706 the college subscribed £60 toward the construction of the third meetinghouse (while the congregation contributed £280), and in 1717 it agreed to pay one-seventh of the cost of its enlargement. *PCSM* 15 (1925):cxix.

21. Pickering, *Life of Timothy Pickering,* p. 11.

22. Apthorp House (1760), which now serves as the Master's residence for Adams House, was built by East Apthorp, first minister of Christ Church and an uncle of and major influence on Charles Bulfinch. The sophisticated design of the first two stories (the third story was added later) may well have been supplied by Peter Harrison, who in the late 1750s designed the church. Called the "Bishop's Palace," the house set standards for opulence in Cambridge in the years just preceding the Revolution. See Wendell D. Garrett, *The Apthorp House* (Cambridge: Harvard University Press, 1960).

23. The suggestion that a design drawn in England was carried to Cambridge by Thomas Hutchinson, who brought the funds from Mrs. Holden, was first made by Samuel Batchelder in *Bits of Harvard History* (Cambridge: Harvard University Press, 1924) and repeated by Bail. Charles A. Cummings first attributed Faneuil Hall to John Smibert in his authoritative article on Boston architecture in Justin Winsor's *Memorial History of Boston* (Boston: James R. Osgood, 1880); John Coolidge has indicated that papers of Bulfinch recently brought to light confirm Cummings' attribution. When Charles Bulfinch enlarged Faneuil Hall in 1806, he retained the design of the typical bay and the detailing of the capitals and base while elongating the proportions to meet delicate Federal standards.

The Scotsman John Smibert (1688–1751) was one of the most important figures in art and architecture in pre-Revolutionary New England. After establishing himself successfully as a portraitist in London, he sailed for Newport, Rhode Island, in 1729 with Bishop Berkeley's Bermuda Group; and he is best known for his painting of the voyagers (1729) now in the Yale University Collection. Smibert married to wealth in Boston and captured the portrait trade of the 1730s and early 1740s with a style that was imitative of that of Sir Godfrey Kneller. Smibert opened a shop for the sale of artist's materials and also organized the first art exhibition held in America. He became architecturally involved in the design of Faneuil Hall in 1740 and of Holden Chapel at Harvard in the following year. For a list of Smibert's works see *Proceedings of the Massachusetts Historical Society* 16 (1878), 17 (1879–80), and 49 (1915–16). See also *The Notebook of John Smibert* (Boston: Massachusetts Historical Society, 1969).

24. For several months in 1768 the college's morning and evening prayers were moved back to Holden when the House of Representatives, exiled to Cambridge by Governor Bernard, requisitioned the larger chapel in Harvard Hall III. For the history of Holden Chapel see Batchelder, *Bits of Harvard History,* ch. 1.

25. The original doorway of Holden Chapel, a tall rectangular opening with a light frame, is clearly shown in Bail, *Views of Harvard,* plates 11 and 29, dated 1767 and 1906; the vestibule with merlons at each corner and a round opening is recorded in a drawing of 1826, plate 46. The facade as it existed in 1850 and as it was then remodeled can be seen in a bound volume of architectural drawings prepared by the office of Gridley Bryant (1816–1899) and dated June 14, 1850, Harvard Archives, UAI.15.10.3pf. A note on Holden Chapel in the card catalogue of Harvard buildings, HUB.1000.5, says that the remodeling of 1812 was probably done by Loammi Baldwin.

26. Each of the three doorways contained a pediment. These were triangular in shape for the end doors, segmental over the false center door. They were still in place in 1806; see the Snyder watercolor in Bail, *Views of Harvard,* plate 29.

27. The committee appointed to rebuild the hall reported on June 18, 1765: "being sensible of his Excellency's superior knowledge in architecture, [we] requested him to favor us with a plan, and having examined and approved the same, we have been carying it into execution." *PCSM* 16 (1925):15.

28. Some members of the committee of legislators appointed to oversee the construction of the new hall favored placing it north of Massachusetts Hall. Governor Bernard, however, counseled, "the next College, if set as a wing to answer Massachusetts Hall would extend to the middle of the highway" (Kirkland Street). He also advised constructing the cornice of stone rather than of wood to impede the spread of any future fire. *PCSM* 16 (1925):15.

29. Photographs of eighteenth-century engraved plans of Harvard Hall III are filed in the Harvard Archives, UAI.15.12vt. The commons was soon outgrown. Before Bulfinch completed University Hall in 1814 one class was forced to eat in Hollis. A low entryway to the basement kitchen is seen in a drawing of 1821 in Bail, *Views of Harvard,* plate 40.

30. The interest in simple, clear volumes and minimal exterior ornament evident in Harvard Hall III are ordinarily associated with the Federal period, somewhat later. This style began to appear in America after the return of Charles Bulfinch in 1787 from his European journey and exposure to the work of Robert Adam.

31. John Coolidge has indicated that Harvard students have documented existence of the royal portraits, which were destroyed in the Revolution, although they are not mentioned in major catalogues of Copley's work. A lost painting of Mount Vesuvius erupting hung over the mantel between them. Full-length portraits by Copley of the donors of Harvard Hall had been taken upstairs to make way for the royal portraits; they are now in the university collection.

32. After fires in Hollis Hall (January 1876) and Stoughton Hall (December 1879) the University constructed a brick fire wall running along the center line of each building. These walls can be seen dividing the central false doors of both facades and interrupting the cornice of the pediment. Comparable walls were constructed in Holworthy in 1880. The fires also required the rebuilding of the roofs of Hollis and Stoughton, and a new roof was added at Holworthy in 1880 when the ceiling of the top floor was raised. These three roofs have similar heavy moldings and broad overhangs, a quality that makes for conformity in their massing but is contrary to the Late Georgian character of Stoughton and Holworthy. The top floor of Stoughton had been cleared of partitions in 1871 at a cost of $4000 to form the theatre and club room for the Hasty Pudding Club.

33. By 1795 Harvard owned all of the block now occupied by Holyoke Center except for one lot at the southeast corner; in the course of the nineteenth century all was sold with the exception of the Bradish lot at the northeast corner (the present site of the Cambridge Trust Company). A thorough examination of the chain of ownership of all property within the original town site was made in 1975 for the Cambridge Historical Commission by Robert Nylander. This information, which corrects many mistakes and false assumptions, is in the files of the Commission in the City Hall Annex.

34. Although today most critics think of the brick Georgian buildings as the most harmonious and beautiful ones at Harvard, this verdict has not always held. Anthony Trollope remarked of them in 1862: "The edifices used for the undergraduates Chambers and for lecture rooms . . . are very ugly red-brick houses standing here and there without order. . . . It is almost astonishing that buildings so ugly should have been erected for such a purpose." Trollope, *North America* (rpt. New York: Knopf, 1951), p. 245.

35. George Santayana, *Persons and Places* (New York: Charles Scribner & Sons, 1943), p. 197.

3. The Early Nineteenth Century

1. The university's economic history is given in a rather episodic fashion in Harris, *Economics of Harvard.* Of particular interest is the relationship between Harvard building construction and the several periods of rapid inflation: 1740–45, the 1770s,

the 1860s, and much of the twentieth century; as well as periods of deflation: 1870–79 and the 1930s.

2. Morison, *Three Centuries of Harvard,* ch. 9. President Kirkland (1810–1828), a Federalist, was one of the most beloved and enlightened presidents of Harvard. Raised on the Berkshire frontier, he was a Unitarian and became pastor of New South Church Boston in 1793. His genuine regard for the individual and his dedication to intellectual advancement (particularly under the impact of German educational theory) produced a well-traveled and informed breed of professors for Harvard. The international experience of professors such as Edward Everett and George Ticknor (who returned from education in Gottingen to a newly established position as professor of Modern Languages) was particularly important. Both Everett and Ticknor purchased books in Europe to enhance Harvard's meager library (Ticknor later established the Boston Public Library), an action directly related to the construction of Gore Hall in the 1840s. For discussion of Ticknor and Everett, see Martin Green, *The Problem of Boston* (New York: Norton, 1966).

3. Harris, *Economics of Harvard,* p. 213.

4. Nathaniel Bowditch, a seasoned sea captain from Salem, received the Magister in Artibus degree from Harvard upon publication of his book *The Practical Navigator* (1802). A self-made man without a college education, Bowditch was fearless, inflexible, and tactless. In 1828 as treasurer he was responsible for the downfall of the enlightened administration of President Kirkland.

5. At the southeast corner of the lot stood the Dana-Palmer House, built in 1822; north of it was the president's house (1860) by E. C. Cabot; after that came three houses constructed by Harvard and rented to faculty: 25 Quincy Street (1844), rented to Professor Walker; 31 Quincy (1844), rented to Professor Pierce; and 37 Quincy (1848), rented to Professor Fenton. See Antoinette F. Downing, Elizabeth MacDougall, and Eleanor Pearson, *Mid-Cambridge,* Cambridge Historical Commission, Survey of Architectural History in Cambridge, Report 2 (Cambridge: M.I.T. Press, 1967), pp. 25, 64.

6. Harris, in *Economics of Harvard,* gives the cost of 14 buildings erected between 1805 and 1869 (he does not say which ones) as $1,290,000; yet the endowment in 1869 was only $2,229,000. Such spending, of course, was not without critics. An anonymous review of Samuel A. Eliot's *Sketches of Harvard College,* in *The North American Review* (1849): 104–107, laments the expenditure on four buildings of $200,000, three-quarters of which was drawn from the college stock. According to the reviewer this was "only about half as much as it might have been but for this insane expenditure within three years upon bricks and stones — this taste for architectural abortions."

7. See Talbot Hamlin, *Greek Revival Architecture in America* (London: Oxford, 1944), pp. 159–186.
Loammi Baldwin (1780–1838), a hero of the Revolution, a citizen of Woburn, and inventor of both the vulcanizing process for rubber and the Baldwin apple, was the father of civil engineering in America. "Founding Fathers," *Journal of the Boston Society of Civil Engineers* 23 (July 1936):173. Setting up an office in 1809 at the Charlestown Navy Yard after a trip to England, Baldwin trained the whole generation of Boston's engineer architects who followed: Alexander Parris (Quincy Markets), Solomon Willard (Bunker Hill Monument), Isaiah Rogers, Ammi B. Young (Customs House), and Gridley J. F. Bryant. As might be expected, his work at Harvard incorporated structural innovation: for example, new windows and doors for Massachusetts Hall and the new, more practical plan for Holworthy.

8. In May 1804 the Corporation, in specifying the location of Stoughton Hall, explained that "in some future time it may be found expedient to extend the College Buildings eastward of the present range of Hollis Hall and the new building now contemplated." Harvard Corporation Records, vol. IV, pt. 2, pp. 14–15 (Harvard Archives UAI.5.30.2).

9. The brewhouse, which stood east of Harvard Hall III, can be seen in Bail, *Views of Harvard,* plate 20; it was burned in 1814 as a prank. A plan of Harvard Yard in 1764,

PCSM 16 (1925), locates the brewhouse and privies as well as the creek that drained the Old Yard. The privies were removed in 1871 after waterclosets were installed in the basements of the dormitories. Andrew Peabody, *Harvard Reminiscences* (Boston: Ticknor & Co., 1888), p. 199.

10. Three unsigned drawings in the Harvard Archives (UAI.15.740pf, 1813), purportedly by Bulfinch, show different arrangements of buildings in the Old Yard. One is the "racetrack"; the second, without the ellipse of trees, places the new hall in the same location as in the racetrack, but on an east-west axis centered between Harvard and Massachusetts Halls. It also has a stair tower (or pavilion) on the narrow western facade that faces those two halls; the building plan is almost identical to the one used for University Hall except for the addition of the western tower with its (redundant) third staircase. The third scheme is much more elaborate and would have more than doubled the then-existing space of the college. The Old Yard was enclosed by two proposed structures corresponding to Hollis and Sever. To the east, in Tercentenary Quadrangle, is a large semicircular dormitory of nine entries opening to the south. At each end of this are buildings with porticos also facing south. The two yards have no visual connection.

11. The choice of granite as a building material became practical after the opening of the Middlesex Canal in 1803, which made it possible to transport the granite by barge from Chelmsford, where it was quarried, directly to the college wharf at the foot of Dunster Street. Bulfinch used stone first at the State Prison, Charlestown (1804–1805), then at Suffolk County Courthouse, Boston (1810–1812), University Hall, and Massachusetts General Hospital (1818–1823).

12. Bail, *Views of Harvard,* plates 32, 46. "The Eastern Front of University Hall," *Harvard Alumni Bulletin* 19, no. 36 (June 14, 1917):713, gives an illustration of the earlier western porch.

13. Peabody, *Reminiscences,* p. 205. Peabody also reports that only the two outside halls were being used for commons in 1824–1828.

14. Pierre de Chaignon la Rose (1871–1941), Harvard A.B. 1895, a Cambridge man of letters and a graduate of Phillips Exeter, taught at Harvard from 1895 to 1902. He did heraldic designs for Yale, Princeton, and the Cathedral of St. John the Divine in New York City, and for the Harvard houses for the Tercentenary in 1936. See Harvard Class of 1895, *50th Anniversary Report,* pp. 538–540.
The seated statue of John Harvard was commissioned from Daniel Chester French (1850–1931) in 1882 and cast in bronze in 1884. This commission thus followed his successful *Minuteman* (1873) for Concord and portrait bust of Ralph Waldo Emerson (1879). The transfer of the statue from its original site on the Delta to a position on axis with Charles McKim's Johnston Gate was intended to give a sense of large-scale planning to the Yard and also to ameliorate the awkwardness of the central portion of Bulfinch's facade of University Hall. The statue symbolically continued to face west in its new location. *Harvard Alumni Bulletin* 26, no. 30 (May 1, 1924):844; Lowell Papers (1922–1925), Harvard Archives, UAI.5.160, folder #566.

15. The first law classes were held in Webber House on Harvard Square; enrollment (down to four students in 1828) did not then require a larger building. To finance the new building, which cost $7000, Nathan Dane agreed to advance $5000 provided the Corporation repay the loan to the endowment of the chair in law that he had just established. The addition was done by Isaac Melvin, a Cambridge housewright.

16. Judge and Supreme Court Justice Joseph Story (1779–1845) was memorialized in marble by his son, the sculptor William Wetmore Story (1819–1895). The life-sized statue, now in Sanders Theatre, launched the career of William Wetmore Story, whose life in the American sculptural colony in Rome inspired Nathaniel Hawthorne's *Marble Faun* (1860) and Henry James's *William Wetmore Story and His Friends* (Boston, 1903).

17. See Jacob Bigelow, *History of Mount Auburn Cemetery* (Cambridge, 1860).

18. The architect Richard Bond was known to have been associated with Isaiah Rogers at the First Parish Church, Cambridge, in 1834. He obtained the commission for Gore Hall in 1838 and was also retained in 1840 for the remodeling of Harvard Hall III.

After Rogers's departure for New York in 1834 Bond succeeded to his practice in Massachusetts. In December of 1838 Bond attended the abortive foundation meeting of the National Society of Architects (superseded in 1857 by the American Institute of Architects) in New York. He may have seen at that time the Gothic designs of New York University (1833–1840), which Ithiel Town and A. J. Davis were then completing; this might explain the up-to-date style of Gore Hall. See Walter H. Kilham, *Boston after Bulfinch* (Cambridge: Harvard University Press, 1946), and files of the Cambridge Historical Commission.

19. The granite used was supplied by Solomon Willard from Quincy quarries. Dressed granite was first used commercially in Boston by Alexander Parris on such structures as Saint Paul's Cathedral (1819) and the Quincy Markets (1822). Harris, *Economics of Harvard,* pp. 234, 295.

20. Charles W. Eliot, *Harvard Memories* (Cambridge: Harvard University Press, 1923).

21. Harris, *Economics of Harvard,* p. 436; Morison, *Harvard in the Seventeenth Century,* p. 297.

22. *American Architect and Building News,* November 23, 1878, p. 172.
Harvard's librarian Justin Winsor had been tapped by President Eliot after his tenure as librarian of the Boston Public Library was threatened. For Winsor's role at the Boston Public Library, see Thomas Boylston Adams, "Enter Politics—and a Great Library Runs Off Course," *Boston Globe,* July 31, 1983, p. A19. Winsor is best known for his monumental *Memorial History of Boston,* 4 vols. (Boston: James Osgood, 1880). See William F. Jordy, *American Buildings and Their Architects,* III: *Progressive and Academic Ideals at the Turn of the Twentieth Century* (New York: Doubleday, 1972), ch. 7, for discussion and further bibliography of metal stack construction and for the historic role of Ware and Van Brunt at Gore Hall.

23. Bunting and Nylander, *Old Cambridge,* p. 159; see also the files of the Cambridge Historical Commission. All the drawings are carefully rendered in color as though for a competition. Gilman submitted four designs (one Gothic, three Romanesque) accompanied by two explanatory letters. Harvard Archives, HUI.15.14pf.

24. Schulze's innovative use of building materials should be noted. The quarry-faced ashlar of his Boylston Hall influenced the young architect H. H. Richardson. Schulze was of German origin and practiced architecture in Boston from 1850 until his move to New York in 1858. After 1877, in partnership with Adolph Cluss in Washington, D.C., he designed many government buildings such as the Arts and Industries Building (1879–1881).

25. President's Report, 1872–73, p. 8.

26. Despite the fact that both Appleton Chapel and Boylston Hall were built with the aid of bequests, the college had to dip into its reserves for $12,200 to finish them. The endowment in 1860 was $975,222.

27. Gridley J. F. Bryant (1816–1899), partner of Arthur Gilman after 1857, is best known for his numerous innovative prison designs such as the Charles Street Jail (1849). See Bainbridge Bunting, *Houses of Boston's Back Bay* (Cambridge: Harvard University Press, 1967), and Robert B. MacKay, "The Charles Street Jail: Hegemony of a Design" (Ph.D. diss., Boston University, 1980).

28. Another remodeling took place in 1877, at which time the interior was subdivided by brick fire walls. President's Report, 1877–78, p. 47. See also "Boylston's Fifth Incarnation by TAC," *Architectural Forum* 113 (July 1960):90–93.

29. Nathaniel J. Bradlee (1829–1888), successor to the practice of George M. Dexter, designed much of Boston's South End between 1850 and 1870. The Dexter and Bradlee drawings are in the collection of the Boston Athenaeum, but the Bradlee drawings for Grays Hall, dated March 13, 1863, are filed in the Harvard Archives, UAI.15.25pf.

30. The three graduates were Francis Calley Gray (1790–1856), A.B. Harvard 1809, who had already bequeathed money for the Museum of Natural History and a remark-

able collection of prints; his brother John Chipman Gray (1793–1881), A.B. Harvard 1811; and their nephew John Chipman Gray (1839), A.B. Harvard 1859, LL.B. 1861, A.M. 1862, LL.D. 1895, son of a third brother, Horace Gray.

31. Grays was the first dormitory to have running water (in the basement, 1869), but it apparently was not very comfortable. Amos Lawrence in a letter of 1869 or 1870 to President Eliot expressed the wish that any new dormitory constructed "not be built like Grays without lathes and plaster which is cold as Greenland. The outside rooms cannot be warmed up to 50 degrees by any process on cold days." Harris, *Economics of Harvard,* p. 325. Steam heat was not added in Grays until 1909.

32. A drawing for College House signed by W. Sparrell, dated March 22, 1832, and one of the enlarged House about 1880, are filed in the Harvard Archives, UAI.15.25pf. The 1880 elevations and plans are in the microfiche collection of the Cambridge Historical Commission.

33. Another dormitory to house law students near the Square was acquired in 1857: Brattle House (1849) by J. C. Merrick, a former hotel with 106 rooms. The purchase price of $22,000, including furniture, was less than half the original cost of $47,500. Nevertheless the college found the venture unprofitable and sold the old hotel in 1865. Bunting and Nylander, *Old Cambridge,* pp. 43, 44; files of the Cambridge Historical Commission.

34. "The Panorama of Athens," painted by Barker and Binford, was purchased by Theodore Lyman II in London in November 1819 and insured for £2000. It was not provided with an exhibition shelter until 1843. Theodore Lyman II (1792–1849) became mayor of Boston (1834–35) and a benefactor of Harvard. Cyclorama painting became very popular in America beginning with John Vanderlyn's *Panorama of Versailles* (1816–19), which was displayed in a special rotunda in New York. Boston's later cyclorama of the Battle of Gettysburg was painted by the French artist Paul Philipoteaux and housed at 539 Tremont Street in a circular building by Cummings and Sears (1884).

35. See Cynthia Zaitzevsky, *Frederick Law Olmsted and the Boston Park System* (Cambridge: Harvard University Press, 1982), ch. 4. Asa Gray (1810–1888), a confirmed Darwinist, carried on the Botany Department alone at Harvard from 1842 to 1872 and was responsible for establishing the herbarium and (with Charles Sprague Sargent) its later offshoot the Arnold Arboretum. Much of the land of the Bussey Institute, Harvard's Department of Agriculture, was used for the Arboretum. The activities of both Gray and his colleague and friend Louis Agassiz were part of the Natural History Museum at Harvard, the first such institution in America, funded by the bequest of Francis Calley Gray (no relation to Asa Gray).

36. The Garden House is one of the few works of Ithiel Town (1784–1844) to reflect the Federal style of Asher Benjamin, with whom Town initially worked. Its unusual roof framing system documents the early engineering contributions of Town, who invented the lattice truss.

37. The West End Field and the Garden House are discussed in Bunting and Nylander, *Old Cambridge,* p. 16. Drawings for the herbarium are filed in the Harvard Archives, UAI.15.25pf.

38. Nathaniel Thayer, Jr. (1808–1883), of Lancaster, Massachusetts, accumulated a vast fortune in finance and railroads. He married Cornelia van Rensselaer in 1846 and was principal of J. T. Thayer and Brother, which in 1864 became Kidder Peabody and Company. His Italianate house by Richard Upjohn on Mount Vernon Street, Beacon Hill (1847), and his sons' lavish mansions by Sturgis and Brigham on Commonwealth Avenue in the Back Bay in the 1880s were the most expensive dwellings in Boston and contrasted sharply with the restraint of his buildings at Harvard. See Vincent P. Carasso, *More than a Century of Investment Banking: The Kidder Peabody Story* (New York: McGraw Hill, 1979). On the old herbarium and the rebuilding in 1909–1915 see Chapter 5, note 21. For the Harvard Press move and the renaming of the building see *Harvard Annual Report,* 1955–1956, p. 79.

39. The estate, brought together beginning in 1650 by Lieutenant Governor Thomas

Danforth, was inherited by his son-in-law, Francis Foxcroft. The formal Georgian mansion, as luxurious as any on Brattle Street, stood on the present site of Lowell Lecture Hall until it burned in 1776. The property was purchased by Daniel Mason, who in 1806 built the mansion known as Shady Hill; four years later he sold the estate to John Phillips, first mayor of Boston. From Phillips it passed in 1815 to Peter C. Brooks, reportedly Boston's first millionaire, and then to Harvard University in 1816. Downing, MacDougall, and Pearson, *Mid Cambridge,* pp. 14, 20, 28.

40. The university sold two other parcels (about 3.5 acres at $600 per acre) on the north boundary of the estate to John Palfrey in 1847 and 1852 but repurchased them in 1919; Downing, MacDougall, and Pearson, *Mid Cambridge,* p. 167. Much of the remaining acreage, which was part of the old Pine Swamp, Harvard probably retained only because it had little resale value. In 1828 the value of the land remaining from the Shady Hill purchase was estimated at only $2,600.

41. Drawings entitled "Proposals for Divinity Hall," one signed by Thomas Sumner and dated March 3, 1825, the other by S. Willard and dated September 2, 18— (paper torn) are preserved in the Harvard Archives, UAI.15.14pf (1825). Both designs are unrealistically grand. Nine years after the building was begun, a third set, signed by W. Sparrell and dated October 25, 1834, were made; these are also filed in the Harvard Archives, UAI.15.25pf. Exactly why they were made remains unclear. The original architect, Solomon Willard (1783–1861), sculptor and architect of the Bunker Hill Monument (1824–1842), left his Boston practice in 1825, moving to Quincy to be near the granite quarries from which he supplied stone to Boston architects. The Harvard drawing and commission were executed just at the time of his retirement from active practice and may well have been executed by Isaiah Rogers, to whom he turned over much of his work and who had been in his office since 1822.

42. The details of the chapel woodwork are masterful, but for suitability in this building the interior should have been painted.

43. Peabody, *Harvard Reminiscences,* p. 32. The new observatory was made possible by a bequest of $100,000 from Edmund Phillips, a recent graduate of the college. It was equipped with a 15-inch equatorial telescope, the largest size then known, which was bought with funds raised by public subscription.

44. Isaiah Rogers (1800–1869) was in the office of Solomon Willard beginning in 1822 and took over when Willard retired in 1826. Rogers experienced immediate success with the Tremont House (1828) in Boston and was associated with Richard Bond on the rebuilding of the First Parish Church in Cambridge (1833–34) just before leaving to set up practice in New York City. Although Rogers remained in New York, he continued to build in Massachusetts.

45. An extensive set of drawings for the Lawrence Scientific School and professor's residence by Gridley J. F. Bryant dating from May and November 1847 are preserved in the Harvard Archives, UAI.15.14pf. (1847). Bryant's Italianate design resembles Bond's, which was used, and Bryant (according to John Coolidge) did the landscaping. Bond may well have been one of many architects who provided designs for Bryant's firm.

46. Before the founding of the M.I.T. School of Architecture in 1867, Lawrence was the only training facility in the Boston area for architectural or engineering education.

47. For the Harvard Branch Railroad see Downing, MacDougall, and Pearson, *Mid Cambridge,* pp. 22–23. The Little Common, a portion of the original Cambridge Common, was a small triangle of land bounded by Kirkland Street and two legs of a street known as Holmes Place. Since 1933 the Little Common has been incorporated into the North Yard.

48. The corporation voted on April 28, 1712: "that the Orchard purchased of Michael Spencer & lately fenced be assigned for a place of recreation & exercise for the Scholars." And on April 19, 1737: "that the Northerly part of the Land improved by the Late President (Wadsworth) and that adjoynes to the playing pasture for the Scholars be Layd open to said playing pasture for the Enlargement of same." *PCSM* 15 (1925):lxxxviii.

49. A letter from J. Moore & Co. to President Kirkland in 1813 estimates the cost of a wooden building with eight baths at $1250; Harris, *Economics of Harvard*, p. 317.

50. Peabody, *Harvard Reminiscences*, p. 120.

51. Edward Clarke Cabot (1818–1901) was president of the Boston Society of Architects from its foundation in 1867 until the end of the century. He worked with George M. Dexter on his first and most famous design, the Boston Athenaeum (1847), and with Arthur Gilman on and off during the 1850s. Octagonally shaped buildings were popular in the 1850s when the gymnasium was designed and had already appeared at Harvard in Isaiah Rogers' Observatory (1843–1851) and the unattributed Panorama Rotunda (1843). See Orson Squire Fowler, *The Octagon House* (New York, 1853; rpt. ed., New York: Dover Press, 1973).

52. College Books, 1875, vol. II, p. 189–227 (*PCSM*, 16). The pamphlet *Harvard Boathouse Memorial*, Harvard Archives HUB1222.128.5, tells us that the upper deck of an 1868 boathouse collapsed when overloaded with spectators during a race on October 20, 1883.

53. Deficits occurred in only four years between 1832 and 1857; Harris, *Economics of Harvard*, p. 216. President Eliot summarizes the deficits and surpluses in his President's Report, 1902–03, p. 323. Besides the Boylston gift for Boylston Hall (1857) and the Appleton bequest for the chapel, the most important gifts to Harvard in mid-century were the Christopher Gore bequest, $100,000 (1834); the E. B. Phillips bequest, $100,000 for the observatory (1848); the A. A. Lawrence gift, $50,000 for the Scientific School (1846); and the F. C. Gray bequest, $50,000 for a museum of natural history (1858). The $369,000 for Memorial Hall, 1865–1876, came from the first large fundraising effort by alumni (a Sanders bequest provided the theatre section).

54. For the role of the picturesque in American culture of the period, see James Early, *Romanticism and American Architecture* (New York: A. S. Barnes, 1965).

4. President Eliot and the Harvard Yard

1. In 1809 Harvard owned 45 acres in Cambridge (22 in Harvard Yard, 2 in the Delta, 21 in the North Yard, Observatory, and Botanical Garden); by 1896 the figure had grown to 83.3 acres. By 1910 the university also owned 63 acres in Boston, 394 in Jamaica Plain, 2000 in the Harvard Forest at Petersham, and 700 in an engineering camp on Squam Lake, New Hampshire. Harris, *Economics of Harvard*, pp. 315, 329, 331; on the Jamaica Plain property see Zaitzevsky, *The Boston Park System*, ch. 4.

2. As cited in Morison, *Three Centuries of Harvard*, p. 253, the *Albany Journal* listed as follows the numbers of graduates receiving A.B. degrees from northern colleges in 1836: Yale 81, Union 71, Princeton 66, Dartmouth 44, Harvard 39, Amherst 38. Harvard's enrollment sagged between 1818 and 1852. Although Harvard first conferred M.A. and Ph.D. degrees in 1873 and Johns Hopkins not until 1878, the faculty and educational program of the latter had been established from the outset (1875) by President Gilman primarily to offer graduate instruction.

3. President Josiah Quincy (A.B. 1790) had already concluded a term as mayor of Boston; Boston's Quincy Markets (1822–1825), depicted in Gilbert Stuart's portrait of him, were erected during his administration. In 1825 the Granite Railway at Quincy-owned quarries (in the town of that name) provided for the first time a means of transporting building stone by rail to the water and thence by sea to Boston and Cambridge; hence Boston's Granite Age (1820–1860). At Harvard President Quincy instituted sound financial reforms, but he was fundamentally uninterested in education, and the repetitious, limited curriculum provided the source of most complaints about his unpopular administration. See Morison, *Three Centuries of Harvard*, pp. 246–272.

4. By 1874 the only required courses were freshman English, a foreign language, two semesters of science, and public speaking. By 1883–84 the elective system was completely in operation. As opposed to the set curriculum in the seventeenth century, Harvard in 1867 offered 92 courses; by 1903, toward the end of Eliot's tenure, there were 456 courses.

5. From a faculty of 32 in 1862, 26 were listed in the *Dictionary of American Biography.* Among the more famous were Louis Agassiz, Asa Gray, Wolcott Gibbs, Henry Wadsworth Longfellow, James Russell Lowell, Benjamin Peirce, and Jeffries Wyman.

6. In the seven-year period 1866–1872 Harvard accumulated a deficit of $27,500, and of this $11,500 developed in 1871–72, a particularly bad year because of losses incurred in the Fire of Boston. Despite heavy expenses in 1869 caused by the purchase of land and a significant increase in salaries, a large deficit for that year was avoided by a rise in tuition (from $104 to $150), rents from a new dormitory (Thayer Hall), and a class subscription of $50,000. Eliot presided over another period of deficits in the early 1900s.

7. One of Eliot's first acts was to raise the salary of the senior faculty—which had increased by only 5 percent since before the Civil War—from $3000 to $4000; this figure changed little until 1906, when salaries could be raised again after a successful $2.5 million endowment drive.

8. The figures do not include temporary or early structures about which insufficient information exists or dwellings built for rental purposes. The early houses at 53 Dunster Street (1841; now Dudley House Master's residence) and Apthorp House (1760; now Master's house for Adams House) were not owned by Harvard in 1869.

9. A review of receipts from rents from four dormitories in the Old Yard in 1857 indicates that the income of $4000 was offset by expenses for repair and cleaning of $3600, leaving but $400 as a return on investment.

10. President Eliot discussed good architecture in a speech at the dedication of the Albright Gallery in Buffalo, published in *The Critic,* August 1905: "In regard to public buildings, however, it is all important that they should not be only noble in design, but also nobly used or occupied. When a just and kindly rich man builds a handsome palace for himself and his family, his lavish expenditure does no harm to the community, but on the contrary provides it with a beautiful and appropriate object of sympathetic contemplation. But when a knave or a gambler lives in a palace, the sight of his luxury and splendor may work injury to the lookers-on. It is the same with regard to public buildings. Their occupation or use must be noble, like that of a Gothic cathedral. They must harbor honest men, not rogues. They must be used to promote large public interests, and must be instinct with public spirit."

11. Professor Coolidge used the terms Industrial, Picturesque, and Imperial Harvard in a seminar, "The Architecture of Harvard," in the spring of 1971.
The model for Imperial Harvard was the World's Columbian Exposition in Chicago (1893). Charles McKim's Columbia University (1893) and his other monumental schemes, such as the plan for Washington, D.C., subsequently provided increasing emphasis on axial alignment and impressive scale.

12. Quoted in George E. Ellis, "Memoirs of Nathaniel Thayer," *PCSM* 2, series 2 (1886).

13. A clipping from an unidentified newspaper dated December 1, 1870, Harvard Archives, HUB1831.2, says that Thayer Hall "is so placed that a line drawn from the front door of Holden Chapel to the center entrance of Appleton Chapel will pass directly through the middle door of Thayer. Nor is the new dormitory exactly on the same line with University Hall; it has been set back a few feet, so as to allow the new Memorial Hall to be seen from the Yard." The article goes on to discuss two alternate locations that were considered and how each would have affected the subsequent building in the Yard.

14. Building materials were still scarce in the early nineteenth century, and in New England the moving of even fairly large masonry structures like Dane Hall was not unknown. See Bunting, *Houses of Boston's Back Bay,* pp. 79, 80, regarding the moving of a much larger granite building, the Hotel Pelham (1857) in Boston.

15. See Wheaton A. Holden, "The Peabody Touch: Peabody and Stearns of Boston, 1870–1917," *Journal of the Society of Architectural Historians* 32, no. 2 (May 1973):114–

131. Matthews Hall is one of the few buildings of Gothic style remaining at Harvard. Others are the Farlow Herbarium (which the same firm designed in 1886), Ware and Van Brunt's Memorial Hall (1866–1878), and Andover Theological School (1910) by Allen and Collens.

Among the work of Peabody and Stearns the stone carving on the Matthews facade is unusual for its quality; it may well have been designed by William E. Barry, who was with the firm in these years. See Margaret Henderson Floyd, "William E. Barry of Kennebunk: The Boston Years," *Maine History News* 19, nos. 3 and 4 (July and Dec. 1983). The papers of William E. Barry, at the Brick Store Museum in Kennebunk, reveal him to have been one of the earliest architects of the Colonial Revival, who must have been interested in the archaeological fragments of the brick foundations of the seventeenth-century Indian College discovered in excavations for Matthews. Barry must have been present in 1870, for he sketched Harvard and Hollis Halls, publishing them in *Pen Sketches of Old Houses* (Boston: James B. Osgood, 1874).

16. See William A. Coles, ed., *Architecture and Society: Selected Essays of Henry Van Brunt* (Cambridge: Harvard University Press, 1969), pp. 1–74. William Robert Ware and Henry Van Brunt had both been students in Richard Morris Hunt's New York atelier in 1858 and 1859. In their Boston office Van Brunt was primarily the designer; Ware, who in the 1860s was asked to establish America's first school of architecture at M.I.T., acted largely as engineer but also as critic. The partnership, begun in 1863, terminated when Ware left Boston to establish the architectural school at Columbia University in 1881 after the firm had produced many of Boston's most important public buildings.

17. Lois Lilly Howe recalled a small girl's wonder at the stores of this building in *Proceedings of the Cambridge Historical Society* 30 (1949–50):41.

18. Cambridge installed a water system with a main along Massachusetts Avenue in 1856. The sewer line was laid out at the same time. See Arthur J. Krim et al., *Northwest Cambridge,* Cambridge Historical Commission, Survey of Architectural History in Cambridge, Report 5 (Cambridge: M.I.T. Press, 1977), pp. 25–26. A letter from the college librarian, T. W. Harris, to President Hill in 1855 indicates that there were then no toilet facilities for women in the Yard, an awkward situation for the female employees of the college library.

19. Jerry Cohen personal communication.

20. Each suite in Holworthy was metered separately to discourage the waste of illuminating gas.

21. The first telephones in Cambridge were installed around 1882 by John Coolidge ('85) and Randolph Coolidge ('83) to connect their rooms in the Yard (this information from their nephew John Coolidge).

22. James F. O'Gorman, *Selected Drawings, H. H. Richardson and His Office* (Cambridge: Department of Printing and Graphic Arts, Harvard College Library, 1974), pp. 144–147. Sever Hall was erected between 1878 and 1880 from an 1871 bequest from James Warren Sever (1798–1871), whose wife confirmed it in her will of 1877. The study for the plan of the Yard, presumably prepared by Richardson's office, suggests his involvement in the selection of the site. See Jeffrey Karl Oschner, *H. H. Richardson, Complete Architectural Works* (Cambridge: M.I.T. Press, 1982), pp. 196–199. The Georgian style of the intricate cut-brick doorway is unique in Richardson's work and surely derived from its Harvard environs. Richardson's Trinity Rectory (1878) and Sever were designed at an important point in the history of brick architecture. Only around 1878 did architectural terra cotta as an ornamental adjunct to rectangular brick become generally available in Boston. Providing ornament more cheaply, it soon replaced cut brick.

23. This observation comes from Robert B. Rettig.

24. The Corporation held a "full discussion" of the location of Sever Hall—the only topic considered—at its meeting of May 17, 1878, but no decision was reached.

25. A history of brick manufacture in the area is found in Krim et al., *Northwest Cambridge,* pp. 27–32. The Sands Brick Company achieved considerable reputation with its fine-quality pressed and cut brick, which it advertised as Harvard Brick. This is not to be confused with the Harvard Brick made by the New England Brick Company after 1890 and used extensively for the Georgian Revival buildings at Harvard in the 1910s and 1920s.

26. See Paul R. Baker, *Richard Morris Hunt* (Cambridge: M.I.T. Press, 1980). Hunt (1827–1895), America's earliest graduate of the Ecole des Beaux Arts, in his mature style was particularly enamored with French classicism.

27. The construction of Robinson and Emerson Halls required that two more of the faculty rental units, 25 and 37 Quincy Street, be moved to other locations. They were destroyed in 1951, amid great controversy, for construction of Allston Burr Hall (see Chapter 9).

Charles Follen McKim (1847–1909) had attended the Lawrence Scientific School in 1867. After his return from Paris in 1870, he worked with H. H. Richardson during the construction of Trinity Church, Boston. Although in practice in New York, in 1887 he won the commission for the Boston Public Library. In the following five years, as his commissions at Harvard began, he also designed several houses and the Algonquin Club (1889) in the Back Bay. McKim's interest in waterstruck brick, which he used for his buildings and gateways for the Yard, reflected his own early interest in Colonial architecture. His influence at Harvard was primarily in terms of planning. See Leland M. Roth, "McKim, Mead and White Reappraised," *A Monograph of the Works of McKim, Mead and White* (New York, 1915; rpt. Benjamin Blom, 1973), pp. 11–73.

28. Guy Lowell (1870–1927), after graduating from Harvard, studied architecture at M.I.T. and then at the Ecole des Beaux Arts. He first opened his Boston office in 1900 when Emerson was designed. He is best known for his Museum of Fine Arts on Huntington Avenue (1906–1915). His commissions at Harvard in the first decade of the twentieth century are close in spirit to those of Richard Morris Hunt and Horace Trumbauer. See Benjamin F. W. Russell, "The Works of Guy Lowell," *Architectural Review* 13 (Feb. 1906):13–40.

29. Alexander Wadsworth Longfellow, Jr. (1854–1934), nephew of the poet, was an admirer and follower of McKim. He went to the Ecole des Beaux Arts after graduation from Harvard and a short attendance at M.I.T. Like McKim before him, Longfellow became one of the senior draftsmen in the office of H. H. Richardson. Designing initially in a style derivative of Richardson's in such works as the Cambridge City Hall (1888) and the Edwin Abbott House (1888; now the Longy School of Music) in Cambridge, Longfellow became a pioneer Boston advocate of accurately used Colonial motifs. After losing the commission for Emerson Hall to Guy Lowell with some rancor in 1900, he subsequently designed numerous buildings at Harvard and Radcliffe as well as an extension to Van Brunt's Episcopal Theological Seminary on Brattle Street. Margaret Henderson Floyd, "The Architecture of Alexander Wadsworth Longfellow, Jr." (Boston: Museum of Fine Arts, Department of American Decorative Arts, in preparation).

30. See "Phillips Brooks Memorial Issue," *Harvard Monthly,* Feb. 15, 1893, pp. 175–220. The architect, A. W. Longfellow, Jr., had been a draftsman in the office of H. H. Richardson. The donor and fundraiser for Phillips Brooks House was Brooks's close friend Robert Treat Paine, who was a client of H. H. Richardson, as was Brooks at Trinity Church. See Margaret Henderson Floyd, "H. H. Richardson, F. L. Olmsted, and the House for Robert Treat Paine," *Winterthur Portfolio* 18 (Winter 1983):227–248.

31. See Bail, *Views of Harvard,* plates 18 and 46; 39; 53. The design for the present fence was authorized by the Corporation and the Memorial Committee. The last portion of this wrought iron fence, extending from the Meyer Gate to the west end of Canaday Hall, honors the class of 1908. The fence was a considerable investment throughout. It was bid at $5 per foot in 1931; only the foundations were constructed then (they extended 4½ feet below grade) because of the Depression; the iron fencing was finished in the middle thirties.

32. Gates and memorials incorporated in the Memorial Fence, in a clockwise order beginning with the Johnston Gate, are:

Johnston Gate, 1889

Class of 1886 memorial

Class of 1881 Gate (in front of Phillips Brooks House)

Class of 1876 Gate

The Bradlee Fountain, 1907

Class of 1879 Gate

Classes of 1887–1888 Gate (exedra form)

Meyer Gate, 1891 (Sever-Fogg axis)

Driveway Gate (south of Emerson Hall)

Class of 1880 Gate (and retaining wall) (facing Quincy Square)

Dexter Gate, 1901 (Wigglesworth Hall, east)

Class of 1877 Gate (opposite south entrance, Widener Library)

Class of 1889 Gate (Wigglesworth Hall, center)

Porcellian (McKean) Gate, 1901

Class of 1857 Gate (opposite Holyoke Center)

Class of 1875 Gate (between Lehman and Straus Halls)

Class of 1873 memorial tablet

See Mason Hammond, "The Enclosure of the Harvard Yard," *Harvard Library Bulletin* 31, no. 4 (Fall 1983):340–383.

33. Harvard Brick were hand made, wood burned, and water struck in the manner of the eighteenth century. Special brick were molded for the water table; other "repressed" brick with a smooth, contrasting surface were made for string courses. Some of the repressed brick were ground to the proper angles to produce voussoirs for flat arches. The source of the brick used for the eighteenth-century Harvard buildings is not known. Initially the bricks were undoubtedly brought to Cambridge by barge and unloaded at the college wharf. The earliest brickyards in Cambridge, near the mouth of Muddy River and Putnam Avenue in Cambridgeport, were not opened until the early nineteenth century. See Krim et al., *Northwest Cambridge*, pp. 27–32.

34. For college ownership and sales of land in Harvard Square, see Bunting and Nylander, *Old Cambridge*, p. 23, and the extensive notes and maps in the archives of the Cambridge Historical Commission.

35. On Higginson, a substantial benefactor of Harvard, see Bliss Perry, *Biography and Letters of Henry Lee Higginson* (Boston, 1921). The long-standing architectural relationship between McKim and Higginson included work on Higginson's home in Pride's Crossing, Massachusetts; Symphony Hall in Boston; and the American Academy in Rome, which McKim had founded (and his firm later designed) and Higginson funded.

36. Thomas Mott Shaw was a principal in the Boston firm Perry, Shaw and Hepburn, which restored Colonial Williamsburg for John D. Rockefeller in the 1920s and 1930s and designed Houghton Library at Harvard in 1937. See Andrew Saint, *Richard Norman Shaw* (New Haven: Yale University Press, 1976), esp. pp. 310–343, for English precedents for the Harvard Union.

37. Of the three streets separating the Yard from the North Yard, only Kirkland Street predates the extension of Harvard ownership into that area. Kirkland Street was in existence as the Highway to Charlestown before Cambridge was founded; Broadway was cut through college land in 1805, Cambridge Street in 1835.

38. The only through street in the North Yard is Oxford Street, which was laid out by private parties in 1840 and 1847, the last portion on a lot on Professors' Row sold by Harvard in 1822.

39. The bibliography on Memorial Hall is long and complex; a selection must suffice: Coles, ed., *Architecture and Society;* Walter Muir Whitehill, "Noble, Neglected, Memorial Hall Turns 100," and Daniel D. Reiff, "Memorial Hall: The Splendor Beneath the Dust," both in *Harvard Bulletin,* March 1972; Robert B. Shaffer, "Ruskin, Norton, and Memorial Hall," *Harvard Library Bulletin* 3, no. 2 (Spring 1949):213–231; Charles Eliot Norton, "Harvard University in 1890," *Harper's Magazine* 81 (1890):591; "Memorial Hall, Harvard University," *Architectural Record Monographs of American Architecture,* vol. 4 (Boston, 1887).

40. Memorial Hall also shows the influence of Viollet le Duc, whose discourses Van Brunt translated in the 1870s. Indeed, its style is a strange mixture of Ruskinism and Viollet le Duc's theories. For example, the diagonally placed columnar corbels of the

balcony above the stage at Sanders are taken directly from illustrations in Viollet's work, then transposed into a Ruskinian environment of revealed wooden construction.

41. The brickwork of Memorial Hall is typically restless, as in Matthews and Weld Halls. Particularly notable is the use of polychromy at points of structural stress such as the voussoirs and haunches of arches. Memorial Hall was built using only rectangular brick and before architectural terra cotta was available in Boston; its ornamental portions are therefore of stone rather than clay, while the polychromy is achieved with tar-dipped, rectangular bricks. The effect of this brickwork differs greatly from the shaped and molded brick used in Sever Hall, a building designed and finished just as Memorial Hall was completed.

The only compromise made in building Memorial Hall was the substitution of brick for freestone (sandstone), which was undoubtedly fortunate because of the superior weathering ability of brick.

42. Harvard enlistments in the Union Army numbered 1311 with 138 dead; for the Confederate Army the figures were 257 and 64. In the formal acceptance of Memorial Hall the Corporation minutes for July 8, 1878, comment: "Memorial Hall is . . . the most valuable gift which the University has ever received, in respect alike to cost, usefulness, and moral significance."

43. A meeting was held on May 12, 1865, to consider Memorial Hall. Charles Eliot Norton spoke with William Robert Ware in order to obtain his reaction before consulting other architects, and on May 29, 1865, a circular was sent to the following architects: E. C. Cabot, William Ware, George F. Meacham, J. E. Colburn, C. D. Gambrell, W. P. P. Longfellow (not to be confused with his younger cousin A. W.), Henry Van Brunt, John Sturgis (who was not an alumnus of Harvard), Hammatt Billings, R. M. Hunt, P. B. White (who had just designed the National Academy of Design in New York City), and Russell Sturgis of New York.

44. The Commencement feast was celebrated in the following locations: Harvard Hall I, 1642–1674; Harvard Hall II, 1677–1763; Harvard Hall III, 1766–1814; University Hall, 1815–1841; Harvard Hall III, 1842–1873; Memorial Hall beginning in 1874.

45. To grace the dining hall fourteen marble busts from the library (Gore Hall) were installed. Portraits from the university's collection transferred to Memorial Hall were cleaned and their frames repaired and regilded in 1874 at a cost of $1787. See Mason Hammond, "The Stained Glass Windows in Memorial Hall," typescript (1978), on deposit in Fogg Museum Library.

46. The use of exposed brickwork on the interior of buildings was a hotly contested issue in the mid-nineteenth century. The anti-stucco school of Gothicists believed that walls of Medieval interiors should be revealed rather than covered with plaster.

47. Walter Whitehill, "A Centennial Sketch," in Marvin E. Goody and Robert P. Walsh, eds., *Boston Society of Architects: The First Hundred Years, 1867–1967* (Boston: Boston Society of Architects, 1967), pp. 15–72, describes site visits by members of the embryonic Society to Trinity Church, Memorial Hall, the Museum of Fine Arts, New Old South Church, and other major recent buildings of the mid-1870s. Van Brunt's disguise of iron reinforcing beams in Sanders Theatre was considered by Sturgis in particular to be out of line with the "honest" objectives of Memorial Hall.

5. The North Yard and Soldiers Field

1. Divinity Hall was sponsored by the Society for Promoting Theological Education at Harvard College, which raised $27,000, mostly in small contributions of less than $50, to build the hall and partially endow three chairs of theology. The University Museum, founded in 1858 as the Museum of Comparative Zoology, was sponsored by the Trustees of the Museum of Comparative Zoology. This organization obtained $100,000 from the Commonwealth and also administered a legacy of $50,000 from Francis C. Gray that had been left "to Harvard or any other institution" to establish a museum of natural history. Harvard donated the land. The museum opened in 1860,

and in 1876 the Trustees relinquished it to Harvard. The Peabody Museum was constructed with a legacy of $150,000 from George Peabody.

2. For the two years that the Museum of Comparative Zoology was being constructed, the staff and collections occupied a two-story, hip-roofed house between Lawrence Hall and the North Avenue Congregational Church (before it was moved). Constructed in 1849 as an auxiliary laboratory for the Scientific School, the entire structure was soon needed for Agassiz's mushrooming collections. When the collections were transferred to the completed museum in 1859, the wooden structure was moved to the present site of the Peabody Museum and remodeled for living quarters for several of Agassiz's assistants. In 1876 it was moved first to Holmes Field as the college hospital, then to a site on Jarvis Street, where the upper floor was used by the Hasty Pudding Club, the lower by the Institute of 1770.

3. Downing, MacDougall, and Pearson, *Mid Cambridge,* pp. 63–65. Henry Greenough (1807–1883) was born in Newburyport, studied in Florence and France, and returned to Boston in 1831. He designed a number of public buildings in Cambridge, including Cambridge City Hall, as well as the house of Louis Agassiz on Quincy Street. George Snell, an Englishman, was an artist and a prominent Boston architect; he had enlarged Christ Church, Cambridge, in 1852. The collaboration between Greenough and Snell seems to have been a one-time affair. Greenough, brother of the sculptor and architectural critic Horatio Greenough, was a sort of gentleman-architect without professional training. He may have felt inadequate for the engineering problems or construction supervision of so large a building as the museum and therefore called on Snell for help.

4. Museums of natural history were an interesting architectural episode of the 1850s; the most influential of these, both designed by Deane and Woodward, were in Dublin (1853) and Oxford (1856).

5. Although President Eliot often spoke and wrote against competitive team sports such as football, which he felt too easily tended to lose its amateur character, he supported individual sports as contributing to good physical health. He discussed the value of athletics in the President's Report for 1880–81.

6. Bruce Langdon Bennett, "The Life of Dudley Allan Sargent, M.D., and His Contributions to Physical Education" (Ph.D. diss., University of Michigan, 1947).

7. "Forty Years of Dr. Sargent," *Harvard Bulletin* 21, no. 32 (May 15, 1919):652–656. Dudley A. Sargent, "The Hemenway Gymnasium: An Educational Experiment," *Harvard Graduates' Magazine* 3, no. 18 (Dec. 1894):169–180. George Meylan, director of the Boston YMCA in the late 1890s and acting director of Hemenway for a short period, obtained the first academic appointment in physical education in America at Columbia University in 1903. McKenzie, who had earlier been at McGill University in Montreal, was also a sculptor and ultimately was appointed to head the program at the University of Pennsylvania. Sargent retired in 1919.

8. Hemenway, the first of a series of athletic facilities designed for Harvard by Peabody and Stearns, was in 1878 the most advanced building of its type and style in America. See Wheaton A. Holden, "The Peabody Touch: Peabody and Stearns of Boston, 1870–1917," *Journal of the Society of Architectural Historians* 32, no. 2 (May 1973):114–131. For the introduction of terra cotta see Margaret Henderson Floyd, "A Terra Cotta Cornerstone for Copley Square: Museum of Fine Arts Boston, 1870–1876, by Sturgis and Brigham," *Journal of the Society of Architectural Historians* 32, no. 2 (May 1973):83–103.

9. See "Austin Hall—Harvard Law School, Cambridge, Mass., H. H. Richardson Architect," *Monographs of American Architecture,* no. 1 (Boston, 1886); O'Gorman, *Richardson Drawings,* pp. 148–154; and John P. Coolidge, "Form and Function: Henry Hobson Richardson and the Making of a Law School," *Harvard Law School Bulletin* 35, no. 2 (Spring 1984):16–21. Correspondence makes clear the autocratic nature of Edward Austin's aesthetic decisionmaking about Austin Hall; see Oschner, *Richardson,* p. 246.

10. Downing, MacDougall, and Pearson, *Mid Cambridge*, p. 17.

11. The contrast between Sever Hall and Austin Hall suggests how strongly Richardson's design for Sever was influenced by the earlier classical buildings and materials used in Harvard Yard. Particularly obvious are the change in the eastern doorway of Sever to Georgian style and its exact axial symmetry. When left to his own devices north of the Yard at Austin Hall, Richardson returned to his own style.

12. Thomas Jefferson Coolidge, *Autobiography* (Boston, 1902).

13. The firm of George Robert Shaw (1848–1937) and Henry Sargent Hunnewell (1851–1931) was responsible for many public and private commissions in Boston between 1873 and 1904. The elegant ornamental carving of Pierce Hall is characteristic. The firm's best-known public building is undoubtedly the Wellesley Town Hall and Library (1881–1883), where they also utilized wreaths of foliage surrounding oculus windows and ornately carved classical swags and garlands. See Margaret Henderson Floyd, "Shaw and Hunnewell at Wellesley, Massachusetts," in *The Architecture of H. H. Richardson and His Contemporaries in Boston and Vicinity* (Philadelphia: Society of Architectural Historians, 1972), pp. 38–41.

14. The two principles are articulated in Charles A. Coolidge, "The Future Physical Development of the University," *Harvard Alumni Bulletin* 28, no. 5 (1925):915–918; and Arthur D. Trottenberg, *Harvard Alumni Bulletin* 67, no. 4 (1964).

15. Edward Clarke Cabot (1818–1901) had designed the President's House at Harvard in 1860. He designed Walter Hastings Hall with the most important of his several partners, Francis W. Chandler (1844–1925), later professor of architecture at M.I.T., who had attended the Ecole des Beaux Arts in Paris with Charles McKim and Robert Peabody in 1867–1870. In the years 1877–1890 the firm also designed the main building for Johns Hopkins University.

16. The elective system not only produced a proliferation of courses (from 92 in 1867–68 to 456 in 1902–03) but also encouraged large survey courses. In 1902–03 13 courses had enrollments over 200, six over 400. President Lowell disapproved of the tendency for students to take numerous introductory courses and thus not to explore any one field in depth.

On the location of Lowell Lecture Hall, see the letter from Guy Lowell to Eliot, June 24, 1901, Eliot Papers, Harvard Archives. The decision to locate Robinson Hall in the Yard was similarly not connected with the advisory committee's deliberations. Its location was determined by Charles McKim, to whom contour maps of the Yard were sent in 1900. See letters of McKim to Eliot, 1899–1909, uncatalogued, Harvard Archives.

17. Wheelwright also designed the Anderson Bridge; see Walter Kilham, "The Anderson Bridge," *Harvard Engineering Journal* 12 (1913). For the *Lampoon* Building (1908) see Samuel Van Dam, "E. M. Wheelwright and the History of the Lampoon Castle" (Senior Honors Thesis, Harvard University, 1971). Wheelwright, who graduated from Harvard in 1876, was one of the seven founders of the *Harvard Lampoon*. He studied at M.I.T., drafted for Peabody and Stearns, then joined Charles McKim on his famous sketching trip with Dr. Bigelow along the New England seacoast. He opened an office in Boston in 1884 and became secretary of the Boston Society of Architects in the following year. In 1888 he joined Parkman B. Haven in partnership as Wheelwright and Haven. Beginning in 1891, as city architect for Boston, he was responsible for numerous public buildings in the city; these were illustrated by Francis W. Chandler in *Municipal Architecture in Boston* (Boston, 1898).

18. See Montgomery Schuyler, "The Architecture of American Colleges," *Architectural Record* 26–29 (1909–1912).

19. Cram's Gothic style was firmly associated with American college campuses and with ecclesiastical architecture by 1910. The nearby Episcopal Theological School (1866–1871), by Ware and Van Brunt, was an early local example. Montgomery Schuyler, "The Work of Cram, Goodhue and Ferguson," *Architectural Record* 29 (1911):4–112, illustrates Cram's collegiate Gothic designs.

20. Allen and Collens were second only to Cram for their elegant if less scholarly

neo-Medieval designs. At the Cloisters (1938) in New York they incorporated fragments of Medieval monasteries; at New York's Riverside Church (1930) they erected a Gothic tower over a steel frame.

21. The old herbarium was an accretion of small connecting buildings strung along a terrace overlooking the gardens. The oldest structure was the Garden House for the director (1810; added to in 1848). A brick herbarium was constructed in 1864 with a gift of $12,000 from Nathaniel Thayer. Although at first referred to as fireproof, by 1909 it was deemed unsafe for the collection. To it were added in 1870 a laboratory and a small auditorium (the gift of H. H. Hunnewell); beyond those were two green-houses. In 1879 a library was added between Garden House and the Thayer Herbarium. Beginning in 1909 its components were replaced one by one with the building of the new Kidder Herbarium in 1909, the Kennedy Library, and the White Laboratory in 1911. These three structures formed a cross at the core of which was the original 1864 herbarium, which was replaced in 1915 by a unit of reinforced concrete construction.

22. Harold C. Ernst, ed., *The Harvard Medical School, 1782–1906* (Boston: 1906).

23. For the stadium's structural innovations the Boston Society of Civil Engineers in 1978 nominated it as a National Historic Civil Engineering Landmark. Anthony Alofsin, "Toward a History of Teaching Architectural History: An Introduction to H. Langford Warren," *Journal of Architectural Education* 37, no. 1 (Fall 1983):2–7.

24. See the following articles in the *Harvard Engineering Journal* 3, no. 2 (June 1904): Ira N. Hollis, "Origin of the Harvard Stadium," pp. 90–108; Lewis S. Johnson, "Material and Design of the Harvard Stadium," pp. 109–130; Henry N. Fox, "Methods of Construction of the Harvard Stadium," pp. 131–144; and H. Langford Warren, "Ancient Stadia and Circuses," pp. 145–152.

25. For the state of concrete construction in 1903 see Henry Russell Hitchcock, *Architecture: Nineteenth and Twentieth Centuries* (Baltimore: Penguin, 1958), pp. 307–321; and Peter Collins, *Concrete: The New Architecture* (London: Faber and Faber, 1959).

26. The stadium was built not only for athletic events but also as a performance area. *Agamemnon* was presented in June 1906, with music composed for the occasion. For another example, Schiller's *Die Jungfrau von Orleans* with Maud Adams was presented there in June 1909, raising $25,000 to benefit the Germanic Museum. One hundred mounted horsemen, a 40-foot reproduction of the facade of Reims Cathedral, a 60-foot oak tree, and a cast of 1500, of whom 600 wore suits of armor, performed on sets designed by John White Alexander; see Sylvia Sanborn, "John White Alexander" (Master's thesis, Tufts University, 1985). This function of the stadium has not been lost: the Classics Club presented Euripides' *The Bacchae* in May 1983; see Pier H. Jebson, "Euripides Conquers Harvard Gridiron," *Harvard Crimson,* 9 May 1983.

27. Briggs Cage was recently attributed to Lowell; see Douglas Bonnell, "The Works of Guy Lowell" (Master's thesis, Tufts University, 1980). The Indoor Athletic Building, including its elaborate interior, is illustrated in *Brickbuilder* 23, no. 11 (July 1933).

28. Since 1866 Harvard had been operating at a deficit, which by 1872 totaled $27,500. Of this amount $11,500 was incurred in 1871–72, a particularly bad year because of the additional losses in the Fire of Boston. Nevertheless, in his first year of office Eliot decided on drastic increases in three areas: the instructional budget, a program of land acquisition, and the bold building program. To some extent these expenses were offset in his first year by an increase in tuition (from $104 to $150 per year), income from a new dormitory (Thayer Hall), and a class subscription of $50,000.

One of Eliot's first acts as president was to raise (from $3000 to $4000) the salaries of the senior faculty, which until then had not been adjusted to meet the serious inflation that accompanied the Civil War. This figure increased by no more than 6 percent until 1906, when salaries could again be raised after a successful $2.5 million campaign for endowment. Even more expensive than the pay raises was the increase in the number of faculty members (seven in Eliot's first year) required by the new elective system.

29. The President's Report for 1881–82, p. 134, is especially helpful in itemizing land purchases. Whereas only $10,387 had been expended for land acquisition in the three years prior to Eliot's administration (1866–1869), he spent $96,500 in his first two years: additions to the Observatory, $13,500; property (marshland) in Brighton, $13,000; university contribution to the Jarvis field purchase, $15,000; Holmes estate, $55,000. The court case of 1869 was 101 Mass. 319, Massachusetts General Hospital vs. City of Somerville.

30. *Report on a Plan for the College Buildings and Grounds* (Harvard Archives, UVII.10.30.96.7) reproduces an 1896 map of the college and gives a good summary of the exchange between the Overseers and the Corporation.

31. The Corporation's objections to a master plan are worth noting: (1) no sufficient knowledge could be had as to future bequests and gifts; (2) including nonuniversity land in such plans would raise its price; (3) the Corporation did not want a standing advisory committee because fund raising required attention to donors' ideas.

32. See *Report on a Plan for the College Buildings and Grounds,* Harvard Archives UVII.10.30.96.7. The reversal of the main facade of Widener occurred between 1896 and 1913, a planning decision that controlled the entire later development of the campus (see Chapter 7). Although Widener was erected shortly after Lowell took office, its design is conceptually a part of the Imperial epoch of the late Eliot years.

33. The committee of architects (Robert Peabody, F. W. Chandler, and G. M. Shaw) reviewed the plan prepared by Shepley, Rutan and Coolidge for a building adjacent to Austin Hall. They advised against the site proposed by the law faculty.

34. Letter to Dr. Francis Peabody, 12 Feb. 1912, quoted in Henry Ames, *Charles W. Eliot* (Boston: Houghton Mifflin, 1930), II, 225.

6. *Buildings for Radcliffe College*

1. Arthur Gilman, "Women Who Go to College," *Century Magazine* 36, no. 5 (Sept. 1888):714–718. LeBaron Russell Briggs, "An Experiment in Faith: Radcliffe College," *Atlantic Monthly,* Jan. 1909, p. 106. This historical sketch relies on Elia Howells, *A Century to Celebrate: Radcliffe College, 1879–1979* (Cambridge: Radcliffe, 1978), which documents extensive research in unpublished materials in the Radcliffe Archives.

2. Arthur Gilman, "The Incorporation of Radcliffe College" (manuscript, Radcliffe Archives, 31 Jan. 1909).

3. Louis M. Lyons, "Heroine of the Children's Hour," *Boston Globe,* 16 Dec. 1928. See Bernice Brown Cronkhite, "Grave Alice," *Radcliffe Quarterly,* Winter 1905, pp. 11–14.

4. Lucy A. Paton, *Elizabeth Carey Agassiz* (Boston and New York: Houghton Mifflin, 1919).

5. Emma Forbes Cary, "Sketch of Mrs. Louis Agassiz," in Caroline Gardner Curtis, *Memories of Fifty Years* (Boston: privately printed, 1947), pp. 115–144.

6. Quoted in Howells, *A Century to Celebrate,* p. 19.

7. On the Gurney and Hooper families see James F. O'Gorman, "A Tragic Circle," *Nineteenth Century* 2 (Autumn 1976):46–49, and Marc Friedlander, "Henry Hobson Richardson, Henry Adams and John Hay," *Journal of the Society of Architectural Historians* 29 (Oct. 1970):231–246.

8. Christina Hopkins Baker, *The Story of Fay House* (Cambridge: Harvard University Press, 1929); Tony E. Laughlin, "A Structural History of Fay House" (manuscript submitted to Professor John Coolidge, Fine Arts 196b, Jan. 15, 1981, Radcliffe Archives). The architect of the mansard roof is not presently known. Vivian May Norris, "A History of Fay House," *Radcliffe Magazine* 2, no. 2 (March 1900):53–62.

9. In the Brattle Street area Longfellow had worked on minor remodelings of Craigie House and had built several houses in Longfellow Park, a space established in 1883 by the family to protect their view to the river.

10. Shurtleff to President L. B. R. Briggs, "Report on the Location of Buildings" (typescript, Radcliffe Archives, 4 June 1906).

11. Montgomery Schuyler, "The Architecture of American Colleges, X: Three Women's Colleges," *Architectural Record* 31, no. 5 (May 1912):512–537. For Radcliffe, see "Tentative Plans for the Development of Radcliffe," *The Boston Evening Transcript,* May 15, 1926.

12. The auditorium at Agassiz followed that at the Carnegie Institute in Pittsburgh (1892), the largest and best-known building by Longfellow and his partners Alden and Harlow. Longfellow had also designed the Brattle Theatre in Cambridge (1890).

13. Radcliffe Annual Report, 1904–5, p. 37; Council Reports, 7 Nov. 1904 and 26 June 1905; and *Radcliffe Magazine,* June 1907, p. 101 all document Sarah Wyman Whitman's stained glass at Radcliffe. A window (Whitman's last work), on display at the St. Louis Fair at the time of her death in 1904, was temporarily placed on the landing of the Agassiz House staircase. It was moved to the library in 1907–08. Whitman also did the large Martin Brimmer window in the south transept of Memorial Hall at Harvard and earlier windows in the parish house of Trinity Church, Boston.

14. Longfellow Hall received the Harleston Parker Medal of the Boston Society of Architects in 1934. See Cronkhite, "Grave Alice," p. 14.

15. See Howells, *A Century to Celebrate,* p. 5. Joseph Randolph Coolidge, Jr. (1862–1928), who was in practice in Boston with Henry O. Carlson (1903–1922), should not be confused with his contemporary Charles A. Coolidge, Harvard's primary designer under President Lowell. Coolidge and Carlson did no other work at Harvard and Radcliffe beyond Byerly Hall and Randolph Hall on the Gold Coast, built as a private dormitory.

16. Guy Lowell, "New Grounds for Radcliffe College" (1902), Radcliffe Archives.

17. R. F. Gourley, later a partner of Josep Lluis Sert (Sert, Jackson and Gourley), designed much later Harvard architecture.

18. Downing, MacDougall, and Pearson, *Mid Cambridge,* p. 65, fig. 116. In the 1960s demolition for new construction was accepted; preservation regulations would restrict such actions today. Shurtleff was principal landscape architect at Williamsburg for the Perry firm.

19. Harrison and Abramovitz had been involved in a number of very large-scale projects, including the United Nations and Lincoln Center in New York. For their work at Radcliffe see "College Dorms for New Lifestyles: Dormitory Complex at Radcliffe College," *Architectural Forum* 136 (June 1972):52–53.

7. Academic Architecture under President Lowell

1. This is an overall figure, including buildings for the Medical and Business Schools.

2. Charles Allerton Coolidge (1858–1936) was first junior partner and later senior partner in the firm of Shepley, Rutan and Coolidge (1886–1915), which succeeded to the practice of H. H. Richardson. From 1915 to 1924 he headed the firm of Coolidge and Shattuck; in 1925 he established Coolidge, Shepley, Bulfinch and Abbott, which in 1952 became Shepley, Bulfinch, Richardson and Abbott. Coolidge also designed for Yale (Sprague Hall) and the University of Chicago (Harper Library; see Jean F. Block, *The Uses of Gothic,* University of Chicago Press, 1983, p. 240). His hospital commissions included work at Massachusetts General, Western Reserve in Cleveland, Rockefeller Institute, Cornell Medical Center, and Childrens' Hospital in Boston. See J. D. Forbes, Shepley, Bulfinch, Richardson and Abbott," *Journal of the Society of Architectural Historians* 17, no. 3 (Fall 1958); Coolidge's obituaries in *Harvard Alumni Bulletin,* 10 April 1936, and *Architectural Forum,* May 1936.

3. Julian Coolidge, "Lawrence Lowell, President," *Proceedings of the Cambridge Historical Society,* vol. 34, p. 951. Drawings and correspondence are to be found in the archives and library of Shepley, Bulfinch, Richardson and Abbott, Boston. The Lowell

Papers (Harvard Archives) contain innumerable examples of President Lowell's involvement (interference) in details of the design and construction of the college buildings. The following examples are typical. Letter to Coolidge, 2 Jan. 1912: "There is only one thing that is not quite right, and that is that the staircase in the center of the east wing does not quite come opposite the division into two rooms . . . I have indicated by pencil dots one method . . ." Letter to Shepley, 24 July 1924: "I enclose a very rough sketch plan, hastily drawn for a dormitory 100 × 24 outside measurement. I think it would work. It has four double studies, or eight men on each floor, and has only about as much floor space per man as the one I showed you for a smaller dormitory yesterday." Letter to Coolidge, 12 Feb. 1923: "Except where I happen to take a personal interest, colors of paint do not seem to have any supervision. Indeed, unless I say something about it, there seems to be a tendency to paint things dirt color. This has just been done on the window jambs of Memorial Hall, Appleton Chapel, and the College fence."

4. The Duquesne plan is reproduced in a pamphlet, "The Future Development of Harvard Square and Its Neighborhood," a report of the committee appointed by the president of Harvard University at the request of the mayor of Cambridge, 1913. A copy is in the Lowell Papers, 1911–14, p. 170. The original drawings have not been located. One recommendation of the report was to widen Massachusetts Avenue by putting the sidewalk under an arcade behind the building facades.

5. The history and activities of the Committee on Plans for the Future Development of Harvard University are summarized in the President's Report, 1923–24, p. 25. In December 1920 the Corporation asked Charles A. Coolidge and Guy Lowell to act as a committee to report on plans for the future development of university buildings. To them were added in May 1922 the president and treasurer of the Corporation, the president of the Board of Overseers, and Professor H. V. Hubbard of the faculty of landscape architecture; a seventh member, Charles Moore, joined in 1924. In December 1923 this committee proposed the cloistering of the Yard and suggested that a model be made to study the change. In June 1924 the Corporation authorized the implementation of the recommendations. Coolidge summarized the recommendations in the *Harvard Alumni Bulletin,* May 7, 1925, pp. 915–918. Minutes of some of the meetings of the committee are found in the Lowell Papers, 1922–25, p. 467.

6. Photographs of the drawings are in the Harvard Archives, UAI.15.740pf, 1900.

7. "Growth and Expenditures of the University Library," Harvard Annual Report, 1982–83, provides these statistics. The Law School Library (1,391,311 volumes), Dumbarton Oaks Research Library (91,149), the University Museum of Comparative Zoology (228,502), and Baker Library at the Business School (539,665) suggest the scale of Harvard's subsidiary collections.

8. The three university architects were Coolidge, Guy Lowell, and Desire Despradelle, a Harvard professor of architecture. On October 12, 1911, eighteen months before construction began, the *Boston Herald* reported the completion of the preliminary design and concluded: "The occasion exists to be seized upon by a munificent donor to bestow a lasting benefit upon a great university and by the same act to build an honorable and enduring monument to a name or a family." Mrs. Widener's son had been lost on the *Titanic.* She had originally planned only a memorial room, but was talked into the whole library by Lowell.

Horace Trumbauer (1868–1938) was born in Philadelphia and founded his own firm there in 1890. At the time of the Harvard commission he had already designed a large house for the Wideners, although his only training had been six years in the firm of Hewitt and Hewitt, 1884–1890. He worked in many styles but has been identified primarily with the large-scale classicism of works such as Widener Library and the Philadelphia Museum of Art (1931–1938). See Alfred Branam, Jr., *Newport's Favorite Architect* (Long Island City, N.Y.: Classical America, 1976), and James T. Maher, *Twilight of Splendor* (Boston: Little, Brown, 1975).

9. John Singer Sargent (1856–1925) had turned to mural painting for the Boston Public Library in the 1890s and was still working on this commission at the time he did the paintings for Harvard. He made sketches for the Widener murals while he was

under commission from the Imperial War Museum, London, sketching troops in France in 1918. In the murals the multiple figures of Everyman have identical faces.

10. Herman Voss, a designer in the Coolidge office, actually conceived of the unique plan of Memorial Church.

11. On the Memorial Church and its interior decoration see Douglass Shand Tucci, "Does the Tower of Old North Church Belong in Harvard Yard?" *Harvard Magazine,* Nov.–Dec. 1982, pp. 44–52. The woodwork was by Irving and Casson of Boston. The sculpture "The Sacrifice" in the memorial section was executed by Malvina Moffman from a design by Joseph Coletti.

12. In fact some sort of screen to isolate the Yard from Harvard Square had been under discussion for some time. President Eliot advocated connecting buildings on the periphery with arcades or a wall. President Lowell asked the architects of the advisory committee to study the feasibility of a screen of buildings as part of their Plan for the Future Development of the University, and they made this one of their first objectives. The Corporation accepted the cloistering solution on 18 June 1924, and authorized the construction of a scale model to study the relation of the existing and proposed buildings. Hammond, "The Enclosure of Harvard Yard."

13. Guy Lowell was not fully committed to the Colonial Revival style but was more influenced by it when working in the Yard in 1911 than he had been at Lowell Lecture Hall (1900) or Emerson Hall (1904).

14. Fogg Art Museum, *Handbook,* 3rd ed. (Cambridge: Harvard University Press, 1936), pp. 222–227; 2nd ed. (1931), pp. vi–viii, xx–xxi.

15. Felix Warburg was the first subscriber to the Fogg Museum building; President's Report, 1930–31, p. 1. "Great Naumburg Collection Begins Journey to Its New Home," *Art Digest* 4, no. 18 (July 1930):7 and cover; Paul J. Sachs, "The Naumburg Bequest," *Harvard Alumni Bulletin* 33, no. 21 (Feb. 19, 1931):632–640.
The woodwork is presumably of English Jacobean origin and dates from the seventeenth century. It had been installed in the Naumburg apartment in the Hôtel des Artistes at One West 67th Street, New York, with rugs and tapestries that were also acquired by the Fogg. The rooms were opened on November 10, 1932.

16. The Naumburg stained glass has been catalogued by Madeline Harrison Caviness, "A Checklist of Stained Glass before 1700 in American Collections," *Studies in the History of Art* (Washington: National Gallery of Art, 1985).

17. R. Clipton Sturgis had designed many notable traditional buildings in Boston, such as the Federal Reserve Bank Building (1922–1923), the Perkins School for the Blind (1917), the Old North Church restoration (1911), and the marble wings of the Massachusetts State House (1917). See William Germain Dooley, "R. Clipton Sturgis, 1860–1951," in Goody and Walsh, *Boston Society of Architects,* pp. 79–80.

18. Harvard University Planning Office, *Long-Range Planning Inventory, Policies, and Recommendations,* 1975, map: "Potential Vehicular Circulation," p. 47. In February 1983 the editors of *Harvard Architecture* sponsored a design competition for a gate to close off Quincy Street. See Robert Campbell, "Modern Style's Harvardgate," *Boston Globe,* March 29, 1983.

19. Between 1910 and 1923 Longfellow produced sketches for three chemistry quadrangles, each designed for a slightly different location. The Chemistry Division was pleased with his designs, and additional units would undoubtedly have been built had not World War I interfered. The Longfellow drawings were shown to Edward Mallinckrodt when the university solicited his gift. By the time Harvard was ready to build a chemistry building in 1925, however, needs had changed, and the administration sought a larger architectural office.

20. See *The Busch-Reisinger Museum, Harvard University,* preface by Seymour Slive, intro. by Charles Hoxthausen (New York: Abbeville Press, 1980); "The New Germanic Museum, Adolphus Busch Hall," *Architectural Review* 1, no. 7 (July 1912). Photographs of the Bestelmeyer plans are filed in the Harvard Archives, UAI.15.25pf.

21. See Alofsin, "Herbert Langford Warren," pp. 2–7. Warren continued in practice after his academic appointment at Harvard. In these years he designed the Gothic Church of the New Jerusalem (1901) opposite the Busch-Reisinger Museum.

22. An illustrated article with plans of the Germanic Museum was published in the *Architectural Forum* 49, no. 4 (1928), by Kuno Francke, director of the museum. In his annual report for 1903, the director wrote, "Professor Bestelmeyer is constantly on the outlook for some old motif in some church or castle that might be fitted into his plan." For interior photographs see Kuno Francke, "The Germanic Museum of Harvard University," *Art and Archaeology* 28, no. 6 (Dec. 1929):233–239.

23. Rindge Technical High School (1932) by Ralph Harrington Doane and Central Square Post Office (1932) by Charles R. Greco are illustrated in Robert B. Rettig, *Guide to Cambridge Architecture* (Cambridge: M.I.T. Press, 1969).

24. "The Harvard Biological Laboratories," *Harvard Alumni Bulletin* 34, no. 17 (Jan. 29, 1932):502–525; "Biological Laboratories, Harvard University," *Architectural Forum* 57, no. 2 (Aug. 1932):129–132; Louise T. Ambler, "About Those Rhinos," *Harvard Library Bulletin* 21, no. 3 (July 1973):271–276. Katherine Ward Lane, who studied at the School of the Museum of Fine Arts, Boston, with Charles Grafly and Brenda Putnam. Lane, an admirer of Anna Hyatt Huntington (who studied animal sculpture in Paris with Antoine Barye), initiated such incised brick sculpture at Harvard. Curiously, similar reliefs appeared almost immediately in England on the Maud Laboratory, Cambridge (1933), in the form of a crocodile by Eric Gill. See Brunskill and Clifton-Taylor, *Brickwork,* p. 139.

25. In their report of 1896 the Overseers criticized the grounds to the President and Fellows: "Jefferson Laboratory faces the rear of the Science School, Austin Hall regards the rear of the gymnasium, Hastings Hall is a feature entirely by itself, the Carey Building is at an angle with everything, and these accidents occur all over the property. A chart is needed by which the ship shall be steered."

26. A special committee to determine the placement of Paine Hall consisted of professor of music Walter Spaulding, chief fund raiser Dave Morris, and President Lowell.
Harvard had acquired the parcel east of Paine Hall in 1815 as part of the Shady Hill estate, but had sold it in 1822 as a portion of one of the lots on Professors' Row and did not repurchase it until 1955; Downing, MacDougall, and Pearson, *Mid Cambridge,* p. 28. Physicist Wallace Sabine, a pioneer in acoustic research, was brought in to check the plans for the music auditorium before construction began.

27. This brick, called "repressed" because of its smooth surface, was made by the New England Brick Company in North Cambridge. Brick employed for the flat segmental arches over windows were specially ground to the proper angles at the factory.

8. The River Houses and the South Yard

1. Harris, *Economics of Harvard,* p. 69. The freshman class numbered 969 in 1929; in 1930 a limit of 1000 was imposed for future entering freshman classes.

2. President's Report, 1893–94.

3. The *Boston Herald* reported on 19 June 1914 that the cheapest room in Harvard's new freshman halls was $35 per year; board was $200, tuition $150.

4. Of the 705 freshmen entering in 1914, 149 (21 percent) lived at home, commuting to the university.

5. Harris, *Economics of Harvard,* p. 78. Before the construction of dining facilities in Randall Hall in 1898 the economical commons had been called the Foxcroft Club, and before that Thayer Commons.

6. The percentage of freshmen entering Harvard from private preparatory schools increased from 62 in 1870 to 77 in 1890 and this trend continued through the Lowell years.
A final club is a social club, usually joined in the sophomore or junior year. A student

can belong to only one final club, although this does not preclude membership in other types of clubs such as the Hasty Pudding or the Signet. In 1936 there were eight final clubs, to which 1.2 percent of the three upper classes belonged: Porcellian Club, 1324 Mass. Ave. (1890); Delphic Club, 9 Linden St. (1902); Owl Club, 30 Holyoke St. (1905); Fox Club, 44 Boylston St. (1906); Fly Club, 2 Holyoke Pl.; Phoenix Club, 72 Mt. Auburn St. (1915); Iroquois Club (a "waiting" club for final clubs), 74 Mt. Auburn St. (1916); and Spee Club, 76 Mt. Auburn St. (1931).

7. According to the 1907–08 *Harvard Catalogue* there were 189 full (two-semester) courses, 254 half courses. By 1902 thirteen survey courses had an enrollment of more than 200, four more than 400.

8. This idea was not new. For a summary of the development of the concept of residential colleges in American universities see George W. Pierson, *Yale: The University College* (New Haven: Yale University Press, 1955), pp. 223–226.

9. The term "South Yard" is not one in general use, but it is a good short designation. To speak of the area as "the houses" is not quite accurate, while the old term, "Riverside," has a specific sociological and political meaning and has come to be applied to the adjacent nonuniversity neighborhood. The designation "South Yard" is as defensible as the term "North Yard" for the contiguous units of university building north of Kirkland Street. For the early history of the Riverside area, see Bunting and Nylander, *Old Cambridge,* pp. 31–32, 41–44.

10. See Bunting, *Houses of Boston's Back Bay,* pp. 361–368.

11. For example, Harvard sold the south half of the Holyoke House lot (known earlier as the Bordman lot and acquired by Harvard in 1794) in 1898 to J. A. Little, who erected a gymnasium and swimming pool attached to Dunster Hall, a private dormitory.

12. A group of alumni, who had raised $50,000 to acquire property fronting DeWolfe Street in order to widen it for a tree-lined carriageway, turned this money over to the Harvard Riverside Associates.

13. For the story of Forbes's fundraising activities and of the various plans that were drawn for the development of the Riverside area see Beth Mandelbaum and Marjorie Fitzsimons, "Edward Forbes, City Planner," in *Edward Waldo Forbes: Yankee Visionary* (Cambridge: Fogg Art Museum, 1971), pp. 45–94. The printed prospectus sent to potential contributors by the Harvard Riverside Associates in 1903 is in the Harvard Archives, Eliot Letters, 1893–1903, box 134, folder 988.

14. For two of these Olmsted plans see Mandelbaum and Fitzsimons, "Forbes," pp. 64, 65.

15. The Warren and Wetmore plan of 1909, drawn by V. H. Bailey, was published in *Harper's Weekly,* 18 Dec. 1909, p. 18. A comparably grandiose scheme, probably also by Wetmore, is illustrated in Mandelbaum and Fitzsimons, "Forbes," fig. 14; it was executed before 1903 (since Westmorely Hall is not shown).

For a discussion of the new Columbia University campus, by McKim, Mead and White, see Francesco Passanti, "The Design of Columbia in the 1890's: McKim and His Client," *Journal of the Society of Architectural Historians* 36, no. 2 (May 1977):69–84.

16. Mandelbaum and Fitzsimons identify "V" as an associate of Guy Lowell; "Forbes," p. 72. Several printed copies of this plan exist; it was doubtless intended for prospective contributors to the freshman halls. Harvard Archives, UAI.17.740pf.

17. President Lowell showed plans and perspectives to Forbes in May 1910 when asking his assistance in the fundraising campaign; Mandelbaum and Fitzsimons, "Forbes," p. 78. The letter, from Coolidge to William R. Thayer and dated October 27, 1912, is in the uncatalogued W. R. Thayer papers at Houghton Library.

18. A hand-colored map from about 1905, probably by Forbes, showing land acquired, under option, and not yet acquired, is reproduced in Mandelbaum and Fitzsimons, "Forbes," fig. 13.

19. Rents from property purchased by the Harvard Riverside Associates were used to pay the mortgage. In case this income was insufficient, the Associates had secured promises of support from a group of guarantors, each of whom would contribute up to $200 per year.

20. A memo of 12 March 1927 in the Lowell Papers indicates that title had passed on eleven properties between DeWolfe Street and Western Avenue and was pending on five others, for a total value of $1,020,000. The President's Report for 1926–27 indicates that by autumn 1926 the university owned most of the land close to the river between Weeks Bridge and Western Avenue. For agreements of the 1970s see Harvard University Planning Office, *Long-Range Planning Inventory, Policies and Recommendations, 1975.*

21. The Wetmore-Coolidge feud is described in an unidentified, undated newspaper clipping in the Harvard Archives, HUB.1000.2; and in the *Boston Advertiser,* 17 Sept. 1898.

Charles D. Wetmore (1867–1941) later became a principal of the architectural firm of Warren and Wetmore, which did such buildings as Grand Central Station (1913) and the Biltmore Hotel (1914) in New York. See "Charles D. Wetmore," *New York Times,* May 9, 1941, p. 21. The official architect for Claverly Hall was George Fogerty of Cambridge, but in fact the young owner, soon to become an architect himself, probably designed it.

22. See Harold Kirker, *The Architecture of Charles Bulfinch* (Cambridge: Harvard University Press, 1969). The firm of Coolidge and Wright was the predecessor of Coolidge and Carlson, which designed Byerly Hall at Radcliffe.

23. The letter from Forbes is quoted in Mandelbaum and Fitzsimons, "Forbes," p. 79.

24. The cost of the three buildings was $1,507,832; this amount divided among 488 students averages about $3090 per student. This unit cost makes interesting comparisons with earlier and later dormitories erected at Harvard.

Date	Name	Students	Total cost	Cost per student
1811	Holworthy Hall	48	$ 24,500	$ 510
1871	Matthews Hall	158	115,000	728
1893	Perkins Hall	155	165,000	1,064
1913	Freshman dorms	488	1,507,000	3,089
1929	Harkness Houses (Lowell, Dunster, Eliot)	837	9,920,000	11,850
1973	Canaday Hall	207	3,120,000	15,072

25. In the spring of 1910 leaders of the class of 1911, in an effort to improve class solidarity, agreed to encourage members to live in the Yard during their last year. This was possible because since 1902 college rooms had been assigned on the basis of seniority. From a class of 382 members, 195 lived in the Yard that year despite the austerity of the quarters. To encourage the class of 1912 to continue the tradition, President Lowell permitted students to apply for quarters in groups of from two to fourteen (a full entry); the drawing for assignment was by group.

26. The principal private dormitories were as follows.

Name	Built	Acquired by Harvard
Little (Harvard) Block	1854	1920
Beck Hall	1876	
Felton Hall	1877	
Fairfax Hall	1869 (enlarged 1900)	
Manter Hall	1882	

Name	Built	Acquired by Harvard
Quincy Hall	1891	
Claverly Hall	1892	1920
Trinity Hall	1893	
Ware Hall	1894	
Dana Chambers	1897	
Dunster Hall	1897	1918
Randolph Hall	1897	1916
Craigie Hall	1897	1920
Apley Court	1897	1920
Westmorely Court	1898, 1902	1920
Brantford Hall	1900	
Russell Hall	1900	1902
Drayton Hall	1902	
Hampton Hall	1902	
Ridgeley Hall	1904	

For the locations of most of these halls see a map of the Harvard Square area showing university buildings, clubs, dormitories, and residences of faculty, Harvard Archives, UAI.15.74pf (1898).

27. All but one of the Coolidge brothers had financed Randolph Hall. Joseph was the architect; Harold, a lawyer, handled business affairs; Archibald managed relations with the university. Professor Julian Coolidge, the youngest brother, refused to participate in the venture, convinced it would lose money—and it did. The Coolidges had acquired Apthorp House, and it was always a part of the project plan.

28. For extensive illustrations see *Harvard Alumni Bulletin* 33, no. 18 (29 Jan. 1931), and 33, no. 20 (12 Feb. 1931). The ten undergraduate houses are:
Kirkland House (Smith Hall, 1914; master's house, 1930; Bryan Hall, 1933)
Winthrop House (Standish and Gore Halls, 1914; additions, 1930)
Leverett House (McKinlock Hall, 1925; additions, 1930; towers, 1958)
Dunster House (1930)
Lowell House (1930)
Eliot House (1931)
Adams House (private dormitories, 1898–1902; additions, 1930, 1931)
Quincy House (Mather Hall, 1930; new portion, 1958)
Dudley House (Lehman Hall, 1925; converted to bursar's offices, 1966)
Mather House (1968)
The story of the Harkness gift of residential halls to both Harvard and Yale is best told in Pierson, *Yale,* ch. 10 and 11; in a more general way in Henry A. Yoemans, *Abbott Lawrence Lowell* (Cambridge: Harvard University Press, 1948), ch. 13. The Yale *Record* spoke of the residential halls as "A Princeton idea being tried out at Harvard with Yale money."

29. If their basic educational concepts were compatible, there were, at first, points of difference. Harkness did not warm to Lowell's idea of an honors college, for he was interested in improving the educational prospects of the average student; but that idea dissolved as the program enlarged. Harkness had expected that the proposed housing would include freshmen, but the president was able to persuade him of the advantages of separate treatment for that group.

30. The contracted figure for the initial Harkness gift for the Harvard Houses was $11,390,000 (later increased to $13,238,870); for Yale it was $11,922,000 for dormitories plus $10,210,000 to endow the Bursary system.

31. Within the Coolidge office, George Will was primarily responsible for designing Smith and Standish Halls, Herman Voss for Gore Hall, Louis Abbott for Eliot House, and Hoedtke and Henry Shepley for Dunster, Lowell, and Adams Houses.

32. One section of Bryan Hall (Entries K, L, M) could not be constructed at the same

time as the rest of the hall and the master's house because of a lease on a building on the site; it was constructed in 1933.

33. The Hicks House originally stood on the site of the Indoor Athletic Building; it was moved to its present location in 1928. See Bunting and Nylander, *Old Cambridge*, p. 83, and Mason Hammond, "Hicks House," *Harvard Library Bulletin*, in press.

34. Herman Voss, chief designer in the Coolidge office who worked on many Harvard projects from 1908 on, recalls that in the initial phase of designing the (then) freshman dormitories — Smith, Gore, and Standish — there was a question as to whether they would be done in the neo-Georgian or Collegiate Gothic manner. Coolidge had alternate designs prepared; interestingly enough, he favored the Medieval designs while most of his office preferred the Georgian. To help resolve the matter he invited a dozen prominent architects to advise him. Among the advisers were R. Clipston Sturgis and Ralph Adams Cram, both of whom also designed in Gothic styles. The reference book most used for details of English architecture was John Belcher, ed., and Mervyn E. MacCartney, *Later Renaissance Architecture in England* (London: Batsford, 1901).

35. Randolph Hall and Apthorp House were acquired in 1916 in exchange for College House on Massachusetts Avenue. Claverly and Westmorely were purchased in 1920 for $420,000; Claverly, while attached to Lowell House, serves as a residential overflow for them all. Construction of the tower block, Entry C, was begun in the spring of 1931. Erected on the site of old Russell Hall (1900), this was the last unit constructed with Harkness funds.

36. For the fort planned for the site of Lowell House, see Bunting and Nylander, *Old Cambridge*, p. 15.

37. On the character of the neighborhood and the house at 17 South Street, whose unusually deep cellar once served as an ice house, see Bunting and Nylander, *Old Cambridge*, p. 42.

38. "Harvard Business School Competition," *American Architecture*, Jan. 28, 1924, pp. 293–308. Competition entries were published in successive issues of *Architecture Magazine* between 1922 and 1926. In a note appended to the last installment, which contained the design by Coolidge, Shepley, Bulfinch and Abbott, the editor, himself a competitor, stated that in his opinion this entry was by far the best one submitted. The winning design of McKim, Mead and White, actually designed by W. M. Kendall of the firm, was selected from forty-nine entrants. The judges for the competition were President Lowell, George F. Baker, Charles F. Adams, John Russell Pope, M. D. Medary, and Louis Ayers. Prominent among the entrants were: Perry, Shaw and Hepburn (with J. J. Hafner); Guy Lowell; Raymond Hood; Aymar Embury; Edgerton Swarthout; H. Van Buren Magonigle; Hewitt and Brown; Mott B. Schmidt; Arthur Holden; and Delano and Aldrich.

39. See Douglass Shand Tucci, "The Houses" and "Charlesbank Harvard," *Harvard Magazine*, Nov.-Dec. 1980.

40. Cotting House was initially planned for the eastern segment of the site and was to have been of modern design. The Cottings, who were committed to the Georgian style for their memorial gift, influenced the shift in site and determined the style of the building.

41. Sturgis, a student of Gropius committed to modernism, drew here on his experience in the office of Shepley, Bulfinch, Richardson & Abbott where he worked from 1952 to 1963. There he had been in charge of the rehabilitation of McKinlock Hall at Leverett House. After establishing his own firm he completed at the Business School the small stucco blocks, final segments of the McKim, Mead and White design.

9. President Conant, Gropius, and Modernism

1. On his presidency, see James Bryant Conant, "Twenty Years," *Harvard Alumni Bulletin* 55, no. 8 (24 Jan. 1953):343–354.

2. The innovative architectural curriculum at Harvard was discussed widely at the time: "Education toward Creative Design," *American Architect* 150 (May 1937):26–30.

3. Conant's own scholarly achievement was substantial. Teddy Lytle, "Bibliographies of James B. Conant," President's Office, Harvard University, 1978, lists more than 120 scientific articles, 90 of which appeared in the *Journal of the American Chemical Society*.

For the General Education Program see "Harvard Present and Future: An Address by President Conant in Sanders Theatre, March 20, 1936," *Harvard Alumni Bulletin* 38, no. 25 (10 April 1936):812–819. Conant's views on education were published in numerous articles in the *Journal of General Education* where a bibliography of his works was reprinted: Virginia Proctor, "James B. Conant," 5, no. 1 (Oct. 1950).

4. "Mr. Conant and Germany: A Presidential Autobiography," *Harvard Alumni Bulletin* 55, No. 8 (24 Jan. 1953):353–354.

5. Bulfinch designed Massachusetts General Hospital after designing University Hall. Both were executed in granite. University Hall was ornamented, while the hospital, leading into the restrained style of the Greek Revival, was not. Littauer follows the second mode.

6. This rear facade of Littauer centers on a slim vertical window derived not from Bulfinch's work but from the firm's White Building at Massachusetts General Hospital. Axially symmetrical, like the front elevation, it is unembellished architecturally, as was much "stripped Classic" protomodern architecture in Boston in these years. On the White Building see Coolidge, Shepley, Bulfinch and Abbott, "Addition to Massachusetts General Hospital in Boston," *Pencil Points* 21 (Nov. 1940):690–700.

7. Coolidge's death marked the end of the full monopoly on Harvard commissions that his firm had held during the Lowell administration. Certainly the firm's last Georgian buildings at Harvard are far inferior to those designed during Coolidge's lifetime. After a period of leveling off, the firm went on to produce under President Pusey excellent modern designs for Quincy and Mather Houses, many of which were planned by Jean Paul Carlhian, who had earlier designed Allston Burr. "SBRA: The Harvard Work," *Architectural Record* 125 (Feb. 1959):159–168.

8. At the insistence of Keyes Metcalf, against Conant's opposition, the Dana-Palmer House (1822) was moved across Quincy Street to allow for the construction of Lamont. A Federal style, hipped-roof structure with an added Greek Revival porch, it had once served as the Harvard Observatory. President Conant lived there during the war while the government occupied the President's House. It is now a university guest house. See Downing, MacDougall, and Pearson, *Mid Cambridge*, pp. 25–26, 28, 57, 105, 113, and ill. 19; Bunting and Nylander, *Old Cambridge*, pp. 21, 155, 164, 166, 189. For the best-known work of the Perry, Shaw and Hepburn firm see "The Restoration of Colonial Williamsburg in Virginia," *Architectural Record* 78, no. 6 (Dec. 1935):355–456.

9. See Christine Fernandez Carvajal, "Art Deco in Boston" (Master's thesis, Tufts University, 1983).

10. Klaus Herdig, *The Decorated Diagram, Harvard Architecture and the Failure of the Bauhaus Legacy* (Cambridge: M.I.T. Press, 1983), Section 3. Herdig's recent work challenges broadly the entire Gropius concept and the pseudo-scientific rationale which he invoked for architectural problem solving. These scientific premises provided justification for eliminating from the design process stylistic or associative reference to historical precedent.

11. James B. Conant, "University Professorships at Harvard," *School and Society* 43, no. 1102 (8 February 1936):205–207. James B. Conant, "Academical Patronage and Superintendence," *Harvard Educational Review* 8, no. 3 (May 1938):312–334. The stature of Gropius was at this time at its highest point as suggested in the following selected examples of contemporary assessment of his work: "A Modernist Scans our Skyline: Gropius, German Architect Bound for Harvard, Sees an Original Style Emerging in America," *New York Times Magazine*, April 11, 1937, pp. 12–24; "Appointment as Professor Architect at Harvard University," *American Architect* 150 (Feb. 1937):19; "Architecture at Harvard," *Architectural Record* 81, no. 5 (May 1937):8–11; "Gropius to Harvard," *Architectural Forum* 66, no. 3 (March 1937):14.

12. On Gordon McKay see "The University," *Harvard Alumni Bulletin* 53, no. 11 (March 10, 1951):456–458.

13. Gropius's belief that architecture should proceed by anonymous collaborative effort is well illustrated by his mode of working with the firm. He insisted that the names of the partners be listed alphabetically (although everyone knew he was the senior partner), and he refused to take individual credit for design. This approach is discussed extensively by Herdig in *The Decorated Diagram*.

For Dean Joseph Hudnut's relationship to Gropius, see Wayland Bowser, "Reforming Design Education," *Journal of Architectural Education* 37 (Winter 1983):12–14.

14. On the Graduate Center see "Dormitories for Harvard University, USA," *Architect's Journal* 109, no. 2817 (Feb. 3, 1949):112, 125–126; "Eclectic Setting; Graduate Commons; Design for Student Living," *Harvard Alumni Bulletin* 51, no. 3 (Oct. 23, 1948):108–109, and 53, no. 2 (Oct. 14, 1950):58–62; "Flexibility at Harvard," *Architectural Forum* 90, no. 1 (Jan. 1949):36, 40; "Harvard Builds a Graduate Yard," *Architectural Forum* 93, no. 6 (Dec. 1950): 61–71; "Harvard Reaffirms an Old Tradition: Proposed Graduate Center, Cambridge," *Architectural Record* 104, no. 5 (Nov. 1948):118–119; "Modern Gets a Bid from the Oldest U.S. University," *Architectural Forum* 89, no. 5 (Nov. 1948):15. On Miró's mural see "Mural by Miró," *Harvard Alumni Bulletin* 54, no. 3 (Oct. 27, 1951):10; "What Is It?" *Harvard Alumni Bulletin* 53, no. 8 (Jan. 27, 1951):347.

15. Walter Gropius, "Tradition and the Center," *Harvard Alumni Bulletin* 53, no. 2 (Oct. 14, 1950):68–71. The conceptual model for the plan of the Graduate Center (despite a presumed derivation from Harvard Yard) was obviously the Bauhaus complex at Dessau (1926); see Walter Gropius, *The New Architecture and the Bauhaus* (rpt. Cambridge: M.I.T. Press, 1965). Connections between the Graduate Center plan and Frank Lloyd Wright's covered walkways at Florida Southern College (1931) have been suggested. See Neil Levine, "Frank Lloyd Wright's Diagonal Planning," in Helen Searing, *In Search of Modern Architecture*, pp. 245–277.

16. The decision on the color of brick was difficult because of the relationship between fenestration and wall surface. A solution opposed to the planar vision of the International Style would have resulted if the window casings had differed in color from the walls.

17. On Allston Burr Hall see H. L. Hopffgarten, Steve Yuen, and Ira Pinkus, "The History of Allston Burr Hall" (paper submitted to Professor Edward Sekler, on file at Carpenter Center, Harvard); "New Buildings," *Harvard Alumni Bulletin* 53, no. 11 (March 10, 1951):456–458; "The University," *Harvard Alumni Bulletin* 54, no. 11 (March 8, 1952):455.

18. The undulating modern facade had already been introduced to Cambridge by Alvaar Aalto at Baker House at M.I.T., but architect Carlhian convincingly claims inspiration from Borromini.

19. Denys Peter Myers, Letter to the Editor, *Harvard Alumni Bulletin,* Dec. 9, 1950, started the debate which continued thereafter for weeks in the winter of 1950–51. Parker's drawings are illustrated in *Harvard Alumni Bulletin* 53 (July 7, 1951):793.

20. M. A. DeWolfe Howe, "Allston Burr," *Harvard Alumni Bulletin* 51, no. 9 (Feb. 12, 1949):372. Burr's long-term concern with undergraduate students, which resulted in the system of Allston Burr tutors in the houses, is well summarized by Thomas E. Crooks, *Harvard Radcliffe Parents' Newsletter,* May 1981. Burr undertook much service for the university during his lifetime, including being chief fundraiser for Memorial Church. When he died in 1949 he left Harvard $2.5 million; part of this was used for the tutorial system and the balance to erect Allston Burr Hall. The inappropriateness of the design given Burr's character was argued in letters to the editor by Richard Wait ('23) and Paul M. Hollister ('13).

21. Sturgis's letters appeared in the *Harvard Alumni Bulletin* 53, no. 2 (Oct. 14, 1950):55, 81, and 53, no. 13 (April 7, 1951):530–531.

22. *Harvard Alumni Bulletin* 53, no. 14 (April 21, 1951):570. The letter (excerpted here) is signed Robin H. Chapman; Eason Cross, Jr., '47; John M. Garber; George S. Goddard, B.Arch. '51; Peter MacGowan, '42; Robert H. Springer, '48; Robert S. Sturgis, '44; Albert Szabo; Felix M. Warburg, '46; Robertson Ward, Jr., '45; Richard H.

Wheeler, '46; Dora Wiebenson. It was actually drafted by Clipston Sturgis's cousin Robert Sturgis, sometime editor of the *Crimson,* who ironically in 1967 would be the architect of Cotting Hall at the Business School.

23. For cartoons of the *World Tree* see "What Is It," *Harvard Alumni Bulletin* 53, no. 8 (Jan. 27, 1951):347, 391, 507, 680, 683, 771.

24. Not accidentally, the Society of Architectural Historians was founded at Harvard in 1940, envisioned (by Kenneth Conant and others) as a means of perpetuating the study of history in the face of Gropius's theories of architectural education. For a perspective on Conant's lifetime work with illustrations see Kenneth J. Conant, "A Majestic Abbey, Long Destroyed, Rises Again—on Paper," *Harvard Magazine,* Jan.–Feb. 1977. Conant's drawings and research on Cluny now form a part of the Loeb Library Collection, Harvard School of Design.

10. President Pusey and the Program for Harvard College

1. See Harris, *Economics of Harvard,* pp. 312, 358–360. Harvard had had four earlier major fund drives: in 1904 for $2.5 million, 1919 for $15.5 million, 1926 for $10 million, and 1936 for $6 million. Two later campaigns were also successful: one for the Medical School in the late 1950s, and one for undergraduate science in 1967.

2. Harris, *Economics of Harvard,* pp. 318–319.

3. "Boylston's Fifth Incarnation by TAC," *Architectural Forum* 113 (July 1960):90–93. Benjamin Thompson was in charge of this project.

4. Harris, *Economics of Harvard,* pp. 315–325.

5. On the Carpenter Center see Eduard Sekler and William Curtis, *Le Corbusier at Work* (Cambridge: Harvard University Press, 1980). Also "Big Change on the Campus: Carpenter Center for the Visual Arts," *Architectural Forum* 118 (March 1963):76–81; A. J. Monk, "Carpenter Centre for the Visual Arts, Harvard University," *Royal Institute of British Architects Journal,* series 3, vol. 70 (May 1963):183–187; J. S. Morris, "Corbusier at Harvard," *Royal Institute of British Architects Journal* 73 (Aug. 1966):360–365; "Le Corbusier at Harvard: A Disaster, or a Bold Step Forward?" *Architectural Forum* 119 (Oct. 1963):104–107; "Le Corbusier Builds at Harvard: New Visual Arts Center," *Architectural Forum* 115 (Dec. 1961):108–111; "Le Corbusier Designs for Harvard: Carpenter Center for the Visual Arts," *Architectural Record* 133 (April 1963):151–158; S. Giedion, "New Ventures in University," *Zodiac* 16 (1966):24–35.

6. Corbusier's early interest in modular concepts continued right through his more baroque phase in the 1960s. See Le Corbusier, *Modulor I and II* (Cambridge: Harvard University Press, 1980).

7. Knod Bastlund, *Jose Luis Sert* (New York: Praeger, 1967); D. Canty, "Harvard Completes a Course in Urban Design," *Architectural Forum* 64 (Jan. 1967):64–77.

8. Josep Lluis Sert, "On Windows and Walls," *Architectural Record* 131 (May 1962):132; "Harvard Health Center Has Redevelopment Plan," *Progressive Architecture* 41 (Feb. 1960):71; "New Work of Sert, Jackson and Gourley: Holyokc Center and World Religions Center," *Architectural Record* 131 (May 1962):132.

9. For Andrews see Jennifer Taylor, *John Andrews: Architecture as a Performing Art* (New York: Oxford University Press, 1982). On Gund Hall see "Gund Hall: Harvard's Graduate School of Design under One Roof," *Architectural Record* 152 (Nov. 1972):95–104; P. Prangnell, "Harvard Graduate School of Design, J. Andrews, Arch.: Some Comments on the Building," *Architectural Forum* 131 (Dec. 1969):62–67; W. Marlin, "Harvard's New Hall," *Architectural Forum* 137 (Dec. 1972):50–55.
The stairs and overhang developed here dramatically by Andrews are concepts Le Corbusier had first suggested in 1933–34 in his design for an unexecuted housing project for M. Durrand in Algeria. Andrews had used the form earlier at Scarborough College, a branch of the University of Toronto.

10. A similarly large space, though different in shape, in Paul Rudolph's Yale Architectural School was disliked by students and subsequently redesigned.

11. In fact in 1983–84 Gund Hall underwent major structural renovation by Don Hisaka, including repair of a leaky roof.

12. F. P. Hosken, "Scale in Cambridge," *Arts and Architecture* 83 (Oct. 1966):6–7; "Six New Yamasaki Projects: Behavioral Sciences Building and Engineering Laboratory," *Architectural Record* 130 (July 1961):126–129; "William James Hall of the Behavioral Sciences," *Architectural Record* 138 (Oct. 1965):138–139.

13. See M. F. Schmertz, "High-density Design for Undergraduate Science at Land Starved Harvard," *Architectural Record* 155 (March 1974):111–118; "Science Center is Precast for Fast Assembly," *Architectural Record* 151 (Feb. 1972):129–132.

14. "New Work of Sert, Jackson and Gourley: Holyoke Center and World Religions Center," *Architectural Record* 131 (May 1962):132. For Sert's own house see Heyer, *Architects on Architecture*, pp. 245–255.

15. See *Architectural Record* 125 (June 1959):15.

16. "Rockefeller Hall, Harvard University," *Architectural Record* 154 (Oct. 1973):148–149.

17. "Faculty Office Building and Classroom and Administration Building for Harvard Law School. Executive Development Complex, Graduate School of Business Administration," *Architectural Record* 151 (Jan. 1972):124–132.

18. "David and Arnold Hoffman Laboratory of Experimental Geology by TAC," *Progressive Architecture* 45 (March 1964):144–147; "P/A Ninth Annual Design Awards: Laboratory Facilities for Research in Experimental Geology for Harvard," *Progressive Architecture* 43 (Jan. 1962):166–169.

19. On Stanley Parker (1881–1965) see *Harvard Class of 1904 50th Anniversary Report*, pp. 349–350.

20. "Six New Yamasaki Projects: Behavioral Sciences Building and Engineering Laboratory," *Architectural Record* 130 (July 1961):126–129.

21. Radcliffe held a limited competition for the gymnasium and athletic facility, specifying the recessive character of the design. Garden Street neighbors organized to control its size and location from the start.

22. Both the Loeb and the Gutman Library projects involved removal of old houses of considerable architectural interest. Fortunately it was possible to save them. The Greek Revival houses from the site of Loeb were moved to St. John's Road, and the two houses from the library site went to Farwell Place. Harvard's more enlightened attitude toward Cambridge houses, in its infancy in the 1950s, is so strong in the 1980s that several more buildings have been moved and restored at great expense: for example, the houses on Prescott Street.

23. See "Drama Center for Harvard," *Architectural Record* 128 (Sept. 1960):151–160; "Loeb Drama Center," *Architectural Record* 126 (Oct. 1959):178–182; "Théâter Automatique: Harvard's New Theater," *Architectural Forum* 113 (Oct. 1960):90–97. Metal grilles appeared on a number of contemporaneous buildings by other architects, for example Yamasaki's Reynolds Aluminum Company Building.

24. "Another Important Design at Harvard: Design by Caudill, Rowlett and Scott for the Graduate School of Education," *Progressive Architecture* 44 (May 1963):67; "Curious Walls of Larsen Hall, Harvard Graduate School of Education," *Architectural Forum* 124 (March 1966):46–53; F. P. Hosken, "Scale in Cambridge," *Arts and Architecture* 83 (Oct. 1966):6–7.

25. Arsenal Square, the small green just north of the Common at the intersection of Concord Avenue, Garden Street, and Chauncy Street, was the site of a Federal brick arsenal and associated buildings erected by the Commonwealth in 1816. These were destroyed in 1887. See Bunting and Nylander, *Old Cambridge*, pp. 46, 47.

26. "Specialized Library for an Urban Campus: the Monroe C. Gutman Library for the Harvard Graduate School of Education," *Architectural Record* 156 (Aug. 1974):98–103.

27. "Countway Library of Medicine of the Harvard Medical School and the Boston Medical Library," *Architectural Record* 133 (March 1963):133–136; "Countway Library at Harvard," *Progressive Architecture* 46 (Nov. 1965):166–177; F. P. Hosken, "Francis A. Countway Library of Medicine of Harvard Medical School," *Arts and Architecture* 83 (April 1966):20–23; "1966 AIA Honor Awards: Countway Library of Medicine, Harvard University Medical School, Hugh Stubbins and Assoc., Arch.," *American Institute of Architecture Journal* 46 (July 1966):48–49.

28. "Eighth House: Quincy House," *Progressive Architecture* 41 (Sept. 1960):134–141; "Harvard Builds Eighth House Designed by SBRA, Quincy House," *ibid.* 39 (Sept. 1958):46; "SBRA: The Harvard Work," *Architectural Record* 125 (Feb. 1959):159–168.

29. "Towered Dorms for Harvard's Leverett House; SBRA," *Architectural Forum* 115 (Sept. 1961):128–129. A comparable relationship of towers, but on a more striking scale, is provided by Trinity Church, Boston (1877), by H. H. Richardson and I. M. Pei's John Hancock Tower in Boston (1967–1975).

30. For Mather House see *Architectural Record* 142 (July 1967):41; Michael O'Hare, "Designing with Wind Tunnels," *Architectural Forum* 128 (April 1968):60; "Better College Living," *Boston Globe,* Nov 8, 1970, p. 30.

31. See "Harvard Married Student Apartments," *Architectural Record* 134 (Sept. 1963):208–209; "Harvard Puts Trust in Principles Instead of Plans," *Architectural Forum* 120 (June 1964):116–119; "Harvard's New Married Student Housing," *Progressive Architecture* 45 (Dec. 1964):122–133; "Married Students' Residence Completed at Harvard," *Architectural Record* 136 (Nov. 1964):12–13.

11. The New Harvard

1. See Paul Heyer, *Architects on Architecture: New Directions in America* (New York: Walker, 1966). Stubbins's own book *Architecture: The Design Experience* (New York: Wiley, 1976) amplifies his views. Although he was a student of Gropius, Stubbins has greater strength as a designer; he is also much influenced by the contextual sense of Alvar Aalto.

2. "Hiding Out in the Harvard Yard (The New Nathan Marsh Pusey Library)," *Interior Design* 47 (Dec. 1976):144–147; M. F. Schmertz, "In Deference to Its Environment the (Nathan Marsh) Pusey Was Built Beneath the Harvard Yard," *Architectural Record* 160 (Sept. 1970):97–102.

3. Icoh Ming Pei was a student of Gropius after graduating from M.I.T. in 1938. He worked initially in the office of Hugh Stubbins. Pei's influence has been as great in twentieth-century Boston as that of Bulfinch in earlier times. He designed Government Center (1961), the Christian Science Church Center (with Arnaldo Cossutta; 1973), the John Hancock Tower (with Harry Cobb; 1973), Harbor Towers (1973), and the west wing of the Museum of Fine Arts (1981). See Peter Blake, "I. M. Pei and Partners," *Architecture Plus* 1, no. 1, pp. 52–59, and no. 2, pp. 20–77; and Muriel Emanuel, *Contemporary Architects* (New York: St. Martin's Press, 1980), pp. 611–612. Records and drawings for the unexecuted Kennedy Center are in the collection of the Kennedy Library, Columbia Point, Boston.

4. Architectural Resources Cambridge, Inc., has designed many other educational buildings, most recently the Cabot Intercultural Center at Tufts University (1980). In most of their projects large overscaled windows and dark mortar for the brick walls have established a clear stylistic identity.
For the Kennedy School see Christopher Reed, "Harvard Dedicates a New School for Public Servants," *Harvard Magazine* 81, no. 3 (Jan.–Feb. 1979):46–51; and Mildred Schmertz, "The Kennedy School of Government: A Purposefully Non-heroic New Gateway to Harvard," *Architectural Record* 165, no. 6 (June 1979):99–106.

5. On Stirling see John Summerson, "Vitruvius Ludens," *Architectural Review* 173, no. 1033 (March 1983):18–25; James Stirling, "Regionalism and Architecture," *Architects Yearbook* 8 (London: Elek Books, 1957), pp. 62–68; and *James Stirling, Buildings and Projects 1950–1974* (New York: Oxford University Press, 1975). For the

Sackler Wing see *James Stirling's Design to Expand the Fogg Museum: A Portfolio of Drawings* (Cambridge: Fogg Art Museum, 1981); John Coolidge, "Stirling: Fogg," *Architectural Review* 173, no. 1033 (March 1983):22–25; Gary Wolf, "Stirling: Fogg," *Architectural Review* 175, no. 1046 (April 1984):35–42; "Stirling to Design Fogg Addition," *Progressive Architecture,* March 1983, pp. 19–21.

6. For the historical language of Post-Modernism see Helen Searing, *New American Art Museums* (New York: Whitney Museum of Art, 1982); Helen Searing and Henry Hope Reed, *Speaking a New Classicism: American Architecture Now* (Northampton, Mass.: Smith College Museum of Art, 1981); and Charles Jencks, *Architecture Today* (New York: Harry N. Abrams, 1981).

7. Jacob Schlesinger, "A Harvard Gatehouse Must Be Special," *Boston Globe,* Aug. 10, 1983.

8. Montgomery Schuyler, "The Architecture of American Colleges I: Harvard," *Architectural Record* 26, no. 4 (Oct. 1909):243–269.

Chronological List of Buildings
Erected or Purchased by Harvard
in Cambridge and Boston

Note: This working list does not include most private residences, clubhouses, and commercial buildings owned or once owned by Harvard.

Only significant alterations are attributed by architect. An asterisk (*) signifies enlargement.

1 Peyntree House (President's House I). Built 1633. Acquired 1638. Demolished 1644.

2 Harvard Hall I (Old College). Built 1638–44. Demolished 1686(?)

3 President's House II. Built 1644. Demolished 1677.

4 Goffe College. Built 1633. Acquired 1651. Demolished 1677.

5 Indian College. Built 1654–56. Demolished 1698.

6 Printing House. Built 1654–55. Demolished: date unavailable.

7 Brew House. Built 1668. Demolished 1814.

8 Harvard Hall II. Built 1674–82. Demolished 1764.

9 President's House III. Built 1680. Demolished 1718.

10 (Old) Stoughton Hall. Built 1698. Demolished 1781.

11 Massachusetts Hall. Built 1718. Altered 1812 Loammi Baldwin; 1870 Ware & Van Brunt; 1924; 1939.

12 Wadsworth House (President's House IV). Built 1726. Altered 1783, 1810*, 1849, 1871.

13 Holden Chapel. Built 1742 John Smibert. Altered 1782; 1850 Gridley J. F. Bryant; 1880.

14 Apthorp House (Adams House Master's Residence). Built 1760 Peter Harrison (attribution).

15 Hollis Hall. Built 1762 Thomas Dawes, Master Builder. Altered 1876, 1898, 1959.

16 Hicks House (Kirkland House), 64 J. F. Kennedy Street. Built 1762. Altered 1929–1930 Coolidge, Shepley, Bulfinch & Abbott. Moved when Indoor Athletic Building was erected.

17 Harvard Hall III. Built 1764 Gov. Francis Bernard, Thomas Dawes. Altered 1842* Richard Bond; 1870 Ware & Van Brunt; 1968 Ashley Myer Smith.

18 Elmwood (President's House VII). Built 1767. Altered 1898*, 1902, 1963.

19 Wiswall House (College House). Built 1769. Acquired 1770. Demolished 1845.

20　Bath House. Built 1800. Demolished: date unavailable.

21　Stoughton Hall II. Built 1804–05 Charles Bulfinch, Thomas Dawes. Altered 1871 Ware & Van Brunt; 1879; 1898; 1968.

22　Fay House (Radcliffe). Built 1807. Altered 1870; 1890–92 A. W. Longfellow, Jr.; 1962; 1982.

23　Botanic Garden House (Asa Gray House). Built 1810 Ithiel Town. Altered 1848, 1910.

24　Holworthy Hall. Built 1811–12 Loammi Baldwin. Altered 1855, 1870, 1871, 1968.

25　University Hall. Built 1813–15 Charles Bulfinch. Altered 1869; 1870; 1898 Pierre La Rose (chapel).

26　Webber House (College House). Built 1750. Acquired 1817. Demolished 1844.

27　Divinity Hall. Designed 1825 Solomon Willard. Altered 1825 Thomas Sumner; 1834 U. Sparrel; 1905 A. W. Longfellow, Jr. (chapel).

28　Matron's House (Divinity School). Built 1825. Demolished: date unavailable.

29　Palfrey House. Built 1831. Altered 1919.

30　Dane Hall. Built 1832. Altered 1844* Isaac Melvin. Moved 1871. Demolished 1918.

31　College House. Built 1832. Altered 1845*, 1859*, 1870*, 1923–26*. Demolished in part 1916, 1956.

32　Warren House. Built 1833. Moved 1900.

33　Dana-Palmer House. Built 1822–23. Acquired 1835. Altered 1839. Moved 1947 for construction of Lamont Library.

34　Gannett House (Law School). Built 1838. Turned east 1938.

35　Sparks House. Built 1838. William Saunders, housewright. Moved 1901. Altered 1909–10*. Moved 1968.

36　Gore Hall (library). Built 1838–41 Richard Bond. Altered 1876* Ware & Van Brunt; 1895; 1906*. Demolished 1913.

37　Fifty-Three Dunster Street (Dudley House Master's Residence). Built 1841 William Saunders, Housewright.

38　Panorama Building. Built 1843. Demolished 1845. Housed Panorama of Athens — gift of Theodore Lyman (1819).

39　Observatory. Built 1843 Isaiah Rogers. Altered 1851*; 1892*; 1931* Coolidge, Shepley, Bulfinch & Abbott; 1954*. Demolished in part 1954–60. See 215, Perkin Building.

40　Twenty-Five Quincy Street (Walker House). Built 1844 Isaac Melvin (attribution). Altered 1904, 1911, 1929. Demolished 1952.

41　Thirty-One Quincy Street (Pierce House). Built 1844 Henry Greenough (attribution). Altered 1878, 1905, 1916. Demolished 1951.

42　Medical School, Boston (North Grove Street). Built 1846 Gridley J. F. Bryant, Jr. Demolished in part.

43　Boat House. Built 1846. Demolished 1869–70.

44　Lawrence Hall (Scientific School). Built 1847 Richard Bond. Altered 1871 Ware & Van Brunt; 1892. Demolished 1970.

45　Thirty-Seven (40) Quincy Street (Felton House). Built 1848. Altered 1900. Demolished 1951.

46　Society Hall (Museum of Comparative Zoology). Built 1849. Altered 1860, 1876. Demolished 1950.

47　Boat House. Built 1856. Demolished 1869–70.

48 Appleton Chapel. Built 1856 Paul Schultze. Altered 1872, 1886, 1919. Demolished 1931.

49 Boylston Hall. Built 1857 Schultze & Schoen. Altered 1871 Peabody & Stearns; 1876 Ware & Van Brunt; 1959 TAC. Housed early Chemistry laboratory.

50 University Museum. Built 1859 George Snell & Henry Greenough. Altered 1871*; 1876* R. H. Slack; 1880*; 1888*; 1900*; 1906*; 1931*; 1971* TAC.

51 Old Gymnasium (Rogers Hall). Built 1859 E. C. Cabot. Altered 1878. Demolished 1933. Germanic Museum 1878–1916.

52 Greenleaf House (76 Brattle Street). Built 1859 by Mary Longfellow Greenleaf; Radcliffe President's House.

53 President's House V (Quincy Street). Built 1860 E. C. Cabot. Demolished 1913.

54 Grays Hall. Built 1862 N. J. Bradlee. Altered 1908, 1961.

55 Herbarium (Garden Street). Built 1864 Ryder & Harris. Altered 1871*, 1876. Demolished 1914.

56 Memorial Hall. Built 1864–78 Ware & Van Brunt. Altered 1897, 1909, 1975. Clock tower burned 1956.

57 Thayer Common (branch railroad station). Built 1850. Acquired 1865. Demolished 1883.

58 Thayer Hall. Built 1869 Ryder & Harris. Altered 1887, 1959.

59 Holyoke House. Built 1870 Ryder & Harris. Altered 1873, 1876, 1909. Demolished 1961.

60 Dental School, Boston (50 Allen Street). Built 1870–71. Demolished 1960s.

61 Bussey Institute Building (Jamaica Plain, Boston). Built 1870–71 Peabody & Stearns. Demolished 1975.

62 Weld Hall. Built 1870 Ware & Van Brunt. Altered 1962 (stairs enclosed).

63 Matthews Hall. Built 1871 Peabody & Stearns. Altered 1887, 1960. Indian College foundations on this site.

64 Harvard Building (101 Arch Street, Boston). Built 1872–73 Peabody & Stearns.

65 Boat House (Flagg Street). Built 1869–70. Altered 1874–76*. Demolished 1901.

66 Hemenway Gymnasium I. Built 1876–78 Peabody & Stearns. Demolished 1938.

67 Sever Hall. Built 1878–80 H. H. Richardson. Rehabilitated 1982–83.

68 Austin Hall (Law School). Built 1881–82 H. H. Richardson.

69 Medical School (Boylston Street, Boston). Built 1881–83 Ware & Van Brunt. Demolished 1966.

70 Jefferson Physical Laboratory. Built 1882–84 Shaw & Hunnewell.

71 Farlow Herbarium (Divinity Library). Built 1886 Peabody & Stearns. Altered 1902*, 1921*.

72 Walter Hastings Hall. Built 1888 Cabot & Chandler.

73 Johnston Gate. Built 1889 McKim, Mead & White. Other gates and fence added 1901–06. Altered 1915*, 1936, 1949. Dudley Gate demolished when Dana-Palmer House was moved.

74 Hunnewell Building (Arnold Arboretum, Jamaica Plain). Built 1890 A. W. Longfellow, Jr. Altered 1895*.

75 Carey Athletic Building (Jarvis Field). Built 1889 A. W. Longfellow, Jr. Altered 1893–94 H. Langford Warren. Demolished 1950. Served as Rotch Building, Architectural School, 1893–1904.

76 Claverly Hall (Adams House). Built 1892 George Fogerty. Altered 1898*.

77 Perkins Hall. Built 1893 Shepley, Rutan & Coolidge.

78 Conant Hall. Built 1893 Shepley, Rutan & Coolidge.

79 Hunt Hall (Old Fogg Museum). Built 1893 Richard Morris Hunt. Altered 1912–13. Demolished 1973.

80 Carey Cage (Soldiers Field). Built 1897 H. Langford Warren, L. J. Johnson.

81 Randolph Hall (Adams House). Built 1897 Coolidge & Wright. Altered 1902*, 1912.

82 Randall Hall Commons. Built 1898 Wheelwright & Haven. Demolished 1962.

83 Phillips Brooks House. Built 1898 A. W. Longfellow, Jr.

84 Hemenway Gymnasium (Radcliffe). Built 1898 McKim, Mead & White.

85 Westmorly Court (Adams House). Built 1898 Warren & Wetmore. Acquired 1902.

86 University Boathouse (Newell). Built 1899–1900 Peabody & Stearns.

87 Stillman Infirmary. Built 1900 Shepley, Rutan & Coolidge. Altered 1904*. Demolished 1964.

88 Semitic Museum. Built 1900–02 A. W. Longfellow, Jr.

89 Pierce Hall. Built 1900 Shaw & Hunnewell.

90 Harvard Union. Built 1900–01 McKim, Mead & White. Altered 1911* (Varsity Club) Thomas Mott Shaw; 1931 Perry, Shaw & Hepburn.

91 Bertram Hall (Radcliffe). Built 1901–02 A. W. Longfellow, Jr.

92 Robinson Hall. Built 1901–04 McKim, Mead & White. Altered 1972–73. Built as Architectural School.

93 Harvard Stadium. Built 1901–03 Ira Hollis, CE; L. J. Johnson, ME; with McKim, Mead & White. Altered 1910 (colonnade); 1930.

94 Lowell Lecture Hall. Built 1902 Guy Lowell.

95 Medical School Campus (Boston). Built 1903–06 Shepley, Rutan & Coolidge.

96 Emerson Hall. Built 1904 Guy Lowell. Altered 1965.

97 Agassiz House (Radcliffe). Built 1904 A. W. Longfellow, Jr.

98 Langdell Hall (Law School). Built 1906 Shepley, Rutan & Coolidge. Altered 1928* Coolidge, Shepley, Bulfinch & Abbott.

99 Weld Boathouse. Built 1906 Peabody & Stearns.

100 Radcliffe Library (Schlesinger Library). Built 1907 Winslow & Bigelow. Altered 1966: Radcliffe (Bunting) Institute; Sarah Wyman Whitman interior stained glass.

101 Eliot Hall. Built 1907 A. W. Longfellow, Jr.

102 Squash Courts. Built 1908 Coolidge & Carlson.

103 *Harvard Lampoon* Building. Built 1909 Wheelwright & Haven. Not owned by Harvard.

104 Kittredge Hall (79 Garden Street). Built 1909 Mowll & Kilham. Altered 1911–14.

105 Dental School (Longwood Avenue, Boston). Built 1909 Shepley, Rutan & Coolidge.

106 Andover Hall (Theological School). Built 1910 Allen & Collens. Altered 1960* (library) Shepley, Bulfinch, Richardson & Abbott.

107 Wolcott Gibbs Laboratory. Built 1911–13 A. W. Longfellow, Jr.

108 President's House VI (17 Quincy Street). Built 1911 Guy Lowell.

109 Barnard Hall (Radcliffe). Built 1912–13 Kilham & Hopkins.

110 Jefferson Coolidge Laboratory. Built 1912–13 A. W. Longfellow, Jr. Demolished 1979.

111 Anderson Bridge. Built 1912–13 Wheelwright & Haven & Hoyt. Not owned by Harvard.

112 Whitman Hall (Radcliffe). Built 1911–12 Kilham & Hopkins.

113 Music Building (Paine Hall). Built 1913 John Mead Howells & Stokes. Altered 1955* Stanley B. Parker (Eda Kuhn Loeb Library addition); 1970* Shepley, Bulfinch, Richardson & Abbott (Fanny Mason Wing).

114 Cruft Laboratory. Built 1913 Warren & Smith, E. Duquesne, Jr. Altered 1952.

115 Widener Library. Built 1913–15 Horace Trumbauer, Julian Abele. Stair murals: John Singer Sargent.

116 Gore Hall (Winthrop House). Built 1913 Shepley, Rutan & Coolidge. Altered 1931 Coolidge, Shepley, Bulfinch & Abbott. Originally freshmen dormitory.

117 Standish Hall (Winthrop House). Built 1913 Shepley, Rutan & Coolidge. Altered 1931 Coolidge, Shepley, Bulfinch & Abbott. Originally freshmen dormitory.

118 Bryan and Smith Halls (Kirkland House). Built 1913 Shepley, Rutan & Coolidge. Altered 1930. Originally freshmen dormitories.

119 Hurlbut Hall. Built 1914 Newhall & Blevins. Acquisition date unavailable.

120 Busch-Reisinger Museum. Built 1914–21 German Bestelmeyer with Warren & Smith.

121 Greenough Hall. Built 1922 Mowll & Rand.

122 Briggs Hall (Radcliffe). Built 1923 Blackall & Elwell.

123 Mower Hall. Built 1924 Coolidge, Shepley, Bulfinch & Abbott.

124 Lionel Hall. Built 1924–25 Coolidge, Shepley, Bulfinch & Abbott.

125 Lehman Hall (Dudley House). Built 1924–25 Coolidge, Shepley, Bulfinch & Abbott. Altered 1965(?) Originally Bursar's Office.

126 Harvard Business School. Competition 1925–26 McKim, Mead & White. Built 1928, Baker Library, dormitories. Completion: 1940s William Campbell; 1963 Robert S. Sturgis.

127 Sinclair Weeks Bridge. Built 1926 McKim, Mead & White.

128 Straus Hall. Built 1926 Coolidge, Shepley, Bulfinch & Abbott.

129 Fogg Art Museum. Built 1925 Coolidge, Shepley, Bulfinch & Abbott. Altered 1932 Coolidge, Shepley, Bulfinch & Abbott (Naumberg Room addition).

130 Briggs Cage (Soldiers Field). Built 1926–27. Designed by Guy Lowell; finished by H. W. Andrews. Altered 1983–84.

131 McKinlock Hall (Leverett House). Built 1925–26 Shepley, Bulfinch, Richardson & Abbott. Altered 1930 Shepley, Bulfinch, Richardson & Abbott; 1959 Shepley, Bulfinch, Richardson & Abbott.

132 Haskins Hall. Built 1926 Robert Allen.

133 Mallinckrodt Laboratory. Built 1927 Coolidge, Shepley, Bulfinch & Abbott. Altered 1953, 1958.

134 Pennypacker Hall. Built 1927 Silverman & Brown. Acquired 1960s.

135 Holden Green; Gibson Terrace; Shaler Lane. Built 1927 Kilham Hopkins Greeley.

136 Converse Laboratory. Built 1927 Coolidge, Shepley, Bulfinch & Abbott. Altered 1966.

137 Continental Hotel. Built 1928–29 Charles R. Greco. Acquired 1972.

200 Countway Library (Medical School, Boston). Built 1963–65 Hugh Stubbins and Associates.

201 Daniels House (Radcliffe). Built 1965–66 Harrison & Abramowitz.

202 Underpass (Cambridge Street). Built 1966–68 C. A. Maguire.

203 Currier House (Radcliffe). Built 1969 Harrison & Abramowitz.

204 Mather House. Built 1967–68 Shepley, Bulfinch, Richardson & Abbott.

205 Faculty Office Building (Law School). Built 1967 Benjamin Thompson.

206 Roscoe Pound Hall (Law School). Built 1968 Benjamin Thompson.

207 Cotting House (Business School). Built 1967–68 Robert S. Sturgis.

208 Gutman Library (School of Education). Built 1968 Benjamin Thompson.

209 Burden Hall (Business School). Built 1968–71 Philip Johnson.

210 Teele Hall (Business School). Built 1969 Kubitz & Pepi.

211 Gund Hall (Graduate School of Design). Built 1969–72 Andrews, Anderson, & Baldwin. Altered 1983 Don Hisaka.

212 Science Center. Built 1970–73 Sert Jackson Associates.

213 McCollum Center (Business School). Built 1970 Shepley, Bulfinch, Richardson & Abbott.

214 Baker Hall (Business School). Built 1970 Shepley, Bulfinch, Richardson & Abbott.

215 Perkin Building (Observatory). Built 1970–72 The Cambridge Seven.

216 Broadway Parking. Built 1971–73 Davies Wolf Bibbins.

217 Everett Parking. Built 1970 Sert Jackson Associates.

218 Rockefeller Hall. Built 1970–71 Edward L. Barnes.

219 Faculty Row (Radcliffe). Built 1971 Gourley & Richmond.

220 Nathan Marsh Pusey Library. Built 1973–76 Hugh Stubbins and Associates.

221 Canaday Hall. Built 1973–75 Ezra Ehrenkrantz.

222 Tozzer Library. Built 1974 Johnson & Hotvedt.

223 Cumnock Hall (Business School). Built 1974 Earl Flansburgh.

224 Soldiers Field Apartments (Business School). Built 1974–76 Benjamin Thompson.

225 Kennedy School of Government. Built 1974–77 Architectural Resources Cambridge, Inc. Altered 1982–84*.

226 Medical Area Total Energy Plant. Built 1976–82 Benjamin Thompson.

227 Indoor Track; Blodgett Pool (Soldiers Field). Built 1977–78 TAC.

228 Seeley Mudd Building (Medical School). Built 1977 TAC.

229 Radcliffe Athletic Center (Garden Street). Built 1978–80 Hoskins Scott Taylor.

230 Biochemistry Building (Divinity Avenue). Built 1979–80 Payette Associates.

231 Sackler Art Museum (Quincy Street). Built 1982–84 James Stirling, Wilford.

232 Guardhouse (Johnston Gate). Built 1983–84 Graham Gund.

Illustration Credits

HUA   Harvard University Archives, Pusey Library
CHC   Cambridge Historical Commission
RCA   Radcliffe College Archives
SBRA   Shepley, Bulfinch, Richardson and Abbott Archives
HBSA   Harvard Business School Archives

1   The Shepard-Hooker-Wigglesworth House: sketch from memory after its demolition in 1844. HUA: 935.57.

2   Map of Cambridge in 1670. CHC: Robert Nylander.

3   Cambridge in 1668 (by H. R. Shurtleff, c. 1933). HUA: HUV2038pf(N).

4   The Old College, Harvard Hall I: north elevation. Conjectural perspective by H. R. Shurtleff, c. 1933). HUA: HUV2038(N).

5   Harvard Hall I: south elevation. Conjectural restoration drawing by Singleton P. Moorhead (c. 1933). HUA: 935.57.

6   Harvard Hall I: first-floor plan. Conjectural restoration drawing by H. R. Shurtleff (c. 1933). HUA: 935.57.

7   Harvard Hall I: second-floor plan. Conjectural restoration drawing by H. R. Shurtleff (c. 1933). HUA: 935.57.

8   Indian College. Conjectural restoration by H. R. Shurtleff (c. 1933). HUA: UAI.15.25pf.

9   Land parcels assembled to make up Harvard Yard, with the years they were acquired. Bunting and Nylander, *Old Cambridge,* ill. 337, by Robert Nylander.

10   Harvard Hall II (1674–1682): detail of Burgis-Price View (1726). HUA: HUV2038.

11   Harvard Hall II: reconstruction of first- and second-floor plans. HUA: UAI.15.25pf.

12   Burgis-Price view (1726), showing Harvard Hall II (1674–1682), Stoughton Hall I (1698) and Massachusetts Hall (1718). HUA: HUV2038.

13   Wadsworth House (1726): south elevation. HUA: HUV46(2–2).

14   Holden Chapel: west front (John Smibert, 1742). HUA: HUV32(4–5a).

15   View of the Colleges: drawing by du Simitière. Original in the possession of the Library Company of Philadelphia. Credit: Colonial Society of Massachusetts. HUA: HUV2168.

16   Hollis Hall: west door (Thomas Dawes, master builder, 1762). HUA: HUV33(8–2).

17 Harvard Hall III: drawing by du Simitière (Gov. Francis Bernard, designer; Thomas Dawes, master builder, 1764). Credit: Colonial Society of Massachusetts. HUA: HUV2168.10.

18 Plan of Havard Hall III: drawing by du Simitière. Credit: Colonial Society of Massachusetts. HUA: HUV2168.10.

19 Harvard Hall III: Library, c. 1790. Conjectural restoration by F. W. Bang after research of John Perkins Brown. HUA: HUV31(1 – 8).

20 Harvard Hall III: addition of two-story porch by Richard Bond, 1842. HUA: HUV31(2 – 4).

21 Harvard Hall III: enlargement by Ware and Van Brunt, 1870. HUA: HUV31(3 – 3).

22 Stoughton Hall II (Charles Bulfinch, architect; Thomas Dawes, master builder, 1804). HUA: HUV34(1 – 4).

23 Plan of Harvard Yard Property, 1799. Bunting and Nylander, *Old Cambridge*, ill. 330A, corrected by Robert Nylander.

24 Holworthy Hall: south elevation (Loammi Baldwin, 1811). HUA: HUV37(2 – 16).

25 "Racetrack" plan of Harvard Yard (Charles Bulfinch, 1812 – 1813). HUA: UAI.15.740pf.

26 University Hall: west facade (Charles Bulfinch, 1813). HUA: HUV39(1 – 4).

27 Dane Hall (1832): western portico. HUA: HUV45(1 – 3).

28 Gore Hall (Richard Bond, 1838 – 1841): perspective drawing. HUA: HUV2240.2.

29 Gore Hall: interior. HUA: HUV48(5 – 1).

30 Gore Library demolition, showing the metal stack wing (Ware and Van Brunt, 1876). HUA: HUV48A(4 – 9).

31 Appleton Chapel (Paul Schultze, 1856). HUA: HUV53(3 – 9).

32 Appleton Chapel interior. From F. O. Vaille and H. A. Clark, *Harvard Book* II (Cambridge, Mass., 1875), p. 121.

33 Boylston Hall as remodeled in 1959 (Paul Schultze and Schoen, 1857; Peabody and Stearns, 1871; TAC, 1959). Harvard News Office.

34 Grays Hall: drawing of north elevation (N. J. Bradlee, 1862). HUA: UAI.15.25pf.

35 College House (1832 – 1870). HUA: HUV81(1 – 4).

36 Asa Gray's Garden House and Herbarium (Ithiel Town, 1810; remodeled by Ryder and Harris). HUA: HUV1204(1 – 1).

37 Land acquisition in the North Yard. Bunting and Nylander, *Old Cambridge*, ill. 359, by Susan E. Maycock.

38 Divinity Hall (design by Solomon Willard, 1825, adapted by Thomas Sumner; chapel interior remodeled by A. W. Longfellow, Jr., 1904). HUA: HUV308(1 – 5a).

39 Harvard Observatory (Isaiah Rogers, 1843 – 1851). HUA: HUV1210(1 – 2b).

40 Lawrence Hall (Richard Bond, 1847; Ware and Van Brunt, 1871), home of the Scientific School. HUA: HUV170(2 – 1b).

41 Thayer Commons railroad station (1849; renovated as a gift of Nathaniel Thayer, 1865). HUA: HUV176(1 – 2a).

42 Old Rogers Gymnasium (E. C. Cabot, 1859). HUA: HUV162(1 – 1a).

43 Rogers Gymnasium interior. HUA: HUV162(3 – 1).

44 Map of Harvard Yard (1856 – 1857). HUA: HUA632pf(N).

45 Eliot Plan of Harvard, 1909. HUA: HUA632pf(N).

46 Thayer Hall (Ryder and Harris, 1869). HUA: HU103.

47 Weld Hall (Ware and Van Brunt, 1870). HUA: HUV40(3-2a).

48 Matthews Hall: architects' sketch (Peabody and Stearns, 1871). HUA: HUV42 (1-7a).

49 Holyoke House (Edward Harris, of Ryder and Harris, 1870). HUA: HUV2329pf, 136 (Paul J. Weber).

50 Harvard Yard: plan of 1870 (Charles W. Eliot). HUA: UAI.15.740pf, series 1860-1899.

51 Bird's-eye view of Harvard Yard proposing Sever Hall (office of H. H. Richardson). HUA: HUV2278pf.

52 Sever Hall: (H. H. Richardson, 1878): east elevation. SBRA.

53 Sever Hall: first-floor plan. SBRA.

54 Hunt Hall (Richard Morris Hunt, 1893), the first Fogg Museum. Fogg Art Museum: Department of Photographic Services.

55 Hunt Hall interior. HUA: HUV54(2-8).

56 Robinson Hall (Charles McKim, 1904), built to house the School of Architecture. Harvard News Office: H67C.

57 Emerson Hall: west facade (Guy Lowell, 1900). HUA: HUV51(1-4).

58 Emerson Hall: north facade. HUA: HUV51(2-5a).

59 Architect's sketch for Phillips Brooks House (A. W. Longfellow, Jr., 1898). HUA: HUV36(1-1).

60 Phillips Brooks House: south facade. Photo: Sylvia Sanborn. HUA: HUV36(2-1).

61 Phillips Brooks House: staircase hall. Photo: Sylvia Sanborn.

62 Harvard Union (Charles McKim, 1902). HUA: HUV144(1-5).

63 Memorial Hall (Ware and Van Brunt, 1866-1878). HUA: HUV166(3-5).

64 Memorial Hall: tower with clock. HUA: HUV166(6-8b).

65 Memorial Hall: final plan. From *Monographs of American Architecture: Memorial Hall* (Boston: Ticknor and Co., 1887), HUA: HUB1556.92F, plate 14.

66 Memorial Hall: drawing of first design. HUA: HUV166(1-2).

67 Memorial Hall: interior of Memorial Transept HUA: HUV166(18-7).

68 Memorial Hall: dining hall looking east. From *Monographs of American Architecture: Memorial Hall.* HUA: HUB1556.92F, plate 10.

69 Memorial Hall: Sanders Theater. HUA: HUV166(17-5).

70 The University Museum as it grew over the years. Bunting and Nylander, *Old Cambridge,* ill. 363, by Susan E. Maycock.

71 University Museum: first section (Richard Greenough and George Snell, 1859). HUA: HUV315(1-1b).

72 University Museum: second section (1871). HUA: HUV315(1-4a).

73 Hemenway Gymnasium (Peabody and Stearns, 1878). HUA: HUV172(2-1).

74 Hemenway Gymnasium interior with Sargent apparatus. HUA: HUV172(1-9).

75 The Carey Athletic Building (A. W. Longfellow, Jr., 1889). HUA: HUV203(1-4).

76 Gannett House (1838). HUA: HUV180(1-3).

77 Austin Hall (H. H. Richardson, 1881-1884). HUA: HUV178(4-1).

78 Austin Hall plan. Harvard Law School Art Collection. From *Monographs of*

American Architecture: Austin Hall (Boston: Ticknor & Co., 1885), HUA: HUB1177.76F, 18.

79 Austin Hall: interior stair hall. Harvard Law School Art Collection.

80 Jefferson Physics: Laboratory (Shaw and Hunnewell, 1882), with Lyman and Cruft Laboratories. HUA: HUV185(1-1).

81 Pierce Hall (Shaw and Hunnewell, 1900). CHC: Neg. 2725.

82 Walter Hastings Hall (Cabot and Chandler, 1888). Harvard University News Office. CHC: Neg. 2722.

83 Perkins Hall: architects' sketch (Shepley, Rutan and Coolidge, 1893). HUA: HUV270(1-1).

84 Langdell Hall (Shepley, Rutan and Coolidge, 1906): eastern elevation with Carey-Rotch Building. HUA: HUV179(2-4).

85 Randall Hall Commons (Wheelwright and Haven, 1898). HUA: HUV302(1-9).

86 Semitic Museum: perspective drawing (A. W. Longfellow, Jr., 1902). HUA: HUV306(1-1).

87 Chemistry Laboratories: perspective drawing of unexecuted project (A. W. Longfellow, Jr., 1911). Harvard University Planning Office.

88 Harvard Divinity School Library (now the Farlow Herbarium) (Peabody and Stearns, 1910). HUA: HUV310(1-1).

89 Andover Hall, Harvard Divinity School (Allen and Collens, 1910). HUA: HU91.

90 Kittredge Hall (William Mowll, 1909-1912) and Observatory Hill. HUA: HUV15(14-2a).

91 Stillman Infirmary (Shepley, Rutan and Coolidge, 1900). Photo: Boston Photo News Company.

92 Harvard Medical School's fifth home (Van Brunt and Howe, 1881-1883). From Moses King, *King's Handbook of Boston* (Boston, 1889), p. 143. HUA: HUV1505 (1-1).

93 Harvard Medical School: Administrative Building (Shepley, Rutan and Coolidge, 1906). HUA: HUV1510(2-4).

94 Harvard Medical School: aerial view of plan. HUA: HUV15(14b-3).

95 Aerial View of Soldiers Field. HUA: HUV15(10-3).

96 Carey Cage, Soldiers Field (H. Langford Warren, 1897). HUA: HUV1336pf.

97 Fence and gatelodge, Soldiers Field (Ira N. Hollis with H. Langford Warren, 1897-1900). Photo: T. E. Marr. HUA: HUV1332pf.

98 Newell Boathouse (Peabody and Stearns, 1900). HUA: HUV1310(1-8).

99 Harvard Stadium (Ira N. Hollis, Lewis J. Johnson. George Bruno de Gersdorff and Charles McKim, consulting architects, 1902). HUA: HUV1331(4-1).

100 Harvard Stadium under construction. From *Harvard Engineering Journal* 3 (1904-05):96. HUA: HUK363.

101 Harvard Stadium with performance of Aeschylus' *Agamemnon* in 1906. HUA: HUD2906.2.5FA.

102 Weld Boathouse (Robert Peabody, 1906-1907). HUA: HUV1305pf.

103 Indoor Athletic Building (Coolidge, Shepley, Bulfinch and Abbott, 1929). HUA: HUV604(1-3).

104 Harvard Overseers Plan (commissioned by Peabody, Hemenway and Shattuck, 1896). HUA: UAI.15.740pf.

105 Founders House, 6 Appian Way. RCA.

106 Fay House, 10 Garden Street (built for Nathaniel Ireland, 1806; altered for Walcott Gibbs, c. 1870). RCA.

107 Fay House as altered (A. W. Longfellow, Jr., 1890). HUA: HUV985(1–4a).

108 Fay House: top-lit library on the third floor. RCA.

109 Fay House hallway (A. W. Longfellow, Jr., 1892). RCA.

110 The western buildings cloistering the Radcliffe Yard. RCA.

111 Unexecuted master plan for Radcliffe (Perry, Shaw, and Hepburn, 1926; Kenneth Conant, delineator). RCA.

112 Aerial view of Radcliffe Yard. Photo: Donald M. Felt. RCA.

113 Agassiz House (A. W. Longfellow, Jr., 1904): second-floor living room. RCA.

114 Agassiz House: theatre auditorium. RCA.

115 Radcliffe Library (Winslow and Bigelow, 1907): Whitman Room, c. 1938 (stained glass by Sarah Wyman Whitman). Photo: Herbert W. Taylor. RCA.

116 Longfellow Hall (Perry, Shaw and Hepburn, 1929): north elevation. RCA.

117 Byerly Hall (Coolidge and Carlson, 1931). Photo: Paul J. Weber. RCA.

118 Greenleaf House (1859), the Radcliffe President's House, 76 Brattle Street. RCA.

119 Cronkhite Graduate Center: unexecuted project drawing (Perry, Shaw, and Hepburn, 1926). RCA.

120 The Radcliffe Quadrangle, Garden Street between Shepard and Linnaean Streets. Photo: Donald M. Felt. RCA.

121 Radcliffe Quadrangle: unexecuted project drawing by Bremer W. Pond of entrance arcade joining Bertram and Eliot Halls. Photo: George H. Davis Studio, Boston. RCA.

122 Bertram Hall (A. W. Longfellow, Jr., 1906): exterior detail. RCA.

123 Bertram Hall: dining room. Photo: H. W. Taylor. RCA.

124 Hilles Library (Harrison and Abramovitz, 1965). Photo: Alexandre Georges. RCA: 856A–17.

125 Plan of Hilles Library and Currier House (Harrison and Abramovitz, 1965). Photo: Harrison and Abramovitz. RCA.

126 Hilles Library: central courtyard. Photo: Ezra Stoller. RCA.

127 Widener Library steps with Weld Hall: drawing by Louis Orr. HUA: HUV2336.10pf.

128 Widener Library (Horace Trumbauer, 1913). HUA: HUV49(4–5b).

129 Widener Library: staircase murals by John Singer Sargent. Photo: Paul J. Weber. HUA: HUV2329pf, 143.

130 Widener Library: reading room. Harvard University Planning Office.

131 Memorial Church (Coolidge, Shepley, Bulfinch and Abbott, 1931). Photo: William M. Rittase. HUA: HUV2332pf,5.

132 Memorial Church interior: view east toward Appleton Chapel. HUA: HUV53A (3–9).

133 Straus and Lehman Halls from the southwest (Coolidge, Shepley, Bulfinch and Abbott, 1924, 1926). HUA: HUV44(1–6).

134 Lehman Hall seen from the Yard. HUA: HUV44(3–1a).

135 Wigglesworth Hall (Coolidge, Shepley, Bulfinch and Abbott, 1930). SBRA.

136 President's House, 17 Quincy Street (Guy Lowell, 1911). Photo: Paul J. Weber. Harvard University Press.

137 The new Fogg Museum of Art (Coolidge, Shepley, Bulfinch and Abbott, 1925): drawing by Hermann Voss. SBRA.

138 Fogg Museum entrance. HUA: HUV155(1–4a).

139 Fogg Museum: first-floor plan. Fogg Art Museum, Department of Photographic Services.

140 Fogg Museum: interior courtyard. Fogg Art Museum, Department of Photographic Services.

141 Fogg Museum: Warburg Room. HUA: HUV155(2–1).

142 Fogg Museum: Naumburg Rooms. Fogg Library, Photographs of Fogg Art Museum Bequests, 87. Fogg 47, C12fe, 1945a, vol. 2.

143 The Faculty Club: architects' drawing (Coolidge, Shepley, Bulfinch and Abbott, 1930). HUA: HUV152(1–1).

144 Aerial view of the North Yard. HUA: HUV15(23–9).

145 Busch Reisinger Museum (German Bestelmeyer and H. Langford Warren, 1914): architectural model. HUA: HUV297(1–2).

146 Biology Laboratories: architects' drawing (Coolidge, Shepley, Bulfinch and Abbott, 1930). HUA: HUV316(1–16).

147 Biology Laboratory entrance, with brick relief sculpture by Katharine Ward Lane. HUA: HUV316(4–4a).

148 Tozzer Library (Johnson and Hotvedt, 1974). HUA: HUV314(1–1).

149 University Herbarium (Shepley, Bulfinch, Richardson and Abbott, 1953). HUA: HUV311(1–5).

150 Music Building and Paine Hall (John Mead Howells, 1913). Photo: Paul J. Weber. HUA: HUV2329pf,129.

151 Mallinckrodt Laboratory (Coolidge, Shepley, Bulfinch and Abbott, 1927), Oxford Street facade, looking toward Memorial Hall. Photo: Paul J. Weber. HUA: HUV2329pf,62.

152 Cambridge Riverside, c. 1896. HUA: HUV15(3–6).

153 Plan for freshman dormitories along the river (Charles Coolidge, 1910). SBRA.

154 Gold Coast Dormitories, Mount Auburn Street, c. 1910. Detroit Publishing Co. CHC: Neg. 2721.

155 Apthorp House (1760); photo c. 1885–1895). MIT Historical Files. CHC: Neg. 2723.

156 Perspective sketch of the River Houses (Coolidge, Shepley, Bulfinch and Abbott, 1928). SBRA.

157 Kirkland House (Coolidge, Shepley, Bulfinch and Abbott, 1913): gable end. Photo: Thomas Ellison. SBRA.

158 McKinlock Hall, Leverett House (Coolidge, Shepley, Bulfinch and Abbott, 1925). SBRA.

159 Gore Hall, Winthrop House (Coolidge, Shepley, Bulfinch and Abbott, 1913). SBRA.

160 Smith Hall Court, Kirkland House (Coolidge, Shepley, Bulfinch and Abbott, 1913). Photo: Thomas Ellison. SBRA.

161 Hicks House (1762). Harvard News Office.

162 Eliot House: courtyard (Coolidge, Shepley, Bulfinch and Abbott, 1930). Photo: William M. Rittase. SBRA.

163 Winthrop House: dining hall (Coolidge, Shepley, Bulfinch and Abbott, 1913). Photo: F. L. Fales. SBRA.

164 Dunster House (Coolidge, Shepley, Bulfinch and Abbott, 1929): perspective drawing by Constantin Perzoff. SBRA.

165 Dunster House: tower. SBRA.

166 Dunster House: dining room walls. Photo: Sigurd Fischer. SBRA.

167 Adams House viewed along Bow Street. Photo: Paul J. Weber. SBRA.

168 Adams House: common room. SBRA.

169 Adams House: interior stair. SBRA.

170 Adams House: courtyard of Randolph Hall. HUA: HUV576(1–7).

171 Lowell House (Coolidge, Shepley, Bulfinch and Abbott, 1929): perspective drawing by Constantin Perzoff. SBRA.

172 Lowell House: courtyard. Photo: William M. Rittase. HUA: HUV606(2–3).

173 Lowell House: common room. SBRA.

174 Harvard Business School: unexecuted competition drawing (Coolidge, Shepley, Bulfinch and Abbott, 1926). SBRA.

175 Alumni Center, Harvard Business School (McKim, Mead and White, 1926). Photo: Laurence Lowry. HBSA: 113–2, Sept./Oct. 1972.

176 Baker Library reading room, Harvard Business School (McKim, Mead and White, 1926). HUA: HUV1467(5–5).

177 Cotting House, Harvard Business School (Robert Shaw Sturgis, 1965). Photo: George Zimberg. Robert S. Sturgis.

178 Cotting House interior. Photo: George Zimberg. Robert S. Sturgis.

179 Littauer Center (Coolidge, Shepley, Bulfinch and Abbott, 1937). HUA: HUV175 (1–9).

180 Littauer Center: north elevation. Photo: Sigurd Fischer. SBRA.

181 Second Hemenway Gymnasium (Coolidge, Shepley, Bulfinch and Abbott, 1938). Photo: Paul J. Weber. SBRA.

182 Houghton Library: (Perry, Shaw and Hepburn, 1941): perspective drawing by R. C. Dean. Houghton Library: pf MS AM, 1964, folder 41.

183 Houghton Library: first-floor plan. Drawing by R. C. Dean. Houghton Library: pf MS AM, 1964, folder 44.

184 Houghton Library: south gallery. Drawing by R. C. Dean. Houghton Library: pf MS AM, 1964, folder 54.

185 Lamont Library (Coolidge, Shepley, Bulfinch and Abbott, 1947). HUA: HUV49C (10–2b).

186 Lamont Library: second-floor poetry room (Alvar Aalto with Coolidge, Shepley, Bulfinch and Abbott, 1947). SBRA.

187 Nuclear Laboratory (Coolidge, Shepley, Bulfinch and Abbott, 1949). HUA: HUV274.

188 Cyclotron, Cambridge Electron Accelerator (Charles T. Main, Engineers, 1946, 1957). Harvard University News Office.

189 Aiken Computation Center (Coolidge, Shepley, Bulfinch and Abbott, 1946; expanded 1964). Photo: Armand J. Dionne. Cruft Photo Lab: Neg. AF363B–1965.

190 Gordon McKay Laboratory (Coolidge, Shepley, Bulfinch and Abbott, 1953). Photo: Robert D. Harvey Studio. SBRA.

191 Graduate Center: exterior elevation with *World Tree* by Richard Lippold. HUA: HUV212(1–6).

192 Graduate Center: Harkness Commons, concourse and ramp. (Walter Gropius and TAC, 1948–1952). HUA: HUV211(5–9).

193 Graduate Center: Harkness Commons with mural by Joan Miro. HUA: HUV211(4–2).

194 Model of the Graduate Center. HUA: HUV211(1–5).

195 Model of Allston Burr Hall (Coolidge, Shepley, Bulfinch and Abbott, 1951). SBRA.

196 Allston Burr plan. SBRA.

197 Allston Burr: large lecture hall interior. SBRA.

198 Allston Burr: west facade. SBRA.

199 Carpenter Center for the Visual Arts (Le Corbusier, with Josep Lluis Sert, 1961). Harvard University News Office.

200 Carpenter Center. Harvard University News Office.

201 Holyoke Center: model with Forbes Plaza (Sert, Jackson and Gourley, 1962–1967). HUA: HUV95(1–6).

202 Holyoke Center: view from the southeast. Sert, Jackson and Gourley.

203 Gund Hall, Graduate School of Design (John Andrews with Anderson Baldwin, 1967–1969). Photo: Steven F. Rosenthal.

204 Gund Hall interior. Photo: Rick Stafford.

205 William James Hall (Minoru Yamasaki, 1963). HUA: HUV303.

206 Undergraduate Science Center (Josep Lluis Sert, 1966–1968). Sert, Jackson and Gourley.

207 Undergraduate Science Center: southeast elevation from overpass. Photo: Steven F. Rosenthal. Sert, Jackson and Associates.

208 Undergraduate Science Center: central hallway with bas-relief sculpture by Constantino Nivola (1950s). Photo: Steven F. Rosenthal.

209 Center for the Study of World Religions (Josep Lluis Sert, 1959). Harvard University News Office.

210 Andover Harvard library (Shepley, Bulfinch, Richardson and Abbott, 1960). SBRA.

211 Rockefeller Hall (Edward Larabee Barnes, 1970). Photo: Richard Cheek: Neg. 2724. CHC.

212 Roscoe Pound Building, Harvard Law School (Benjamin Thompson Associates, 1968). Photo: James Morrison. Harvard Law School Art Collection.

213 Music Building: Eda Kuhn Loeb Library Wing. Drawing by Stanley B. Parker, 1955. From *Harvard Alumnae Bulletin* 57 (4 June 1955): 659. Eda Kuhn Loeb Music Library.

214 Music Building: Fanny Mason Wing. Drawing by James F. Clapp, Jr., for Shepley, Bulfinch, Richardson and Abbot, 1970. SBRA.

215 Engineering Sciences Laboratory (Minoru Yamasaki and Associates, 1962). Harvard University News Office.

216 Sears Tower (Isaiah Rogers, 1843) and Harvard Observatory Additions (1892, 1931, 1954, 1960, 1970). Photo: Laurence Lowry. Neg. 450–16, July '76.

217 Loeb Drama Center (Hugh Stubbins, 1959). Photo: Molitor Photography. Hugh Stubbins Associates.

218 Larsen Hall, School of Education (Caudill, Rowlett and Scott, 1964). HUA: HUV812(1–1).

219 Gutman Library, School of Education (Benjamin Thompson, 1969). Photo: Lilian Kemp, Neg. 82-5-15(6). Harvard School of Education Publications Office.

220 Aldrich Hall, Harvard Business School (Perry, Shaw and Hepburn, 1953). HBSA.

221 Kresge Hall, Harvard Business School (Perry, Shaw and Hepburn, 1953). HBSA.

222 Baker Hall, Harvard Business School (Shepley, Bulfinch, Richardson and Abbott, 1970). HBSA.

223 McCollum Center, Harvard Business School: view toward the Charles River. HBSA.

224 Burden Hall, Harvard Business School (Phillip Johnson, 1968). HBSA.

225 Soldiers Field Apartments (Benjamin Thompson, 1974). Photo: Nick Wheeler, 1976, 00506. Harvard University Planning Office.

226 Countway Library, Harvard Medical School (Hugh Stubbins, 1973). Photo: Louis Reens. Hugh Stubbins and Associates.

227 Countway Library: curved central staircase. Photo: Louis Reens. Hugh Stubbins and Associates.

228 Quincy House: courtyard (Shepley, Bulfinch, Richardson and Abbott, 1958). SBRA.

229 Quincy House: courtyard entrance with library. SBRA.

230 Leverett House: perspective drawing of southwest elevation (Shepley, Bulfinch, Richardson and Abbott, 1958–1959). SBRA.

231 Leverett House: library. SBRA.

232 Mather House: tower (Shepley, Bulfinch, Richardson and Abbott, 1968). SBRA.

233 Mather House: dining hall. SBRA.

234 Peabody Terrace (Sert, Gourley and Jackson, 1963). Sert, Jackson and Gourley.

235 Peabody Terrace. Sert, Jackson and Gourley.

236 Canaday Hall (Ezra Ehrenkrantz, 1973). Photo: Steven F. Rosenthal, Neg. 10-14-74, 4.

237 Pusey Library: entrance (Hugh Stubbins, 1973). Photo: Edward Jacoby. Hugh Stubbins and Associates.

238 Pusey Library. Photo: Edward Jacoby. Hugh Stubbins and Associates.

239 Pusey Library interior. Photo: Steven F. Rosenthal. Hugh Stubbins and Associates.

240 John F. Kennedy School of Government and Library: project model of unexecuted design (I. M. Pei, 1974). I. M. Pei and Partners.

241 John F. Kennedy School of Government (Architectural Resources Cambridge, Inc., 1977). Photo: Nick Wheeler. Architectural Resources Cambridge, Inc.

242 John F. Kennedy School of Government: interior. Photo: Nick Wheeler. Architectural Resources Cambridge, Inc.

243 Sackler Museum from the northwest. Photo: Steven F. Rosenthal.

244 Sackler Museum (James Stirling, 1981) from the southwest. President and Fellows of Harvard College and James Stirling: Neg. 1982–140.29.

245 Sackler Museum: axonometric drawing. President and Fellows of Harvard College and James Stirling: Neg. 1982-140.36.

246 Guardhouse at the Johnston Gate (Graham Gund Associates, 1982). Photo: Steven F. Rosenthal. Graham Gund Associates.

Index

Athletics (*Continued*)
116–123. *See also* McKenzie, R. Tait;
Meylan, George L.
Austin, Edward, 101, 123, 151, 211, 300n9
Austin Hall, 43, 56, 100–103, 301n11,
303n33; and neighboring buildings, 96,
107, 173, 211, 246, 307n25; and
donor, 101, 300n9
Austin, Samuel, 101
Ayers, Louis, 311n38

B&B Chemical Company, 217
Bailey, V. H., 308n15
Baker, George, 205, 311n38
Baker Hall, 255, 257, 258
Baker House Dormitory (M.I.T.), 216,
313n18
Baker Library, 206–208, 213, 255, 305n7
Baldwin, Loammi, 40, 286n14, 287n25,
289n7
Barker and Binford, 51, 292n34
Barnard Hall, 140, 142
Barnes, Edward Larabee, 245
Baroque style: of Guy Lowell, 78, 109,
124; of Ecole des Beaux Arts, 78, 109,
124, 167, 181; English, 92, 109, 197;
and South Yard plans, 180, 181; of
modern buildings, 228, 234, 238
Barry, William E., 296n15
Barye, Antoine, 307n24
Bauhaus, 219, 313n15
Beaux Arts, Ecole des, *see* Ecole des
Beaux Arts
Beck Hall, 309n26
Benjamin, Asher, 292n36
Benjamin Thompson Associates, 101, 174,
246, 253, 257. *See also* Thompson,
Benjamin
Berkeley, Bishop, 287n23
Bernard, Sir Francis, 30, 287n24, 288n28
Bertram Hall, 140, 142–144
Bestelmeyer, German, 168, 235, 306n20,
307n22
Betts lot, 16
Bigelow estate, 39
Billings, Hamatt, 299n43
Biltmore Hotel, 309n21
Biological Laboratories, 169–171, 172,
219; and University Museum com-
pound, 111, 167, 168, 171, 246
Bok, Derek, 246
Bond, Richard, 32, 44, 55, 290n18,
293nn44,45
Bond, William C., 54–55
Bordman, Andrew, 35
Bordman estate, 34
Bordman lot, 308n11
Borromini, 313n18
Boston, 292n34, 293n39, 294nn1,3,
296n22; funds from, 15, 46, 59, 96;

ministers, 16, 37, 82, 285n6; architecture, 25, 26, 49, 103, 111, 130, 159,
189–190, 215, 291n29,
293nn41,44,46, 296n16, 297n29,
300n3, 301nn13,17, 316n3; and
Medical School, 27, 109, 112, 115,
167, 254, 257; Fire of 1872, 105,
295n6, 302n28; and Business School,
254; and Kennedy Library, 275
Boston Athenaeum, 294n51
Boston City Hall, 145, 249, 257
Boston Public Library, 115, 289n2,
291n22, 297n27, 305n9
Boston Society of Architects, 294n51,
299n47, 301n17, 304n14
Boston Society of Arts and Crafts, 139
Boston Society of Civil Engineers, 302n23
Boston University, 115
Boston YMCA, 300n7
Botanic Garden, 51, 112, 219, 294n1
Botanic Garden Apartments, 219
Bowditch, Nathaniel, 39, 289n4
Bowdoin College, 38, 60, 98
Boylston Hall, 24, 49, 51, 70, 176,
291n24; and neighboring buildings, 40,
67, 159; and donor, 49, 291n26,
294n53; renovations to, 51, 231
Boylston, Ward Nicholas, 49, 294n53
Bradish lot, 235, 286n16, 288n33
Bradlee Gate, 298n32
Bradlee, Nathaniel J., 51, 67, 291n29
Brantford Hall, 310n26
Brattle House, 292n33
Brattle Theatre, 304n12
Brattle, William, 16
Briggs Cage, 123, 302n27
Briggs Hall, 140, 142
Brigham and Women's Hospital, 257
Brighton, 179, 303n29
Brookline, 5
Brooks, Peter Chardon, 287n18, 293n39
Brooks, Phillips, 82, 297n30
Brown University, 21, 60
Bryan Hall (Kirkland House), 190,
310nn28, 32
Bryant, Gridley J. F., 49, 289n7, 291n27,
293n45; and Holden Chapel, 35,
287n25
Buck, Paul, 222
Buckingham House, 134–135, 137, 140
Bulfinch, Charles, 30, 54, 83, 130, 280,
316n3; and New Stoughton, 39; and
University Hall, 41–43, 67, 74, 96,
290nn11,14; and plan of Harvard Yard,
41–42, 49, 290n10; and Old North
Church, 157; and uncle Apthorp, 184,
287n22; and Federal style, 215,
287n23, 288n30
Bunker Hill Monument, 289n7, 293n41
Bunting Institute, 133

Lippold, Richard: *World Tree*, 221, 225, 229, 314n23
Lisbon earthquake (of 1755), 22
Littauer Center, 65, 210–212, 217, 312nn5,6; and neighboring buildings, 173, 241
Little Common, 56, 84, 101, 293n47; traded to Harvard, 57, 166
Little, J. A., 308n11
Little's Block, 83, 309n26
Loeb Drama Center, 140, 252–253, 271, 315n22
Loeb, Eda Kuhn, Library (Music Building), 248–249
Loeb, Frances, Library, 238
Longfellow, A. W., Jr., 54, 123–124, 297nn29,30, 303n9; and Phillips Brooks House, 81–82, 130; and Carey Athletic Building, 98, 117; and Fay House, 107, 124, 130, 133; and Semitic Museum, 109, 167; and chemistry quadrangle, 109, 110, 167, 176, 306n19; and Agassiz House, 133, 137, 139, 304n12; and Bertram and Eliot Halls, 140, 142
Longfellow, Alice Mary, 128, 130, 139, 141
Longfellow Hall, 134, 138, 139, 140, 252, 304n14
Longfellow, Henry Wadsworth, 116, 128, 130, 140, 295n5
Longfellow Park, 271, 303n9
Longfellow, W. P. P., 299n43
Lowell, A. Lawrence, 109, 161, 205, 210, 230–231, 262; and Georgian Revival, 107, 124, 150, 151, 209; and curriculum, 150, 301n16; land acquisition and planning, 150, 151, 174, 183; and funding, 151, 183, 186, 187; and Charles Coolidge, 151, 152, 183, 231, 312n7; and Edward Harkness, 151, 187, 310n29; interest in architecture, 151, 305n3, 307n26, 311n38; and Harvard Yard, 152, 166, 306n12; and undergraduate housing, 177–179, 184–187, 222
Lowell, Guy, 123–124, 297n28, 305nn5,8, 308n16, 311n38; and Emerson Hall, 78, 81; and Lowell Lecture Hall, 109, 301n16; and Radcliffe Quadrangle, 109, 140; and Briggs Cage, 123, 302n27; and President's House, 159, 306n13
Lowell House, 152, 187, 188, 197, 203–205, 310nn28,31; cost, 309n24; and Claverly, 311n35
Lowell, James Russell, 295n5
Lowell Lecture Hall, 64, 109, 169, 293n39, 301n16, 306n13

Lyman Laboratory, 103, 105, 171, 172, 174
Lyman, Theodore, Jr., 51, 292n34

MacGowan, Peter, 313n22
Maginnis and Walsh, 140
Magonigle, H. Van Buren, 311n38
Main, Charles T., Engineers, 219
Mallinckrodt, Edwin, 306n19
Mallinckrodt Laboratory, 167, 173, 174–176, 250, 276
Manning, William, 20
Mansart, 206
Manter, Hall, 309n26
Marrett estate, 34
Mason, Daniel, 293n39
Mason, Fanny, Wing (Music Building), 248–249
Massachusetts Bay Colony, 11; fundraising by, 1, 15; building appropriations, 2, 5, 22, 23–24, 27, 28
Massachusetts, Commonwealth of: funding from, 35, 37–38, 42, 64, 115, 299n1
Massachusetts General Hospital, 115, 176, 290n11, 304n2; and Littauer, 211, 217, 312nn5,6
Massachusetts Hall, 21, 22–23, 70, 82, 189, 286n11, 290n10; and neighboring building, 20, 28, 34, 36, 43, 68, 158, 288n28; remodelings, 23, 35, 62, 286n14, 289n7; and Johnston Gate, 279
Massachusetts Institute of Technology, 62, 115; Baker House Dormitory, 216, 313n18; School of Architecture, 293n46, 296n16, 297n28, 301nn15,17, 316n3
Massachusetts State House, 228, 306n17
Mathematical School, 30
Mather Hall (Leverett House, now Quincy House), 197, 262, 310n28
Mather House, 265–267, 310n28, 312n7, 316n30
Mather, Increase, 16
Matthews Hall, 5, 14, 67–68, 70, 299n41; and neighboring buildings, 25, 43, 158, 159; and Gothic style, 111, 296n15; cost, 309n24
Maud Laboratory (Cambridge, England), 307n24
McCollum Center, 255, 257, 259
McIntire, Samuel, 215
McKay, Gordon, Laboratory, 174, 176, 220–221, 226, 241, 312n12
McKenzie, R. Tait, 98, 300n7. *See also* Athletics
McKim, Charles, 112, 205, 280, 297nn27,29, 298n35, 301nn15,16,17; and Memorial Fence and gates, 75, 82,

Radcliffe College, founding of, 128–130
Radcliffe Gymnasium (1898, Hemenway), 133, 137, 139
Radcliffe Library, 133, 134, 137, 139
Radcliffe Quadrangle, 109, 140, 142–149
Radcliffe Quad Recreational Facility, 149, 251, 315n21
Radcliffe Yard, 109, 133–139, 140, 142, 254
Randall Hall, 46, 108, 109, 178, 307n5
Randolph, Edward, 18
Randolph Hall (Adams House), 184, 185, 202, 300n15, 310nn26,27; acquired, 51, 186, 311n35; and Adams House, 187, 197
Randolph Trust, 51
Regency style, 255
Renaissance style, 25, 67, 98; and Harvard Hall II, 16, 18, 19
Revolution (American), 27, 112, 288n31, 289n7; and building styles, 24, 25, 287n22; and financial difficulties, 37
Reynolds Aluminum Company Building, 315n23
Richardson, H. H., 109, 123–124, 277, 280, 281, 316n29; and Sever Hall, 74–75, 81, 171, 296n22, 301n11; and Charles McKim, 83, 297n27; and A. W. Longfellow, Jr., 98, 130, 297nn29,30; and Austin Hall, 101–103, 301n11; and Charles Coolidge, 304n2
Rice University, 276
Ridgeley Hall, 310n26
Rindge Technical High School, 171, 307n23
Riverside, 179–183, 308nn9,13
Riverside Church (New York), 302n20
Robinson Hall, 64, 77, 78, 81, 82, 161; and School of Architecture, 78, 117, 220; location of, 297n27, 301n16
Rockefeller Hall, 245–246
Rockefeller Institute, 304n2
Rockefeller, John D., 298n36
Rogers Gymnasium (later Rogers Hall), 57, 58, 166, 168; and athletic program, 96, 98
Rogers, Isaiah, 25, 289n7, 293nn41,44; and Observatory, 54, 250, 294n51; and First Parish Church, 49, 279, 290n18
Romanesque style, 46; Richardson Romanesque, 75, 103
Roosevelt, Theodore, 98
Roscoe Pound Building, 101, 174, 246, 247
Rotch Building (formerly Carey Athletic Building) 98–101, 107, 117; and neighboring buildings, 174, 307n25
Royal Naval Hospital (Greenwich), 206
Royce, Josiah, 78

Rudolph, Paul, 314n10
Ruskin, John, 67, 87, 298n40
Russell Hall, 310n26, 311n35
Ryder and Harris, 52, 65, 123

Sabine, Walter, 307n26
Sackler, Arthur M., 276
Sackler Museum, 276–279, 317n5
Sage, Mrs. Russell, 186
Saint Catherine's Hall (Cambridge), 285n2
Saint Michaels (Marblehead), 285n5
Saint Paul's Cathedral (Boston), 291n19
San Biagio, Montepulciano, 163
Sanders, Charles, 92, 294n53
Sanders Theatre, 90, 92, 290n16, 294n53, 299n40; and Commencement, 49, 87; and neighboring buildings, 237
Sands, J. L., and Sons, 75, 297n25
Santayana, George, 36, 78
Sargent, Charles Sprague, 292n35
Sargent, Dudley Allen, 98, 139, 300n7
Sargent, John Singer, 154, 305n9
Scarborough College, University of Toronto, 314n9
Schlesinger Library, 133
Schmidt, Mott B., 311n38
School of Architecture, 78, 98, 101, 106, 116, 117, 119. See also Graduate School of Design
School of Dentistry, 116
School of Government, 210, 238; John F. Kennedy School of Government, 272–276
Schulze, Paul, 46, 49, 291n24
Schuyler, Montgomery, 167, 280
Science Center, see Undergraduate Science Center
Sears Tower, 250, 251
Semitic Museum, 64, 109, 110, 167–168, 169
Sert, Jackson and Gourley, 235, 240, 267
Sert, Josep Lluis, 235, 243, 245, 257, 280, 304n17
Sever, Anne, 70, 296n22
Sever estate, 123
Sever Hall, 70–75, 81, 277, 290n10, 301n11; and Tercentenary Quadrangle, 65, 152; brickwork of, 74–75, 171, 296n22, 299n41; location of, 74, 296nn22,24; and Austin Hall, 301n11
Sever, James Warren, 70, 296n22
Sever Quadrangle, 63, 74, 81, 82, 152, 166
Sewall lot, 39
Sewell, Samuel, 13
Shady Hill estate, 56, 59, 84, 109, 307n26; land transactions, 39, 52, 292n39, 293n40
Shattuck, George, 126
Shaw and Hunnewell, 103–105, 123, 301n13

347 *Index*